On the Verge of a
Planetary Civilization

On the Verge of a Planetary Civilization

A Philosophy of Integral Ecology

Sam Mickey

ROWMAN &
LITTLEFIELD
——— INTERNATIONAL
London • New York

Published by Rowman & Littlefield International, Ltd.
16 Carlisle Street, London, W1D 3BT
www.rowmaninternational.com

Rowman & Littlefield International, Ltd. is an affiliate of Rowman & Littlefield
4501 Forbes Boulevard, Suite 200, Lanham, Maryland 20706, USA
With additional offices in Boulder, New York, Toronto (Canada), and Plymouth (UK)
www.rowman.com

Copyright © 2014 by Sam Mickey

All rights reserved. No part of this book may be reproduced in any form or by any electronic or mechanical means, including information storage and retrieval systems, without written permission from the publisher, except by a reviewer who may quote passages in a review.

British Library Cataloguing in Publication Information Available
A catalogue record for this book is available from the British Library

ISBN: HB 978-1-7834-8136-1
PB 978-1-7834-8137-8
EB 978-1-7834-8138-5

Library of Congress Cataloging-in-Publication Data

Mickey, Sam, 1981–
On the verge of a planetary civilization : a philosophy of integral ecology / Sam Mickey.
pages cm
Includes bibliographical references and index.
ISBN 978-1-78348-136-1 (cloth : alk. paper)—ISBN 978-1-78348-137-8 (pbk. : alk. paper)—ISBN 978-1-78348-138-5 (electronic)
1. Deleuze, Gilles, 1925–1995. 2. Ecology—Philosophy. I. Title.
B2430.D454M53 2014
194—dc23
2014017957

∞™ The paper used in this publication meets the minimum requirements of American National Standard for Information Sciences Permanence of Paper for Printed Library Materials, ANSI/NISO Z39.48-1992.

Printed in the United States of America

Contents

Acknowledgements — vii

1. Introduction — 1
   - Becoming Ecological — 10
   - Becoming Integral — 16
   - Becoming Humourous — 24
   - Becoming Speculative — 29
   - Notes — 35

2. Beginning — 45
   - Opening — 47
   - Decision — 55
   - Examples — 63
   - Chorology — 73
   - Chaosmos — 79
   - Notes — 87

3. Middle — 101
   - Sense — 105
   - Rhizomes — 112
   - Nomads — 122
   - Omnicentric — 128
   - Anthropocosmic — 135
   - Notes — 144

4. Ending — 161
   - Apocalypse — 167
   - From Globe to Planet — 172
   - Planetary Love — 177
   - Cosmopolitics — 183
   - Notes — 192

5. Conclusion — 207
   - Refrain — 209
   - Compost — 212
   - The SF Mode — 219
   - On the Verge — 223

Notes	230
References	239
Index	257

Acknowledgements

Philosophy is a joint effort. This book would not be possible without support and collaboration provided by so many who have shared in the loving struggle of philosophy with me. Firstly, writing a work on ecological and planetary issues, I have been continually reminded that I live on a planet. It is a wondrous and humbling reminder of the immense support granted to me by water, plants, respiration, sunlight, bacteria, soil, gravity, and innumerable other features of existence on Earth. Regarding institutional support, I am grateful to faculty, students, and staff at the University of San Francisco, Pacifica Graduate Institute, Dominican University of California, and the California Institute of Integral Studies, and I am grateful to Sarah Campbell and everyone at Rowman & Littlefield International. I am also indebted to everyone involved with the Forum on Religion and Ecology at Yale, with particular thanks to the directors of the Forum, Mary Evelyn Tucker and John Grim, two living examples of integral ecologists. I cannot forget George James, Irene Klaver, and Keith Wayne Brown, without whom I would never have found my way to phenomenology. I am still learning from them and from the other environmental philosophers at the University of North Texas. Much appreciation goes to Sean Kelly, Brian Swimme, and Catherine Keller for their encouraging guidance and for their extensive comments on earlier drafts of this work. Many thanks go to Sean Esbjörn-Hargens for supporting my work with integral studies and welcoming my participation in conferences and publications on that topic. Many dear friends have wandered with me along the meandering path of the geophilosophy of Deleuze and Guattari. Along those lines, Adam Robbert, Whitney Bauman, Elizabeth McAnally, and Luke Higgins all deserve special thanks for reading, writing, and talking with me. Extra special thanks go to Kimberly Carfore for her love, partnership, and intellectual solidarity throughout the writing and publication of this work. I want to express deep gratitude to all those who have nurtured me and supported this work, all those nearest and dearest to me, my family, friends, loved ones, and so many others who have been my companions and coconspirators—too many others to name, multiplicities of multiplicities folded together in the chaosmos.

ONE

Introduction

This book presents philosophical contributions to integral ecology—an emerging approach to ecology that crosses the disciplinary boundaries of the humanities and sciences (natural and social) with the aim of responding to the increasingly complex and perplexing ecological problems pervading the planet. "A book", according to Gilles Deleuze, "is not worth much on its own", but "can respond to a desire only in a political way, outside the book".[1] Like any book, this book of integral ecological philosophy finds its real value in its response to what happens outside its pages, in the connections the book makes with other people, with other problems and questions. This book is an invitation to make those connections—to experiment to make something happen to respond to your desires. Can the book respond to a desire for a comprehensive understanding of ecological problems? Can it respond to a desire for a more peaceful and just tomorrow for humans and for all the beings composing our planetary home, our *oikos*? The answer is simple. Experiment.

This book allies itself with the philosophy of Gilles Deleuze (1925–1995) and some of his colleagues and successors, particularly those who, like Deleuze, consider the task of philosophy to be an experimental effort to forge new connections, to create something and become different. Deleuze and his writing partner Félix Guattari express this sense of philosophy when they say, "Philosophy is the discipline that involves *creating* concepts".[2] A similar definition of the task of philosophy comes from Jacques Derrida (1930–2004), a friend and colleague of Deleuze and another close ally of mine throughout this book. Derrida is well known for his writings on deconstruction, and although deconstruction might sound as if it would yield a destructive approach to philosophy, it is also (and perhaps primarily) creative. It works in a way that opens new possibilities: "Deconstruction is inventive or it is nothing at all; [. . .] it opens up a passageway, it marches ahead and marks a trail [. . .]. Its *process* involves an affirmation".[3]

For thinkers like Deleuze and Derrida, philosophy is not just about talking or debating. Neither is it primarily a matter of thinking or reflecting. It is creative, inventive, or it is nothing at all. A philosopher's task is to facilitate the emergence of new events, new realities. Along these lines, the contemporary philosopher Graham Harman mentions that the "creation of concepts" proposed by Deleuze and Guattari is not just a creation of thoughts or images in human consciousness. Concepts are "independent forces traversing and apportioning reality", such that philosophy is not simply a creation of intellectual ideas but is also a creation of independent forces, which is to say, a "creation of objects" or *integral units*.[4]

Philosophers create concepts, and these concepts are not simply representations in human minds. They are events, objects, occasions. One can participate in them by following clues and decoding signs that express strange, unknown, and mysterious things. Along these lines, Deleuze says that a philosophy book should be like a detective novel or science fiction book, which is not to say that philosophical writing should be fiction as opposed to fact, but that it should "intervene" in and "resolve local situations" (problems not unlike the murders, thefts, time travel, aliens, and artificial intelligences of detective and sci-fi situations).[5] A concept is a specific event resolving specific problems, ranging from small-scale problems (e.g., a jewel heist or an intelligent robot) to large-scale problems (e.g., alien invasions and intergalactic politics) in the entangled temporalities (e.g., time travels) of presents, pasts, and futures.

Making things happen, concepts adapt and change along with the problems in which they intervene. "They are alive, like invisible creatures", like organisms changing with the dynamics of the events, problems, and other concepts that make up its environmental conditions.[6] Concepts can be thought of as "centers of vibrations, each in itself and every one in relation to all the others", and even when they do not cohere or correspond, they still "resonate" with one another (like Aristotle's concepts resonating with Plato's even when they disagree), and they have a "nondiscursive resonance" that vibrates in practises, actions, and bodies. To get a sense of how a concept does something, it might help to imagine a concept as a lens, bearing in mind that a concept is not merely a tool but is more of nascent practise. A philosopher does things with concepts in much the same way that, through the lenses of eyeglasses, a detective might see something that should be looked at by a molecular biologist with the more powerful lens of a microscope, which might then provide evidence that calls for someone's arrest or liberation, or perhaps the evidence leads to the discovery that alien intelligences have been interacting with Earth for millennia.

A concept shifts and transforms as it tracks problems, and in doing so, it opens possibilities for engaging specific situations and for creating new situations. This is exactly what is set to work in the practise of deconstruction. As John Caputo says in commenting on a question that came up in conversation with Derrida, "to 'deconstruct' does not mean—how often do we have to say this?—to flatten out or destroy but to loosen up, to open something up so that it is flexible, internally amendable, and revisable".[7] In short, philosophy can provide ways of participating in the local contexts of problems—here and now—whilst also calling for something else, something new, another context, summoning new possibilities.

A crucial question is whether philosophy can summon new possibilities not just for human existence but also for the nonhuman denizens of Earth. In contrast to much of the history of philosophy, which has been too focused on human existence, too anthropocentric and humanistic, Deleuze and Guattari (abbreviated henceforth as D&G) conceive of their philosophy in terms of a philosophy of Earth (i.e., geophilosophy) in which nature and human culture are not diametrically opposed.[8] The entanglement of nature and culture was precisely what interested them about the philosophy of nature. In 1988, Deleuze said that he and Guattari hoped to "produce a sort of philosophy of Nature, now that any distinction between nature and artifice is becoming blurred".[9] A few years later, D&G explicitly developed their concept of geophilosophy (see the section on "Rhizomes" in this book). However, even their earlier works express their antagonism to human exceptionalism. D&G always argued against understanding the human "as a king of creation", proposing instead that humans are on the same plane with other beings, immersed in "intimate contact with the profound life of all forms or all types of beings", such that a human is never responsible only for itself or other humans but is "responsible for even the stars and animal life".[10] Even the stars! Perhaps such an extraplanetary extension of responsibility sounds like a controversial point. However, with many people becoming increasingly concerned about the effects of asteroids, meteors, and solar flares on human life, it is not as controversial of a point as it used to be.

The humans and nonhumans on Earth are inextricably entangled with one another in ecological relationships, which are themselves situated within the dynamics of an evolving universe. Humans are not effectively understood if they are thought to be an exclusive group over and above the rest of the natural world. Deconstruction is inventive for humans and nonhumans, or it is nothing at all. The creation of concepts summons new possibilities for everything and everyone, whether human, nonhuman, or otherwise. As D&G put it, the "creation of concepts in itself calls for a future form, for a new earth and people that do not yet exist".[11] The conceptual inventiveness of philosophy is a practise that calls for transformation and renewal. Whose renewal? How much transformation? How can one respond to desires for transformation and renewal? These are the questions taken up in this book, *On the Verge of a Planetary Civilization*, particularly insofar as these questions touch on the ecological problems imprisoning and endangering the humans and nonhumans of our planetary home. Those problems are varied and numerous, affecting the natural environment, social and political institutions, and human health, well-being, and existential fulfilment.

Ecological problems can be found lurking in all activities, big and small: when I'm drinking water or eating food, when a species goes extinct, when I brush my teeth whilst the tap water runs, when a new road, factory, or hospital is built, when a nuclear reactor malfunctions, when fossil fuels burn, when wildfires burn, when chemically treated grass grows in my neighbour's backyard, when contaminated food is recalled, when crops are killed by drought, when I use Wi-Fi or check a Twitter feed, when a hurricane makes landfall, when a political leader is elected or overthrown, or when I drive a car to a nearby grocery store. These events connect to issues like water scarcity, global climate change, globalization, the loss of biological and cultural diversity, war, poverty, energy and resource use, food safety, consumption and consumerism, technological innovation, social and economic progress, happiness, hopelessness, despair, and so much more. These are serious problems threatening the future of life on Earth and the meaning of human existence, threatening to unravel the boundaries tying together the fabric of planetary coexistence. Although those problems are often referred to collectively as an "environmental crisis", it is important to remember that we humans are inextricably woven into the causes and effects of those problems, such that the environmental crisis is simultaneously a crisis of humanity. In Neil Evernden's laconic saying, "We are not *in* an environmental crisis, but *are* the environmental crisis".[12] To put it another way, the environmental crisis is a crisis of the integration of human and Earth systems. Such a crisis cannot be adequately addressed without crossing disciplinary boundaries to engage the interconnections between humans and nonhumans in the meanings and matters of ecological problems. Furthermore, such problems call for philosophies that can work (and play) with integral ecology to bring about the creation of new ideas, new concepts, new events that can make things happen to open some chance of a future.

This creation of new ideas resembles an approach to philosophy found in the writings of Plato, whose dialogues present the rejuvenated life of his teacher, Socrates. In Plato's *Theaetetus*, Socrates describes himself as a midwife's son and says that he is himself a midwife; that is, a practitioner of the "maieutic art" of facilitating birth.[13] Socrates is not saying that he literally helps women in the process of giving birth. Rather, his saying is a metaphor for his practise of educating humans. Using ideas in the same way a midwife uses her hands to deliver babies, Socrates facilitates the birth of latent capacities of human existence. In a more general sense, every midwife and every mother is a philosopher, birthing humans into being. With this approach to education, Socratic philosophy supported the emergence of Plato's Academy and the subsequent developments of universities and educational institutions that, with incredible irony, did not consider mothers and midwives as particularly important models for attaining knowledge. Furthermore, what those universities and institutions spread was far from ecological learning or Earth literacy. They spread human exceptionalism, which privileges rational human-human interactions and relegates human-Earth relations to an unconsidered or unimportant background.[14]

Shifting from the ancient to the modern world, another example that points out the effectiveness of philosophy to facilitate transformation can be found in the seventeenth-century philosopher René Descartes. Resonating with Plato's legacy, Descartes perpetuates the privilege of humans over the rest of the natural world. In the sixth part of his *Discourse on the Method*, Descartes proposes to replace the speculative thinking of ancient and medieval philosophy with a philosophy that is "very useful to life", a "practical philosophy" that would allow humans to become "masters and possessors of nature".[15] With a concept of method that seeks mastery of nature, Cartesian philosophy gets things done. Indeed, the concepts developed by Descartes have facilitated extensive scientific and technological developments (often called "progress"), which have helped make humans the Earth-shaping force we are today. Cartesian philosophy did not just change the ways that philosophy and science were done. It changed the ways that people lived their lives and the ways they related to the natural world, for better and for worse. In the centuries since Descartes, numerous technologies have come to populate the world, things like railroads, cars, aeroplanes, computers, telecommunications, nuclear reactors, social media, and genetically modified organisms, radically transforming human existence, altering the course of life, and changing the face of Earth. Of course, Descartes did not do all of that himself. Cartesian philosophy is among many factors that facilitated modern technological developments. Indeed, the effects and transformations of Cartesian philosophy exceed anything Descartes said or intended.

When philosophers aim to create concepts that open possibilities and make things happen, they cannot determine or preprogram what will emerge from their creations. This is not to say that philosophers are not responsible for what they write, think, and speak. The point is that their creations surpass their own philosophies, such that the transformative power of a philosophy book is not in the book, but takes place "in a political way, outside the book", in the ways the book interfaces with different things and plugs into different systems and networks.[16] As Plato says in his letters, his writings do not disclose his conception of reality, for such a conception arises through his communion with the object of his study—the "thing itself" (*pragma auto*).[17] Likewise, the scientific and technological revolutions facilitated by Cartesian philosophy are not necessarily indicative of Descartes's own understanding of the world. Indeed, they probably go far beyond anything he could have imagined. Similarly, the revolutionary philosophy of Karl Marx changed the world, but not in ways he could determine or predict in advance. Marx is not directly responsible for every communist revolution or even for all things Marxist. Indeed, Marx himself is reported to have said, "I am not a Marxist".[18]

In short, Marx does not endorse all things Marxist, Plato does not necessarily support the Platonism expressed in many of his dialogues, and Descartes cannot be convicted as a card-carrying Cartesian. What is at stake here is not whether philosophers endorse their own philosophies. In most cases, they are probably sincerely invested in what they write, even if that sincere investment is brief, full of doubt, or masked by metaphors or other rhetorical devices. The point is that the creations of philosophers take on lives of their own, invisible critters growing amidst ecologies that entangle ideas, societies, and natural environments. Working with such unruly creatures is a joint effort. Philosophy cannot be done alone.

Philosophers create concepts by working and playing with others. This includes reworking and replaying other philosophies and transforming them in ways that go beyond whatever they initially intended or accomplished. In other words, philosophical thinking is thinking with others, in the way that Isabelle Stengers—another close ally in this book—says she is "thinking with" philosophers like Deleuze and Alfred North Whitehead in an effort to enact a "free and wild creation of concepts".[19] In the work of Aristotle, for example, we find a philosopher who is thinking with Plato, Pythagoras, Empedocles, Heraclitus, and others. When we read works of Thomas Aquinas, we find him thinking with numerous ancient and medieval thinkers, including Aristotle, Augustine, Maimonides, Ibn Rushd (Averroes), and many more. From the ancient to the contemporary world, philosophers think with one another, whether in consensus or in contrast, in discussion or in debate, in person or on the phone, in print or online.

It is important to add here that philosophers do not think only with other philosophers. They also think with nonphilosophical companions, like Deleuze (a philosopher) thinking with Guattari (a psychotherapist) to compose cowritten books, including Deleuze's last book, in which he says (with Guattari) that "the non-philosophical is perhaps closer to the heart of philosophy than philosophy itself".[20] At its core, philosophy seeks to create concepts that resonate outside of philosophy, outside of philosophical books and philosophical ways of knowing. Philosophers think with "a sort of groping experimentation" into nonphilosophical ways of knowing (e.g., "dream", "pathological processes, esoteric experiences, drunkenness, and excess") and even into modes of existence outside the human ("an animal, a molecule, a particle"), such that "one does not think without becoming something else", becoming different not just cognitively but ecologically.[21] In Derrida's terms, one could say that philosophy at its core deconstructs itself, practicing hospitality and welcoming differences and others into its ecology, welcoming strangers into its home. "Hospitality is the deconstruction of the at-home; deconstruction is hospitality to the other".[22]

In this book, I think with Deleuze, Derrida, and many other companions—philosophers, historians, theologians, environmentalists, cosmologists, dogs, plants, poets, elements, political movements, technologies, and many others—to facilitate the creation of integral ecological concepts. Such concepts resonate with calls for a new Earth and new people, an Earth and people that are mutually enfolded into what can be called, tentatively and tenderly, a planetary civilization. Not simply a global civilization where humans around the world participate in (or react against) the homogenizing spread of worldwide trade and information networks that benefit a miniscule few at the expense of the health and well-being of the vast multitude of planetary beings, the concept of a planetary civilization conveys—hopefully—the possibility of becoming otherwise, the possibility of inventing new modes of togetherness, intensifying the vibrant coexistence of humans with one another and with all of the habitats and inhabitants of Earth. In particular, throughout this book, I focus on the creation of concepts that provide a sense of the boundary issues of planetary coexistence: the uncertainty of our limits and edges, the ambivalence of boundaries that can protect or oppress, the complex connections that separate us (who?) and bring us together, and the partitions that allow some things to be seen and heard whilst others remain invisible and voiceless, nonsense.

Are we in the middle of a planetary emergency? Is a planetary civilization emerging? Who decides? Who is included in the "we" of a planetary civilization? Where did we come from? Where are we going? Questions about who we are, where we come from, and where we are going are some of the fundamental questions addressed by philosophy as well as science and religion, and today, they are some of the most pressing questions facing the human species. They call for concepts that resonate with our efforts to understand and respond to the increasing complexity and uncertainty of human-Earth relations. They call for ideas about how to exist in a time of immense ecological challenges, a time out of joint.

"The time is out of joint". So says Shakespeare's Hamlet, who is dismayed over the state of affairs in his homeland, Denmark, and equally dismayed that his task is "to set it right".[23] It is true that the time is out of joint, and not only for Hamlet's Denmark. It is true everywhere throughout the current global civilization, a world that is marked by multiple ecological problems and ongoing crises. Like Hamlet, many people today hear the challenging call to set it right, including scientists, activists, political leaders, community organizers, religious practitioners, economists, artists, educators, children, corporate executives, and many others. This book is a contribution to efforts to set it right, to cultivate a better tomorrow, not by following Hamlet but by following the concepts of philosophers.

In Derrida's analysis of this saying of Hamlet, he suggests that it implies two different ways of being out of joint, that is, "two disadjustments": (1) our time is unjust, and (2) time bears an "untimeliness" that folds the past into the present, an "anachrony" that complicates "the very presence of the present" by spreading the present, unfolding its inheritance of the past and opening it up for a time to come.[24] Similarly, in his account of Hamlet's phrase, Deleuze also suggests that this saying is not only about injustice but is also, in another sense, about the spreading or unfolding of time: "Time itself unfolds".[25] Derrida and Deleuze suggest that, on the one hand, to say that time is out of joint is to say that our time is unjust, violent, or broken. In our time, humans are becoming increasingly aware of ruptures, breaks, and disorder in the natural environment, in social institutions, and in human consciousness. This is particularly evident in the current proliferation of ecological crises endangering multiple forms of human and nonhuman existence. On the other hand, there is another way of interpreting this disjointed time. To say that time is out of joint is to say that time is evolutionary: an open-ended, unfolding process. This process is not accounted for in most ordinary notions of time (e.g., time as a preestablished measuring system containing sequences of now-points). Far stranger than the notion of time as a container for events or as a sequence of nows, a disjointed time is an untimely time, in which our experiences are never simply on time but are always complicated, always already late and early, unfolding the past and folding into an unforeseen future. Our time is out of joint in each of those distinct senses: unjust and evolutionary. Ironically, as we realize that time is an unfolding process, we are also awakening to the injustices of our time. At the same time that humans are entering into a widespread recognition of our evolutionary context, we are recognizing that our context is riddled with injustice that humans are committing.

Mary Evelyn Tucker, a scholar in the field of religion and ecology, articulates a similar point in her account of the twenty-first-century planetary situation, where she describes how the new story—the story of an evolving universe—"is beginning to dawn on humans as we awaken to a new realization of the vastness and complexity of this unfolding process":

At the same time that this story becomes available to the human community, we are becoming conscious of the growing environmental crisis and of the rapid destruction of species and habitat that is taking place around the globe. Just as we are realizing the vast expanse of time that distinguishes the evolution of the universe over some thirteen billion years, we are recognizing how late is our arrival in this stupendous process. Just as we become conscious that the Earth took more than four billion years to bring forth this abundance of life, it is dawning on us how quickly we are foreshortening its future flourishing.[26]

For philosophy to respond creatively to contemporary problems, it must participate in the recognition that our time is out of joint, that planetary coexistence is situated in evolutionary relationships undergoing crisis. In other words, for philosophy to make something happen in today's world, philosophy must become ecological, which is not just about practises for "going green" (e.g., recycling, eating locally, and buying eco-friendly products) but is more primarily about attending to the unpredictable intricacies of evolutionary relationships and responding to conditions of crisis or injustice. The importance of becoming ecological is well recognized by many (yet still not enough) scholars, researchers, policymakers, and activists working with ecological problems, and it is a fundamental point for this book.

To give an introductory orientation to this book, I describe the task of becoming ecological and, following that, I describe three other aspects of the philosophical contributions that this book presents: integral, humourous, and speculative. This introduction thus provides an outline of an approach to philosophy that, by becoming ecological, integral, humourous, and speculative, creates concepts that call for responses to the complex boundaries of planetary coexistence.

BECOMING ECOLOGICAL

In 1866, the German biologist Ernst Haeckel coined the word *oecologie* (from the Greek *oikos*, meaning "household" or "dwelling") to develop an inquiry into the household of nature. Haeckel intended for ecology to further the development of the evolutionary theory articulated by Charles Darwin in *The Origin of Species* in 1859. Defining ecology as the scientific study of relations between organisms and their environmental conditions, Haeckel says that "ecology is the study of all those complex interrelations referred to by Darwin as the conditions of the struggle for existence".[27] The influence of Darwin on ecology led the environmental historian Donald Worster to describe Darwin as the "single most important figure in the history of ecology over the past two or three centuries".[28] With roots in evolutionary theory, ecology started as an extension of biological science. Biologists were focusing only on the nutrition and reproduction of organisms whilst ignoring the relations that each organism has with its environment. By focusing on complex interrelations, Haeckel's ecology extended biology to include more thorough explanations of the conditions of existence for living beings.

First developed as an extension of evolutionary biology to include the study of relations between organisms and environmental conditions, ecology facilitates knowledge of both of the ways in which our time is out of joint: knowledge of evolution (e.g., species are constituted over time in relation to dynamic environmental conditions) and of disjointed ecologies (e.g., ecological damage, crisis, injustice). In a time that is out of joint, humans are becoming ecological, becoming aware of our evolutionary household and of the critical conditions therein.

Becoming ecological is not merely a scientific endeavour. Although many forms of ecological research continue to be part of theories and practises in biology and environmental sciences, the meaning of the word *ecology* has exploded, far exceeding its initial definition as a biological science. Indeed, for Haeckel himself, ecology is conceived not only as a science but also as a theological vision for which evolution "now leads the reflecting human spirit" to a metaphysical truth about the "order of the cosmos".[29] In other words, ecology as Haeckel understood it is both science and spirituality, a model for analyzing biological phenomena and a model for living one's life.

Since its nineteenth-century beginnings, ecology has become a "household" word with a wide range of meanings and connotations. It is a pervasive part of human civilization. Even if it is not referred to explicitly, ecology shows up in many ways throughout mainstream media and popular images that circulate through the technologically developed world. The natural environment can no longer be conceived as the background of human existence but is becoming an increasingly active part of everyday events, making regular appearances in the news, showing up in reports on various topics: global climate change, a polar vortex, a nuclear disaster in Japan, an oil spill in the Gulf of Mexico, tornadoes and hurricanes wreaking record-breaking havoc, "eco-friendly" products and technologies, celebrity environmentalists, "green" businesses, extinct or newly discovered species, fossil fuels and alternative energies, food contaminations and recalls, droughts and floods, asteroids and meteors.

Ecology can be found in popular films, often in films that portray human civilization as alienated or disconnected from the natural world. In some cases, the civilization portrayed is our own, as can be seen in the numerous documentaries focusing on the dangers of human-caused (anthropogenic) environmental problems like global climate change, deforestation, mass extinction of species, water scarcity, and habitat destruction. In other cases, the disconnected civilization is a fictitious one that bears striking resemblances to our own, exhibiting traits of consumerism or military-industrial colonialism.[30]

Ecology is also in hip-hop—a genre of popular music typically associated less with the natural environment than with critical perspectives on socioeconomic and cultural issues (e.g., urbanization, drug use, sex, crime, poverty, racism, etc.). For example, whilst on a world tour, the hip-hop artist Jay-Z (Shawn Carter) worked in collaboration with the United Nations and with the cable television network MTV to raise awareness about the global water crisis, which is the focus of the UN's International Decade for Action 2005 to 2015, "Water for Life".[31] This eco-hip-hop collaboration included the production of a video special, *Diary of Jay-Z: Water for Life*, which followed Jay-Z as he visited places around the world that have been affected by the global water crisis and spent time with children who experience water scarcity firsthand.

Not only is it in popular media and in news about current events. Ecology is also everywhere in scientific inquiry and other forms of academic research. Since Haeckel first coined the word, ecology has developed into numerous subfields and schools of thought, with ecological perspectives emerging in many areas of academic study, spanning the biophysical sciences (e.g., agroforestry, ecosystem ecology, and population ecology) as well as the social sciences (e.g., ecological economics, ecopsychology, and political ecology) and the humanities (e.g., environmental ethics, environmental aesthetics, and religion and ecology).

Ecological themes are everywhere today, present in various ways throughout current events, mainstream media, and numerous forms of research. The ubiquity of ecology overflows the limits of its standard definition. In other words, ecology has become more than a biological study of the interrelations that comprise the Earth "household" (*oikos*). It has become a "household" word with a vast spectrum of meanings and connotations within and beyond scientific and academic communities. That sounds like good news, insofar as it indicates the widespread dissemination of ecological perspectives. However, differing approaches to ecology occasionally impede one another's efforts, as when scientific researchers degrade religious perspectives as mere superstition or naïve belief, or when people engaging in political ecology fail to consider recent developments in scientific research. Comprehensive responses to ecological problems require the crossing of disciplinary boundaries.

Whilst there have been attempts to develop more inclusive or integrative approaches to ecology, many of these attempts only include perspectives modeled on ideals of scientific objectivity (e.g., biophysical, social, and systems sciences). Such approaches can be beneficial for coordinating the efforts of biologists, atmospheric scientists, economists, and policymakers, but they fail to address phenomena investigated in the humanities (e.g., ethical values, cultural traditions, religious communities, metaphysical speculations, and personal experiences). If they are to be comprehensive, effective, and long term, ethical and political responses to a time out of joint must include multiple approaches to the meanings and mysteries of the natural world. They must include sciences along with the environmental humanities, addressing the ways in which evolutionary unfolding and environmental crisis relate to the experiences, values, ideas, meanings, cultures, and traditions that shape and are shaped by ecological problems.

The task of becoming ecological, then, does not end with an understanding of the crises and evolutionary dynamics of our disjointed time. It also involves an integrative task: responding to ecological problems by crossing boundaries between disciplines of the sciences and humanities in a way that accounts for ecological realities in their numerous and varied aspects. Such an understanding of the task of becoming ecological is formulated in *The Three Ecologies* by Félix Guattari, who articulates a "generalized ecology"—an ecological philosophy he also calls *ecosophy*, which responds to ecological disturbances and the degradation of the exterior environment as well as the progressive deterioration of "human modes of life, both individual and collective".[32] The guiding question of ecosophy is this:

> [H]ow do we change mentalities, how do we reinvent social practices that would give back to humanity—if it ever had it—a sense of responsibility for its own survival, but equally for the future of all life on the planet, for animal and vegetable species, likewise for incorporeal species such as music, the arts, cinema, the relation with time, love and compassion for others, the feeling of fusion at the heart of the cosmos?[33]

Ecosophy—a generalized or integral ecology—aims to reinvent modes of human existence in relationship to three ecologies: the mental, social, and environmental.[34] *Mental ecology* is not mental in the sense of cognitive. Rather, the whole dimension of subjectivity and the processes that constitute subjectivity (i.e., "subjectification") are included in mental ecology: "mental ecosophy will lead us to reinvent the relation of the subject to the body, to phantasm, to the passage of time, to the 'mysteries' of life and death".[35] Mental ecology studies relationships between organisms, environments, and ideas, but it is much more than that. It is also a commitment to existential transformation, advocating the development of innovative experiments and practises that promote the ongoing production of free and creative subjects, who can understand and express themselves affirmatively in relation to the rest of the world.

Guattari's *social ecology* addresses collective relations of subjectification, including relations of politics, economics, "social struggle", movements of "mass consciousness-raising", and "the technological evolution of the media", all with the aim of emancipating individuals and social systems from unjust conditions, particularly the unjust conditions of "Integrated World Capitalism"—Guattari's term for the network of financial and commercial relations homogenizing the planet, turning everything and everyone into resources and dollar signs.[36] Taking the singularities of mental and social subjectivity into account, Guattari calls for ecology to question "the whole of subjectivity and capitalistic power formations", thus opening up ecology beyond its association with, on the one hand, "a small nature-loving minority" for whom ecology is associated with parks and the great outdoors, and on the other hand, "qualified specialists" for whom ecology is primarily about environmental science and policy.[37]

Environmental ecology corresponds roughly to what is normally included in the environmental or ecological sciences, which study the complex interrelations of organisms and ecosystems. Guattari mentions that it is possible to "rename environmental ecology *machinic ecology*", where machines are not the passive, inert, controllable objects of mechanistic materialism but are better described as self-organizing (i.e., autopoietic) systems, events, or affective assemblages, which are composed of interrelated parts and have capacities for acting and being acted upon.[38] In short, environmental ecology studies the complex interrelations of machinic assemblages at multiple scales (e.g., organisms, populations, species, and ecosystems), and at any scale, the development of the system is wildly contingent and uncertain. Anything could happen. The self-organizing dynamics of assemblages are radically open. Guattari formulates this point into a "principle specific to environmental ecology: it states that anything is possible—the worst disasters or the most flexible evolutions".[39] It is important to add here that environmental ecology does not exclude human assemblages. Each of the three ecologies overlaps with the others. Cosmic and human events are brought together as ecosophy studies the interactive processes of all assemblages, including their stratified and organized structures as well as the chaos, disequilibrium, and flexibility that mark their breakdowns and evolutionary breakthroughs. The inclusion of human practises in environmental ecology underscores the importance of environmental ethics for a generalized ecology. Ecosophy is a vision of ethics adapted to a complex and uncertain world in which anything can happen. Weaving together the three ecologies requires "an ecosophical ethics adapted to this terrifying and fascinating situation".[40]

Guattari's ecosophy works towards liberating singularities in each of the three ecological registers, carefully attending to singularities—the unique and compelling capacities of things. "The demands of singularity are rising up almost everywhere" during our time of ecological crisis, such that the question of ecology "becomes one of how to encourage the organization of individual and collective ventures, and how to direct them towards an ecology of resingularization".[41] Such resingularization restores the uniqueness that makes individuals different from one another, not to isolate them but to open possibilities for more complex modes of togetherness and community. "Individuals must become both more united and increasingly different".[42] A resingularization of a river, for instance, would unleash the unique capacities whereby that river persists in becoming a river. Liberating the singularity of the river frees up possibilities for the river to intensify its existence, which means entering into relationships that develop its powers to affect and be affected by other environments, societies, and subjects, and breaking any relationships that dull those powers. That river would not be assimilated into a capitalist homogeneity where everything is reduced to dollar signs within the same system of monetary exchange. Homogeneity clearly dulls the river's affective capacities. Can an artistic rendering of the river into painting enhance its affective capacities? Can an irrigation project? Everything depends on the specifics. Who or what is impacted? How much? Some paintings liberate singularities, and some paintings are cliché, dulling affective capacities through the overuse and monotonous repetition of images. Likewise, some irrigation projects are more enhancing than others.

The point is not to save nature, save the world, or preserve some supposedly natural or pristine state of affairs. The point of a generalized ecology—an ecosophy—is to develop conditions for resingularization: conditions for new existential values ("a nascent subjectivity"), social transformation ("a constantly mutating socius"), and environmental revitalization ("an environment in the process of being reinvented").[43] To generalize ecology is to respond creatively to the demands of singularities. It requires the navigation of the complexity and uncertainty of problems that entangle multiple aspects of ecological realities, including environmental, social, and subjective. It requires becoming integral.

BECOMING INTEGRAL

The phrase *integral ecology* emerged four times independently throughout the twentieth century.[44] It was first used by Hilary Moore in a 1958 marine ecology textbook, in which Moore proposes that ecologies that focus on ecosystems (synecology) and on their component organisms (autecology) should be supplemented by an "integral ecology" that would reconnect the ecosystem and its components into a whole.[45] Moore's effort to integrate disparate ecological schools is indicative of the holistic impulse of integral ecology, but Moore's strictly scientific approach yields a relatively narrow sense of integral ecology compared with the integral ecologies that would arise later. In the meantime, numerous ecologically oriented disciplines continued emerging, not only in the biophysical sciences but also in the humanities and social sciences; for example, fields of environmental ethics, ecofeminism, ecopsychology, ecological economics, and deep ecology. That proliferation of ecological research cleared a path for approaches to ecology that would work across the boundaries of all of those areas of inquiry. In 1995, three different theorists used the word *integral* to call for such boundary-crossing approaches to ecology: the cultural historian and "Earth scholar" (or "geologian") Thomas Berry, the liberation theologian Leonardo Boff, and the Integral theorist Ken Wilber. A brief overview of each will elucidate the task of becoming integral.[46]

Berry used the phrases *integral cosmology* or *integral ecology* at least as early as 1995 to refer to his work with the new story of the evolving universe.[47] For Berry, the historical mission of humans today—our "Great Work"—is for us to reinvent ourselves and our cultural traditions so that our contact with the Earth community becomes mutually beneficial instead of destructive. The destruction currently afflicting our planetary community is largely the result of forms of human consciousness and behaviour that dissociate humans from the natural world and thus fail to develop a conscience that participates in "a single integral community of the Earth".[48] Accordingly, our Great Work is "to reinvent the human", creating new modes of consciousness and conscience that participate in an integral Earth community. Such a community can only be built with the support of renewed engagements in many sources of wisdom, including those of contemporary sciences, the world's religious traditions, indigenous communities, and women.[49] With those sources of wisdom, humans can accomplish the mission of our times: "We are here to become integral with the larger Earth Community".[50] Our Great Work is becoming integral.

Deriving from the Latin word for a "whole" or "complete entity" (*integer*), the word *integral* bears connotations of unity or wholeness. Based on that definition, becoming integral with the Earth community suggests that humans would understand themselves as members of one single yet multiform community that includes all of the planet's habitats and inhabitants, ideas and societies, humans and nonhumans. This definition of integral in terms of wholeness does not touch on everything that is implied in the word's meaning. Indeed, it does not touch on the sense of touch implicit in the meaning of *integral*. Touch is at the heart of "integral". Etymologically, the word *integral* could be defined as "untouched" or "intact", like an undivided whole.[51] This does not mean that integral ecology is simply holism. Nor does it mean that integral ecology calls for humans to stop touching the natural world and let it return to some pristine or original state (as if that were even possible). The untouched is the limit of touch, where touch makes contact with something else, something different. Integral ecology calls for a touch that attends to its limits, its contacts. It calls for humans to reinvent themselves so that their touch is tactful, so that their practises enhance ecological relations instead of dulling and destroying them. In other words, becoming integral with the Earth community is a matter of carrying out a transition to a tactful mode of contact with the world, where tactful touch means not touching too much, touching lightly and tenderly.

An objectifying touch is not tactful. It fails to leave intact the agency or existential value of what is touched. The touched entity becomes *merely* an object and is no longer touching. It is stripped of its agency. According to Berry, everything we touch is an agent or subject, so when we touch something, it is not only touched by us, it is also touching us. "We are touched by what we touch".[52] Our Great Work is to learn how to touch the beings in our planetary home in ways that leave their forms of subjectivity intact. We must learn how to touch in a way that does not reduce touching subjects to mere objects but participates in the complex relationality that intertwines touching and touched, intangible and tangible, subjective and objective.

Tactful touch entails recognizing that the universe is not composed of mere objects but is a "communion of subjects".[53] To be sure, the universe is made up of different objects, but these objects are not merely touched. They are subjects touching other subjects. Ultimately, when we touch anything, we are participating in the reciprocal relations of a vast and complex network of touching, a communion of touch that embraces the Earth and the cosmos as a whole. Berry articulates this in terms of "three basic principles: differentiation, subjectivity, and communion", which resonate with Guattari's environmental, mental, and social ecologies, respectively.[54] Altogether, these principles are known as the "cosmogenetic principle", which Berry developed with the cosmologist Brian Swimme.[55] According to this principle, all evolutionary processes involve an objective or tangible exterior that differentiates things from one another, a subjective depth or self-organization (i.e., autopoiesis) that provides the interior articulation or agency of things, and a relational communion whereby subjects connect with one another in collective or social milieus. The cosmogenetic principle is at work on all levels of the Earth community, including the air (atmosphere), water (hydrosphere), and rock (geosphere) as well as all forms of life (biosphere) and human consciousness (noosphere). Integral ecology includes all these spheres into "an integral Earth study".[56]

Integral ecology, for Berry, is a matter of becoming integral with the Earth community by attending to the threefold cosmogenetic principle. It is a matter of cultivating mutually beneficial relations with the natural world through tactful contact, tender tenacity, holding the members of our planetary home in communion, touching and being touched. We must touch lightly and tenderly, leaving intact the intangible subjectivity that makes our Earth community thrive in mutually enhancing communion. Such tactful contact would leave a vibrant planetary home for future generations, a planetary home that "can be lived on with grace and beauty and at least a touch of human and earthly tenderness".[57] This is our Great Work: to develop an integral touch, a touch of tenderness. This is integral ecology for Berry, cultivating a tender touch that would support the flourishing of the Earth community for present and future generations.

In 1995, whilst Berry was developing his integral ecology, the Brazilian theologian Leonardo Boff began describing his approach to ecology as an "integral ecology". In an introduction to the special issue of the theology journal *Concilium* dedicated to ecology and poverty, Boff (with coauthor Virgilio Elizondo) calls for an integral approach to ecology that brings together the approaches that have emerged in the sciences, humanities, and in movements of conservation, preservation, and environmentalism. "The quest today is increasingly for an *integral ecology*" that can bring together those approaches in efforts to create

> a new alliance between societies and nature, which will result in the conservation of the patrimony of the earth, socio-cosmic wellbeing, and the maintenance of conditions that will allow evolution to continue on the course it has now been following for some fifteen thousand million years.
>
> For an integral ecology, society and culture also belong to the ecological complex. Ecology is, then, the relationship that all bodies, animate and inanimate, natural and cultural, establish and maintain among themselves and with their surroundings. In this holistic perspective, economic, political, social, military, educational, urban, agricultural and other questions are all subject to ecological consideration. The basic question in ecology is this: to what extent do this or that science, technology, institutional or personal activity, ideology or religion help either to support or to fracture the dynamic equilibrium that exists in the overall system.[58]

Since this 1995 proposal, Boff has further developed his concept of integral ecology. His personal website has sections on four different approaches to ecology: environmental, social, mental, and integral, again recalling Guattari's three ecologies plus his more general ecosophy.[59] The *environmental* approach engages ecological issues through sciences and technological development. The *social* approach addresses issues of social justice and sustainable social institutions (education, health care, economy, etc.). Moreover, social well-being in this context is not exclusively human, "it must also be socio-cosmic. It must attend to the needs of the other beings in nature, the plants, the animals, the microorganisms, because all together they constitute the planetary community, in which we are inserted and without whom we ourselves could not exist".[60] Focusing on consciousness, the *mental* approach (also called "deep" or "profound") indicates that ecological problems call not only for healthier and more sustainable societies and environments but also for healthier processes of subjectivity, processes that revitalize sociocosmic well-being by renewing vital engagements with the natural world and with cultures, gender roles, religious worldviews, and unconscious desires.

Those first three approaches (environmental, social, and mental) include the various fields of ecology that have emerged from the biophysical sciences, social sciences, and humanities. *Integral* ecology includes those three ecologies and presents a new vision of Earth, wherein humans and Earth are situated in the evolutionary becoming of the cosmos, which is to say, situated in processes of cosmogenesis. Echoing the cosmogenetic principle of Swimme and Berry, Boff enumerates three aspects of cosmogenesis: (1) "Complexity and differentiation", which structures the objective or exterior facets of things; (2) "Self-organization and consciousness", which structures the subjective depth or interior facets of things; and (3) "Reconnection and relation", which structures the ways things come together not merely as a collection of different objects but as communicating agents, communing subjects.[61] Boff's three aspects of cosmogenesis are parallel to his three ecologies: environmental (differentiation), mental (consciousness), and social (relation). Whereas his three ecologies are ways of studying phenomena, the three aspects of cosmogenesis refer to dimensions of real processes of becoming.

Boff (writing with Mark Hathaway) finds a paradigmatic example of integral ecology in the Earth Charter, which is an international document that presents a shared vision of values and principles for a peaceful, just, and sustainable global society.[62] The Earth Charter calls for the emergence of a global society grounded in a shared vision and principles that embrace democratic political participation, human rights, social and economic equity, nonviolence, ecological integrity, and respect for life. "The Earth Charter springs forth from a holistic, integral vision" that, according to Boff and Hathaway, presents "an affirmation of hope" with its proposal for "inclusive, integrated solutions" to the interlocking crises of the environment, society, and consciousness.[63]

The exemplary role of the Earth Charter for integral ecology indicates Boff's commitment to liberation. As a Catholic liberation theologian, Boff's personal and professional efforts engage spirituality, tradition, and scripture to support the liberation of humans from conditions of injustice. Thus, the work of liberation is not only about personal salvation but also about social justice. Furthermore, Boff's works point to a crossover between liberation theology and ecology, which have in common an aim to "seek liberation" in response to cries that express "bleeding wounds": the wounds of social oppression ("the cry of the poor"; theology) and environmental degradation ("the cry of the Earth"; ecology).[64] Boff's integral ecology thus asks the question of *integral liberation*: "How can we move forward toward an integral liberation for humanity and the Earth itself"?[65] Whereas liberation is normally defined "in the personal sense of spiritual realization or in the collective sense of" social justice, integral liberation includes both senses of liberation and situates them "in a wider, ecological—and even cosmological—context".[66] In its cosmological context, the process of integral liberation can be understood as the "conscious participation of humanity" in the cosmogenetic processes of differentiation, subjectivity, and communion.[67]

Boff's integral ecology has many parallels to that of Berry, including the importance of liberation, as Berry's integral ecology also attends to the connections between social injustice and environmental degradation.[68] In addition to their focus on liberation, Berry and Boff both come from Catholic theological backgrounds, which is evident in their inclusion of religious perspectives within their integral visions and in their influential roles within the study of ecological theology and the broader field of religion and ecology.[69] The most direct parallel between Berry's and Boff's integral ecologies is their use of the threefold cosmogenetic principle, which Boff derives from Berry to designate the three areas of study included in integral ecology.

Boff uses other sources along with Berry to articulate his threefold vision of integral ecology. One notable example is Guattari. Whilst the parallel between Guattari's three ecologies and the cosmogenetic principle of Swimme and Berry seem like a case of independent invention and not influence, the terminology for Boff's environmental, social, and mental ecologies comes explicitly from Guattari, thus establishing a moment of crossover between liberation theology and the poststructuralism associated with Guattari (along with Deleuze and Derrida). Boff says that the violent aggression of humans towards the natural world indicates "a failure to integrate the three main directions of ecology as formulated by F. Guattari: environmental ecology, social ecology, and mental ecology".[70] Boff also draws on Guattari's concept of "transversality", which Boff uses to describe a "peculiar feature of ecological knowledge" whereby it crosses multiple dimensions of knowledge simultaneously, relating ecological community and complexity to the future and the past and to "all experiences and all forms of comprehension".[71] Integral ecology thus calls for an "understanding of the transversality (interconnected or cross-disciplinary nature) of knowledge".[72] It is through a transversal movement that integral ecology can liberate the singularities of environmental, social, and mental ecologies.[73] In short, contributions to integral ecology come from many different directions, of which Berry, Boff, and Guattari are just a few. One can also find contributions coming from scholars and practitioners working with the Integral theory of Ken Wilber—the person most commonly associated with the word *integral*, or, more specifically, *Integral* (capitalized so as to distinguish it from other integral approaches).

Wilber's writings and theories have become more intricate and more refined throughout his career, beginning with the publication of his first book, in which he accounts for the roles of different forms of psychology, therapy, and spirituality in facilitating the development of the human being through different levels of consciousness.[74] In his more recent works, Wilber has extended his thinking to include everything, literally. He articulates his Integral vision in terms of a "Theory of Everything" (TOE)—a theory that "attempts to include matter, body, mind, soul, and spirit as they appear in self, culture, and nature".[75] Wilber himself notes that all attempts at such a theory always "fall short" and are "marked by the many ways in which they fail", not necessarily because of any deficiencies on the part of the theorist, but because theoretical categorization could never encompass the expansiveness of everything:

"the task is inherently undoable".[76] Along those lines, Wilber is constantly revising his approach, having moved through several distinct phases in his career, from his initial phase of psychological and spiritual writing, through phases of developmental and evolutionary thinking, into his most recent phases developing and applying his Integral framework.[77]

Wilber first proposed his Integral framework in *Sex, Ecology, Spirituality: The Spirit of Evolution*, which was published in 1995, the same year that Boff and Berry independently proposed their versions of integral ecology. As the title suggests, Wilber applies his Integral framework to ecology, including a proposal for "Integral environmental ethics", although without explicitly using the phrase *integral ecology*.[78] To articulate his framework, Wilber presents a diagram that is supposed to function as a map of everything: the AQAL model, an "all-quadrant, all-level" map.[79] The four quadrants are as follows: individual subjectivity in the upper-left quadrant, individual objectivity in the upper-right quadrant, collective subjectivity (i.e., intersubjectivity) in the lower-left quadrant, and collective objectivity (interobjectivity) in the lower-right quadrant. Becoming integral, for Wilber, means integrating all quadrants—the subjective, objective, individual, and collective dimensions of different ways of being and knowing. Furthermore, becoming integral requires that one account for the quadrants as they are situated in evolutionary and developmental processes, which are mapped as "levels" (e.g., levels of matter, life, and mind).

By simplifying the right-hand quadrants, the model can be simplified into "The Big Three": subjectivity ("I"), intersubjectivity ("we"), and objectivity (which includes individual and collective "It/s"; that is, "It" and "Its").[80] The Big Three is roughly parallel to Guattari's three ecologies, with "I", "We", and "It/s" corresponding to mental, social, and environmental ecologies, which themselves correspond to the subjectivity, communion, and differentiation of the cosmogenetic principle.[81] Furthermore, like Wilber's Integral vision, the integral ecologies of Guattari, Boff, and Berry situate these three dimensions of being and knowing in the evolutionary processes of a creative and unpredictable universe. To be sure, these thinkers are very different from one another, yet they point towards a shared commitment of integral ecologies: accounting for subjective, social, and environmental ecologies as they are situated in the dynamic processes of a cosmos in which anything can happen. That shared commitment is taken up by Sean Esbjörn-Hargens and Michael Zimmerman in their monumental book applying Wilber's Integral framework to ecology, *Integral Ecology: Uniting Multiple Perspectives on the Natural World*.

Esbjörn-Hargens and Zimmerman draw on the works of Guattari, Boff, Berry, and many others in an effort to use the AQAL model to map the vast multiplicity of ecological perspectives. Their book is the most systematic presentation of an integral approach to ecology thus far. Yet although it seeks to integrate over two hundred distinct approaches to ecology, including approaches from sciences, humanities, arts, and social movements, it is still "only the briefest sketch", as "much more work remains to be done" by various kinds of integral ecologists engaging in ongoing efforts to map the complexity, depth, and mystery of relationships in the natural world.[82] Much work remains, and it is more than any single approach can accomplish. Multiple approaches are needed, multiple ways of becoming integral, and each approach needs to draw on the appropriate philosophical concepts: transversal concepts that can cross boundaries between different perspectives and facilitate efforts to cultivate comprehensive responses to ecological problems.

BECOMING HUMOUROUS

This book presents concepts of integral ecology, which is to say, concepts for becoming ecological and becoming integral in a civilization of planetary interconnectivity. Although such concepts are serious, I claim that a philosophy of integral ecology must also deploy concepts for becoming humourous. A humourous tone is indicated by the somewhat silly structure of the book, wherein the beginning, middle, and ending chapters are designated as "Beginning", "Middle", and "Ending", as if a planetary civilization would neatly follow a well-known order, as if its tangled and unpredictable boundaries could ever be so clear and distinct or so readily available for exploration in three easy steps. The titles indicate that those chapters, themselves situated in a middle between introductory and concluding chapters, introduce an element of play into well-known orders and easy-to-follow steps, making fun of philosophy books that purport to encapsulate in written form the meanings, matters, and mysteries of reality. At the same time, the chapters of this book are not just the expressions of a person trying to be funny. They call sincerely for different ways of thinking about philosophy, about boundaries, and about planetary coexistence.

Ecological problems are extremely serious, as are questions about the emergence and future of a planetary civilization. The future of life is at stake. Without taking away from that seriousness, I want to add that these problems are also humourous and that jokes, silliness, play, and laughter provide effective ways of expressing these problems. The truths and facts about ecological problems are real, and they are also really humourous. This is not to say that they are laugh-out-loud funny. They are humourous in the sense that their boundaries are tricky, weird, and ambiguous, sometimes confusing, sometimes scandalous, sometimes vague, and always entangled with numerous opinions, fictions, forgeries, and hidden motives. I do not mean to suggest that these problems should be objects of cynical detachment or that they should not be taken seriously, in which case it would be dismissive and inappropriately irreverent to say that these problems are humourous. Humour here is less about a careless detachment and more about ethically provocative playfulness.

This playfulness is not unlike what is called "clowning" by Theodor Adorno, a philosopher and member of the Frankfurt school of social theory. For Adorno, clowning is a practise that allows one to respond respectfully to things instead of mastering or controlling them.[83] Clowning acknowledges the "heterogeneous" dimension of things; that is, a dimension of irreducible difference ("nonidentity") that exceeds the limits of anything one can know or identify.[84] "No object is wholly known", so philosophers must include "a playful element" that prevents their concepts and methods from ruling over things.[85] Aware that things cannot be entirely known, the philosopher must still "talk as if" they were entirely known, and such talk involves "clownish traits"; that is, it brings the philosopher "to the point of clowning", talking about things in a way that acts as if they are entirely known whilst acknowledging that they far exceed what is known. An example of clowning comes from Deleuze in his rhetorical question, "How else can one write but of those things which one doesn't know, or knows badly"?[86] Deleuze recognizes that we only have something to say if we write "at the frontiers of our knowledge, at the border which separates our knowledge from our ignorance and transforms the one into the other".[87] Deleuze is not saying that to apologize for not knowing philosophy as well as he should. He is clowning.

Clowning, philosophers speak as if they have knowledge of things, all the whilst knowing how ridiculous their claims to knowledge are. "Philosophy is the most serious of things, but then again it is not all that serious".[88] With humour, the philosopher is divided: ridiculously serious, seriously playful. Along similar lines, the contemporary philosopher Simon Critchley proposes that an ethics of responsibility must include what he calls *"the experience of an ever-divided humorous self-relation"*, wherein one experiences oneself from the outside, on others' terms: "In this way, I can bear the radicality of the ethical demand because I can laugh at myself. I find myself ridiculous, which is to say that I do not find my *self*, whatever that might mean, but rather see myself from outside and smile".[89] This ethically provocative clowning is not unlike that found in comedies of ancient Greece and in stories about trickster figures told in many indigenous traditions. Consider *The Clouds*, a comedy written by the Greek playwright Aristophanes in the fifth century BCE. This play portrays a caricature of Socrates teaching at a "think tank" (*phrontisterion*).[90] Aristophanes uses this caricature to show the humourous problems of philosophers (or scientists, intellectuals, scholars, etc.) who have their heads in the clouds and cannot effectively relate to the conventions and norms of mainstream society. This is a very old joke that is still funny today: intelligent people exhibiting tendencies to be nerdy and socially awkward. Aristophanes enjoins these thinkers to keep their feet on the ground, to develop healthy bodies and not just wondrous intellects, and to make their ideas relevant to society. This does not necessarily mean taking your head out of the clouds. Perhaps keeping our heads in clouds of wonder and question is crucial for developing materially grounded and socially relevant philosophies and theologies.[91] In whatever manner we deal with the clouds (and the weather and the climate, for that matter), it might be best to incite some laughter and make jokes about the situation rather than simply scolding people for their errors and lamenting the difficult stretch involved in keeping one's feet on the ground with a head in the clouds. To meet the challenges of integrating knowledge into the messy boundaries of embodied and social existence, it is instructive to keep in mind the English proverb laughter is the best medicine.

In many indigenous traditions, the ethical force of comedy is often expressed in stories involving trickster figures, which are frequently figured as animals, thus ensuring that ethics is never entirely divorced from environmental concerns. In Native American traditions, trickster figures include animals like the coyote, rabbit, and raven. These animals are said to cross conventional boundaries, shift the social order, deliver divine messages, and play tricks, sometimes for better and sometimes for worse. A trickster is "a boundary-breaker but also an important boundary-maker: a destroyer of order and an institutor of order".[92] Tricksters decode and recode the meanings and matters of the world. The trickster is such a compelling and instructive figure, engaging the trickster figure is of crucial importance for anyone trying to learn how to live amidst the ambiguities and uncertainties of the real world. This point is made by Donna Haraway, a contemporary feminist theorist of science and technology, who suggests that hopes for a better world, "for accountability, for politics, for ecofeminism, turn on revisioning the world", such that the world is envisioned not as a totality of objects or a passive background for human experience but as a wildly active trickster animal, Coyote—"a coding trickster with whom we must learn to converse".[93] There is nothing in the real world that escapes the boundary-making and boundary-breaking play of trickster coding. Everything happens in the contexts of trickster texts. This resonates with Derrida's provocative claim that there is no nontext or outside-text (*hors-texte*), which is to say, there is nothing that escapes the complex and ambiguous boundaries of contexts.[94] We must learn to stay with the trouble of our various contexts, avoiding any tendency to find a foundation or to certify some certainty that escapes from the trickster's play of codes.

An example of a Coyote trickster comes from the Lillooet, a First Nations people who live northeast of Vancouver in British Columbia, Canada. In their language, the word for "one animal" (*pépla7*) also means "another one", and they tell a story that plays with this ambiguity in a way that emphasizes the messy boundaries between oneself and another and between originals and copies.[95] In this story, two coyotes are walking together, and the first coyote tells the other, "Everybody knows that I am a Coyote. But you are not a Coyote, you are 'Another one.'" They disagree and argue, and then, to prove who is really a coyote, the first coyote crosses a garden where people call out in recognition, "Hey, there is a Coyote going there". Then the other coyote crosses the garden, and people call out, "There goes another one, it's another one that is going there". The joke is that the "other" coyote is indeed a coyote—one coyote, "one animal"—and is at the same time not a coyote but merely "another one", other than or secondary to the first coyote.[96] The story teaches about the ambiguous boundaries between self and other and between originals and their repetitions or copies.

Drawing on indigenous stories about tricksters, ancient Greek comedies, and many other sources of humour, one can argue that comedy plays a key role in grounding ethical responses to ecological problems, particularly insofar as comedy is celebratory and joyous in its engagements with the messy, ambiguous, and confusing boundaries that limit human attempts to lead a good life, whereas tragedy laments those boundaries and laments the absence of a morality that transcends limitations.[97] Along those lines, Marc Bekoff's research into animal behaviour (ethology) shows that animals learn codes of conduct during play, which suggests that play is fundamental to the evolution of social morality, such that play could be described as a "foundation of fairness".[98] Bekoff's work suggests that ethical responses to ecological problems could benefit from taking animals seriously, which entails taking play seriously. Or is it taking seriousness playfully? It is a question of integrating play, laughter, and humour with serious ethical discourses and practises: learning to laugh at the ambiguities and confusions that mark even the most serious of situations, and learning to play with animals and play as animals.

Play is an important part of the integral ecology of Boff and Hathaway. Although "the struggle for integral liberation is certainly a serious matter", seriousness does not exclude play:

> To be truly effective, all our actions for change must be infused with the playfulness and celebration inherent in all creative endeavors, including the creativity of the cosmos itself. Play, in particular, lies at the very heart of our humanity [. . .]. Indeed, authentic joy, celebration, and play seem to capture a spirit that is deeply subversive to the dominant system's controlling dynamics: music, dance, and laughter lie at the very heart of our struggle for life. In Colombia, for example, in the midst of one of the most violent situations in the world, human rights activists know the value of going out for an evening of dancing [. . .] to continue in the struggle—what some of them call "dancing the revolution".[99]

A philosophy that dances, plays, and laughs becomes capable of inspiring an integral struggle. Becoming humourous, philosophical concepts are capable of subverting systems of control. One can find that kind of subversive humour in Nietzsche, who describes his style as "a dance, a play of symmetries of every kind, and an overleaping and mocking of these symmetries".[100] This playful style is not unlike that of a trickster, making and breaking the boundaries and signs that code and decode the world. This tricky style is also expressed by Haraway, whose writing finds "ways of blocking the closure of a sentence, or of a whole piece, so that it becomes hard to fix its meanings. I like that, and I am committed politically and epistemologically to stylistic work that makes it relatively harder to fix the bottom line".[101]

With our planetary future at stake, philosophers more than ever are called to create concepts that work, concepts that effectively get something done in response to the challenges of becoming ecological and becoming integral. At the same time, philosophers are called to create concepts that play, concepts that subvert unjust systems and cultivate fairness and responsibility through joyous and celebratory encounters with the uncertain and messy boundaries of ecological problems. The creative task of philosophy is work and play, passion and humour.

BECOMING SPECULATIVE

Ecological problems call with urgency for humans to learn the truth about them so as to respond to their challenges, their questions: What is happening? Who is affected? How much? What is to be done? Whilst humour celebrates the tricky boundaries of problems and the play within systems, humour alone cannot provide the impetus for the invention of new boundary projects and new systems. Along with becoming humourous, a philosophy of integral ecology must also become passionate about the environmental, social, and subjective realities of the Earth community. Passion and humour are key ingredients for creative responses to serious problems. Our conceptions of reality need to resonate with what Stengers calls a "humor of truth", celebrating the ambiguous boundaries, relative contexts, and uncertain perspectives that condition ecological problems, as well as a "passion for truth", responding creatively to the real events that constitute problems.[102] Resonating with humour and a passion for truth, philosophy becomes speculative, involved in figuring out what is happening and enacting new possibilities, inventing new events. The task of becoming speculative is to resonate with humour and passion, diagnosing ecological becomings and facilitating the invention of new becomings, new ecological modes of existence.

Articulating a philosophy for diagnosing becomings, Stengers draws on D&G, who themselves draw on Nietzsche to articulate a philosophical process—"a becoming-philosophical"—that seeks truth in the invention of new modes of existence and not solely in reflection on the past (the history of philosophy) or on a realm beyond change (eternal philosophy).[103] The philosopher thus takes up the task of performing a "diagnosis of becomings" as part of a *"speculative* operation, a thought experiment" that makes risky investments in projects for "creating possibles", which is not about doing something probable (something likely, something that could probably be done) but about doing something that was not previously thought possible, a new mode of existence, a new becoming.[104] The task of creating possibles requires thought to take a leap into the unthought, a leap that can be provoked by the force of imagination. Stengers follows Whitehead's speculative philosophy in calling for the use of "imaginative rationality" to provoke a "flight of experience" that creates heretofore unthought events.[105] A speculative integral ecology is an ecology of possibles, an imaginative ecology that diagnoses and invents becomings, activating transformative capacities of environments, societies, and subjects. An ecology of possibles does not just analyse events. It makes events happen.

Performing experiential and experimental flights of thought to create new possibilities, speculative philosophy sounds like it might follow the slogan that the telecommunications company AT&T began using in 2010—"Rethink Possible"—which might sound affirmative but is just as ambiguous as their image of Ma Bell, a maternal figure whose mothering euphemizes a smothering monopolization.[106] It can be very beneficial to rethink possibilities, and speculative philosophies can support such rethinking. By exploring and trying to expand the boundaries of what can happen, people can gain access to more and better opportunities, connections, products, and services—in short, more access to the world: a bigger piece of the global pie. However, despite AT&T's historical roots in the inventive practises of Alexander Graham Bell and his Bell Telephone Company, the possibilities currently articulated by AT&T are all too probable. The experiments of speculative philosophy aim to create something new and not merely expand boundaries to obtain a bigger or better version of what is already given. Speculative philosophy aims to create a new pie. Along those lines, the slogan of speculative philosophy seems best expressed by the Native American activist Winona LaDuke (who, incidentally, does not call herself a speculative philosopher): "We don't want a bigger piece of the pie, we want a different pie".[107] Moreover, this "different pie" does not necessarily mean a slightly different pie, like a pie made only out of organic ingredients instead of ingredients produced with chemical pesticides and fertilizers. The pie of speculative philosophy is more risky and surprising than that. It is a pie that creates events. Maybe it is like a pie thrown in the face, a common device of many comedies, or it could be more like a pie that has a file or some tool baked into it so that it can be smuggled to a prisoner who needs to escape in time to do something that will save the planet from imminent danger. A pie for escaping is precisely the sort of pie baked in the philosophy of D&G, who present a speculative concept of a world in which "everything escapes, everything creates", a world in which "there is always something that flows or flees, that escapes" any imprisoning organizations, codes, or structures.[108] In any case, the point here is not analogies about pies and telecommunications companies, but the risky inventiveness of becoming speculative.

Speculative philosophy does not entail simply reflecting on plausible scenarios or thinking about events that can or could happen. It entails creating new fields of what is possible, exceeding the coordinates of probabilities. For Stengers, philosophy is "referred to specifically as 'speculative' in the sense of a struggle against probabilities".[109] Probabilities work with what can happen within a certain horizon of possibility, like getting different pieces of the same pie or playing different characters in the same game. Struggling against probabilities, speculative philosophy responds to ecological problems by affirming that there are always more possibilities for bodies and environments. We cannot fully control or determine what environments and bodies can do. Anything can happen. As Deleuze says, "We do not even know what a body *can do* [. . .] what a body is capable of, what forces belong to it or what they are preparing for".[110] Similarly, the philosopher Bruno Latour—a friend and colleague of Stengers—suggests that we should address ecological problems by maintaining an experimental openness, a "situation of ignorance", in which we recognize that "no one knows what an environment can do".[111]

With this experimental openness, a philosopher responds creatively to the different becomings of human and nonhuman beings (Latour's "actors" or "actants") in ongoing efforts to allow for the participation of "a greater number of actants" in the process of cosmopolitics; that is, the process of composing a shared world, a "collective".[112] For Stengers, this is what is unique about philosophy, "the singular affinity between philosophy and the question of becoming".[113] As the discipline that involves creating concepts, philosophy is unique among fields of inquiry for its power to question becomings, challenging practises to create new possibilities amidst many different yet coordinated problems. This is the task of speculative philosophy: to diagnose and transform becomings, thus allowing humans and nonhumans to produce new alliances and compose a shared world, a *planetary collective*.[114]

It is important to mention that speculative philosophy in this context of Stengers and her allies (Whitehead, D&G, and Latour) does not entail that different truths about the world are merely constructs fabricated by humans and their thought experiments (social constructionism, constructivism), nor does it entail the opposite claim: that truths about the world are simply given in immediate experience or in scientific measurement untainted by human perspectives (realism). Speculative philosophy struggles against the reduction of events to plausible dichotomies between human society (subjects) and the natural world (objects). Accordingly, it is not hard for a speculative philosopher to imagine a conception of biology that would recognize that frogs are real and that we have access to that reality only indirectly through a process of mediation like measurement and interpretation. Does this mean that to become speculative is to avoid becoming constructivist or realist? Not entirely. Those senses of constructivism and realism are very narrow, if not stereotypical, and they fail to do justice to the commitments of some of the speculative philosophers who call themselves constructivists or realists.

Stengers calls her speculative philosophy "constructivist" precisely to affirm the "coconstruction of identity", where events are constituted amidst interrelationships that cannot be neatly bound into categories of subjectivity and objectivity or values and facts.[115] Her "openly constructivist approach" to philosophy "affirms the possible" and resists the probabilities given within the confining oppositions that separate objective facts, faithful descriptions, and absolute knowledge from subjective values, relative beliefs, and fictions.[116] Constructivism in this sense is about affirming the creative process as the matrix or field in which things come into existence. "Constructivism", as D&G put it, "requires every creation to be a construction on a plane that gives it autonomous existence", and this includes every creation—humans, organisms, ecosystems, technologies, and even the concepts created by philosophers. Concepts are not on a different level than the real world. They happen on the same plane as other things. Concepts are things, too, invisible critters, "things in their wild and free state".[117] They are events soliciting and provoking the dynamic participation of complex assemblages of humans and nonhumans. Creating a concept is thus not an attempt of humans "over here" to socially construct a reality "over there". Indeed, for constructivism, the very idea of the humanities mutates, changing into posthumanities or inhumanities to account for the inextricable entanglements of humans with nonhumans.[118]

Constructivism is not about attending to the ways that humans construct concepts of reality. It is about attending to the creative process whereby a thing comes to exist. In Whitehead's terms, "'construction' is 'process'" and includes the constitutive operations of all actors, which he calls "actual entities".[119] Accordingly, Whitehead could be considered a constructivist along with Stengers and D&G. Yet in affirming the possibility of knowledge (however indirect) of a real world outside the horizons of human interpretations, Whitehead, Stengers, and D&G can also be considered realists, although not realists for whom things simply are what they appear to be as presented immediately in experience (naïve realism) or as described and formalized in sciences (scientific realism). For instance, Whitehead describes his philosophy as a "provisional realism" in which "nature is a structure of evolving processes. The reality is the process", but the process is never fully grasped in the immediacy of experiences or in scientific abstractions.[120] Similarly, Latour's works could be considered both constructivist and realist. Indeed, Latour uses both of those terms to describe his philosophy. Latour's "constructivism" or "compositionism" attends to the process of composition for all actors and does not assimilate the world into a social/natural or subject/object dualism.[121] His "realism" attends to the reality not of objective facts uncontaminated by subjectivity but to the reality of actors; that is, the reality of all humans and nonhumans as active participants or agents in the ongoing process of composition.[122]

Latour's orientation to the reality of actors is analogous to the "agential realism" proposed by the physicist and feminist philosopher Karen Barad, who argues that the world is not made up of interacting separate individuals that are either active subjects or passive objects, but is made up of "intra-acting" agencies, where "intra-action" refers to *"the mutual constitution of entangled agencies"*.[123] Commenting on the constructivism-realism debate, Barad describes agential realism as

> an epistemological-ontological-ethical framework that provides an understanding of the role of human and nonhuman, material and discursive, and natural and cultural factors in scientific and other social-material practices, thereby moving such considerations beyond the well-worn debates that pit constructivism against realism, agency against structure, and idealism against

materialism. Indeed, the new philosophical framework that I propose entails a rethinking of fundamental concepts that support such binary thinking.[124]

The work of contemporary theorists like Barad, Latour, and Stengers is indicative of an emerging trend in philosophy: speculative realism, which includes diverse positions that have in common at least two commitments: affirming the importance of philosophical speculation about metaphysical questions (e.g., What is real? What makes up the world? What is the meaning of existence?), and affirming a realism that overcomes the tendencies of philosophies to conceptualize reality only in terms of human access to reality or some kind of correlation between subjective thinking and objective being.[125]

By affirming speculative philosophy, speculative realists renew engagements with metaphysical questions, which have generally been prohibited in modern philosophy, especially since the late eighteenth century when Immanuel Kant developed a critical philosophy that was supposed to show that rationality is too limited to grant humans access to knowledge about metaphysical questions.[126] By affirming realism, speculative realism overcomes human-centred philosophies for which reality is only ever articulated in terms of human access to reality, and it makes way for the creation of concepts capable of facilitating the composition of a planetary civilization that cultivates complex connections between humans and nonhumans. In this context, an integral ecological philosophy that is becoming speculative can create concepts for getting real, for understanding and responding creatively to ecological problems as they entangle environmental, social, and subjective modes of existence in an unpredictable universe. For a philosophy of integral ecology, a humour and passion for truth come together in efforts to create concepts capable of summoning a new Earth and new people, summoning a new planetary collective.

This book presents some concepts for a speculative philosophy of integral ecology. They are concepts for navigating the complex and paradoxical boundaries of ecological problems, boundaries that entangle nature and culture, matter and meaning, cosmos and politics, facts and fictions, pasts and futures, beginnings and endings, and so much more. They are concepts for creating new liberating becomings and new values that support planetary coexistence, concepts that might assist proponents of the Earth Charter in efforts to articulate "basic values to provide an ethical foundation for the emerging world community".[127] They are concepts for a planetary civilization, concepts on the verge—the limit, edge, boundary, threshold—of a planetary civilization. In other words, by focusing "on the verge", I am focusing on conceptions of the boundaries of planetary coexistence. As indicated by the ongoing proliferation of ecological crises, those boundaries are becoming increasingly tricky, looking less like stable points of departure (beginning) and arrival (ending) and more like complex and uncertain becomings—ongoing intervals of interconnectedness, intermezzos, creative processes that are always interrupting . . . irrupting in the middle of things. A beginning is not a stable origin that lies back in a position of control to organize rigid orders and borders, and an ending is not a closure or cataclysmic apocalypse that determines, finally, once and for all, the values of a life, an ecosystem, a person, or a civilization. Beginnings and endings are like the edge effects produced by ecotones—the transitional boundary zones where ecosystems make contact and create tension between one another.[128] To negotiate the boundaries of beginnings and endings, one must stay in the middle of their becomings, staying on edge, affirming the troublesome tensions of transitions. By rethinking beginnings, middles, and endings, a philosophy of integral ecology can work and play with concepts of the complexity and uncertainty of boundaries in an effort to facilitate creative experiments with the composition of a planetary civilization.

NOTES

1. Gilles Deleuze, *Desert Islands and Other Texts 1953–1974*, translated by Michael Taormina (Los Angeles: Semiotext[e], 2004), 220.
2. Gilles Deleuze and Félix Guattari, *What Is Philosophy?* translated by Hugh Tomlinson and Graham Burchell (New York: Columbia University Press, 1994), 5.
3. Jacques Derrida, "Psyche: Inventions of the Other", translated by Catherine Porter and Phillip Lewis, in *Reading De Man Reading*, edited by Lindsay Waters and Wlad Godzich (Minneapolis: University of Minnesota Press, 1989), 42.
4. Graham Harman, *Towards Speculative Realism: Essays and Lectures* (Winchester: Zero Books, 2010), 34; Harman, *Guerrilla Metaphysics: Phenomenology and the Carpentry of Things* (Chicago: Open Court, 2005), 118, 248.
5. Gilles Deleuze, *Difference and Repetition*, translated by Paul Patton (New York: Columbia University Press, 1994), xx.
6. Gilles Deleuze, *Two Regimes of Madness: Texts and Interviews 1975–1995*, translated by Ames Hodges and Michael Taormina (New York: Semiotext[e], 2007), 238.

7. Jacques Derrida, *Deconstruction in a Nutshell: A Conversation with Jacques Derrida*, edited by John D. Caputo (New York: Fordham University Press, 1997), 130.

8. D&G is also the name of one of the brands produced by the Italian fashion company Dolce & Gabbana. Abbreviating Deleuze and Guattari as D&G is a way of deconstructing or deterritorializing the corporate logo, repeating the company's refrain with a difference. On the production of deterritorialized refrains, see the "Refrain" section of this book's concluding chapter.

9. Gilles Deleuze, *Negotiations, 1972–1990*, translated by Martin Joughin (New York: Columbia University Press, 1995), 155. Three notable anthologies (one special issue of a journal and two books) explore D&G's transdisciplinary contributions to the philosophy of nature and to ecological theory and practise, including contributions from their individual and cowritten works, with topics ranging from science, technology, politics, philosophy, art, and culture: Dianne Chisholm, "Deleuze and Guattari's Ecophilosophy", *Rhizomes* 15 (2007), http://www.rhizomes.net/issue15/index.html; Bernd Herzogenrath, ed., *Deleuze/Guattari & Ecology* (London: Palgrave Macmillan, 2009); and Herzogenrath, *An [Un]Likely Alliance: Thinking Environment[s] with Deleuze/Guattari* (Newcastle upon Tyne: Cambridge Scholars, 2008). A significant shortcoming in those anthologies is their lack of attention to D&G's many contributions to engagements with religious perspectives on ecology. One can find accounts of those contributions elsewhere, especially in the works of Catherine Keller, "Talking Dirty: Ground Is Not Foundation", in *Ecospirit: Religions and Philosophies for the Earth*, edited by Laurel Kearns and Catherine Keller (New York: Fordham University Press, 2007); Roland Faber, "Becoming Intermezzo: Eco-Theopoetics after the Anthropic Principle", in *Theopoetic Folds: Philosophizing Multifariousness*, edited by Roland Faber and Jeremy Fackenthal, 212–35 (New York: Fordham University Press, 2013); Luke Higgins, "Toward a Deleuze-Guattarian Micropneumatology of Spirit-Dust", in *Ecospirit: Religions and Philosophies for the Earth*, edited by Laurel Kearns and Catherine Keller (New York: Fordham University Press, 2007); Clayton Crockett and Jeffrey Robbins, *Religion, Politics, and the Earth: The New Materialism* (New York: Palgrave Macmillan, 2012); and Anthony Paul Smith, *A Non-Philosophical Theory of Nature: Ecologies of Thought* (New York: Palgrave Macmillan, 2013).

10. Gilles Deleuze and Félix Guattari, *Anti-Oedipus: Capitalism and Schizophrenia*, translated by Robert Hurley, Mark Seem, and Helen R. Lane (Minneapolis: University of Minnesota Press, 1983), 4.

11. Deleuze and Guattari, *What Is Philosophy?*, 108.

12. Neil Evernden, *The Natural Alien: Humankind and the Environment* (Toronto: University of Toronto Press, 1985), 134.

13. Plato, *Theaetetus*, 149a–151c, 161e, 184b, 210b–d.

14. Consider what Socrates says in Plato's *Phaedrus* (230d): "You see, I am fond of learning. Now the country places and the trees won't teach me anything", whereas "the people in the city do".

15. Descartes, *Discourse on the Method*, translated by George Heffernan (Notre Dame: Notre Dame Press, 1994), 87.

16. Deleuze, *Desert Islands*, 220.

17. In the second and seventh of Plato's *Epistles* (314c, 341c), Plato distinguishes his own studies from what is written in his dialogues. In his seventh letter, Plato says that his pursuit of his studies cannot be expressed verbally, but emerges through sustained communion with "the thing itself" (*to pragma auto*) and "is brought to birth in the soul on a sudden, as light that is kindled by a leaping spark, and thereafter it nourishes itself" (341c).

Introduction 37

18. Marx's statement that "all I know is that I am not a Marxist" is reported by Friedrich Engels, who worked with Marx and coauthored *The Communist Manifesto*. Tom Bottomore, ed., *A Dictionary of Marxist Thought*, 2nd ed. (Malden: Blackwell, 1991), 347.

19. The phrase "free and wild creation of concepts" (the subtitle of Stengers's book, *Thinking with Whitehead*) is also translated as "a free and savage creation of concepts", and as Stengers notes, this phrase indicates a commitment to situating our knowledge and judgement in the creative process of adventure, and it is not about "savagery" or "an appetite for destruction" (27). The phrase "free and wild creation of concepts" comes from Deleuze and Guattari, *What Is Philosophy?*, 105. In much of her philosophy, Stengers is thinking with Deleuze and with Whitehead, as indicated by the title of one of her essays, "Thinking with Deleuze and Whitehead". For her account of the importance of Deleuze's commitment to cowriting books with Guattari and to engaging nonphilosophy, see Stengers, "Gilles Deleuze's Last Message".

20. Deleuze and Guattari, *What Is Philosophy?*, 41.

21. Ibid., 41–42.

22. Jacques Derrida, *Acts of Religion*, ed. Gil Anidjar (New York: Routledge, 2002), 364.

23. Shakespeare, *Hamlet*, 1.5.184–88.

24. Jacques Derrida, *Specters of Marx: The State of the Debt, the Work of Mourning, and the New International*, trans. Peggy Kamuf (New York: Routledge, 1994), 22. As Derrida says elsewhere, "the anachronism *spreads* the present"; that is, the enfolding of the past into the present opens the present to that which exceeds it, that which is otherwise than presence (Derrida, *Circumfession: Fifty-Nine Periods and Periphrases*, in *Jacques Derrida*, Geoffrey Bennington and Jacques Derrida [Chicago: University of Chicago Press, 1993], 150f).

25. Deleuze, *Difference and Repetition*, 88.

26. Mary Evelyn Tucker, *Worldly Wonder: Religions Enter Their Ecological Phase* (Chicago: Open Court Publishing, 2003), 3.

27. Haeckel, quoted in Carolyn Merchant, *American Environmental History: An Introduction* (New York: Cambridge University Press, 2007), 178.

28. Donald Worster, *Nature's Economy: A History of Ecological Ideas*, 2nd ed. (New York: Cambridge University Press, 19), 114.

29. Ernst Haeckel, *Monism as Connecting Religion and Science: The Confession of Faith of a Man of Science*, trans. J. Gilchrist (London: Adam and Charles Black, 1895), 32–33.

30. There are many readings that address ecological issues implicit in popular film since the middle of the twentieth century, including issues regarding wilderness, animals, economic development, technology, ecoterrorism, and environmental disaster. Some recent works include the following: Robin L. Murray and Joseph K. Heumann's *Ecology and Popular Film: Cinema on the Edge* (Albany: SUNY Press, 2009); Sean Cubitt's *EcoMedia* (New York: Rodopi, 2005); Pat Brereton's *Hollywood Utopia: Ecology in Contemporary American Cinema* (Portland: Intellect Books, 2005); and David Ingram's *Green Screen: Environmentalism and Hollywood Cinema* (Exeter: University of Exeter Press, 2004).

31. Brigitte Stark-Merklein, "Rap Star Jay-Z's Video Diary to Spotlight Water Crisis in Angola and Worldwide", *UNICEF*, October 11, 2006.

32. Félix Guattari, *The Three Ecologies*, trans. Ian Pindar and Paul Sutton (London: Ahtlone Press, 2000), 27.

33. Félix Guattari, *Chaosmosis: An Ethico-Aesthetic Paradigm*, trans. Paul Bains and Julian Pefanis (Bloomington: Indiana University Press, 1995), 119–20.

34. Guattari, *Three Ecologies*, 28, 41, 52. Guattari also discusses "the three ecologies" of "the environment, the socius and the psyche" in *Chaosmosis*, including an entire chapter on the object of ecosophy (20, 119ff).

35. Ibid., 35. Guattari's mental ecology adapts the "ecology of ideas" proposed by the social theorist Gregory Bateson (54). Guattari quotes Bateson in the epigraph: "There is an ecology of bad ideas, just as there is an ecology of weeds" (492). For a thorough overview of Bateson's approach to ecology, see Noel Charlton, *Understanding Gregory Bateson: Mind, Beauty, and the Sacred Earth* (Albany: State University of New York Press, 2008).

36. Guattari, *Three Ecologies*, 31, 62.

37. Ibid., 52.

38. Ibid., 66. This concept of machine used by Guattari (and by Deleuze) is analogous to concepts articulated in complexity sciences, such as the concept of machine presented in the "complex thought" of the French theorist Edgar Morin. According to Morin, "every physical being whose activity includes work, transformation, production can be conceived as a machine". Morin's "machine-beings" include planets, organisms, social institutions, technologies, and more (Morin, *Homeland Earth: A Manifesto for the New Millennium*, trans. Sean M. Kelly and Roger LaPointe [Cresskill: Hampton Press, 1999, 68]). Like Morin's notion of machine, that of D&G overcomes "the distinction between the artificial and the natural" (Deleuze and Guattari, *A Thousand Plateaus: Capitalism and Schizophrenia*, trans. Brian Massumi [Minneapolis: University of Minnesota Press, 1987, 141]). There is a distinction that D&G "propose between *machine* and *assemblage*: a machine is like the set of cutting edges" whereby an assemblage undergoes events of transformation, mutation, and variation (ibid., 333). A machinic assemblage is a structure of interrelated parts (assemblage) enacting capacities for transformation (machine).

39. Guattari, *Three Ecologies*, 66.

40. Ibid., 67.

41. Ibid., 31, 65.

42. Ibid., 69.

43. Ibid., 68.

44. A succinct account of the history of the phrase *integral ecology* in its "four independent usages" (Hilary Moore, Leonardo Boff, Thomas Berry, and Ken Wilber) is given in Sean Esbjörn-Hargens, "Ecological Interiority: Thomas Berry's Integral Ecology Legacy", in *Thomas Berry, Dreamer of the Earth: The Spiritual Ecology of the Father of Environmentalism*, edited by Ervin Laszlo and Allan Combs (Rochester: Inner Traditions, 2011), 95–99.

45. Hilary Moore, *Marine Ecology* (New York: Wiley, 1958), 7.

46. More thorough accounts of the integral ecologies proposed by these three thinkers are given in the anthology edited by Sam Mickey, Adam Robbert, and Sean Kelly, *Integral Ecologies: Nature, Culture, and Knowledge in the Planetary Era*, forthcoming.

47. Berry's early uses of the phrases *integral cosmology* and *integral ecology* are mentioned by Sean Esbjörn-Hargens, who learnt of this aspect of Berry's work from "the inspiring eco-justice poet Drew Dellinger", a former student of Berry who was a fellow student with Esbjörn-Hargens in the Philosophy, Cosmology, and Consciousness program at the California Institute of Integral Studies in San Francisco (Esbjörn-Hargens, "Ecological Interiority", 93).

48. Thomas Berry, *The Great Work: Our Way into the Future* (New York: Bell Tower, 1999), 4.

49. Ibid., 159. Berry refers to these sources of wisdom as "a fourfold wisdom", which can "guide us into the future" (ibid., 176).

50. Ibid., 48.

51. The prefix of the word *integral* (*in-*) has a negative or privative force (like *un-* in English), and the *-teg-* shares the same derivation as the Latin word *tangere* ("to touch"), which is the source of English words like *tact*, *tangible*, *tag*, *tangent*, and *contact* (*Oxford English Dictionary Online*).

52. Berry, *Great Work*, 81.

53. Ibid., 82.

54. Ibid., 16, 162.

55. Brian Swimme and Thomas Berry, *The Universe Story: From the Primordial Flaring Forth to the Ecozoic Era—A Celebration of the Unfolding of the Cosmos* (San Francisco: HarperCollins, 1992), 66–78.

56. Berry, *Great Work*, 90.

57. Thomas Berry, *The Christian Future and the Fate of Earth* (Maryknoll: Orbis Books, 2009), 10.

58. Leonardo Boff and Virgilio Elizondo, "Ecology and Poverty: Cry of the Earth, Cry of the Poor", *Concilium: International Journal of Theology* 5 (1995): ix–x.

59. The following quotations come from the four parts of the "Ecology" section of Boff's website, http://leonardoboff.com/, which is accessible in English, Spanish, and Portuguese.

60. Boff and Elizondo, "Ecology", para. 2.

61. Ibid., para. 4.

62. Drafted by scholars, scientists, political leaders, religious leaders, and others (including Leonardo Boff), the Earth Charter was released in June 2000 and has since been endorsed by many individuals and more than 4,500 organizations, including groups from governments, religious communities, nongovernmental organizations, and universities (Earth Charter Associates, "Read the Charter", http://www.earthcharterinaction.org/content/pages/Read-the-Charter.html). For more on the Earth Charter, see the website for The Earth Charter Initiative: http://www.earthcharterinaction.org/content (Earth Charter Associates, "Earth Charter Initiative", http://www.earthcharterinaction.org/content).

63. Mark Hathaway and Leonardo Boff, *The Tao of Liberation: Exploring the Ecology of Transformation* (Maryknoll: Orbis Books, 2009), 300.

64. Leonardo Boff, *Cry of the Earth, Cry of the Poor*, trans. Phillip Berryman (Maryknoll: Orbis Books, 1997), 104.

65. Hathaway and Boff, *Tao of Liberation*, 61.

66. Ibid., xxv.

67. Ibid., 292.

68. The importance of issues like justice, law, and rights in Berry's work is articulated in Cormac Cullinan's *Wild Law: A Manifesto for Earth Justice* (Devon: Green Books, 2011).

69. On the role of Berry and Boff in ecotheology, see John Hart, "Catholicism", in *The Oxford Handbook of Religion and Ecology*, ed. Roger Gottlieb (New York: Oxford University Press, 2006), 80–87. For an account of Berry's significance for the field of religion and ecology, see John Grim and Mary Evelyn Tucker, *Ecology and Religion* (Washington, DC: Island Press, 2014), 4–9. For an overview of the many facets of Berry's profound intellectual journey, see the anthology edited by Heather Eaton, *The Intellectual Journey of Thomas Berry: Imagining the Earth Community* (Lanham: Lexington Books, 2014).

70. Boff, *Cry of the Earth*, 216.

71. Boff, *Cry of the Earth*, 4. Boff does not cite Guattari explicitly with regard to transversality, but Boff's use of Guattari elsewhere leaves room for extrapolation. Boff uses the term in a way similar to Guattari, who developed the concept of transversality as a way of figuring complex connections and processes that

could not or should not be assimilated into binaries or hierarchies that set up simple oppositions between subject and object, oneself and another, individual and collective, vertical and horizontal, and more. "Transversality is a dimension that tries to overcome both the impasse of pure verticality and that of mere horizontality; it tends to be achieved when there is a maximum communication among the different levels and, above all, in different meanings" (Félix Guattari, *Molecular Revolution: Psychiatry and Politics*, trans. Rosemary Sheed [New York: Penguin Books, 1984, 18]). Writing with Deleuze, Guattari describes "a transversal movement", which "sweeps one *and* the other away, a stream without beginning or end that undermines its banks and picks up speed in the middle" (Deleuze and Guattari, *A Thousand Plateaus*, 25).

72. Hathaway and Boff, *Tao of Liberation*, 337.

73. Guattari, *Three Ecologies*, 69.

74. Ken Wilber, *The Spectrum of Consciousness* (Wheaton: Quest Books, 1977).

75. Ken Wilber, *A Theory of Everything: An Integral Vision for Business, Politics, Science, and Spirituality* (Boston: Shambhala Publications, 2000), xii.

76. Ibid.

77. For an overview of the phases of Wilber's thinking, see Allan Combs, *The Radiance of Being: Understanding the Grand Integral Vision; Living the Integral Life*, 2nd ed. (St. Paul: Paragon House, 2002), 136–41.

78. Ken Wilber, *Sex, Ecology, Spirituality: The Spirit of Evolution*, 2nd rev. ed. (Boston: Shambhala Publications, 2000), 543.

79. Ibid., 127–35.

80. Ibid., 149–53.

81. Similar threefold visions of ecology are proposed variously by many theorists and researchers. For instance, it can be found in Richard Evanoff's transactional approach to ethics, which brings together local (bioregional) and global perspectives on ethics in an effort to harmonize self (human well-being), society (justice), and nature (sustainability). Evanoff, *Bioregionalism and Global Ethics: A Transactional Approach to Achieving Ecological Sustainability, Social Justice, and Human Well-Being* (New York: Routledge, 2011). This approach to ecology also resembles Edward Wimberly's pragmatic approach to environmental ethics based on a "nested ecology", in which humans and decision-making processes are situated in "an integrated whole" that includes all of the mutually enfolded (i.e., nested) hierarchies of ecology, including "personal, social, environmental, and cosmic ecologies" as well as an "ecology of the unknown" that resonates with "terms of spirituality and religion" (Wimberley, *Nested Ecology: The Place of Humans in the Ecological Hierarchy* [Baltimore: Johns Hopkins University Press, 2009], 4).

82. Sean Esbjörn-Hargens and Michael E. Zimmerman, *Integral Ecology: Uniting Multiple Perspectives on the Natural World* (Boston: Integral Books, 2009), 16, 487. Esbjörn-Hargens and Zimmerman affirm the emergence of "a rich variety of integral ecologies", and they recognize that those integral ecologies "need not be contained within any single framework". Ibid., 485, 540.

83. Although Adorno's negative dialectics is helpful for respecting the unknowable nonidentity of things, his thinking is not entirely amenable to ecological issues, particularly insofar as Adorno focuses primarily on human subjectivity and not on the value of nonhumans apart from their relations to humans. Jane Bennett points out that "Adorno is reluctant to say too much about nonhuman vitality", and he is quick "to remind the reader that objects are always 'entwined' with human subjectivity" (Bennett, *Vibrant Matter: A Political Ecology of Things* [Durham: Duke University Press, 2010], 16).

84. Theodor Adorno, *Negative Dialectics*, trans. E. B. Ashton (New York: Seabury Press, 1973), 5.
85. Ibid., 14.
86. Deleuze, *Difference and Repetition*, xxi.
87. Ibid.
88. Adorno, *Negative Dialectics*, 14.
89. Simon Critchley, *Infinitely Demanding: Ethics of Commitment, Politics of Resistance* (London: Verso, 2007), 86. Critchley goes on to say that this kind of humourous self-relation is what the Irish playwright and poet Samuel Beckett calls the *risus purus* ("pure laugh"), which Beckett describes in his novel *Watt*: "It is the laugh of laughs, the *risus purus*, the laugh laughing at the laugh, the beholding, the saluting of the highest joke, in a word the laugh that laughs—silence please—at that which is unhappy" (Beckett, *Watt* [New York: Grove Press, 2009], 39).
90. Aristophanes, *Clouds*, line 94. For more on Aristophanes and on the importance of comedy for philosophy, see Bernard Freydberg, *Philosophy and Comedy: Aristophanes, Logos, and Eros* (Bloomington: Indiana University Press, 2008).
91. For more on the importance of staying with the clouds, see Catherine Keller, *Cloud of the Impossible: Theological Entanglements* (forthcoming).
92. Arnold Krupat, "Native American Trickster Tales", in *Comedy: A Geographic and Historical Guide*, Vol. 2, ed. Maurice Charney (Westport: Greenwood Publishing Group, 2005), 448. Although I am focusing on indigenous examples of tricksters, it is important to note that tricksters are found in many religions and not just indigenous traditions. In the context of Christianity, for instance, Marion Grau's postcolonial feminist theology develops the figure of a "transgendered trickster Christ"—a cross-dressing, boundary-crossing Christ facilitating liberation by unsettling oppressive hierarchies of gender, class, and race. Grau, *Of Divine Economy: Refinancing Redemption* (New York: T&T Clark, 2004), 223.
93. Donna Haraway, "Situated Knowledges: The Science Question in Feminism and the Privilege of Partial Perspective", in *Simians, Cyborgs, and Women: The Reinvention of Nature* (New York: Routledge, 1991), 201.
94. "*There is nothing outside of the text*". Derrida, *Of Grammatology*, trans. Gayatri Chakravorty Spivak (Baltimore: Johns Hopkins University Press, 1976), 158.
95. Bill Edwards and Jan P. van Eijk, "The Two Coyotes: A Humorous Lillooet Story", in *Salish Myths and Legends: One People's Stories*, eds. M. Terry Thompson and Steven M. Egesdal (Lincoln: University of Nebraska Press, 2008), 305.
96. Ibid.
97. Shagbark Hickory, "Everyday Environmental Ethics as Comedy and Story: A Collage", *Ethics and the Environment* 8.2 (2003): 80–105. Also see Hickory et al., "Further Thoughts on Everyday Environmental Ethics as Comedy and Story: A Conversation with Shagbark Hickory", *Canadian Journal of Environmental Education* 9.1 (2004): 82–91, and Joseph Meeker, *The Comedy of Survival: Literary Ecology and a Play Ethic*, 3rd ed. (Tuscon: University of Arizona Press, 1997).
98. Marc Bekoff, *Minding Animals: Awareness, Emotions, and Heart* (New York: Oxford University Press, 2002), 120.
99. Hathaway and Boff, *Tao of Liberation*, 391.
100. Nietzsche says this in a letter from February 1984 to his friend Erwin Rohde (Friedrich Nietzsche, *Selected Letters of Friedrich Nietzsche*, ed. and trans. Christopher Middleton [Indianapolis: Hackett Publishing, 1996], 221).
101. Donna J. Haraway, "'There Are Always More Things Going on Than You Thought!' Methodologies as Thinking Technologies: Interview with Donna Har-

away", in *Bits of Life: Feminism at the Intersections of Media, Bioscience, and Technology*, eds. Anneke Smelik and Nina Lykke (Seattle: University of Washington Press, 2008), 33–34.

102. Isabelle Stengers, *Cosmopolitics I*, trans. Robert Bononno (Minneapolis: University of Minnesota Press, 2010), 4. Humour is not relativism. It is not a detached irony that dismisses ecological problems as mere fabrications of human interpretations or political ideologies (24). The humour of truth does not posit a "relativity of truth" but celebrates "the truth of the relative" (11). The distinction between "a relativity of truth" and "a truth of the relative" comes from D&G, who make the point that truth is indeed relative to partial observers, but the observers are not simply humans but include many other agents or "forces" that "belong to the things studied". Deleuze and Guattari, *What Is Philosophy?*, 130.

103. "The *diagnosis* of becomings in every passing present is", according to D&G, "what Nietzsche assigned to the philosopher as physician, 'physician of civilization,' or inventor of new immanent modes of existence. Eternal philosophy, but also the history of philosophy, gives way to a becoming-philosophical" (Deleuze and Guattari, *What Is Philosophy?*, 113). In *The Gay Science*, Nietzsche says that he is "still waiting for a philosophical *physician* in the exceptional sense of the term—someone who" takes up the "task of pursuing the problem of the total health of a people, time, race or of humanity" (*The Gay Science*, trans. Josefine Nauckhoff [New York: Cambridge University Press, 2001], 6).

104. Stengers, *Cosmopolitics I*, 12. Stengers notes that her sense of "possible" and "probable" corresponds to Deleuze's "virtual" and "possible" respectively, such that the creation of possibilities would be described in Deleuze's terms as a creation of virtual events (263n10).

105. Isabelle Stengers, *Thinking with Whitehead: A Free and Wild Creation of Concepts*, trans. Michael Chase (Cambridge: Harvard University Press, 2011), 255. For Whitehead, speculative philosophy must work with "imaginative rationalization", which makes thought take "flight" in order to create concepts ("fundamental ideas", "general ideas") through which "every element of our experience can be interpreted". Alfred North Whitehead, *Process and Reality: An Essay in Cosmology*, corrected edition eds. David Ray Griffin and Donald W. Sherburne (New York: Free Press, 1978), 3, 5.

106. Vitaly Demen, "Is It Possible to Rethink Possible"? *EMG Strategy Consulting*, April 2010, para. 1.

107. Winona LaDuke, quoted in Jay Walljasper, "Winona LaDuke: Voice of Native Cultures", in *Visionaries: The 20th Century's 100 Most Important Inspirational Leaders*, eds. Satish Kumar and Freddie Whitefield (White River Junction, VT: Chelsea Green Publishing, 2001), 56.

108. Deleuze and Guattari, *A Thousand Plateaus*, 142, 216.

109. Stengers, *Cosmopolitics I*, 17.

110. Deleuze, *Nietzsche and Philosophy*, trans. Hugh Tomlinson (New York: Columbia University Press, 2006), 39. Deleuze is echoing the seventeenth-century philosopher Baruch (Benedict) Spinoza, who claims in his *Ethics* that "no one has yet determined what the Body can do" (*Ethics*, in *Collected Works of Spinoza, Vol. 1*, 2nd printing with corrections, ed. and trans. Edwin Curley [Princeton: Princeton University Press, 1988], IIIP2S).

111. Latour, *Politics of Nature*, 80, 156, 197.

112. Latour, *Politics of Nature: How to Bring the Sciences into Democracy*, trans. Catherine Porter (Cambridge: Harvard University Press, 2004), 80–81. Latour uses Stengers's concept of cosmopolitics to refer to this process of composing a "collective"—"that which *collects us all* in the cosmopolitics envisaged by Isa-

belle Stengers". Cosmopolitics overcomes the "bipolar power source" that separates the world into "nature" (cosmos) and "society" (politics) (Latour, *Pandora's Hope: Essays on the Reality of Science Studies* [Cambridge: Harvard University Press, 1999], 297).

113. Stengers, *Cosmopolitics I*, 60.

114. The idea of such a planetary collective is supported by a group of filmmakers, thinkers, and media creatives who are called, not incidentally, Planetary Collective. For more on their multidisciplinary and multimedia work, see http://www.planetarycollective.com.

115. Stengers, *Cosmopolitics I*, 38. Affirming the complex interpenetration of subjectivity and objectivity is a common commitment among speculative philosophers. Accordingly, Whitehead's speculative philosophy is not exclusively rationalist or empiricist. Embracing "its rational side and its empirical side", Whitehead's philosophy accounts for the "dipolar character" whereby all entities have a "physical pole" (providing "an objective side of experience") and a "mental pole" (providing a "subjective side of experience") (Whitehead, *Process and Reality*, 3, 277). Similarly, in the speculative philosophy of the nineteenth-century German philosopher G. W. F. Hegel, a "speculative proposition" involves a "proposition of identity" that affirms a complex unity in which the dualistic subject/object structure of ordinary judgements and propositions "is destroyed" (Hegel, *Phenomenology of Spirit*, trans. A. V. Miller. [Oxford: Oxford University Press, 1977], 38).

116. Ibid., 57. This echoes the constructivism of D&G. "Constructivism unites the relative and the absolute". Deleuze and Guattari, *What Is Philosophy?*, 22.

117. Deleuze, *Difference and Repetition*, xx.

118. "In truth, there are only inhumanities, humans are made exclusively of inhumanities, but very different ones, of very different natures and speeds". Deleuze and Guattari, *A Thousand Plateaus*, 190.

119. Whitehead, *Process and Reality*, 151.111.

120. Whitehead, *Science and the Modern World* (New York: Free Press, 1967), 72. Whitehead also calls his philosophical position "organic realism" (Whitehead, *Process and Reality*, 309).

121. Latour follows Stengers on this point. "Like Stengers, I am a constructivist but not a social constructivist" (Latour, "Interview with Bruno Latour", in *Chasing Technoscience: Matrix for Materiality*, ed. Don Ihde and Evan Selinger [Bloomington: Indiana University Press, 2003], 26). To help distinguish his position from the simplistic positions of the realism-constructivism debate, Latour considers calling his constructivism "compositionism" (Latour, "The Promises of Constructivism", in *Chasing Technoscience: Matrix for Materiality*, eds. Don Ihde and Evan Selinger [Bloomington: Indiana University Press, 2003], 40).

122. Latour calls his position a "more 'realistic realism'" (Latour, *Pandora's Hope*, 15). In contrast to naïve realism, for which the nonhuman world is a collection of uncontestable facts of passive objects, Latour's realism is more realist insofar as it affirms that nonhumans "have a *history*, too", including "the multiplicity of interpretations, the flexibility, the complexity"; in short, the agency, which has been attributed exclusively to humans in accordance with the subject-object dualism that pervades modern thinking (16).

123. Karan Barad, *Meeting the Universe Halfway: Quantum Physics and the Entanglement of Matter and Meaning* (Durham: Duke University Press, 2007), 33.

124. Ibid., 26.

125. A shared commitment of speculative realists is to follow the critique of "correlationism" expressed by Quentin Meillassoux, one of the four founding figures of speculative realism (along with Ray Brassier, Iain Hamilton Grant,

and Graham Harman). Correlationism is Meillassoux's term for "the idea according to which we only ever have access to the correlation between thinking and being" (Meillassoux, *After Finitude: An Essay on the Necessity of Contingency*, trans. Ray Brassier [New York: Continuum, 2008], 5). Harman uses the phrase *philosophies of access* to refer to philosophies of correlationism (Graham Harman, *Prince of Networks: Bruno Latour and Metaphysics* [Melbourne, Australia: re.press, 2009], 165, 222). For more on speculative realism, see the groundbreaking anthology of essays edited by Levi Bryant, Nick Srnicek, and Graham Harman, *The Speculative Turn: Continental Materialism and Realism* (Melbourne: re.press, 2011).

126. Having woken from his "dogmatic slumber" after being exposed to David Hume's sceptical (antimetaphysical) philosophy, Kant inquired into the limits of human reason and the very possibility of metaphysical knowledge of the real world, coming to the conclusion that humans "can know objects only as they appear" to human senses (the realm of phenomena) and "not as they are in themselves" (the realm of noumena) (Immanuel Kant, *Prolegomena to Any Future Metaphysics That Can Qualify as a Science*, trans. Paul Carus [Chicago: Open Court, 1997], 7, 35). According to Nietzsche, this Kantian prohibition against knowing things in themselves supported the emergence of scientific reductionism (i.e., scientism), which is first heard in the nineteenth century with the "Rooster's crow of positivism"—a school of thought developed by Auguste Comte, according to whom the only statements considered meaningful are those that correspond to experimentally verifiable facts, and any metaphysical value or articulation of any fundamental principle of reality (e.g., God, the good life, the true world, actuality, etc.) is considered unscientific, and thus meaningless (Nietzsche, *Twilight of the Idols*, trans. Richard Polt [Indianapolis: Hackett Publishing, 1997], 23). Following Hume's skepticism, Kant's critical turn, and positivism, antispeculative biases continued throughout the nineteenth and twentieth centuries, although they did not prevent the speculative tradition from surviving in Romanticism, speculative idealism, and German "nature philosophy" (*Naturphilosophie*). In the twentieth century, metaphysical speculation was prohibited in favor of scientific knowledge and linguistic analysis in "analytic" (i.e., Anglo-American) philosophy, and attention to immediate experience (phenomenology), critique (post-Kantian and post-Marxist theorists), and language games in "continental" (i.e., mainland European) philosophy. In the early twenty-first century, the use of the term *metaphysician* has remained "as brutal an insult" for continental philosophers as for scientists and Anglo-American philosophers (Harman, *Towards Speculative Realism*, 106).

127. Earth Charter Associates, "Read the Charter", para. 6.

128. The transitional tension of an ecotone is indicated by the etymological derivation of *ecotone* from the Greek word for "tension" (*tonos*).

TWO
Beginning

In any event, is beginning happening? Is every day a new beginning? Is every moment? Is every boundary or borderline? In any case, beginnings abound. When and where a beginning happens, it leads to new events and possibilities. Leading to different and often unpredictable occasions, beginning irrupts and flows with a dynamic movement. Whether the beginning of the day or the beginning of the universe, beginning overflows any attempt to contain it in some distant and unchanging background. Waking up in a bad mood at the beginning of the day can affect my mood all day, as if I cannot contain what opens out after waking up on the wrong side of the bed. Likewise, the dynamics of the beginning of the universe are not over and done with. They are still active in the ongoing evolution of life and the laws of nature. This means that the laws of nature are not static and unchanging rules set down at the origin of the universe to govern all times and all places at all scales. Rather, as Whitehead says, the laws of nature are more appropriately described as "habits of nature" insofar as these laws are always situated within the limits of specific temporal contexts.[1]

In the process of becoming, the beginning of the universe pulses in every beating heart. The Big Bang echoes in the honking of geese. The births and deaths of stars shine in the greening of the grass. As the American poet Walt Whitman says in his "Song of Myself", "I believe a leaf of grass is no less than the journeywork of the stars".[2] Beginnings of stars, galaxies, and leaves of grass are not static points. Beginnings are journeywork. The boundaries of beginnings cannot be constrained into a neatly fixed position. They open out, continually producing variations and differences (including closures) between things, between times, between spaces. Perhaps a preliminary definition of beginning could propose that a beginning is an opening or, more specifically, a "liminal" opening.[3] In other words, to begin is to open out from the limits, boundaries, and edges between things: the beginning of a forest opening out from the boundary of a prairie; the beginning of a shore opening out from the edge of a sea; a new community or national identity opening out in a revolutionary moment between regimes.

An image of the intimate relationship between beginning and boundary (or between beginning and limit, margin, borderline, edge, and other liminal figures) appears in the circumference of a circle, along which any point can simultaneously mark a beginning and a limit of the circle. This resonates with the words of the pre-Socratic philosopher Heraclitus, for whom beginning occurs together with limit: "beginning [*archai*] and limit [*peras*] are shared [*xunon*]" (DK 22b103).[4] A similar interpretation of the relation of beginnings and limits is expressed by the twentieth-century German philosopher Martin Heidegger in his recovery of the ancient Greek sense of "boundary" (*peras*): "A boundary is not that at which something stops but, as the Greeks recognized, the boundary is that from which something *begins its presencing*".[5] Heidegger affirms the togetherness of boundaries and beginnings, but only insofar as a boundary is that from which a beginning takes place. In her articulation of "Boundaries on the Edge", the environmental philosopher Irene Klaver supplements Heidegger's statement by saying that a boundary not only marks that from which something begins but also marks its own beginning: "Boundaries themselves begin their own 'presencing'."[6]

Consider the Berlin Wall: it marked the border from which East and West Germany began, and from its construction in 1961 through its fall in 1989, the wall also marked the beginning of its own "presencing" as an imposing border and a remnant of war. The wall was a symbol of the Cold War era—a political era of two superpowers, the capitalist United States and the communist Soviet Union—and the hole in the wall opened possibilities for profound transformation, possibilities for "new power relations/constellations that far exceed the boundaries of any unity". Klaver notes that, when the wall came down, the first hole "made in the wall symbolized hope: a promise of an open future, while at the same time a witness of a once imposing border".[7] The opening of the boundary shows the beginning of an uncertain future, and at the same time, it shows an imposing wall that closes off and blocks. There is thus a complex play at the border: the opening of the wall conveys the indeterminacy and uncertainty of future possibilities while also testifying to the wall's presence as a blockage and closure of possibilities.

Furthermore, the wall coming down entangles nature and culture, as it initiated not only political and cultural changes but also ecological changes. With a lack of military activity, Russian and Polish grasslands reforested, depriving migrating geese of their foraging grounds. While Marxist academics changed their understandings of communism and moved to new fields of study, the geese moved to new fields as well. While the academics started theorizing globalization and cultural pluralism, the geese "found new grazing grounds on their migration route, such as a large Dutch wetland area, the Oostvaarders Plassen, itself a result of intricate relations between nature and culture".[8] Once the geese arrived in the Netherlands, they began affecting Dutch politics by raising issues of environmental policy and management. The hole in the wall thus opened possibilities for crisscrossing the porous and tentative boundaries of nature and culture, such that "something like the fall of a wall can cause flocks of geese to descend on wetlands in the Netherlands" and effect change in Dutch environmental policy. Just as the piece of the wall that the primatologist and activist Jane Goodall carries with her to symbolize her own efforts "to counter apathy with hope", the opening in the wall can give us a sense of hope for ecological and sociopolitical transformations, hope for new possibilities for connections between nature and culture. "Just as dried soil needs to be opened up, to be broken, for the water to percolate, so our conceptual schemes need always to be opened for connections to be seen—or to be made—in order to understand. We need to create open situations".[9]

OPENING

Supplementing the philosophical understanding of boundaries from Heraclitus to Heidegger, Klaver's work indicates how engagements with ecological theories and practises become engagements with the indeterminacy and complexity of boundaries, engagements that attend to limits, borders, and edges as they open interactions that connect opposites like nature/culture, human/nonhuman, theory/practise, and even opening/closure. An opening is thus not necessarily opposed to a closed or static structure. In fact, some openings occur precisely with the aim of closing in on new structures. An example of such an opening comes from the Occupy Wall Street movement, which began in the fall of 2011 with a series of protests taking place across the United States (and to a lesser extent internationally). Although the aims of that movement include open-ended dialogue and the creation of open places of resistance to the hegemony of corporations and global capitalism, those aims are part of a larger aim to find new leaders, create new communities, and develop alternative structures of economic and political organization. To emphasize this point, Slavoj Žižek addresses the aim of the Occupy movement by referring to a quotation from the early twentieth-century writer G. K. Chesterton: "Merely having an open mind is nothing; the object of opening the mind, as of opening the mouth, is to shut it again on something solid".[10]

In emphasizing the importance of boundaries, Klaver draws on the "boundary projects" of Donna Haraway. Boundary projects are sites of production that transform matters and meanings. They are sites of material-semiotic production where humans and the world constitute one another, coding, decoding, and recoding one another, such that the world is envisioned as a "coding trickster with whom we must learn to converse".[11] Figured as a trickster, the world is not simply natural or cultural. It is a complex of boundary projects or "boundary formations", which are composed of coconstitutive flows of the flesh (material) and the word (semiotic), wherein matters and meanings are entangled "figures", which can be defined variously as "material-semiotic nodes or knots" or "naturalcultural contact zones".[12] Along with nodes, knots, contact zones, and boundary projects, Haraway speaks of "the open" to refer to these "mortal entanglements [. . .] for which we are responsible and in which we respond".[13] Heidegger is known for developing a concept of "the open", but Haraway opens up Heidegger's concept to a more enriched sense of nonhuman worlds, so that the open is not solely the property of human existence.[14] The open is a place of mutual response between humans and nonhumans, a place of naturalcultural contact.

To transform boundary projects is to transform the open, to create new practises for responding to the open. "New openings will appear because of changes in practices, and the open is about response".[15] Becoming responsible for the open and responding in the open are not only human practises but also are practises of *companion species*, where the word *species* conveys the interactive play between species as kinds (universality) and species as specifics (singularity). Haraway focuses extensively on human-dog relations, including her relationship to her dog, Ms. Cayenne Pepper, an Australian Shepherd. However, Haraway does not restrict the word *species* to kinds of pets or even to kinds of organisms, but opens it up to all kinds of beings. "Not much is excluded from the needed play" of companion species, "not technologies, commerce, organisms, landscapes, peoples, practices".[16] All specific things and kinds of things are included in the play of companion species taking place in the boundary projects of the open. In short, the different kinds of matter, life, and consciousness in the cosmos are different ways of becoming in the open. This resonates with the claim of Elizabeth Grosz, who draws on Deleuze's philosophy, feminist theories of sexual difference, and Charles Darwin's evolutionary theory to develop a "philosophy of becoming" for which the real world is figured as a "dynamical open-endedness", wherein new modes of existence emerge through the opening up and destabilization of fixed identities.[17]

The generative knots and nodes of the open are sites of the interspecies practise of "becoming with", and this coconstitutive practise leads Haraway to ask how "becoming with" is also "a practice of becoming worldly".[18] By opening questions about practises of becoming with and becoming worldly, new possibilities open up for coding and recoding the world. More specifically, Haraway is interested in how these questions of becoming facilitate efforts to counter "militarized neoliberal models of world building" by "nurturing a more just and peaceful other-globalization" (*autre-mondialization*), an "other globalization" that is neither neoliberal economic globalization nor a reactionary "anti-globalization" (*alter-globalization*).[19] Facilitating a more just and peaceful globalization, responsibility for the open is a practise of integral ecology—an approach to ecology that engages the coconstitutive relations of becoming with, which entangle the human and nonhuman members of the Earth community in material-semiotic knots. However, before elaborating, I interrupt this proposal for a more open globalization (deferring it until the "Ending" chapter), and I turn back to further consider the openings of beginnings and boundaries.

To conjoin beginnings with boundaries is not to assert that beginnings are identical with boundaries, limits, or edges. If they are identical, their identity is not simple or static. They are much more complex than that. As Heraclitus's fragment suggests above, beginnings and limits are conjoined in sharing. To convey this sharing, Heraclitus uses the word *xunos*, which, as Klaver mentions, is "a small word with tremendous range and importance for it connotes connectivity, relatedness: 'together, with, common, shared'".[20] In contrast to a simple identity or undifferentiated unity, a relation of sharing includes differences, divergences, and flows of becoming. Sharing happens in the open, in the complex entanglements of becoming with. Beginnings and boundaries do not simply enclose one another in static identity. They open out in complex connectivity: boundaries shaping beginnings shaping boundaries. To articulate the beginnings of boundaries or the boundaries of beginnings is not a matter of simply locating a point in space or time, but of articulating configurations of sharing and practises of becoming with. Entangled with boundaries through connectivity, togetherness, and sharing, beginning is a relational opening, not a simple or static origin.

The distinction between beginning and origin is made by Edward Said, a Palestinian American theorist of postcolonialism. In *Beginnings: Intention and Method*, Said uses the word *origin* to denote a passive and static meaning ("X *is the origin of* Y"), whereas "beginning" is an active movement of becoming ("The beginning A *leads to* B").[21] An origin dominates from a central position or linear point that is taken as absolute, and in contrast, a beginning "encourages nonlinear development" as it unfolds within the contested contexts of historical situations.[22] On one hand, an origin assimilates everything into the same dominant order, and on the other hand, "beginning is *making* or *producing difference*".[23]

Keller draws on this distinction between origin and beginning in the theology of becoming she constructs in *Face of the Deep*. An origin functions as a linear and absolute foundation that, in contrast to the relationality of beginnings, needs nothing—no relation, no context—in order to create. An example of such an origin can be found in the Christian doctrine of "creation out of nothing" (*creatio ex nihilo*), according to which God creates from a transcendent position and imposes order onto the world. As such an origin, God lies back from a position that subordinates and dominates anything that follows from it or that fails to conform to its central position.[24] To participate and flourish in creation, everyone and everything must be aligned with the origin, for to be unaligned is to be an object of exclusion and violence. Insofar as God is figured as transcendent and male, this origin legitimates structures of domination that turn complex relations into binary oppositions wherein unbelievers are subordinate to believers, immanent nature to transcendent divinity, women to men, body to mind, emotion to reason, animals to humans, and more.

The open relations of beginnings are suppressed and oppressed with the rigid hierarchies of origins. These hierarchies reduce complex relationships to binary oppositions in which one term always subordinates the other. Origins thus legitimate what the ecofeminist philosopher Karen Warren calls the "logic of domination", wherein hierarchies are imposed upon relations in such a way as to give one term of the relation a superior position and the other term a subordinate position.[25] Val Plumwood calls this the "logic of colonization", and it is at work in dualisms such as male/female, human/nature, ego/world, self/other, culture/nature, reason/emotion, mind/body, and civilized/primitive.[26] The colonized term is under or subordinate to the superior term. To use a different spatial metaphor, the colonized term is marginalized by a superior centre. In this case, the logic of domination is what Plumwood calls "hegemonic centrism", which sets up a mutually exclusive opposition between centre and periphery, such that whatever is central has power or control over that which is peripheral or marginal.[27]

This logic of domination is evident not only in a transcendent God dominating immanent nature, but also in modern and secular forms of domination, including classism, racism, and sexism, according to which wealthy white men hold positions that marginalize the poor, minorities, women, immigrants, and others. Furthermore, the logic of domination also involves naturism and speciesism, which justify the subordination of nonhuman organisms and ecosystems to human interests. The logic of domination, or what Keller calls "dominology", is subverted by the dynamic relations of beginnings.[28]

For Keller, beginning "does not lie back" from a position of domination, but it opens out with dynamics of relationality.[29] This relational opening marks a deconstruction of origins and of structures that perpetuate domination. The opening of beginning thus contributes to a deconstruction of the dominant image of a God who creates *ex nihilo*, an image that, moreover, does not appear in the biblical scriptures themselves. For Keller, oppressive origins expressed in religions can be overcome with the beginnings expressed in religions. This is in stark contrast to Said, who associates religions primarily with origins, which are marked by the privileged position held by divinity and myth, as with the example of the transcendent male God. For Said, sacred origins are opposed to secular beginnings, which are produced by humans in historical contexts. One might wonder whether Said's opposition simply reverses the logic of domination, repeating the appeal to a dominant origin by privileging the secular as a dominant social order that subordinates religious traditions and opposes the sacred to the secular.

Beginnings are not the sole property of the secular, but neither are they exclusively sacred. Rather, if beginnings open connections and relations of togetherness, then one could conjecture that a beginning involves an interconnection between the sacred and the secular, so that the sacred-mythological can never be found without the secular-historical, and vice versa.[30] In any case, regardless of whether the sacred and secular are mutually enfolded, beginnings can happen in sacred and secular contexts. The same is true for origins. They occur in secular contexts and not only in transcendent deities. Consider scientists who reduce personality and consciousness to origins in genetics or neuroscience. Consider politicians who think society originates in a contract between rational individuals, a contract from which religious (i.e., nonrational) discourses must be excluded.

The logic of domination did not stay contained within the Christian doctrine of creation out of nothing, nor is its beginning simply located in that doctrine. "Gradually it took modern and then secular form, generating every kind of western originality".[31] For example, the logic of domination at work in the doctrine of creation out of nothing appeared in a more secular form in the colonization of Australia in the eighteenth century by Europeans who justified their colonization with a legal doctrine according to which the Australian land and its inhabitants (including humans) were reduced to *terra nullius* ("land of no one"; "no man's land").[32] More recent examples can be found in the innovations constantly emerging in contemporary global technoculture, where innovations are supposed to be "new and improved" and not repeat the past. It is as if innovation mimics the original creativity of the divine, for which any repetition of the past would compromise the omnipotence and transcendence of the original creative act. Similarly with avant-garde art, the production of new works often involves a suppression of the entanglements of historical contexts, always to be new and transcend, never repeat. Such a suppression of one's context is what Haraway calls a "god trick" and, as with Keller's understanding of the dominological trick of origins, the god tricks of contemporary technoculture are never simply sacred or secular but are always woven into a "sacred-secular technoscientific web".[33]

Like an appeal to origins, a god trick involves positing an absolute Truth (or Word) that rests completely outside of or in a superior position to the materiality, heterogeneity, and multiplicity in which all knowledge is situated.[34] Such an un-situated truth is the "god-trick of seeing everything from nowhere", and this "view of infinite vision", regardless of whether it posits relativism (e.g., all perspectives are valid) or totalization (e.g., all perspectives are contained in my perspective), "is an illusion".[35] For instance, a god trick in an Abrahamic monotheism could say that, for all times, all places, and all people, God is a masculine figure or a particular man. A secular biotechnological god trick could say that every organism is reducible to a genetic origin (e.g., Richard Dawkins's "selfish gene"). The gene is a domineering origin and goal. Insofar as biotechnological research in genetics promises the fulfilment of modern secular ideals of progress and the restoration of human nature, the figure of the gene resembles the incarnate messiah of salvation history of sin and redemption. "Genes", in more provocative words, "are a bit like the Eucharist of biotechnology".[36] Giving various examples of ways in which discourses related to the Human Genome Project resemble narratives of a salvation history, Haraway lists some suggestive titles from a variety of publications and television programmes, including the title of an article, "In the Beginning Was the Genome".

Appealing to un-situated origins and absolutes, god tricks prevent respectful engagements with the irreducible complexity and specificity of the open. They presuppose prefabricated answers that short-circuit the question that emerges in the open: "Which historically situated practices of multispecies living and dying should flourish?"[37] Haraway reminds us that, to respect companion species, this question must be kept open, such that our answers respond to the unique material-semiotic practises in which interspecies relations are situated. "There is no outside from which to answer that mandatory question; we must give the best answers we come to know how to articulate, and take action, without the god trick of self-certainty".[38] Without god tricks, humans can engage the complex and messy entanglements of the open rather than pretending to exist in some un-situated space of self-certainty and innocence.

A god trick or an appeal to a foundational origin could subordinate the sacred to the secular or vice versa, but an appeal to beginnings affirms the opening in which sacred and secular boundaries are entangled in messy and uncertain ways. The material-semiotic knots of the open intertwine the sacred and secular, just as they intertwine other opposites: the flesh with the word, the historical with the mythological, and the natural with the cultural. One could say that beginning in the open is not exclusively sacred, nor is it secular, but is perhaps more accurately described as *postsecular*.[39]

This sacred-secular openness is evident in the "sacramental consciousness" that marks Haraway's upbringing as a Catholic.[40] Growing up Catholic, she experienced the sacrament of communion, wherein the food of bread and wine is seen as the body and blood of Jesus Christ. She recognized "that the Real Presence was present under both" senses of "species"—the general sign (Word) and the particular bread and wine (Flesh): "Sign and flesh, sight and food, never came apart" for Haraway after she partook of "that hearty meal".[41] However, Haraway's Catholicism is not entirely Catholicism, as her appreciation of sacramental consciousness is countered by her antagonism towards god tricks that fail to respond respectfully to the contact zones of the open. This ambivalence is expressed in Haraway's simultaneous affirmation of her Catholic/Christian heritage and her commitment to atheism. Consider the following passage from an interview:

> Well, you know, I am of course a committed atheist and anti-Catholic, anyway at some level. You cannot live in the Christian United States, the right-wing United States, and not be anti-Christian. But that theological tradition is a very deep inheritance for me, and I think it affects my style very deeply.[42]

Identifying oneself as "anti-Christian" is not necessarily the most effective way of describing a complex response to one's deep inheritance of the Christian tradition. In *How Like a Leaf*, Haraway gives more nuanced examples of her complex "Catholic sacramentalism".[43] "My inability to separate the figural and the literal comes straight out of a Catholic relationship to the Eucharist".[44] Haraways goes on, adding, "I have a very Catholic sensibility as a theorist even though I am opposed to Catholicism".

Haraway affirms the sacramentalism of Catholicism, yet she remains uncompromising in her opposition to the god tricks performed in that tradition. However, one might wonder whether she, like Said, is overstating an opposition to religion. She opposes all god tricks committed throughout the sacred-secular web of contemporary global culture, yet never describes herself as antiscience or antidemocracy. In any case, Haraway's oppositional rhetoric notwithstanding, she conveys the task of becoming with and becoming worldly as a task to navigate sacred-secular networks worldwide in such a way as to overcome the god tricks of origins and respond affirmatively to the knotty openings of beginnings. Furthermore, this task of becoming responsible for the open, in the open, requires an open way of being—that is, an open style. Haraway is thus committed to her open style of writing, a style that finds "ways of blocking the closure of a sentence, or of a whole piece, so that it becomes hard to fix its meanings".[45] In sum, to become responsible in and for one's material-semiotic context is to open interconnections and loosen up oppressive hierarchies, forging connections between religious as well as secular contexts, between women and men, between cultures, and between yourself and the companion species that make up all of your relations. In opening, beginnings overflow the dominating structures of origins and god tricks. A decision to overcome the origins of domination is a decision to begin in the open.

DECISION

The openness of beginning is implicit in the etymological sense of "beginning" as it derives from the Old Teutonic word *be-ginnan*, which contains the verb *ginnan* ("to cut open, open up, begin, undertake") and relates to a variety of cognates, including the Old English verb *gínan* ("to gape, yawn").[46] A beginning is not a mere point on a linear continuum, but is a complex delimitation, a cut that opens connections, relations, and transitions. Perhaps rather than defining a beginning as a liminal opening, it would be more etymologically correct to define it as a cutting open or an opening cut. The cut of beginning resonates with another cut, the scission of decision. To decide is "to cut away" (from Latin, *decidere*). As Whitehead says, "'Decision' does not here imply conscious judgment, though in some 'decisions' consciousness will be a factor. The word is used in its root sense of a 'cutting off'".[47] For Whitehead, decision is what makes an actual thing actual, cutting away some possibilities and actualizing others. Indeed, decision "constitutes the very meaning of actuality".[48]

Keller notes that Whitehead's sense of decision is anticipated by Nachmanides, a medieval philosopher and Kabbalist for whom the verb "to create" (*bara*) at the opening of the biblical creation narrative in Genesis means "to cut away" or "set a boundary".[49] Consider how the days of creation in the Genesis narrative involve God setting boundaries: on the first day, dividing light/day from dark/

night; on the second day, creating a firmament that divides the waters above from the waters below; on the third day, dividing the sea from dry land; on the fourth day, putting lights in the firmament that divide the light of day from the light of night; on the fifth day, bringing forth birds and sea creatures, which repeat the difference between the firmament and the waters below, respectively; on the sixth day, bringing forth land animals and humans and differentiating the two by creating the latter in the divine image and telling them to subdue the rest of creation; and on the seventh day, cutting the previous six days off from a day of rest. In short, acts of creation set boundaries. In Heraclitean terms, *archai* are shared with *peras*. In that sharing (Heraclitus's *xunos*), beginnings decisively actualize some possibilities while cutting away others.

There is thus something of a paradoxical condition to decision: on one hand, a decision cuts away possibilities (including whatever possibility is actualized; its possibility is cut away by becoming actual and thus no longer possible), and on the other hand, a decision incorporates possibilities into an actual occasion. This paradox can be read in the ambiguity of the prefix *de-* in *decision*, which could mean "cut away" or "cut off" as well as incorporate; for example, "un-cut" or "de-cut": the former cuts something away, the latter undoes the cut.[50] John Llewelyn draws attention to this paradox in his reflections on the interpretations of decision given by Derrida, who himself draws on the works of the nineteenth-century Danish philosopher Søren Kierkegaard, for whom decision is a moment of madness that constitutes the self in its existential relation to itself and others.[51] Decision is not an origin that would establish rigid limits or hierarchies between connection and disconnection. Rather, decision moves in two directions at the same time, marking an unruly entanglement between connection and disconnection, a sharing or intertwining, "a chiasmic crossing where there takes place a disconnecting connection", which is not only paradoxical but also "paralogical".[52] Paralogy is not just a fallacious argument or mental illusion, as in Immanuel Kant's paralogisms, but can also be a condition of creativity.[53] More than making a new move in the same game, paralogy invents new games.[54] If you develop an innovation or create a new object that stays within the lines of what is measurable and calculable, you have made a new move but have not invented a new way of moving. As a process of paralogical invention, decision welcomes novelty that opens the limits of what is currently measurable or calculable, such that those limits open onto a greater sensitivity to differences, incommensurability, and mystery.

An important distinction must be made here regarding the inventive process of decision. When Lyotard is discussing invention, he is talking about human inventiveness, whereas Whitehead and Keller are working with a concept of decision that applies to all actual occasions, including humans as well as atoms, reptiles, slime moulds, elephants, and indeed, everything. Much to the chagrin of humans who have a species superiority complex—a mixture of chauvinism and narcissism writ large—humans are not the only agents in the cosmos. All actual occasions act, becoming actual, decisively: actualizing and cutting away possibilities. This is not a crude leveling of the differences between humans and other beings, nor is it an anthropomorphic projection of human agency as the norm for all other actors. Every actor acts, and every actor acts differently. Human decisions are quite different than the decisions of polar bears or tectonic plates, which are themselves different from the decisions of apples and oranges, and even apples and oranges are commonly said to be radically different, even incomparable.

Always different and differentiating, decisions take place throughout the universe and are not restricted to human deliberations. This cosmological scope of decision is articulated in the evolutionary narrative expressed by Brian Swimme and Thomas Berry in *The Universe Story*. Swimme and Berry describe the evolution of a star as "a series of decisions on a branching tree of possibilities". A star evolves with "a coordinated sequence of transitions", and each transition is a decision for one branchpoint instead of others. In short, "at each branchpoint in the universe a fundamental decision is made determining that particular direction".[55] Such decisions move into the future with some degree of interdependent freedom or agency, but their movement is also set within determined limits, for the actualization of each branchpoint only takes place within the conditions of the particular series of possibilities that presents itself at that point. These dynamics of decision are also evident in organisms. Imagining a population of woodpeckers that "finds itself at the edge of the world", where a familiar valley and its maples and beech trees "begin to give way to the firs and brush of the mountain biome", Swimme and Berry wonder: "What if some of them decided to enter a new world to find their grubs, to mate, to make their nests, and to enjoy in every way the life here in the world of the mountains"?[56] Those woodpeckers would enter a different world with new pressures from natural and sexual selection, pressures that could lead to new genetic variations and adaptations, new modes of existence (e.g., new shapes in their wings or beaks, different diets and eating habits, or new mating practises). Similarly, consider bison and horses: although they share a common hoofed ancestor, their decisions have led them to diverge into two different species with two different orientations towards the world: the bison deciding to charge enemies head on and the horse deciding to flee predators.[57]

Decisions open transitions into new and different worlds, whether these are the decisions that form stars, the decisions of an organism entering a foreign ecosystem, the decisions of a female responding to the advances of potential mates, or the decisions of bacteria to follow certain temperature gradients and concentrations of nutrients. In much the same way that the decisions of the common ancestors of bison and horses are still at work in the lives of bison and horses today, decisions have enduring consequences that reach into the unforeseeable future. For example, decisions of humans to domesticate and control the natural world will still be at work in future generations. Humans have "taken over such extensive control" of the Earth community that "the future will be dependent on human decision to an extent never dreamed of in previous times".[58] Humans are deciding the boundaries of wilderness, deciding what species will flourish or perish, and deciding the chemical composition of the atmosphere and the planet's soil and water. In other words, humans have "decisively inserted themselves into the ecosystemic communities throughout the planet. [. . .] The future of Earth's community rests in significant ways upon the decisions to be made by the humans who have inserted themselves so deeply into even the genetic codes of Earth's process".[59] No matter how humans make those decisions, they cannot ensure that everything will have a future in the Earth community. Some things will be incorporated and others cut away. Many species, landscapes, and cultures might not make it, and for many it is already too late.

For better and for worse, decisions always involve the exclusion of some possibilities. Accordingly, Keller indicates that beginnings are far from innocent. "A cloud of missed possibilities envelops every beginning: it is always *this* beginning, *this* universe and *not* some other".[60] This is why beginnings are so formidable, why they are, as the DJ/scholar Paul Miller puts it, "always the hard part. Once you get into the flow of things, you're always haunted by the way that things could have turned out. This outcome, that conclusion. You get my drift. The uncertainty is what holds the story together".[61] Things become actual within a disorienting cloud of possibilities, a haunting mist in which many possibilities are missed. The question is how to stay in that haunting mist of beginning instead of suppressing it beneath the dominant certainty of an origin. In Deleuzian terms, an origin imprisons events in a judgement, whereas a beginning is a nonjudgemental decision, which opens up new events in a way that integrates rather than suppresses the uncertainties and oscillating possibilities whirling around them. Before elaborating on Deleuze's distinction between judgement and decision, it is important to note that, like Whitehead, Deleuze does not restrict decision to humans as opposed to nature. Deleuze affirms the intimate intertwining of the human and the natural.

As Deleuze says with Guattari in their coauthored *Anti-Oedipus*, the human is to be understood not as an imperial force of domination that subordinates nature, not "as a king of creation, but rather as the being who is in intimate contact with the profound life of all forms or all types of beings, who is responsible for even the stars and animal life".[62] In other words, Deleuze (as well as Guattari) makes "no distinction" between humans and nature, affirming instead a mutual enfoldment of "the human essence" of the natural world and "the natural essence" of the human. In *A Thousand Plateaus* (the second volume of *Capitalism and Schizophrenia*, of which *Anti-Oedipus* is the first), D&G further develop concepts that overcome the opposition between human culture (or language, words, signs, meaning) and nature (or matter, energy, body, biology). "It is no longer even appropriate", declare D&G, "to group biological, physico-chemical, and energetic intensities on the one hand, and mathematical, aesthetic, linguistic, informational, semiotic intensities, etc., on the other".[63] To overcome those nature/culture oppositions, D&G transform philosophy into a "synthesizer" that conjugates flows and opens material-semiotic connections. This synthesizer places everything in "continuous variation", such that heterogeneous intensities interconnect and flow into one another. With this synthesizer, D&G "witness the incorporeal power" of matter and "the material power" of language and form. In other words, they witness "a passage to the limit" where opposites open into interconnected flows of becoming.[64]

D&G contrast their philosophical synthesizer with judgement. "The synthesizer has taken the place of the old 'a priori synthetic judgment'".[65] Unlike the synthesizer, the Kantian "a priori synthetic judgment" does not open flows between the phenomena experienced by humans and the real (noumenal) things of the cosmos, but only interconnects humans and the cosmos insofar as they are subordinated to prior foundations, which are necessary, universal, and not subject to variation in experience or thought. In contrast, the synthesizer puts everything in continuous variation in a flowing material-semiotic cosmos in which thought is not separate from the cosmos but is one cosmic force among others. "Philosophy is no longer synthetic judgment; it is like a thought synthesizer functioning to make thought travel, make it mobile, make it a force of the Cosmos".[66] Functioning without foundation, origin, or judgement, the operation of the synthesizer is the generative operation of decision.

"A decision", according to Deleuze, "is not a judgment". A decision "springs vitally from a whirlwind of forces that leads us into combat", and such combat is not to be confused with war.[67] This is not militaristic combat. It is a vitality that enriches and intensifies whatever it engages. Judgement turns the vitality of combat into war. It colonizes the whirlwind of forces with transcendental criteria that are imposed on all times and places. A decision facilitates the emergence of new modes of existence, whereas a judgement manipulates forces and prevents anything new from emerging, suppressing instead of engaging the whirlwind of forces flowing in combat. Moreover, to renounce judgement in favor of decision is not to renounce all criteria for distinguishing between different values or different beings. Criteria are immanent to the decision, such that the cut of decision opens up new modes of existence according to their own demands and obligations, including the demand to continue existing and becoming actual, which means continuing to engage the whirlwinds and clouds of possibilities without suppressing them or assimilating them into some preexisting schema. "Herein, perhaps, lies the secret: to bring into existence and not to judge".[68]

It is important to note that Deleuze's affirmation of decision is not a decision theory or decisionism, for that would assimilate decision into a schema that organizes the vertiginous clouds of possibilities and answers questions instead of letting them remain open. Decision theory provides answers to the problems of agency and freedom instead of engaging the whirling mist. Deciding is not a matter of answering questions or putting an end to problems. It is a matter of integrating a whirlwind of minute inclinations and unconscious orientations in such a way as to produce differences and encourage the development of new modes of existence. This integration does not assimilate or appropriate differences into a homogeneous unity, but intensifies their consistency to generate new events. This stands in contrast to what Deleuze calls the "philosophical decision" of Plato, which is really a judgement more than a decision, as it does not involve producing differences to create new events but consists in "subordinating difference to the supposedly initial powers of the Same and the Similar", "declaring difference unthinkable in itself" and sending it "back to the bottomless ocean".[69] A nonjudgemental decision integrates rather than suppresses the mist and clouds condensing out of the oceanic abyss of difference. "Everything starts out in the abyss".[70]

The sense of decision as a creation of new events and an integration of differences and missed possibilities exhibits some resonance with Derrida's writings on decision, where decision is not about a theory of subjective autonomy, nor is it a decisionism that would perpetuate a dichotomy between freedom and the limits of law or determinism. Decision is a deconstructive process of welcoming new events by responding to the profound differences marked by every difference, the profound otherness of every other.[71] As mentioned above, Derrida draws on Kierkegaard's understanding of decision as the constitutive act of subjectivity and of faith, claiming that all decisions must involve a leap beyond knowledge and beyond any calculation or anticipation of what is to come. There is thus "a paradoxical condition of every decision": a decision can only be known or decided in a moment that breaches the horizon of what is able to be known or decided. That is the paradox faced by the woodpeckers at the edge of the world, deciding to leave a familiar valley and move toward an unknown mountain. Moving "outside of knowledge or given norms", decisions move through "the ordeal of the undecidable".[72]

Derrida repeats Kierkegaard's saying that "the instant of decision is madness".[73] If decisions were not mad, entranced, wild, and crazy, they would not become decisions, but would be programmed reactions or calculations that assimilate differences rather than responding creatively to them. In other words, to decide is to respond to one's entanglement with differences and others, and this response is mad insofar as it interrupts or disturbs one's own horizon of what can be signified or said. To connect with the singularity of the other and respond to all of the other's alterity (otherness), a decision must cut the other off from oneself so that the other is really other and not assimilated into my horizon. In the madness of decision, one is "alone, entrenched in one's own singularity" and thus cut off from "the absolute singularity of the other", and that cut is so profound that, for biblical religions, it is imagined as a repetition of the cut between oneself and the "absolute other", God.[74] Cut off from the other, decision is always secretive. It is not a secret that could be communicated (not even to oneself or to God), not an unknown that could be known, but a secret that breaks through structures of communicability and knowledge, displacing the habituated boundaries of the known and the unknown and responding to the singularity of the other.[75]

A decision does not only cut oneself off from the other, but also cuts the other off from the other others who call for a response. If one is responsible to some other, then one sacrifices one's responsibility to other others, as in the biblical case of Abraham's response to God calling him to sacrifice his son, Isaac.[76] In the event of a decision, the compelling force of the wholly other comes from every other. Entrenched in one's own singularity, the wholly other is every other, not only God. Every other manifests the absolute singularity of the wholly other. This is conveyed in a palindrome—the French phrase *tout autre est tout autre*, which can be translated as "every other (one) is every (bit) other".[77] Every other (*tout autre*) calls with the absolute singularity of the wholly other (*tout autre*), making it impossible to decide who or what is calling or decide which other(s) will receive a response: every other, wholly other, haunting every decision with undecidability. "The undecidable remains caught, lodged, as a ghost [. . .] in every event of decision. Its ghostliness [*sa fantomaticité*] deconstructs from within all assurance of presence, all certainty or all alleged criteriology assuring us of the justice of a decision".[78]

A decision does not put an end to the differences, uncertainties, and missed possibilities whirling around every event. Decision integrates every other precisely as that which is wholly other and unable to be assimilated, calculated, appropriated, or integrated. Welcoming others, welcoming the arrival of new events, the cut of decision opens up to the ghosts of undecidability. These ghosts not only haunt human-divine relations or human-human relations, but also relations between humans and "places, animals, languages".[79] Decision opens cuts between every other, differential relations through which people, places, symbols, divinities, and all inhabitants of the planet and of the cosmos share in the undecidable entanglement of responsibility. Although Derrida differs from Whitehead and Deleuze insofar as his writings do not explicitly address nonhuman modes of existence nearly as much as theirs do, Derrida is like Whitehead and Deleuze in attempting to overcome human/nonhuman dualisms and to thus conceive of things "before the opposition of nature and culture, animality and humanity, etc.".[80] Decision is always ecological and cosmological, a generative process of differentiation far exceeding the limits of humanity. The ghost of undecidability haunts all relationships, even Derrida's decision to feed his cat.[81] With so many other cats in the world, how could he decide which to feed? How could he respond in this situation, with so many other others calling for food? To make a decision to feed oneself or another is to make a cut between the hunger and satiety of others and ultimately a cut between their living and dying, a cut in the web of life. This ecology of decision resonates with an observation made by the American poet and environmental activist Gary Snyder: "There is no death that is not somebody's food, no life that is not somebody's death".[82]

Every decision to eat and every responsibility for feeding another is haunted by the living and dying of others, haunted by all other hungry mouths in the world, including future generations of others, haunted by the cloud of possibilities surrounding the whole Earth community. Every decision and every responsibility is haunted by the open chaos of undecidability. The ethico-religious and legal order of decision and responsibility are "founded upon a bottomless chaos", and chaos here "refers precisely to the abyss or the open mouth, that which speaks as well as that which signifies hunger".[83] In the open, decisions emerge from an abyss of difference without a stable foundation. Far from equilibrium, decisions begin in chaos, an opening—uncertain, undecidable, haunting—which interrupts the dominological judgements and origins that support the ecological devastation ravaging planetary coexistence.

EXAMPLES

To provide philosophical contributions to integral ecology, a concept of beginning as liminal opening or as an opening decision needs to be relevant to specific examples related to ecological realities. Before discussing some specific examples, it is important to consider more about how examples are used. After all, becoming an example is not always thought of as a good thing. Imagine a teacher telling a student, "I am going to make an example out of you". If the student had taken a test and given the correct answers to the questions, then becoming an example could feel like a reward or an honour. If the student was being disruptive, not following rules, or not properly answering questions, then becoming an example might feel a lot more like pain and punishment than an honour. Even if it is an honour, becoming an example might mean that you are just a copy, an ectype, one instance or case of the exemplary structure or paradigm of school rules. Alternatively, becoming an example might mean that you are the exemplar, the archetype or model against which others can and should be measured. Who sets the boundary between model and copy? Who decides what examples are exemplary?

Consider how Rachel Carson's well-known 1962 publication, *Silent Spring*, ignited the environmental movement and increased awareness of the dangers of the pesticide DDT by making an example out of birdsong, warning the public that continued use of chemical pesticides may lead to devastating environmental and human impacts, including the possibility of a "silent spring" when no more birdsongs can be heard, because the birds have gradually died off, unable to produce offspring due to the eggshell-thinning effect of the DDT that accumulated in the birds.[84] Along different lines, consider how some environmentalists and scholars make an example out of the ecological sensibilities of indigenous peoples. Attempting to honour indigenous environmental ethics, they treat indigenous peoples as an example of "ecological noble savages", innocent and harmonious with the natural world—an example that can do more harm than good insofar as it perpetuates nostalgic and romanticized stereotypes that fail to do justice to the actual existence of indigenous persons and the singularity of indigenous lifeways.[85]

Derrida describes a paradoxical tension at work in the problem of exemplarity. "The example", on one hand, "is not substitutable".[86] Its uniqueness and singularity cannot be replaced, repeated, copied, or modeled, but paradoxically, it is precisely because an example is irreplaceable that one can make an example out of it. Through irreplaceability, it can become a good example, worthy of being copied and repeated universally, an exemplary example. It is its irreplaceability that makes it exemplary, its singularity that makes it universalisable. Every example cuts open the paradoxical decision of choosing the singular *and* the universal. This opens political and ethical problems tending to the universality and singularity of every other (*tout autre*), as example and exemplar implode into the undecidability of the *exemplum*, which ambiguously conveys a universal model, a specific example, and a compelling moral anecdote. The force of undecidability sets to work the deconstruction of any hegemonic original model that would reduce differences to mere copies or otherwise efface the nonsubstitutable uniqueness of examples. With its affirmation of irremediable difference (Derrida's *différance*), deconstruction can mobilize resistance to the logic of domination that colonizes the world with its origins, models, and foundations.[87]

Deconstruction cuts through the opposition between example and exemplar, so that an example is not wielded like an exemplary origin or identity but a beginning—an open question or problem that calls for responsibility to the universality and singularity of any example/exemplar. In other words, like Carson's birds, Derrida's cat (Lutece), or Haraway's dog (Ms. Cayenne Pepper), an exemplary example is one that calls in the open for respect for species in their specificity and generality. As Deleuze would put it, an exemplary example (i.e., Platonic Idea, archetype) "'corresponds' to the essence of the problem or the question as such", a correspondence that resonates with Kant's description of the Idea as "a problem permitting of no solution".[88] An exemplar is a particular problem, a problem like Lutece, a problem like Ms. Cayenne Pepper, a problem like Maria. Each being is a complex question, an opening decision. "It is as though there were an 'opening', a 'gap', an ontological 'fold' which relates being and the question to one another".[89] Deleuze can thus support efforts like those of Elizabeth Grosz, who uses Deleuze, feminism, and evolutionary theory to cut open hegemonic systems and destabilize any "frozen set of archetypes" that are founded on "a nature whose openness has been misunderstood".[90] Deleuzian archetypes are thawed and defrosted. They are moving multiplicities—openings and folds of differential relations. Nothing is simply a copy of a transcendent origin. Each thing has its beginning as "a multiplicity, which unfolds and becomes within its own spatiotemporal coordinates (its own 'internal metrics'), in perpetual relation with other multiplicities".[91] Every multiplicity is a singular example and a universal exemplar. In other words, everything becomes a *unique* example, having its own irreducible and singular differences, and at the same time, everything becomes an *ordinary* example, a universalisable and regular series of differences at the intersection of other multiplicities. "'Everything is ordinary'! and 'Everything is unique'"![92]

Dealing with examples requires a problematic decision that takes place amidst the whirling forces of the one and the many, the regular and the unique, the universal (exemplars) and the singular (examples), the species and the specifics. The problem does not call for a solution as much as it calls for an engagement with the questions raised in the mist and clouds of its whirling forces. To engage the whirling clouds of decisions, one should not limit oneself to asking the Socratic question of "What is . . . "? (e.g., "What is justice"? or "What is nature"?). Privileging the transcendent Being of what something *is*, the Socratic question suppresses dynamic relations of multiplicities, studying the clouds by dispelling them, explaining them away with a rationalization that loses touch with immanent existence.[93] As a problem, an exemplary example opens questions of the immanent intensities of events, questions of becoming. "Who"? "How"? "How much"? With problematic Ideas, "the questions 'How much'?, 'How'?, 'In what cases'? and 'Who'? abound".[94] A good example does not solve problems, nor does it refer questions to a transcendent origin or model. It opens up different responses to questions, making a difference, producing connections among multiplicities.

An exemplary beginning opens out and produces differences, problems, and decisions that engage the whirling material-semiotic forces of events, which are unique (singular) and ordinary (universal). Any example of beginning can become an exemplary example, such that the example raises problems not simply about what a beginning is but how it becomes, who it becomes, in what cases it happens, how much it happens, and so on. The point is not to use the example as a representation of the determinations of an established map or model but to let the example raise problems that invite experimental contact with events. Consider the ways in which beginnings take place in the following three examples: (1) a shore that begins at the edge of a sea, (2) a forest that opens in a prairie, and (3) a community that begins in the opening between two regimes.[95]

In the first example, a shore begins at the boundary where it is touched by the sea. Every sea/shore boundary is a decision or a complex of decisions. Decisively, the seashore boundary actualizes the shoreline while possibilities for the shoreline are cut away. The cut of the shoreline brings sea and shore together while holding them apart. The boundaries of the sea share in the constitution of the shore, and the shore shares in the constitution of the boundaries of the sea. The sea shapes the shore, and yet it does not simply invent the shore, but finds the shore already there, already at the limit of the sea. Rachel Carson, the American biologist, nature writer, and environmental activist, describes this relationship between shore and sea in *The Edge of the Sea*. "Once this rocky coast beneath me was a plain of sand; then the sea rose and found a new shore line. And again in some shadowy future the surf will have ground these rocks to sand and will have returned the coast to its earlier state".[96] For Carson, the "coastal forms merge and blend in a shifting, kaleidoscopic pattern", a pattern of "earth becoming fluid as the sea itself".[97] The beginning of the shoreline is a limit, a cut from which land and sea open into one another coconstitutively: the becoming-sea of the shore, the becoming-shore of the sea. While the coast limits the reach of the sea, the sea affects the shape of the shore, changing it from sand to rock and eventually back to sand. Furthermore, the present appearances of these sea/shore boundaries are connected with their pasts and futures. Just as Carson describes the future of these boundaries in terms of the uncertainty of some shadowy future, she notes in *The Sea Around Us* that past beginnings are also shadowy, with no eyewitnesses to shed light on certain details. "Beginnings are apt to be shadowy, and so it is with the beginnings of that great mother of life, the sea".[98]

Beginning in the sea, the conditions of life were shaped by an environment without much oxygen, and the subsequent evolution of life shaped its environment, oxygenating the water and air through photosynthesis, and thus creating the conditions for respiration—the breath of life. The present conditions of the sea are connected with past and future coevolutionary interactions whereby the sea transforms and is transformed by life. Like these coevolutionary interactions, the coconstitutive relations between sea and shore show that "the present is linked with past and future".[99] The sand in the shadowy future of coastal rocks opens out from the beginning of those rocks and even from the very beginning of the planet, such that "each grain on a beach is the result of processes that go back into the shadowy beginnings of life, or of the earth itself".[100] Opening out from the shadowy beginnings of the planet, the shadowy beginnings of the sea, the shore, and life converge with the shadowy beginning of humans. Indeed, the edge of the sea is "the place of our dim ancestral beginnings".[101]

In the second example, let's move from the seashore to a place where a forest begins from within a prairie, a place that the American forester and conservationist Aldo Leopold describes as an "oak opening". In *A Sand County Almanac*, Leopold tells of how prairie fires in Wisconsin would burn everything in the prairie except for the bur oaks, which came into the prairie as "shock troops sent by the invading forest to storm the prairie".[102] The "groves of scattered veterans" who survived the fire were "known to the pioneers as 'oak openings'".[103] These groves of oaks provided new beginnings from which the forest could open out, and fires provided new beginnings from which the prairie could open out. Leopold notes that botanists can read twenty thousand years of history in this relationship between prairie and forest, or as he puts it, this "war" between prairie and forest. During some periods, the forest retreated almost to the northern border of Wisconsin at Lake Superior, and during other periods, the forest "grew to and beyond the southern border of Wisconsin". Furthermore, Leopold's use of war metaphors to describe oak openings (e.g., "shock troops", "invading forest", "scattered veterans") raises vital questions about the place of war and violence in the liminal openings of beginnings (Whose war? How much violence? In what cases?), particularly insofar as the violent conflicts that take place in beginnings are real events and not merely literary tropes.

Regarding the third example, although it is possible to refer metaphorically to the openness and the violent conflict that happen in beginnings, Žižek describes the beginning of a new community in which this violence and openness were presented quite literally. Reflecting on the Romanian Revolution of 1989, Žižek depicts

> the unique picture from the time of the violent overthrow of Ceauşescu in Romania: the rebels waving the national flag with the red star, the Communist symbol, cut out, so that instead of the symbol standing for the organizing principle of the national life, there was nothing but a hole in its center. [. . .] The enthusiasm which carried them was literally the enthusiasm over this hole, not yet hegemonized by any positive ideological project.[104]

What is important in this example is that "the masses who poured into the streets of Bucharest 'experienced' the situation as 'open'".[105] This openness was manifest literally in the open hole in the Romanian flag, and the violence of this new beginning was not a mere metaphor but involved riots and fighting that claimed hundreds of human lives. Between two regimes and amidst violent conflict there appeared the openness of a new beginning for Romania.

With a shore, a forest, and a new community, the decisive opening of beginning becomes apparent. The cuts and conflicts involved in beginnings raise questions about what kinds of control or power take place in the shifting and shadowy kaleidoscopic patterns of beginnings. Can struggle and conflict become peaceful? How? How much and in what cases are beginnings scenes of war or violence? Whose beginnings? Whose war? These are open questions, and the responses to them are varied and diverse, changing depending on the context. The militarism and violence of oak openings have a different intensity than the conflict of the Romanian revolution, which are both quite different from the fractal contact between sea and shore. Could it be that the challenge is not eliminating conflict but cultivating forms of conflict that create differences and new modes of existence rather than annihilate differences and homogenize the diversity of existence? For example, consider Heraclitus, for whom the sharing (*xunos*) that connects beginning with limits also connects war to all beings, such that everything has its birth in shared conflict.[106]

Is it possible to participate in the struggles of war and strife as loving struggles, friendly struggles? This is not unlike the position of Empedocles, who describes a mixing of "love" and "strife" (*eros* and *eris*) at the roots of things.[107] Llewelyn notes that, for Heraclitus, "to whom Empedocles may have been indebted, love as harmony enters on the scene as that which gets expressed in the idea of a friendly struggle (*polemos*) that is said to go on among all things".[108] Such struggle is part of "the struggle for integral liberation" involved in the work and play of integral ecology, a "struggle for life" that draws on "authentic joy, celebration, [. . .] music, dance, and laughter".[109] If struggle is part of all beginnings, perhaps it can become an integral struggle, creative and life-affirming, like the conflict produced by the "war machine" articulated by D&G, a machine that "*in itself does not have war for its object*" but functions like the combat of decision, a cutting edge that "opens and multiplies connections" by integrating (not suppressing) the whirl of forces.[110] In any case, however loving and creative a beginning might be, beginning is always haunted by possibilities of domination, oppressive hierarchies, and destructive violence. Although the war machine can function creatively, it can also be appropriated for the sake of destruction, war, and militarism. This is evident when one considers how the Israeli Defense Forces (IDF) appropriated concepts from D&G for use in their military strategies against the Palestinians.[111]

The place of war and violence in beginnings is further complicated when considering that war is frequently associated with patriarchal domination, such that the inclusion of war in beginnings perpetuates sexism, heterosexism, homophobia, and other structures that efface the multiplicities of sexual difference. This patriarchal connotation of war is indicated in Heraclitus, for whom the conflict that generates all things is figured as masculine and as sovereign: "war is the father [*pater*] of everything" as well as "the king [*basileus*] of everything" (DK 22b53). However, if beginnings emerge with the cutting edge of a decision that opens and multiplies connections, then even under extremely oppressive conditions, beginnings harbour the power to undo the homogenizing hegemony of the father/king and any hierarchy of dominant privilege, power, and position. Instead, beginnings open becomings—the becoming-sea of the shore and the becoming-shore of the sea—which generate new coevolutionary contacts that entangle presents and futures with the shadowy beginnings of their ancestral past. Deleuze and Guattari map out a multiplicity of "becomings", including becoming-woman, becoming-animal, becoming-molecular, becoming-cosmic, becoming-intense, becoming-imperceptible, and more.[112] A becoming is less a matter of identifying with an entity or event and more about entering into a mutually enfolded relationship with its anomalous difference and thereby intensifying one's own life and the material-semiotic process of life itself.

D&G make an example out of becoming-woman. It is not simply one line of becoming among others, but is "the key to all the other becomings", such that "all becomings begin with and pass through becoming-woman".[113] Sexual difference is crucial to encounters with all kinds and degrees of difference. Becoming-woman has a pivotal role because it facilitates the dismantling of the rigid structures of patriarchal domination, and once those structures are cut open, it is possible for other becomings to flow. Moreover, as Grosz says in her engagement with Deleuze's concepts, it is not that becoming-woman is for men only or that women do not need to pass through becoming-woman. "If one *is* a woman, it remains necessary to become-woman as a way of putting into question the coagulations, rigidifications, and impositions required by patriarchal [. . .] power relations".[114] With their concept of becomings, D&G open possibilities for the decisive struggle of beginnings to engender not a dominant father/king that wages war on immanent becoming, but to engender a multiplicity of creative experiments that open new possibilities for subjects, societies, and environments to become different.

The place of conflict and struggle in beginnings is even further complicated insofar as unprecedented beginnings are currently taking place for the entire human species and, indeed, for all life on Earth. At the time I am writing, the world is on edge. It is an uncertain and undecidable edge, marking the threshold of what could become a new beginning. Is it possible that a new era of civilization is beginning to dawn, one characterized by a commitment of humans worldwide to share in the development of complex relations and novel connections that intertwine humans with one another, with other species, and with the planet? Ecological and economic crises globally are forcing humans to respond to and take responsibility for their inextricable entanglement with others. For better and for worse, with advances in telecommunications and the democratization of biotechnologies and information technologies, humans are enacting unprecedented transformations of one another and of land, air, water, and life on Earth. The unprecedented scale of these transformations is evident in a variety of examples: the development of nuclear technologies that provide sources of energy as well as sources of mass destruction; human interventions in evolutionary processes to produce genetically modified organisms (GMOs); the spread of free trade and the deregulation of markets through capitalist models of economic globalization; the destabilization of the planet's climate through human activities that involve excessive emissions of greenhouse gases (especially carbon dioxide).

It is a widespread scientific observation that "no ecosystem on Earth's surface is free of pervasive human influence".[115] Human influence is so pervasive that some scientists and philosophers have proposed that the geological epoch that began around twelve thousand years ago, the Holocene, has reached its end, and a new epoch is beginning, the Anthropocene, wherein there is no longer any nature or wilderness that is not to some extent anthropogenic.[116] As Swimme and Berry say, humans are currently facing the challenge of recognizing that "our decisions have immediate effects on the macrocosmic reality throughout the Earth community", such that the well-being of humans and the whole Earth community is threatened any time "we fail to take the macrophase meaning of the Earth and universe into our microphase species projects".[117] This is an immense change for all modes of planetary existence. Indeed, the term *Anthropocene* only tells a small part of the story. Humans are not only transforming their geological epoch (spanning twelve thousand years) within the encompassing sixty-five million years of one geological era, the Cenozoic. They are transforming the very geological *era* in which they live. The "new life" of the Cenozoic era is undergoing a profound and uncertain transformation.[118] The incredible biological diversity that has defined this era is currently undergoing a mass extinction, which human actions have largely caused and which human actions must mitigate for the sake of the survival of the species currently inhabiting Earth, including the human species.[119] This is the sixth mass extinction of species that has taken place in the history of the Earth. The previous mass extinction event, ending the Cretaceous period and the whole Mesozoic era, occurred sixty-five million years ago with the extinction of the dinosaurs. Anthropogenic factors are causing the extremely fast rate of the current mass extinction, which is estimated to be between one hundred and one thousand times faster than the background rate found in the fossil record.[120] Not least of these anthropogenic factors are those that contribute to habitat destruction through global warming. The very climate of the planet is changing unpredictably and becoming a much more precarious habitat for life, far more precarious than is conveyed in the rather benign phrases *global warming* and *climate change*.[121]

As we humans cross the threshold into an era of planetary interconnectedness, our survival and well-being (and the survival and well-being of all life on Earth) depends in part on the ways in which we respond to the dynamics at work at this threshold. The possibility of a beginning for a planetary civilization is shaped by the dynamics of beginning and the concepts with which we respond to those dynamics. If the beginning is conceived as a dominating origin imposing itself unilaterally, colonizing and oppressing all others, then crossing the threshold of a planetary civilization would found a destructive global hegemony, "effacing the folds" of difference with what Derrida calls "the hegemony of the homogeneous".[122] If beginnings are conceived as generative limits that produce decisive dynamics of openness and connectivity, then the beginning of a planetary civilization would initiate relations of mutual enfoldment and sharing between members of the Earth community.

To avoid global hegemony and facilitate the emergence of a planetary civilization of complex relationality, humans need to participate creatively and responsibly in the openings of beginnings. Humans need to respond decisively to their place in the open. To further explicate this place in the open, I turn back to earlier beginnings, before our global society, before our environmental crisis. I turn back to the beginnings expressed in Plato's *Timaeus*, particularly with respect to the discourse on *chora*—place, milieu, the middle (*milieu*) in which all being and becoming take place (*lieu*). This turn back provides a clue about the place of humans on a planet in an evolving and chaotic cosmos, the chaosmos. The chaosmos provides the shifting grounds that will let a thousand new ecologies bloom, integral ecologies with which humans can responsibly engage boundary projects in the opening of a planetary civilization.

CHOROLOGY

The beginning of a planetary civilization could be measured against the Paleolithic beginnings of human societies, which could, in turn, be measured against the beginnings of life, the beginnings of Earth and its solar system, and the beginning of the universe. In other words, to understand the beginning of a planetary civilization, one could consider its relationship to all prior beginnings. Furthermore, an understanding of these beginnings presupposes some concept of beginning. To inquire into the possibility of a new beginning for civilization thus requires a turn back, a turn to inquire about how other beginnings have begun and how those beginnings are examples of the nature of all beginning, of all origination, generation, production, birth, creation, invention, and so on. The question of how to create concepts for a planetary civilization is not unlike the question faced by ancient Greek philosophers regarding concepts of the city (*polis*). In particular, Plato's *Timaeus* raises the question of how the actualization of an ideal city requires a turn back to prior human beginnings (the first city, an archaic Athens), which itself requires a turn back to the beginning that takes place in the creation of the cosmos. With all of this turning, the dialogue of the *Timaeus* is full of interruptions, cutting through the dualisms typical of Platonism (e.g., being/becoming, intelligible/sensible, logic/myth) and recovering a milieu—*chora*—a liminal place percolating through the cracks in the hierarchies of origins and judgements, opening possibilities for new modes of existence. Turn back, then, and consider how the whirling discourse of the *Timaeus* harbours concepts that help us turn back, engaging the place of beginning in a way that interrupts the dominology of origins.

"One, two, three".[123] With these words the *Timaeus* begins, and yet this beginning is already referring to an earlier beginning. Socrates is counting the number of people present who participated in a discussion that took place the day before. Counting three people (Timaeus, Hermocrates, and Critias), Socrates interrupts his counting to ask about the place, the whereabouts, of a fourth person: "Where, my dear Timaeus, is the fourth of our guests of yesterday"?[124] *Where*, indeed? The fourth is never identified, and never mentioned again in the dialogue, but the absence of the fourth provokes the opening question of the dialogue, a question concerning the place of real bodies, a question that asks about whereabouts. Filling in for the absent fourth, the dialogue continues as they remember the topics of their discussion from the day before. Socrates reminds those present that the discourse from the day before was concerned with "the kind of constitution [*politeia*]" that would be best, "and the character of its citizens".[125] Socrates goes on to recapitulate this prior discussion, which bears many resemblances to the discussion of an ideal city in Plato's *Republic*.[126] The problem is that the ideal city is not becoming. It does not move and change. It is a merely transcendent archetype—a "pattern" that exists only "in heaven" and does not exist "anywhere on earth".[127] Socrates wants to see the ideal political constitution take *place* in an actual community, some*where* on Earth. To describe the ideal city as it takes place in motion, on Earth, is to describe the city as it participates in multiple struggles (including "military actions" and "verbal negotiations"). Aware of his own inability to give that description, Socrates says that "none could deal more adequately" with this task than the three in his company (Timaeus, Hermocrates, and Critias).[128] With his only speech in the dialogue, the nominally *herm*eneutic Hermocrates says that they will indeed take up this task.[129] After Critias and Timaeus agree with Hermocrates, they begin, starting with a speech from Critias, who recounts a story about the excellent deeds of an archaic Athens.

Critias interrupts his telling of the myth of archaic Athens to draw attention to the fact that his telling of this myth is itself not mythical. It is a way of transporting the myth of the political community "into the realm of fact", which Socrates considers an "all-important" aspect of Critias's story: it must be "no invented fable [*muthon*] but genuine history [*logon*]".[130] With this nonmythical myth, Critias thereby interrupts the opposition between myth and *logos*. In his reading of the *Timaeus*, John Sallis notices that Socrates and Critias are enacting a "reconstitution of the very opposition" between *muthos* and *logos*, an interruptive and paradoxical reconstitution for which Socrates's account of the ideal city is viewed not as ideal *logos* but as constructed myth, and the true *logos* is expressed by Critias in a myth of archaic Athens.[131] Immediately following this interruption and paradoxical reconstitution of the myth/logic opposition, Critias again interrupts his account of the archaic Athens, this time to let Timaeus give a speech, "beginning with the origin of the Cosmos and ending with the generation of mankind".[132] Just as in the first lines of the dialogue, a beginning is interrupted to refer back to another beginning. This dialogue is an eruption of mythic/logical interruptions. It is in the intervals opened by these interruptions that a political constitution takes place.[133]

To describe the beginning of the cosmos, Timaeus distinguishes between two kinds of things: (1) that which is perpetually being (*to on aei*) and is not generated, and (2) that which becomes through generation (*to gigomenon*) and is subject to destruction.[134] For Timaeus, then, the question of the cosmos is a question of whether it is being or becoming—a basic formula of Platonic dualism. Perpetual being is understood through reasoning (logic), whereas becoming is grasped through the senses (irrationally) and only discloses matters of opinion and belief. Being exists eternally, whereas a sensible thing is generated as a copy of its original ideal, an image of its paradigm. The distinction between being and becoming thus corresponds to a distinction between, on one hand, the intelligible (*to noeton*), logic, and truth (*aletheia*), and on the other hand, the sensible (*to aistheton*), myth, and belief (*pistis*).[135] As with the *muthos/logos* schema, this schema, too, is interrupted. This interruption shakes preconceptions about Plato and Platonism, but even more than that, it shakes the very origin of the cosmos.

While Timaeus is discussing necessity (*ananke*), claiming that it is "necessary" for the cosmos to have a beginning as a copy (because it is sensible, and all sensible things are generated as copies of ideal forms), he interrupts his account of cosmogenesis with an injunction: "it is most important to begin at the natural beginning".[136] At this point of interruption, Socrates says his final words of the dialogue, words of acceptance for Timaeus's speech, a speech accepted "wondrously" (*thaumasios*).[137] If "philosophy begins in wonder" (*thaumazein*), as Socrates says in the *Theaetetus*, then Socrates's acceptance marks not only the beginning of his silence for the remainder of the dialogue, but the beginning of philosophy.[138] Philosophy begins in the opening of an interruption that turns back in wonder to the natural beginning. As Socrates receives this speech in silence, Timaeus begins again to describe the beginning of the cosmos. Following a lengthy discourse on the details of a demiurgic god who produces the cosmos as a sensible copy of an intelligible form, Timaeus returns to an inquiry into the role of necessity (*ananke*) in the beginning of the cosmos.[139] The cosmos is generated not only through the formal cause of ideal being but also through necessity, which is "the Errant Cause": nomadic, vagabond, and vague, wandering creatively outside the limits of the intelligible. This suggests that the cosmos has its beginning not simply through a demiurge stamping an ideal form on it, but also through a creative wandering that interrupts the schema of intelligible origin and sensible copy. Not simply intelligible or sensible, this cause bears traces that can be called elemental. The world of sense includes traces of elemental matters (fire, water, air, and earth), traces that take place without the demiurgic stamp of ideal being, like copies without a model.[140]

The errant cause marks an elemental beginning, a generative movement of wondrous wandering. This wandering interrupts the enumeration of the two kinds (being and becoming), exceeding the limits of Platonism, slipping through the cracks of dualisms as a "third kind" (*triton genos*). The third kind is conceived of as the "receptacle" (*hupodoche*) or "recipient" (*dechomenon*), wherein all forms come into being and pass away. This receptacle is also described as a mother, as the nurse of all generation, and as *chora* (also transliterated as *khora*) sometimes translated as "place" in English (*locus* in Latin, *lieu* in French).[141] Recapitulating the opening lines of the dialogue, the counting of three kinds ("One, two, three") opens onto the question of whereabouts. According to Timaeus, place generates all things. Its elemental wandering makes room for everything in the cosmos. As a matrix where all being and becoming take place, *chora* shakes things up, raising multiple problems. A theological problem is that any temporal priority and (omni)potency of God is disturbed by *chora*, for God's creative work is situated somewhere, limited, in place, which is not to say that place is the origin of God and all things (*chora* is precisely *not* original being), but that place is their preoriginal matrix, their elemental context.[142] A cosmological problem is whether other worlds have taken place before or alongside our 13.8-billion-year-old cosmos, such that our universe is one of many worlds in a multiverse.[143] An ecological problem is how much *chora* has to do with the plurality of actual places on Earth, such as animal habitats, biodiversity hotspots, mines, ecovillages, national parks, fisheries, nuclear test sites, and concentrated animal feeding operations (CAFOs). Is place one underlying field, or is place always one among many places? A concept of *chora* seems like it would be more relevant to ecology if responding to *chora* entails responding to a plurality of actual places (pluralism) rather than responding to place as a single underlying field (monism). Perhaps *chora* makes room for what D&G call a "magic formula", which they emphasize in capital letters, "PLURALISM = MONISM".[144]

Chora seems to silently receive all forms (in the way Socrates has silently received Timaeus's discourse, and in the way that Hermocrates has kept his hermeneutic mouth hermetically sealed). Yet this reception is not a mere passivity but is causally effective. *Chora* is quite generative (in the way Socrates initiates philosophy through silent wonder, in the way Hermocrates makes room for Critias and Timaeus to give speeches). *Chora*, an errant cause, is said to move "like an instrument which causes shaking".[145] The receptacle undulates, "sways unevenly in every part, and is herself shaken" by the forms she receives "and shakes them in turn as she is moved".[146] As the movement of *chora* makes room for interactions between being and becoming, Timaeus's discourse on *chora*—a chorology—opens places between the related dichotomies of myth/logic, sensible/intelligible, and belief/truth. *Chora* is "apprehensible by a kind of bastard reasoning", a dark dream wherein hardly anything knowable or believable comes to light: "we dimly dream and affirm that all that exists should exist in some spot [*topo*]" and "some *place* [*choran*]".[147] The Athenian understanding of "bastard" indicates that this oneiric reasoning is born of a citizen father and an alien mother, in this case, Timaeus and *chora*, respectively.[148] Although the presence of a father and mother might suggest stable heteronormative gender relations, the undulating receptacle shakes up all dualisms, including masculine/feminine, male/female, and sex/gender. Chorology is a strange, quirky, and hybrid discourse, a dreamy affirmation that sways and wanders through rational discourses (*logoi*) and stories (*muthoi*). The entire dialogue of the *Timaeus* can be read as a chorology that shakes with eruptions of interruptions to make room for discourses, stories, and dreams about the receptive place of beginnings: the beginning of a dialogue, the beginning of a city, the beginning of philosophy, the beginning of the cosmos.

Timaeus proposes the chorology in following the injunction to begin at the natural beginning. Rather than functioning like an origin that lies back, *chora* is another kind of beginning: a dynamic and receptive opening, a place that perpetually sways and shakes, errantly undulating, making room for things to come into being and pass away. This kind of beginning is described and comprehended through a dreamy discourse that makes room between the poles of dualistic oppositions (to which Plato's dialogues are often crudely reduced), oppositions such as being/becoming, intelligible/sensible, divine/material, citizen/foreigner, and logical/mythical. In the way *chora* errantly shakes all that she receives and makes room for the existence of all things, chorology makes room for dualistic schemas while wandering through them and shaking them up. Presumably, the chorology would also shake up the politics of the ideal city that Socrates articulated and the archaic Athens that, for Critias, exemplifies the ideal city in motion. Although Timaeus's cosmology comes to an end before Critias can begin to finish his account of the archaic Athens and articulate the ideal city as it takes place on Earth, it is possible to give an indication of a politics of *chora*. Sallis claims that "a politics of the χώρα [*chora*] will never be a simple linear discourse, one that could be confident of having begun at the beginning, one that could with assurance dispense with all need to double back upon itself".[149] Furthermore, chorological politics would not provide prescriptions or proscriptions for producing a civilization, but would instead attend to whatever is at play in the boundary projects involved in any such production. A chorological politics is one that resists the logic of domination and puts politics in its place, in its complex relational matrix, its knotty entanglements in the open. This has been emphasized by feminist theorists such as Judith Butler and Luce Irigaray, both of whom write about *chora* as a place that cannot be directly controlled or shaped by anything transcending it.[150] Keller also expresses this choric resistance: "A feminist politics now resistant to any fixed difference as well as to any indifference to difference, folds in and out of this khoric indeterminacy".[151]

Interrupting the hegemony of the homogeneous, chorological politics leads us to wander with wonder amidst the whirling forces of decision, opening a place, perhaps, for the emergence of a planetary civilization flourishing with biological and cultural diversity. Without prescriptions or models, *chora* engenders a dreamy wandering that, on the one hand, makes room for ideals to become manifest and, on the other hand, shakes up all ideals and identities by attending to the limits that interrupt ideals and interrupt the very opposition between intelligible ideals and sensible manifestations. That sort of approach to politics may sound strange. Indeed, discourses and practises in Western traditions have tended to suppress *chora* and assimilate this third kind into binaries of natural/cultural, sensible/intelligible, myth/logic, matter/form, becoming/being, and more, binaries that are used as justification for the domination of the subordinate or marginalized term by the superior or central term. The suppression of *chora* can be found in Aristotelian and neo-Platonic reductions of places to formless matter and modern reductions of places to abstract grids and calculable sites.[152] Casey's philosophical history of place articulates some ways in which a sense of place is recovered by diverse twentieth-century philosophers, including Whitehead, Heidegger, Bachelard, Foucault, Derrida, Deleuze and Guattari, Irigaray, and others.[153] "Philosophy", for these thinkers as for the poet Gary Snyder, "is thus a place-based exercise".[154] Furthermore, many place-based philosophers explicitly draw on the Platonic *chora* to develop their concepts, and they do so in many different ways.[155] The point I want to emphasize is not which interpretation of *chora* is correct or best. Rather, the point is to experiment with chorological concepts, letting them mutate and adapt with the aim of opening decisions and creating new events to facilitate the emergence of a planetary civilization.

Philosophical efforts towards a recovery of place are, to some extent, efforts towards a recovery or reconstruction of Platonism, not the Platonism that is hastily reduced to a matter/form dualism, but a more open and receptive Platonism, a chorological Platonism that limits hegemonic ideals and puts dualism in its place. The various efforts to recover place are ways of remaining open for another Platonism to come, keeping vigil for a more chorological Platonism. As Derrida says, "We are today on the eve of Platonism".[156] This is similar to Deleuze's effort to reverse or overturn Platonism, which is not about closing all possibilities for thinking with Plato, but about opening Platonic schemas so that they cease supporting systems that subordinate differences to an origin. When differences are not colonized by model/copy hierarchies, they "rise to affirm their rights" and their "positive power", undoing hierarchies in working towards a "condensation of coexistences".[157] This recovery of place and chorology makes room for a new beginning: for Platonism, for humans, for concepts, for God, for planetary coexistence. In the milieu of such a beginning, humans become situated in the cosmos, not an enclosed cosmos dominated by ideal form, a divine demiurge, or any sort of hegemonic homogeneity, but an open cosmos that shakes, sways, and undulates with the intense fluctuations of its receptive matrix. In other words, the chorological recovery of place makes room for a beginning in which humans become participants in a chaotic cosmos — the chaosmos.

CHAOSMOS

For concepts of integral ecology to support the beginning of planetary civilization, those concepts must not be mere ideals. They must be events that summon a response to the call for a new Earth and new people, events that set a planetary civilization in motion. The beginning of a planetary civilization must happen in place, which is to say, it must open out from the receptive matrix that makes room for things to come into being and pass away. Insofar as it takes place, the beginning of a planetary civilization recapitulates the dynamics at work in all prior beginnings, including the beginnings of human communities, the beginnings of philosophy, and the beginning of the cosmos. On the one hand, the beginning of a planetary civilization involves ideals and models that are set into motion, and on the other hand, this beginning limits the hegemony of ideals and ideologies by interrupting them with the fluctuations of the receptive matrix in which they take place. A planetary civilization is thus situated not in an ideally ordered "cosmos", but in a cosmos that is always shaking, swaying, and wandering through undulations of "place" (*chora*), undulations that could be described as "chaos".

Derrida cautions us against hastily associating chaos with *chora*, which is not to say that they do not resonate with one another's undulating openness. Associations with chaos are often viewed as bad, scary, and terrifying, such that projecting chaos onto *chora* would impose on *chora* "the anthropomorphic form and the pathos of fright".[158] *Chora* is chaotic, but it is not neatly amenable to dualisms of order and disorder or good and bad. Contrary to the dominant tendencies in Western civilization, chaos is not some undifferentiated abyss that must be controlled, suppressed, and dominated for civilization to emerge. To associate *chora* with chaos, one must be careful to acknowledge that chaos is not opposed to the order of the cosmos but is the openness necessary to keep the cosmos moving and changing. As Keller puts it, the deep opening of chaos "would not lie below as an interior or undifferentiated potency but would *capacitate* beginning".[159] This capacitating power of chaos is studied in thermodynamics, where the chaos of dissipative systems, which are far from equilibrium, generate pattern and order, as indicated in the title of the groundbreaking book on this topic by Ilya Prigogine and Isabelle Stengers, *Order Out of Chaos*.[160] The generativity of chaos is also studied in chaos theory, which analyses the iteration of fractals (self-similar geometrical patterns) emerging from the chaotic dynamics of a relational openness. That openness is described as "sensitive dependence on initial conditions" (also known as the "Butterfly Effect"), whereby an input of minute differences in a system can have large-scale effects on the output, like a butterfly flapping its wings in California and thereby causing a storm halfway around the world weeks later.[161] That which incapacitates and disorders is somehow folded together with the power to create order and capacitate new events. As Swimme and Berry observe, "The universe is both violent and creative, both destructive and cooperative. The mystery is that both extremes are found together" at "every level of existence: the elemental, the geological, the organic, the human".[162]

For the cosmos to evolve and become inhabitable by life and humans, it must be a *profoundly* chaotic cosmos. For a planetary civilization to take place, it must take place in the chaosmos. In short, the beginning of a planetary civilization is the beginning of a civilization situated in the chaosmos. The word *chaosmos* was coined by the Irish novelist James Joyce in *Finnegans Wake*:

> every person, place and thing in the chaosmos of Alle anyway connected with the gobblydumped turkery was moving and changing every part of the time: the travelling inkhorn (possibly pot), the hare and the turtle pen and paper, the continually more and less intermisunderstanding minds of the anticollaborators, the as time went on as it will variously inflected, differently pronounced, otherwise spelled, changeably meaning vocable script-signs.[163]

Like the text of *Finnegans Wake*, the chaosmos is a world that is constantly "moving and changing". It is not a world dominated by the hegemonic homogeneity of ideal form or of schematic dualisms of origin/copy or sensible/intelligible. It is a world open to "intermisunderstanding minds of the anticollaborators", open to infection from various inflections, altered pronunciations, and alternative spellings. It is a world that is "whirled without end to end". Here, chaos is not all disorder, but is more like "the beginning of all thisorder".[164]

The chaosmos is not a stable or simple cosmos, nor is it a Kosmos with a capitalized *K* (*kappa*) that would encapsulate all the complexities and uncertainties of chaos. We need to decapitate any such capitalized Kosmos.[165] Like the word "*chora*", the words *chaos* and *chaosmos* each begin with a lowercase *ch*, a transliteration of the Greek lowercase *chi* (χ), which is marked as an asymmetrical crisscrossing figure, which contrasts to the symmetrical order of the capital *chi* (X). This chiastic beginning of the chaosmos suggests a crucial crisscrossing, an asymmetrical interweaving of order and disorder that would interrupt any attempts to neatly encapsulate chaos and capitalize on it with an all-embracing order. Isn't it laughable to attempt to encapsulate the fluctuations of chaos within such an order? Ha! With a burst of laughter, the "ha" inside of the cosmos is liberated, and the c(ha)osmos is encountered as the chaosmos. Thinking with Joyce is an exercise in the philosophical task of becoming humourous.

The text of *Finnegans Wake* manifests the style of the chaosmos, moving errantly, like a trickster, wandering outside of any simple schema or linear progression. This errancy is evident in the line with which *Finnegans Wake* begins, which can be read as the end of the line with which the book closes, such that the closing is simultaneously the opening. In this opening line, Joyce refers to a "commodius vicus of recirculation"—a cyclical path alluding to Giambattista Vico (*vicus* is a pun on Vico) and his account of history in terms of cyclical repetition.[166] According to Deleuze, this *vicus of recirculation*, like Friedrich Nietzsche's "eternal return", resists the simple homogeneity and order of a cosmos and opens up a "world of differences implicated in one another", where every "difference passes through all the others"—"a complicated, properly chaotic world", a "chaosmos".[167]

A related conception of the chaosmos is expressed in the "complex thinking" of the contemporary French social theorist Edgar Morin. Grounded in principles of complexity, his thinking "endeavors to connect that which was separate while preserving distinctiveness and differences".[168] Making no mention of the use of the term in Joyce or Deleuze, Morin's use of the word *chaosmos* occurs in the title to the third section of the first chapter in *La Nature de la Nature* (the first of Morin's six-volume series, *La Méthode*).[169] The image of the chaosmos is fundamental to Morin's thinking because it describes the world in terms of a complex relationship, and not with a restricted or stabilized complexity, but an open complexity that intertwines unity and order with multiplicity and disorder.[170] According to Morin, "We are in a universe in which chaos is at work and that patterns its action through a dialogue between order and disorder".[171] In short, chaos and cosmos are inextricably interwoven: "Le Cosmos est le Chaos et le Chaos est le Cosmos".[172] However, as Morin notes, the idea of this chaotic cosmos has still not emerged on a collective level: "the new cosmos has not penetrated our minds".[173] Just as Western civilization supported the suppression of place in favor of calculable spaces and controllable sites, so the chaos of the chaosmos, too, has been suppressed.

The human domination of place, whereby the matrix that makes room for the creation of the cosmos is assimilated into binaries and oppositional schemas, is closely tied to the suppression and control of differences and the domination of those beings associated with difference or disorder (e.g., wild, female, poor, disabled, immigrant, nonhuman, etc.). Consider, for example, the domination of chaos in biblical religions, particularly as this domination is expressed in certain readings of the opening verses of the creation narrative in Genesis (1:1–2): "In the beginning when God created the heavens and the earth, the earth was a formless void and darkness covered the face of the deep, while a wind from God swept over the face of the waters". For Keller, this passage indicates that, contrary to dominant theological interpretations of the last two thousand years, the Hebrew vision of the creation is not a simply ordered whole that God creates out of nothing (*ex nihilo*) but is more like Joyce's chaosmos — a cosmos that emerges from the watery and shadowy chaos of "the deep": "'the chaosmos' coined in the thick darkness of *Finnegans Wake* offers itself as a transcription of 'the creation'".[174] The creation is thus understood not as an "imposition of order but as a fractal cascade of indeterminacy and form".[175] However, Keller shows how such an affirmation of the chaosmos — a chaotic world created out of the deep (*ex profundis*) — has been suppressed throughout the history of Western civilization, particularly in the theological doctrine of *creatio ex nihilo*, for which the world is an imposed order that God created out of nothing, an order defined by the mastery and domination of the chaotic waters of the deep.

The mastery and domination of chaos has deep historical roots, which can be traced back to Babylonian antecedents to the biblical creation narrative. The Hebrew word for *deep* is *Tehom*, and as Keller notes, this is "the Hebrew rendition of *Tiamat*" — the mother goddess embodied in the chaotic waters that are conquered by the warrior-hero Marduk in the *Enuma Elish* (the Babylonian creation epic).[176] The *Enuma Elish* contains the germinal expression of the Western understanding of the supremacy of order over chaos, which corresponds with the distinction between father god (order) and mother goddess (chaos). Marduk's conquest of Tiamat is echoed in the biblical account of the conquest of the deep by God, who divides the waters on the second and third days of creation, separating waters above the sky from the waters below the sky (day 2), and separating the latter waters from the earth (day 3) (Gen. 1:6–10). For Keller, this supremacy of the divine order of the father over the chaos of the feminine waters is indicative of "an incipient *tehomophobia*" (in contrast to *tehomophilia*) in biblical religions, a phobia that "prepares the way for the *creatio ex nihilo*".[177] The suppression of chaos is symptomatic of the logic of domination, which subordinates differences to an original identity — an identity that is "ideally" that of a straight, rich, white, male human and not something or someone "different"; for example, a female, a person of colour, or a nonhuman animal.

In affirming the creation as a chaosmos, Keller is reconstructing the tehomophilic elements of scripture and of theological discourses, making room for a theology of becoming, which subverts the dominology of biblical religion and opens up possibilities for responding decisively to the complexities and knotty entanglements of relationships between humans and one another, other species, and the whole Earth community. Furthermore, Keller's interpretation of the chaosmos engages articulations of the chaosmos in literature, sciences, and philosophies. She also touches briefly on other religious worldviews, cutting across any East/West divide by including other biblical traditions as well as Asian traditions. For instance, she indicates a connection between the chaotic matrix of Tehom and the flowing and creative "Way" (*Dao*) expressed in the Daoist myths of ancient Chinese religion.[178] Keller's account of the chaosmos thus appears as a fluctuating and wandering interpretation, a "tehomic hermeneutic" opening hybridized discourses that cut open disciplinary boundaries, interrupting any simple binary of sacred/secular, mythical/logical, East/West, theology/philosophy, or humanities/sciences.[179]

Situated in the depths of the chaosmos, integral ecology works and plays with just such hybridized discourses. Could this mean that integral ecology is interdisciplinary? Or multi-, trans-, para-, or post-disciplinary? The important thing is not whether tehomic discourses move within, between, across, under, beside, or after disciplines. The point is that tehomic discourses (like chorologies) do not take disciplinary boundaries for granted, but constitute a "polydoxy", which affirms the multiplicity and relationality of all of the *doxa* (perspectives, beliefs, expectations) whereby disciplinary boundaries are forged, enfolded, unfolded, and broken.[180] Tehomic and choric discourses interrupt determinations of the limits of disciplinarity and open possibilities for moving between disciplines, multiplying disciplines, or transcending disciplines. With such discourses, integral ecology can perhaps be described best as transdisciplinary insofar as it cuts across the very limits of disciplinarity, transgressing them and opening them up to multiple horizons, multiple configurations of research, knowledge, theory, and practise.

Whereas the suppression of place and chaos impedes the emergence of a planetary civilization by effacing its embeddedness within the chaosmos, integral approaches to ecology can experiment with transdisciplinary interpretations of the chaosmos to facilitate the emergence of a planetary civilization, a civilization that is based in place, grounded in the shifting grounds of the open. There are many resources for transdisciplinary engagements with concepts and representations of the chaosmos. For instance, Philip Kuberski recovers a variety of figures of the chaosmos expressed throughout the history of science, literature, philosophy, and religion. "Whether one turns to Werner Heisenberg, James Joyce, Jacques Derrida, or Lao Tsu, one sees this interpenetration of disorder and order, chance and necessity, improvization and adherence, differentiation and relationship".[181] In the works of those and many other figures, and in many of the world's creation myths (in Genesis, Hesiod, Ovid, or Daoism), one can detect a sense of the world as

> unitary and yet untotalized, a chiasmic concept of the world as a field of mutual and simultaneous interference and convergence, an interanimation of the subjective and objective, an endless realm of chance which nevertheless displays a persistent tendency toward pattern and order. Everything in the world can be seen as chaosmic.[182]

One of the philosophers Keller thinks with in her transdisciplinary account of the chaosmos is Deleuze, who adapts Joyce's term and puts it into play in his own creation of metaphysical concepts. For Deleuze, all beings take place in the errant motion of the chaosmos. To say that beings emerge from the chaosmos is to say that they emerge from a "chaodyssey" (*chao-errance*) — a chaotic odyssey of productive differences.[183] Beings do not emerge simply from an ordered universe but from the opening of the chaosmos, "the Grand Canyon of the world", the matrix that makes room for the world to come into being.[184] Deleuze's account of the chaosmos grounds his ontology, which is an ontology that opens up to the errant and eccentric odyssey of the chaosmos. "Ontology", according to Deleuze, "is the dice throw, the chaosmos from which the cosmos emerges".[185] To be is to wander through an unpredictable odyssey of becoming: "divergent series endlessly tracing bifurcating paths".[186]

Furthermore, Deleuze suggests that a concept of the chaosmos is implicit within the concept of the receptacle/*chora* expressed in Plato's *Timaeus*. Deleuze makes this connection with the image of a screen — "a formless elastic membrane, an electromagnetic field, or the receptacle of the *Timaeus*" — that makes possible the production of events within "a chaotic multiplicity".[187] Deleuze also finds the concept of the chaosmos at work in Whitehead's metaphysical cosmology (although Whitehead never used the term *chaosmos*). Their shared sense of a chaosmos is evident in their shared sense of Plato's *chora*. As Roland Faber puts it, for Deleuze and Whitehead, *chora* is "the 'space' of a *chaosmic multiplicity* that is always in the process of becoming, or better, is the *process of becoming*".[188]

According to Deleuze, Whitehead presents an affirmation of the chaosmos insofar as he articulates "a condition of opening" according to which all events are "directly connected to each other" within the creative process; which is to say, all prehension is "*already* the prehension of another prehension", "naturally open, open onto the world, without having to pass through a window".[189] This condition of opening is expressed in Whitehead's account of Plato's receptacle. Whitehead considered twentieth-century physical sciences to be closer to the doctrine of the receptacle than any science articulated since Plato, particularly insofar as the receptacle is an active process (a moving and shaking place, not a passive substance as modern science generally supposed), and this process generates relations of internal connectedness between occasions without imposing those relations on them.[190] This active and relational receptacle resonates with the active and relational universe disclosed through quantum and relativity physics, evolutionary biology and cosmology, ecology, and complexity sciences.[191] Active and relational forces pervade the universe from its earliest to its most recent phases of development. Even the singular point of the universe's beginning did not come out of nothing, but out of an active and relational matrix.[192]

The receptacle is a network of mutual immanence; that is, a "community of locus" — "the necessary community within which the course of history is set, in abstraction from all the particular historical facts".[193] The community of locus is the chaosmos, which makes room for events to become internally interconnected. This chorological community is open to the intertwining of order and disorder. There is "no sharp division" between the institution of a dominant order and the chaotic frustration of that order, for every instance of order is always already in "transition", and such transition "is the realization of that vibrant novelty which elicits the excitement of life".[194] Whitehead's attention to "the rush of immediate transition" is indicative of his affirmation of the chaosmos, which limits the hegemony of binaries by making room for novelty and creative differences.[195]

The chaosmos articulated by Keller, Deleuze, Whitehead, and others makes room for beings to become, without being colonized by a transcendent or original order. However, as Keller's theology of becoming shows, this does not rule out any God or Beyond in the chaosmos. As Faber points out, "Whitehead and Deleuze—with Derrida—tend to interpret it [the Beyond] as an untapped *plentitude* of multiplicity of becoming-otherwise". There is thus a "chaosmic fluency of the Beyond". [196] The chaosmos is thus a place open to unpredictable possibilities for transformation, for something different, for becoming otherwise.

Concepts of the chaosmos can replace origins with beginnings, empowering decisions to participate in the creative struggle for integral liberation, the struggle for a flourishing planetary civilization. Keller provides a compelling expression of this point. "Amid the chaosmos of our relations, the particularlity of this time, this place, reveals itself with a new vividness. It invites novelty of response".[197] Regardless of whether it is officially sacred or secular, such novelty of response requires faith. It requires "the confidence to act in the face of an open-ended future" and thus "act in great humility and in great love", the confidence "to throw ourselves into a planetary struggle for" a more peaceful, just, and sustainable Earth community, the confidence "to sustain this struggle creatively, knowing that creation itself is a chaosmos of new beginnings".[198]

NOTES

1. Alfred North Whitehead, *Modes of Thought* (New York: Free Press, 1968), 154. Whitehead asks the following rhetorical question: "Why talk about 'the laws of nature' when what we mean is the characteristic behaviour of phenomena within limits at a given stage of development in a given epoch—so far as these can be ascertained"? "People make the mistake of talking about 'natural laws'. There *are* no natural laws. There are only temporary habits of nature" (Whitehead, *Dialogues of Alfred North Whitehead* [Boston: David R. Godine, 2001], 342, 363).

2. Walt Whitman, *Leaves of Grass* (New York: Oxford University Press, 2005), 22.

3. The word *liminal* derives from the Latin *limen*, meaning "threshold" or "limit" (*Oxford English Dictionary*).

4. Translations of Heraclitus are modified based on various sources I consulted, including the following: Charles H. Kahn, *The Art and Thought of Heraclitus: An Edition of the Fragments with Translation and Commentary* (Cambridge: Cambridge University Press, 1979); Richard D. McKirahan, *Philosophy before Socrates: An Introduction with Texts and Commentary* (Indianapolis: Hackett Publishing, 1994); Brooks Haxton, *Fragments: The Collected Wisdom of Heraclitus* (New York: Viking Press, 2001).

5. Martin Heidegger, "Building Dwelling Thinking", in *Poetry, Language, Thought*, trans. Albert Hofstadter (New York: Harper & Row, 1971), 154.

6. Irene Klaver, "Boundaries on the Edge", in *Nature's Edge: Boundary Explorations in Ecological Theory and Practice*, eds. Charles S. Brown and Ted Toadvine (Albany: SUNY Press, 2007), 122.

7. Ibid., 125.

8. Ibid., 126.

9. Ibid., 125–26.

10. Quoted in Slavoj Žižek, "Occupy First. Demands Come Later", *The Guardian*, October 26, 2011, para. 5.

11. Donna Haraway, "Situated Knowledges: The Science Question in Feminism and the Privilege of Partial Perspective", in *Simians, Cyborgs, and Women: The Reinvention of Nature* (New York: Routledge, 1991), 201.

12. Donna Haraway, *When Species Meet* (Minneapolis: University of Minnesota Press, 2008), 4, 7, 31.

13. Ibid., 226.

14. Heidegger's concept of the "open" conveys a "clearing" that makes room for beings to be (Heidegger, "The Origin of the Work of Art", in *Off the Beaten Track*, trans. Julian Young and Kenneth Haynes [Cambridge: Cambridge University Press, 2002], 30). The open could be described as a material-semiotic entanglement where the meaningful horizon of the world comes into interactive tension with the ground of Earth. "To the open belongs a world and the earth" (31). However, Haraway differentiates her sense of "the open" from that of Heidegger, because Heidegger limits the open to humanity, as if animals, plants, and stones do not make contact with the opening of Earth and the world (221, 334, 367). For Haraway, the open is a complex multispecies relationship that cannot be untangled into a neat dichotomy between humans and nonhumans. For an analysis of Heidegger's articulation of the open and its place in the history of human/animal relations in Western thought, see Giorgio Agamben, *The Open: Man and Animal*, trans. Kevin Attell (Stanford, CA: Stanford University Press, 2004). Agamben's concept of the open is still anthropocentric. Nonetheless, Mick Smith shows that, despite the anthropocentrism of Heidegger and Agamben, their concepts of the open still have much to offer an ecological philosophy. Smith, *Against Ecological Sovereignty: Ethics, Biopolitics, and Saving the Natural World* (Minneapolis: University of Minnesota Press, 2011), 113.

15. Haraway, *When Species Meet*, 90.

16. Haraway, *When Species Meet*, 19. Although some companion species are companion animals or "pets" (e.g., dogs, cats, ant farms, potbellied pigs, bunnies, etc.), companion species are also more than this. Haraway uses the category of companion species in a way that is "more rambunctious" than mere companion animals (16). This category figures the complex contact whereby species (including humans) become intimately entangled with one another in mutually constitutive relationships. This is not to say that species are already constituted, and subsequently enter into relation with other species. "The partners do not precede their relating; all that is", according to Haraway, "is the fruit of becoming with: those are the mantras of companion species" (17). In other words, "I am who I become with companion species" (19). Companion species are "significant others" (15).

17. Elizabeth A. Grosz, *Becoming Undone: Darwinian Reflections on Life, Politics, and Art* (Durham, NC: Duke University Press, 2011), 2, 41.

18. Haraway, *When Species Meet*, 3.

19. Ibid.

20. Irene Klaver, "The Implicit Practice of Environmental Philosophy", in *Environmental Philosophy and Environmental Activism*, eds. Don Marietta Jr. and Lester Embree (Lanham: Rowman & Littlefield, 1995), 74. From *xunos* derive numerous words that contain prefixes of togetherness, including the Greek *syn-* and *sym-* (e.g., *synthesis, symbiosis, symbol*) and the Latinate *cum/com-, con-,* and *co-* (e.g., *community, connection, cohabitation*) (77n). *Xunos* is also related to *koinos* ("common").

21. Edward Said, *Beginnings: Intention and Method* (New York: Columbia University Press, 1985), 6.

22. Ibid., 373.

23. Ibid., xvii. Although Said's distinction is helpful for understanding how creativity or generative forces can involve rigid structures of domination (i.e., origins) or structures that encourage nonlinear development (i.e., beginnings), it is important to note that beginnings and origins are not always differentiated in this way. There are many ways to do things with the words *beginning* and *origin*. As Said himself says, these words are part of a "constantly changing system of meaning" (Said, *Beginnings*, xvii).

24. Catherine Keller, *Face of the Deep: A Theology of Becoming* (New York: Routledge, 2003), 5, 158–61.

25. Karen Warren, *Ecofeminist Philosophy: A Western Perspective on What It Is and Why It Matters* (Lanham, MD: Rowman & Littlefield, 2000), 24, 47–50.

26. Val Plumwood, *Feminism and the Mastery of Nature* (New York: Routledge, 1993), 43.

27. "A hegemonic centrism is", according to Plumwood, "a primary-secondary pattern of attribution that sets up one term (the One) as primary or as centre and defines marginal Others as secondary or derivative" or "as deficient in relation to the center". (Plumwood, *Environmental Culture: The Ecological Crisis of Reason* [New York: Routledge, 2002], 101)

28. Keller, *Face of the Deep*, xvii, 6.

29. Ibid., xv.

30. As Keller says (rephrasing Said's words), "beginning and beginning-again are historical-secular and *therefore also* mythological/theological" (*Face of the Deep*, 160).

31. Keller, *Face of the Deep*, xvi.

32. Whitney Bauman, *Theology, Creation, and Environmental Ethics: From Creatio Ex Nihilo to Terra Nullius* (New York: Routledge, 2009).

33. Donna Haraway, *Modest_Witness@Second_Millennium.FemaleMan©_Meets _OncoMouse™*. (New York: Routledge, 1997), 2.

34. Ibid., 134–8. Haraway's account of god tricks resonates with Bruno Latour's claim that "the West thinks it is the sole possessor of the clever trick that will allow it to keep on winning indefinitely" (Latour, *We Have Never Been Modern*, trans. Catherine Porter [Cambridge: Harvard University Press, 1993], 9).

35. Haraway, "Situated Knowledges", 189, 191–96.

36. Haraway, *Modest_Witness*, 44.

37. Haraway, *When Species Meet*, 88.

38. Ibid.

39. *Postsecularism* and *postsecular* are terms that some scholars have suggested for describing the contemporary situation of civilization, which is marked by "a deconstruction or breakdown of any strict opposition between the religious and the secular" (Clayton Crockett, *Radical Political Theology: Religion and Politics after Liberalism* [New York: Columbia University Press, 2011], 160). Furthermore, Crockett explicitly relates contemporary postsecularism to concepts developed

by postmodern philosophers and theologians, including Heidegger's concept of the open (149).

40. Haraway elaborates on the material-semiotic complexity of sacramental consciousness. "As a person cursed and blessed with a sacramental consciousness and the indelible mark of having grown up Irish Catholic in the United States, I'm saddled with a kind of indelible understanding that the sign is the thing in-itself [. . .] the implosion of semioticity and materiality always simply seemed the case about the world". Haraway, "Birth of the Kennel: A Lecture by Donna Haraway", The European Graduate School, August 2000, http://www.egs.edu/faculty/haraway/haraway-birth-of-the-kennel-2000.html.

41. Haraway, *When Species Meet*, 16.

42. Donna Haraway, "'There Are Always More Things Going on Than You Thought!' Methodologies as Thinking Technologies: Interview with Donna Haraway", in *Bits of Life: Feminism at the Intersections of Media, Bioscience, and Technology*, eds. Anneke Smelik and Nina Lykke (Seattle: University of Washington Press, 2008), 35.

43. Haraway, *How Like a Leaf: An Interview with Thyrza Nichols Goodeve* (New York: Routledge, 2000), 24.

44. Ibid., 141.

45. Haraway, "There Are Always More Things", 33–34.

46. Keller, *Face of the Deep*, xv; see also *Oxford English Dictionary*.

47. Alfred North Whitehead, *Process and Reality: An Essay in Cosmology*, corr. ed. eds. David Ray Griffin and Donald W. Sherburne (New York: Free Press, 1978), 43.

48. Ibid.

49. Keller, *Face of the Deep*, 160.

50. John Llewelyn, *Margins of Religion: Between Kierkegaard and Derrida* (Bloomington: Indiana University Press, 2009), 69.

51. Ibid. Jacques Derrida, *The Gift of Death*, trans. David Wills (Chicago: University of Chicago Press, 1995), 65.

52. Llewelyn, *Margins of Religion*, 69.

53. In the "Transcendental Dialectic" in his *Critique of Pure Reason*, Kant distinguishes between "logical paralogism", which is an argument that is false because of its form, and "transcendental paralogism", which has a proper syllogistic form but leads to illusion insofar as it tries to rationally assert the existence of objects that are outside the limits of possible experience, objects such as self, world, and God (*Critique of Pure Reason*, trans. Paul Guyer and Allen Wood [Cambridge: Cambridge University Press, 1998], B399, 411).

54. This is Jean-François Lyotard's sense of paralogy. For Lyotard, "the quest for paralogy" is the aspect of "the postmodern condition" that involves commitments to any way of thinking that supports the invention of new modes of existence, or in Lyotard's terms, commitments to any "little narrative" (*petit récit*) that supports "imaginative invention". Lyotard, *The Postmodern Condition: A Report on Knowledge*, trans. Geoff Bennington and Brian Massumi (Minneapolis: University of Minnesota Press, 1984), 60, 66. Commitments to little narratives provide a positive definition of postmodernism, in contrast to the negative or critical definition of postmodernism as "incredulity toward metanarratives" (xxiv). Moreover, this incredulity is directed not towards any narrative that addresses other narratives or encompassing questions (e.g., the meaning of life, the nature of the universe, the global challenges of the environmental crisis, etc.). Rather, Lyotard considers postmodern incredulity to be directed towards two types of metanarratives: narratives of the progress of knowledge (e.g., Hegelian dialectics of Spirit), and modern Enlightenment and Marxist narratives of

emancipation (of which Habermas is the most prominent of contemporary proponents). By legitimising the assimilation of differences and new events into their programmed discourses, such metanarratives of progress and emancipation actually impede the very futures they would seek to attain. A little narrative could be understood as a paralogical metanarrative, a narrative that seeks not to assimilate differences but to inventively multiply differences, decisively facilitating the creation of new ways of being.

55. Brian Swimme and Thomas Berry, *The Universe Story: From the Primordial Flaring Forth to the Ecozoic Era—A Celebration of the Unfolding of the Cosmos* (San Francisco: HarperCollins, 1992), 70–71.

56. Ibid., 129.

57. Ibid., 129–32, 136–7.

58. Ibid., 4.

59. Ibid., 14.

60. Keller, *Face of the Deep*, 160.

61. Paul D. Miller (DJ Spooky That Subliminal Kid), *Rhythm Science* (Cambridge: MIT Press, 2004), 4.

62. Gilles Deleuze and Félix Guattari, *Anti-Oedipus: Capitalism and Schizophrenia*, trans. Robert Hurley, Mark Seem, and Helen R. Lane (Minneapolis: University of Minnesota Press, 1983), 4.

63. Deleuze and Guattari, *A Thousand Plateaus: Capitalism and Schizophrenia*, trans. Brian Massumi (Minneapolis: University of Minnesota Press, 1987), 109.

64. Ibid.

65. Ibid., 95.

66. Ibid., 343.

67. Deleuze, *Essays Critical and Clinical*, trans. Daniel W. Smith and Michael A. Greco (London: Verso, 1998), 134.

68. Ibid., 135.

69. Deleuze, *Difference and Repetition*, trans. Paul Patton (New York: Columbia University Press, 1994), 127. Deleuze's image here of Plato sending difference back to the bottomless ocean is echoed in *The Logic of Sense*, first released in 1969, one year after *Difference and Repetition*. Deleuze says that, for Plato, the difference that escapes the identity of the Idea is "never sufficiently hidden, driven back, pushed deeply into the depth of the body, or drowned in the ocean" (*The Logic of Sense*, trans. Constantin V. Boundas [New York: Columbia University Press, 1990], 7). Deleuze does not want to suppress difference and the abyss of oceanic depth, but wants to let them return to the surface. "*Everything now returns to the surface*" (7).

70. Deleuze, *The Logic of Sense*, 188.

71. Derrida, *Deconstruction in a Nutshell: A Conversation with Jacques Derrida*, ed. John D. Caputo (New York: Fordham University Press, 1997), 137.

72. Derrida, *Gift of Death*, 77, 5.

73. Ibid., 65.

74. Ibid., 60, 66.

75. Regarding the secrecy of decision, consider the etymological derivation of the word *secret* from the Latin *secretus*, a form of *secernere* ("to set apart"), where *cernere* ("to separate") shares a root with the Greek *krinein* ("to decide" or "to separate") (*Oxford English Dictionary*).

76. The near-sacrifice of Issac by Abraham is described in Genesis 22:1–18. This biblical event has been the focus of much philosophical interpretation, including Kierkegaard's account, where he argues that God's call for the sacrifice of Isaac shows that faith requires a "teleological suspension of the ethical"— for the sake of responsibility to the wholly other (God), one suspends one's

general ethical obligations to other others. Emmanuel Levinas counters Kierkegaard with a reading for which the near-sacrifice of Isaac includes an ethical responsibility to the other, particularly insofar as Abraham heard God's call while keeping enough distance from the sacrificial act so as to hear the call of the angel who told him not to harm Isaac. Derrida supplements these readings by pointing to the deconstruction of the boundary between the ethical and the religious, such that the religious relationship to the wholly other is implicit in ethical relationships to any others. The ethico-religious decision makes cuts between oneself and every (wholly) other. On the relationship between Kierkegaard, Levinas, and Derrida in their readings of Genesis 22, see Llewelyn, *Margins of Religion*, 34–44.

77. Derrida, *Gift of Death*, 68, 77.

78. Derrida, *Acts of Religion*, ed. Gil Anidjar (New York: Routledge, 2002), 253.

79. Derrida, *Gift of Death*, 71.

80. Derrida, *Of Grammatology*, trans. Gayatri Chakravorty Spivak (Baltimore: Johns Hopkins University Press, 1976), 70.

81. "How would you ever justify the fact that you sacrifice all the cats in the world to the cat that you feed at home every morning for years, whereas other cats die of hunger at every instant? Not to mention other people"? Derrida, *Gift of Death*, 71. For more on Derrida's relationship with his cat, see his account of being seen naked by his cat. Derrida, *The Animal That Therefore I Am*, ed. Marie-Louise Mallet, trans. David Wills (New York: Fordham University Press, 2008), 3. Also see David Wood, "Thinking with Cats," in *Animal Philosophy: Essential Readings in Continental Philosophy*, eds. Matthew Calarco and Peter Atterton (London: Continuum, 2004), and see the chapter on Derrida and animals in Matthew Calarco, *Zoographies: The Question of the Animal from Heidegger to Derrida* (New York: Columbia University Press, 2008), 103.

82. Gary Snyder, *The Practice of the Wild: Essays* (Washington, DC: Shoemaker & Hoard, 1990), 244.

83. Derrida, *Gift of Death*, 84–86. The chaos of the open mouth also comes to expression in Derrida's account of "an abyssal and *chaotic* desert" as the ground of a messianic call for justice, "if chaos describes first of all the immensity, excessiveness, disproportion in the gaping hole of the open mouth" (Derrida, *Specters of Marx: The State of the Debt, the Work of Mourning, and the New International*, trans. Peggy Kamuf [New York: Routledge, 1994], 28).

84. Rachel Carson, *Silent Spring* (Boston: Mariner Books, 2002).

85. Douglas J. Buege, "The Ecological Noble Savage Revisited", *Environmental Ethics* 18.1 (1996): 71–88.

86. Derrida, *Demeure: Fiction and Testimony*, trans. Elizabeth Rottenberg (Stanford: Stanford University Press, 2000), 41.

87. According to the deconstructionist Mark C. Taylor, *différance* "can provide a critique and response to the religious and political neofoundationalism that threatens to sunder our world". However, many practitioners of deconstruction neglect the creativity called for in their work, focusing instead on the critical (destructive) aspects of deconstruction, thus failing to "provide the constructive gesture so desperately needed to respond to today's raging neofoundationalism" (Taylor, *After God* [Chicago: University of Chicago Press, 2007], 306, 309).

88. Deleuze, *Difference and Repetition*, 64. Kant, *Critique of Pure Reason*, B510:506. On Deleuze's response to Kant's theory of ideas, see Deleuze, *Difference and Repetition*, 168–76, and see Daniel W. Smith, "Deleuze, Kant, and the Theory of Immanent Ideas," in *Deleuze and Philosophy*, ed. Constantin V. Boundas (Edinburgh, UK: Edinburgh University Press, 2006). Deleuze's concept of

problematic Ideas also resonates with his concept of sense. Deleuze "redefines the nature of structures along the lines of the open-ended and virtual assemblages", which he defines "as 'transcendental Ideas' in *Difference and Repetition* or as 'sense' in *The Logic of Sense*" (Paul Patton and John Protevi, "Introduction", in *Between Deleuze and Derrida*, eds. Paul Patton and John Protevi [London: Continuum Press, 2003], 2).

89. Deleuze, *Difference and Repetition*, 64.

90. Grosz, *Becoming Undone*, 150–51.

91. Smith, "Deleuze, Kant", 52.

92. Deleuze, *The Fold: Leibniz and the Baroque*, trans. Tom Conley (Minneapolis: University of Minnesota Press, 1992), 91.

93. This Socratic rationalization is what Aristophanes parodies in *The Clouds* (see the section "Becoming Humourous"). I am not arguing that Socrates himself had such a simplistic sense of the "what is" question.

94. Deleuze, *Difference and Repetition*, 188.

95. Klaver discusses the function of boundaries in these three examples in "Boundaries on the Edge", 120–21, 125.

96. Rachel Carson, *The Edge of the Sea* (New York: Houghton Mifflin, 1998), 249.

97. Ibid., 249–50.

98. Rachel Carson, *The Sea Around Us* (New York: Oxford University Press, 2003), 3.

99. Carson, *Edge of the Sea*, 37.

100. Ibid., 125.

101. Ibid., xii.

102. Aldo Leopold, *A Sand County Almanac and Sketches Here and There* (London: Oxford University Press, 1968), 27.

103. Ibid.

104. Slavoj Žižek, *Tarrying with the Negative: Kant, Hegel, and the Critique of Ideology* (Durham: Duke University Press, 1993), 1.

105. Ibid.

106. Heraclitus says "war is shared with all beings" (*polemon eonta xunon*) and "everything is born from strife" (*ginomena panta kat' erin*) (DK 22b80). This war and strife are not opposed to peace and justice. They are struggles for peace and justice, such that Heraclitus can say "strife is justice" (*diken erin*).

107. As Empedocles, things "never cease continually interchanging, at one time all coming together into one by Love and at another each being borne apart by the hatred of Strife" (14.19). For a translation of this passage from Empedocles and an analysis of the Empedoclean concepts of love and strife, see McKirahan, *Philosophy before Socrates*, 236, 260–62.

108. Llewelyn, *Margins of Religion*, 133.

109. Mark Hathaway and Leonardo Boff, *The Tao of Liberation: Exploring the Ecology of Transformation* (Maryknoll: Orbis Books, 2009), 391.

110. Deleuze and Guattari, *A Thousand Plateaus*, 513.

111. The use by the IDF of the concepts of D&G and other postmodern theorists is discussed by Eyal Weizman, "Walking through Walls: Soldiers as Architects in the Israeli-Palestine Conflict," *Radical Philosophy* 136 (2006): 8–22. Žižek provides a brief summary of the appropriation of D&G by the IDF. "It was recently made public that, in order to conceptualize the Israeli Defense Forces' urban warfare against the Palestinians, the IDF military academics systematically refer to Deleuze and Guattari, especially to *Thousand Plateaus*, using it as 'operational theory'". Žižek continues, describing how the IDF uses the distinction D&G articulate between "smooth" and "striated" space. "The IDF now

often uses the term 'to smoothe out space' when they want to refer to operation in a space as if it had no borders. Palestinian areas are thought of as 'striated' in the sense that they are enclosed by fences, walls, ditches, roadblocks, and so on". Žižek, *In Defense of Lost Causes* (New York: Verso, 2008), 204.

112. These becomings are expressed in numerous places in Deleuze and Guattari's *A Thousand Plateaus*, particularly in the tenth "plateau" or chapter, "1730: Becoming-Intense, Becoming-Animal, Becoming-Imperceptible . . . " (232–309).

113. Ibid., 277.

114. Elizabeth A. Grosz, *Volatile Bodies: Toward a Corporeal Feminism* (Bloomington: Indiana University Press, 1994), 176. Although D&G open up possibilities for integrating sexual difference, it is important to consider how D&G overlook some issues of sexual difference that are articulated by feminist theorists. For instance, Lorraine Tamsin compares the concept of becoming-woman with the account of sexual difference given by Luce Irigaray. Whereas D&G engage the multiplicity of flows of sexual difference, Irigaray's work shows how this engagement fails to consider how flows of becoming-woman involve different inflections for women and for men. Becoming-woman could run the risk of denying women certain specific sexual pleasures that would not be denied if more attention were given to the ambiguity and apparent duality of sexual difference (Tamsin, *Irigaray and Deleuze: Experiments in Visceral Philosophy* [Ithaca: Cornell University Press, 1999], 81–88). For more on the convergences and divergences between Deleuze and feminist theory (including that of Irigaray), see Dorothea Olkowski, *Gilles Deleuze and the Ruin of Representation* (Berkeley: University of California Press, 1999). For a variety of perspectives on the contributions and limitations of Deleuze for feminist and queer theories, see Ian Buchanan and Claire Colebrook, eds., *Deleuze and Feminist Theory* (Edinburgh: Edinburgh University Press, 2000); Chrysanthi Nigianni and Merl Storr, eds., *Deleuze and Queer Theory* (Edinburgh: Edinburgh University Press, 2009).

115. P. M. Vitousek, H. A. Mooney, J. Lubchenco, and J. M. Melillo, "Human Domination of Earth's Ecosystems," *Science* 277 (1997): 494.

116. Holmes Rolston III, *A New Environmental Ethics: The Next Millennium for Life on Earth* (New York: Routledge, 2012), 44–48.

117. Swimme and Berry, *Universe Story*, 57.

118. The word *Cenozoic* derives from the Greek *kainos* ("new") and *zoe* ("life") (*Oxford English Dictionary*).

119. As Esbjörn-Hargens and Zimmerman note, scientific communities are in consensus that a mass extinction is currently taking place, but the specific details of this extinction (e.g., how many species lost and how fast) are quite uncertain, which is due to, among other things, the ambiguities in different concepts of species and to the lack of data about how many species are on the planet today (Sean Esbjörn-Hargens and Michael E. Zimmerman, *Integral Ecology: Uniting Multiple Perspectives on the Natural World* [Boston: Integral Books, 2009]). Esbjörn-Hargens and Zimmerman also claim that the ethical implications of species extinction are not certain and that species extinction can be good or bad depending on the perspective. From a short-term perspective, the sixth mass extinction appears bad for the species today, but on an evolutionary scale, extinction can facilitate speciation, and mass extinction events have been followed by "an exponential leap" in biodiversity (653).

120. Millennium Ecosystem Assessment (MEA), *Ecosystems and Human Well-Being: Synthesis* (Washington, DC: Island Press, 2005), 5–36; United Nations Environment Programme, *Global Environmental Outlook (GEO-4): Environment for Development* (Valletta, Malta: Progress Press, 2007), 157–92.

121. The cognitive linguist George Lakoff makes the point that the phrase *global warming* does not convey the seriousness of the current climate crisis. In an interview where he urges environmentalists to "watch their language", Lakoff indicates that this is a problem of "framing", which is a term he uses to refer to the way language shapes thinking. "'Global warming' is the wrong term: 'Warm' seems nice". With the word *warm*, the climate crisis is framed in a way that has close associations with comfort and coziness. People in cold climates might like the idea of a warmer globe. However, the phrase *climate change* has problems as well, as it lacks any connation of value. "'Climate change' is the attempt to be scientific and neutral. 'Climate crisis' would be a more effective term. Climate collapse. Carbon dioxide strangulation. Suffocation of the earth. But it's not easy to change these things once they get into the vocabulary" (Katy Butler, "Winning Words: George Lakoff Says Environmentalists Need to Watch Their Language", *Sierra* 89.4 [2004]: 54).

122. Derrida, *Monolingualism of the Other: Or, the Prosthesis of Origin*, trans. Patrick Mensah (Stanford: Stanford University Press, 1998), 40.

123. Plato, *Timaeus*, trans. R. G. Bury (Cambridge: Harvard University Press, 2005), 17a.

124. Ibid.

125. Ibid., 17c.

126. John Sallis points out some problems with the traditional identification of the discourse of the *Republic* with the prior discourse mentioned in the *Timaeus*, particularly in light of some incompatibilities between the current events to which each dialogue refers. "Yet, regardless of whether a connection can be established between the dramatic dates of the two dialogues, there can be no question but that, as regards content, the discourse recapitulated in the *Timaeus* corresponds in considerable degree to that narrated in the *Republic*". Sallis, *Chorology: On Beginning in Plato's* Timaeus (Bloomington: Indiana University Press, 1999), 23. Furthermore, like the *Timaeus*, the *Republic* (511b) opens the question of the best city and its citizens while also asking a question of beginnings, employing hypotheses to reach "the beginning of the whole".

127. Plato, *The Republic*, 2nd ed., trans. Allan Bloom (New York: Basic Books, 1991), 592b.

128. Plato, *Timaeus*, 19c–20b.

129. It is important to note that Hermocrates, with his *herm*eneutic name, remains silent for the remainder of the dialogue, thus interrupting the opposition between silent listening and discursive interpretation. "Indeed, silent audition, silent apprehension, will prove to belong to, to be called for by [. . .] certain things that are not yet things" (Sallis, *Chorology*, 35). Those things are elemental traces that flee from discourse, traces that discourse attempts to capture "with such words as *fire, air, water,* and *earth*. Silence will thus prove to be a decisive moment in the *Timaeus*" (35).

130. Plato, *Timaeus*, 26c–e.

131. Sallis, *Chorology*, 39.

132. Plato, *Timaeus*, 27a. As Sallis notes, this "is a matter of a palintropic move, of a turn through which one beginning (archaic Athens) is referred back to a still earlier beginning (the generation of the cosmos)" (Sallis, *Chorology*, 45).

133. For more on the politically constitutive function of the interruption of myth, see the chapter "Myth Interrupted" in Jean-Luc Nancy, *The Inoperative Community*, trans. Peter Connor, Lisa Garbus, Michael Holland, and Simona Sawhney (Minneapolis: University of Minnesota Press, 1991), 43.

134. Plato, *Timaeus*, 27d–28a.

135. Ibid., 28b–c.

136. Ibid., 29b
137. Ibid., 29d.
138. Socrates, *Thaeatetus*, 155d. On the place of wonder in philosophy, including its relevance to questions of opening and decision in continental thought, see Mary-Jane Rubenstein, *Strange Wonder: The Closure of Metaphysics and the Opening of Awe* (New York: Columbia University Press, 2008).
139. Timaeus says that his discourse thus far "has been an exposition of the operations of Reason; but we must also furnish an account of what comes into existence through Necessity" (Plato, *Timaeus*, 47–48a).
140. Ibid., 48a–48b.
141. Ibid., 48e–49a, 50d, 52d, 52b.
142. The chorological challenge to omnipotence undoes theologies that seek order, certainty, and power. In contrast, Caputo's deconstructive "theology of the event" is "happy down below with *khora*", for that is where the "weak force of God" has room to disturb the boundaries of dominant orders and call insistently for new events to take place (John D. Caputo, *The Weakness of God: A Theology of the Event* [Bloomington: Indiana University Press, 2006], 39). God in the sense of a powerful being does not exist. God's weak force insists in the dynamics of *chora*, which Caputo describes as the spacing of "may-being" (*peut-être*), the "perhaps" that opens possibilities for the arrival of events that exceed the limits of what is currently possible (Caputo, *The Insistence of God: A Theology of Perhaps* [Bloomington: Indiana University Press, 2013], 13).
143. Although *chora* opens up questions of the multiverse, Plato's *Timaeus* (31a) discounts the possibility of "many or infinite" universes, claiming that the singularity of the universe is based on the singularity of its paradigmatic origin (ideal Being). For a discussion of this point in the *Timaeus*, see Mary-Jane Rubenstein's philosophical exploration of concepts for and against multiple worlds (a multiverse) throughout the history of Western cosmologies. Rubenstein, *Worlds without End: The Many Lives of the Multiverse* (New York: Columbia University Press, 2014), 23.
144. Deleuze and Guattari, *A Thousand Plateaus*, 20. In the "Middle" chapter of the present work, I discuss in more detail this monism/pluralism question ("Nomads") and the complex relationship between finite places and the infinite ("Omnicentrism").
145. Plato, *Timaeus*, 53a.
146. Ibid., 52e. The undulating motion of the receptacle is further indicated by the derivation of *hupodoche* ("receptacle") from the verb *hupodekhomai*, which means, among other things, "to receive beneath the surface of the sea". Casey, *The Fate of Place: A Philosophical History* (Berkeley: University of California Press, 1997), 357n. *Chora* is not altogether unlike Carson's sea, that "great mother of life" that interacts with coastal forms in a "shifting, kaleidoscopic pattern" with a shadowy beginning and a shadowy future. Carson, *Edge of the Sea*, 249. Carson, *Sea Around Us*, 3.
147. Plato, *Timaeus*, 52b.
148. Sallis, *Chorology*, 118–20.
149. Sallis, *Platonic Legacies* (Albany: SUNY Press, 2004), 44.
150. Judith Butler, *Bodies That Matter: On the Discursive Limits of "Sex"* (New York: Routledge, 1993), 17, 39–42; Luce Irigaray, *The Speculum of the Other Woman*, trans. Gillian C. Gill (Ithaca, NY: Cornell University Press, 1985), 168–79. As Casey puts it in his philosophical history of *The Fate of Place*, there is thus "a specific choric resistance to (male) imposition and subjection", including resistance to designations such as masculine or feminine, male or female, sex or

gender. Edward S. Casey, *The Fate of Place: A Philosophical History* (Berkeley: University of California Press, 1997), 467.

151. Keller, *Face of the Deep*, 166.

152. In his *Physics* (209b), Aristotle misrepresents the *Timaeus* and equates *chora* with matter (*hule*), saying nothing of a third kind that interrupts the binary opposition of matter/form.

153. Casey, *Fate of Place*, 210–15, 301–30.

154. Gary Snyder, *Practice of the Wild: Essays* (Washington, DC: Shoemaker & Hoard, 1990), 69.

155. Roland Faber gives a cogent analysis of the convergences and divergences between the conceptions of *chora* in Whitehead, Derrida, Deleuze, Irigaray, Butler, and Kristeva (Faber, "Introduction: Negotiating Becoming," in *Secrets of Becoming: Negotiating Whitehead, Deleuze, and Butler*, eds. Roland Faber and Andrea M. Stephenson [New York: Fordham University Press, 2011], 28–40.

156. Derrida, *Dissemination*, trans. Barbara Johnson (Chicago: University of Chicago Press, 1981), 107.

157. Deleuze, *Logic of Sense*, 262. "Overturning Platonism, then, means denying the primacy of original over copy, of model over image" (Deleuze, *Difference and Repetition*, 66). Deleuze's overturning of Platonism is not simply against Platonism. Deleuze recovers a concept of Ideas (Platonic) while bringing the transcendence of Ideas back into contact with immanence and becoming (anti-Platonic). Accordingly, Murray Code suggests that Deleuze's reconciling of "the immanent and transcendent aspects of experiencing" produces a vitalistic ontology "that can be described as an anti-Platonistic Platonism" (Code, *Process, Reality, and the Power of Symbols: Thinking with A. N. Whitehead* [New York: Palgrave, 2007], 222).

158. Derrida, *On the Name*, ed. Thomas Dutoit (Stanford: Stanford University Press, 1995), 103.

159. Keller, *Face of the Deep*, 166.

160. Chaotic "fluctuations and changes at the local levels of a system" generate "its instability and complexity but, importantly, also guarantee its order and regularity at the macrolevel". Ilya Prigogine and Isabelle Stengers, *Order Out of Chaos: Man's New Dialogue with Nature* (New York: Bantam Books, 1984), 206.

161. James Gleick, *Chaos: Making a New Science*, rev. ed. (New York: Penguin Books, 2011), 8.

162. Swimme and Berry, *Universe Story*, 51.

163. Joyce, *Finnegans Wake* (New York: Penguin Books, 1982), 118. Quite unrelated to Joyce's sense of the term, *chaosmos* is also the name of a board game in which players, facing the impending end of the universe, seek cosmic conquest through the attainment of a unique and powerful object.

164. Ibid., 582, 540. The conceptions of the chaosmos developed by Keller and Deleuze, described below, depend upon this confabulation of the chaosmos in Joyce.

165. This follows the "deconstructionist hermeneutics" advocated by John Caputo, who engages "in the de-capitalization, the decapitation of the most dangerous Capitals—geographic, philosophical, and economic". Caputo's radical thinking aims "to put a cap on this excess" of Capitals (Caputo, *More Radical Hermeneutics: On Not Knowing Who We Are* [Bloomington: Indiana University Press, 2000], 85).

166. Joyce, *Finnegans Wake*, 3. For Vico's account of history as a circulation through three stages (gods/theocratic, heroes/aristocratic, and humans/democratic), see Giambattista Vico, *New Science: Principles of the New Science Concern-*

ing the Common Nature of Nations, trans. David Marsh (London: Penguin Books, 2000).

167. Deleuze, *Difference and Repetition*, 57. For Deleuze, the relation between the affirmations of the chaosmos in Nietzsche's "eternal return" and in Joyce's *vicus of recirculation* indicates that "Joyce is Nietzschean" (Deleuze, *Logic of Sense*, 264). In *Thus Spoke Zarathustra*, Zarathustra's animals tell him that he is *"the teacher of the eternal recurrence"* — the doctrine that "all things recur eternally and we ourselves with them, and that we have already existed an infinite number of times before and all things with us" (Nietzsche, *Thus Spoke Zarathustra: A Book for Everyone and No One*, trans. R. J. Hollingdale [New York: Penguin Books, 1969], 237).

168. Morin, *Homeland Earth: A Manifesto for the New Millennium*, trans. Sean M. Kelly and Roger LaPointe (Cresskill: Hampton Press, 1999), 114.

169. Joyce coined the word *chaosmos* in the 1939 publication of *Finnegans Wake*, and Deleuze used the word in the 1968 and 1969 publications of *Différence et répétition* [*Difference and Repetition*] and *Logique du sens* [*The Logic of Sense*]. Morin's *La Nature de la nature* was first published in 1977, and Morin's first use of "chaosmos" occurs in 1980 with the second edition of this work (Morin, *Method: Towards a Study of Humankind. Vol. 1 of The Nature of Nature*, trans. J. L. Roland Bélanger [New York: Peter Lang, 1992], 26).

170. J. L. Roland Bélanger, "Chaosmos: Edgar Morin's Basic Analogue for Viewing Life", *French Cultural Studies* 8.24 (1997): 375–86.

171. Morin, *Homeland Earth*, 29.

172. Morin, quoted in Bélanger, "Chaosmos", 376.

173. Morin, *Homeland Earth*, 30.

174. Keller, *Face of the Deep*, 12.

175. Ibid., 194.

176. Although "the scripture brooks no conscious remembrance of any other deity", Keller observes that the text "seems secretly to commemorate" *Tehom* as "the name of the First Mother", particularly insofar as "the grammatically feminine *Tehom*" appears like a proper name (with no preceding article) (Keller, *From a Broken Web: Separation, Sexism, and Self* [Boston: Beacon Press, 1986], 82). On Tiamat and Marduk in the *Enuma Elish*, see Anne Baring and Jules Cashford, *Myth of the Goddess: Evolution of an Image* (London: Penguin Books, 1993), 282.

177. Keller, *Face of the Deep*, 26. Moreover, with trickster queerness playing with the boundaries of words no less than the boundaries sex/gender relations, it is worth noting that you cannot spell *tehomophobia* without *homophobia* (ibid., 23, 62).

178. Ibid., 14–15. Religious historian Norman Girardot likewise finds a chaosmos at the beginning of Daoism. "The dynamic chaotic order, or chaosmos, of the Tao is the harmony of the creation time, the 'concordant discord' of the beginnings", and returning "to the primitive chaos-order or 'chaosmos' of the Tao" is the "secret of salvation" (Girardot, *Myth and Meaning in Early Taoism* [Berkeley: University of California Press, 1983], 3, 43).

179. Keller, *Face of the Deep*, 103–4, 108, 117–22.

180. Catherine Keller and Laurel C. Schneider, "Introduction", in *Polydoxy: Theology of Multiplicity and Relation*, eds. Catherine Keller and Laurel C. Schneider (New York: Routledge, 2011).

181. Philip Kuberski, *Chaosmos: Literature, Science, and Theory* (Albany: SUNY Press, 1994, 2).

> All literature is chaosmic, to some degree, presenting knots in the forms of fictions, metaphors, and symbols which oscillate between

poles of reference. The most complex literary texts in the first half of the twentieth century began to find the chaosmos everywhere, while in the second half of the century it has found a contrapuntal philosophical medium in the works of Heidegger, Derrida, Lacan, Deleuze and Guattari, Norman O. Brown, and others. (192)

182. Ibid., 3, 38.
183. Deleuze, *Logic of Sense*, 264.
184. Ibid., 176.
185. Deleuze, *Difference and Repetition*, 199.
186. Deleuze, *Fold*, 81.
187. Ibid., 76.
188. Faber, "Introduction", 32.
189. Deleuze, *Fold*, 80–81. In *Process and Reality*, Whitehead argues that an "actual entity" (or "actual occasion") is not a passive object but is a process of "feeling" or "prehension" whereby the occasion is situated in the world, receptive to every other occasion, the prehensions of which are expressed throughout the antecedent universe (73). With Whitehead's concept of prehension, all occasions become mutually immanent monads, like open windows that allow each monad to prehend the prehensions of others. In *Adventures of Ideas* (New York: Free Press, 1967), Alfred North Whitehead contrasts the openness of his monads with the closed condition of Leibnizian monads, which are "windowless for each other" and only have windows in relation to God (133–34).
190. Whitehead, *Adventures of Ideas*, 134.
191. Kuberski, *Chaosmos*, 45–50.
192. "Cosmologists sometimes claim that the universe can arise 'from nothing.' But this is loose language. Even if shrunk to a point or a quantum state, our universe is latent with particles and forces: it has far more content and structure than what a philosopher calls 'nothing'" (Martin Rees, *Our Cosmic Habitat* [Princeton: Princeton University Press, 2001], 142).
193. Whitehead, *Adventures of Ideas*, 150, 187, 201.
194. Whitehead, *Modes of Thought* (New York: Free Press, 1968), 87.
195. Whitehead, *Process and Reality*, 129.
196. Faber, "Introduction", 28, 30.
197. Catherine Keller, *God and Power: Counter-Apocalyptic Journeys* (Minneapolis: Augsburg Fortress, 2005), 151.
198. Ibid.

THREE
Middle

Beginning does not occur out of nothing, but happens in place (*chora*), emerging out of the deep (*ex profundis*), out of the profound chaos of the chaosmos. It does not lie back and control everything that follows from it. It is not a hegemonic origin or transcendent foundation, although, to be sure, it can become one. Not in all times and places, but in the limits of some contexts—the particularity of this here, this now—beginning is an ongoing creative process, opening out amidst multiplicities, amidst the unfathomably complex boundaries of the chaosmos. Sometimes, in some examples, beginning happens in the middle of things. Questions of beginning involve theoretical issues that complicate the relationships of original models and paradigms to specific cases and examples, and they also involve practical issues in which claims to an original identity (e.g., species, race, class, gender, ability) are used to justify the domination of that which is different or other than the established identity. Instead of opposing identity to difference, concepts of beginning can help us stay in the middle of things, opening places of creativity, subverting the logic of domination that supports the theories and practises currently spreading injustice and destruction throughout the Earth community. In this sense, concepts of beginning contribute to an integral sense of ecology, for which ecology engages the complex boundaries of ecological realities so as to facilitate the emergence of a vibrant planetary civilization.

As beginning stays in the middle of things, in the between, in the interstices and intermezzos, concepts of beginning open up concepts of middles, such that a middle becomes a place of creative opening, not an apathetic position or a lukewarm average, and not a "hegemonic centrism" that dominates the marginal or peripheral.[1] I follow Luke Higgins in his proposal for an approach to philosophy and theology that stays "in the middle of things", an approach that affirms "the inter-flowing ecological multiplicities upon which life on this planet depends" instead of suppressing them "with statically ordered lines of social transmission (in Whitehead's terms) or reverting to a plane of transcendence (in Deleuze-Guattari's terms)".[2] Such an approach "finds the greatest depth and intensity of feeling not in any definitive beginning or ending points, but always in the harmonics of becoming resonating from the middle of our interflowing multiplicities".[3] Roland Faber, another thinker of the Deleuze-Whitehead assemblage, makes a similar point about the ecology of the middle. "Ecoconsciousness and ecoconscience" are matters of "becoming intermezzo", immersing oneself in the middle, learning to "become 'in between' and 'become interbeing'", which "always means to follow multiplicities in their deconstructive complexity within and without, to unsettle the boundaries and clear borders of forced identities".[4] To develop concepts for becoming intermezzo is to develop a new sense of the world and the place of humans amidst its interflowing ecological multiplicities. Indeed, concepts that keep us in the middle of things engender a new sense of sense, which I describe as an integral sense.

According to the contemporary French philosopher Jean-Luc Nancy, the environmental, social, and existential crises of the present age can be understood as different aspects of a "crisis of sense".[5] This is not merely a crisis of perception. It is a crisis of the world. In Nancy's philosophy, sense refers to the world, not simply to a property or quality of the world, but to the world itself, such that "the world *no longer has* a sense, but it *is* sense".[6] Furthermore, to say that the world is sense does not imply that the world is fundamentally material or sensible and not semiotic or sensitive. Rather, sense is material and semiotic, sensible and sensitive. In other words, sense is multidimensional. It involves complex relations between intelligible or semiotic sense (meaning), perceptual or aesthetic sense (materiality), subjective sense (apprehending; sensitive), objective sense (apprehended; sensible), and so much more: "The sense of the word *sense* traverses the five senses, the sense of direction, common sense, semantic sense, divinatory sense, sentiment, moral sense, practical sense, aesthetic sense, all the way to that which makes possible all these senses".[7] The crisis of sense is a crisis in which the many senses of sense are increasingly subject to forces of control, homogenization, colonization, and domination. The complex multiplicities of the world are increasingly effaced and erased as they are partitioned into a hierarchical order where differences are subordinate to a hegemonic identity or transcendent ideal. This is theorized in Jacques Rancière's conception of politics as a "partition of the sensible", where the world of sense undergoes a partition or "distribution" (*partage*) that separates those who have political power or representation from those who are marginalized and disenfranchised, those who are not visible or audible.[8] The dominant partition pervading contemporary global civilization colonizes the many senses of sense with hegemonic models that subordinate and marginalize all those who are different or other than the preferred identity. This is not unlike the god tricks of scientific rationality, wherein scientific truths are posited as if they have a view from nowhere, separated from the heterogeneities and multiplicities of concrete contexts. Such partitioning can be described as "imperialistic bad sense".[9] With such imperialistic bad sense, the logic of domination expands and legitimates itself as it traverses the multiplicities of sense.

The imperialistic domination of sense is evident in the partition of the sensible expressed among ancient Greek philosophers like Plato, who opposed "the sensible" (*to aestheton*) to "the intelligible" (*to noeton*), the former composing an apparent world of illusory images and perception and the latter composing a true world of ideal forms. This rift between the sensible and the intelligible deepened throughout subsequent historical transformations, eventually leading to a crisis of sense that is endangering and destroying the world, including the ideals and values of the true world and the vital forces and matters of the apparent world. The history of this rift is expressed by Nietzsche, who cogently describes the path that ends in the eradication of any true or apparent world, demarcating six stages in the history of the "True World".[10] The first stage begins with Plato's initial positing of a true world over against an apparent world. In this case, the true world is something that a wise and virtuous person can attain. In the famous allegory of the cave in Plato's *Republic*, Socrates distinguishes between the apparent world of illusory shadows and the realm of the idea of the good, which is the source of all truth and phenomena. While describing the image of the cave, Socrates tells Glaucon that the idea of the good is attainable. It is the last thing seen in the soul's assent from the cave into the world, "and that with considerable effort".[11] The true world, the highest good, appears for those who put forth the required effort. Although the allegory presents the true world as attainable, the gap between the apparent world and the true world is opened, and it becomes increasingly unbridgeable as the stages of history progress.

The second stage Nietzsche marks off begins when the idea of truth becomes Christian. In this case, the true world is "unattainable for now, but promised ... 'to the sinner who does penance'".[12] The true world is attainable, but not now. It is only attainable after death or after Christ returns.[13] The ideal goal (*telos*) of life is, in this stage of history, unattainable until the end (*eschaton*). At the third stage, the true world can neither be attained nor promised, but its connection to human rationality nonetheless obliges us to act in its accord. Alluding to Kant, who lived in Königsberg, Nietzsche calls this stage "Königsbergian".[14] For Kant, the structure of human rationality permits access to phenomena, but not to things in themselves—the noumenal true world.[15] The goal of life is no longer the attainable presence or promised presence of the true world, but merely the presence of a "good will" that acts according to universal principles of rationality.[16] The fourth stage is positivism, which restricts meaningful statements to those that correspond to experimentally verifiable facts. Metaphysical claims about the true world do not point to an ideal world or even to moral obligations, but to superstition and to ignorance of scientific truth. "The true world—unattainable? In any case, unattained. And if it is unattained, it is also unknown. And hence it is not consoling, redeeming, or obligating either".[17] The true world cannot even be inferred, and thus it cannot obligate. It is simply an unknown question that should not be asked. In the fifth stage, the true world, after losing its obligating power, has "become useless, superfluous, *hence* a refuted idea: let's do away with it"![18] In its declaration of the meaninglessness of metaphysical claims, the positivistic stage was the last to deal with the true world, dealing with it by negating it. Now that it has been refuted, we can and must completely do away with any notion of a true world. This loss of the true world can be heard in the declaration that Nietzsche puts in the words of a madman: "God is dead".[19]

With the loss of the true world, the sixth and final stage of Nietzsche's history realizes the significance of this loss for the apparent world. "*Along with the true world, we have also done away with the apparent*"![20] The loss of truth is the converse of a loss of the world of sense. With the death of God comes the death of nature.[21]

This is the outcome of a civilization orienting itself towards the sundering of the world into a dualistic hierarchy (God/nature, truth/appearance): sense is divided and conquered, the meanings and matters of its multiplicities desolated. The loss of the world is the advent of nihilism. A saying from one of Nietzsche's notebooks from 1887 describes nihilism with the following: "What does nihilism mean? *That the highest values devaluate themselves.* The aim is lacking; 'why?' finds no answer".[22] Our supposed truths are the attempts of human beings "to render the world estimable" by positing themselves "as the meaning and measure of the value of things", dividing and conquering the world so as to "maintain and increase human constructs of domination".[23] The task now, according to Nietzsche, is to overcome the nihilistic rift separating the values of the true world from the world of sense. The task now is to lead meaning (*Sinn*) back to sense (*Sinn*), staying in the middle of multiplicities to participate in the recuperation and redistribution of the sense of the world.[24]

SENSE

Many philosophers throughout the twentieth century have worked towards the rehabilitation of sense. Phenomenology is exemplary here. Indeed, phenomenology can be defined as "a philosophy of 'sense'", which is a point made by Paul Ricoeur in his account of the phenomenology of Edmund Husserl, whose teaching and writing has influenced many prominent phenomenologists (e.g., Martin Heidegger, Maurice Merleau-Ponty, and Emmanuel Levinas).[25] For Husserl, the term *sense* is used with the "broadest possible extension", such that *sense* designates the ground of all inquiry into ways of knowing and being.[26] This extension is further elaborated by Merleau-Ponty, who provides an "ontological rehabilitation of the sensible", wherein subjectivity and objectivity are expressions of one ground—a crisscrossing tissue or "intentional fabric" that he calls the "flesh", which is both the "self-sensing" flesh of my body and the sensible flesh of the cosmos.[27] Husserl and Merleau-Ponty made and are continuing posthumously to make important contributions towards a rehabilitation of sense. However, with the residual subjectivism and idealism accompanying its focus on lived experience, phenomenology still harbours tendencies to privilege identity over difference and to repeat the logic of domination that marks the current crisis of sense. Accordingly, feminist theorists such as

Luce Irigaray, Judith Butler, and Elizabeth Grosz have pointed out that phenomenological accounts of sense or flesh tend to perpetuate male-centred perspectives that fail to honor sexual difference and the irreducible otherness of bodies.[28] Rather than rejecting phenomenology, those theorists adapt phenomenological insights to make them more extended and open to difference and otherness. Such openness to difference and otherness is a prominent feature of the concepts of sense that emerged with a school of continental thought that came to be known as "postmodernism", which can be summarily described in terms of the efforts of philosophers such as Jacques Derrida, Gilles Deleuze, and Michel Foucault to get thought moving after it had become stagnant and alienated. To get thought moving, these and other thinkers transformed "the metaphysical concept of essence (the transcendent)" into a more immanent and relational concept—a "concept of sense", which is grounded in a "non-sensical" structure opening up the mystery, the question at the heart of being.[29]

To say that sense is grounded in a nonsensical structure is to say that sense is not grounded in a fixed identity or origin but in difference, otherness—that which exceeds the fixed boundaries of various determinations of sense. This sense of nonsense is expressed by Deleuze in *The Logic of Sense*—a book that aims to liberate the irreducible singularity of events from false dichotomies of subjects/objects and transcendence/immanence. Deleuze's concept of sense liberates the "pure event"; in other words, it works "to liberate the singularities of the surface" where transcendent ascent meets immanent descent and subjective interior meets objective exterior, to liberate every unit or monad so that they become "nomadic singularities" wandering outside the restrictive lines of organization and representation.[30] Sense is not merely a process of signifying or denoting, but it is an unfolding process of relational events that create different distributions of signifiers and signifieds, words and worlds. Sense is composed of multiplicities of mutually enfolded vectors, which are entangled in networks that are material as well as meaningful and semiotic. The multiplicities of sense are effects or products of a creative process. This is news that Deleuze celebrates: "that sense is never a principle or an origin, but that it is produced" as part of a generative process.[31] Sense is produced out of a generative matrix that Deleuze calls nonsense. "Nonsense is that which has no sense, and that which, as such and as it enacts the donation of sense, is opposed to the absence of sense".[32] Nonsense is not a negation or absence of sense, but it is the presence of forces that enact multiple vectors of sense while infinitely exceeding them. As nonsense is the positive process whereby sense is enacted, there is thus a "co-presence of sense and nonsense".[33] To engage this process is to enter the realm of "pure becoming"; that is, the realm of the pure event—a positivity that "transcends affirmation and negation".[34] "The event is the identity of form and void", not unlike that expressed in Zen Buddhism.[35] Deleuze's concept of (non)sense can be described as a concept of integral sense (drawing on the etymological meaning of *integral* as *untouched*). An integral sense is a sense that is copresent with nonsense, copresent with that which is not touched by sense. Accordingly, Deleuze's concept of sense is exemplified by the sense of touch insofar as tactile contact happens when touch encounters a limit where touched meets untouched, surface meets depth.[36] An integral touch contacts the nonsensical process of pure becoming through which the multiplicities of sense are generated. With an integral touch, concepts of sense stay in the middle, amid the flows of becoming. They liberate the multiplicities of the chaosmos from the dualistic schemas that put sense down, the schemas that subordinate the heterogeneities and materialities of sense to an ideal origin or transcendent truth.

Deleuze's concept of integral sense resonates with Nancy's concept of the sense of the world.[37] For Nancy, sense is the world, and "sense is touching", a reminder of the touch at the heart of becoming integral.[38] Adapting phenomenological and postmodern concepts of sense, Nancy's concept of touch affirms intangible otherness and differences by adhering to the complex events of entanglement *and* differentiation that take place in touch.[39] Along with philosophical sources, Nancy draws on Christian scripture to express his philosophy of touch. He describes Christianity as a "religion of touch", and he devotes specific attention to the biblical scene in which Mary Magdalene comes upon the recently resurrected Jesus, who tells her, "Do not touch me".[40] That scene expresses "the word and the instant of relation and revelation between two bodies".[41] Contact with the revelation of the resurrected Jesus is supposed to leave Jesus intact, untouched. This illustrates a sensitive point about touch in general. To really make contact with a being, one must paradoxically leave untouched everything one touches. One must touch with tact, opening up to the "gap intrinsic to touch"—an "insurmountable edge-to-edge" relationship that unites while also differentiating.[42] Tactful touch is like the touch of love or the touch of truth. "Love and truth touch by pushing away: they force the retreat of those whom they reach, for their very onset reveals, in the touch itself, that they are out of reach. It is in being unattainable that they touch us, even seize us".[43]

In tactful touch, "you are unable to hold or retain anything, and that is precisely what you must love and know".[44] This resonates with the postcolonial theology articulated by Mayra Rivera, who explores a "touch, which does not quite touch", thus conveying an integral sense of "a transcendence in the flesh of others whom we touch, but may never fully grasp".[45] However, one need not posit transcendence to conceive of this integral touch. For example, drawing on Whiteheadian and Deleuzian concepts of immanence, Faber describes the "mutual immanence" of multiplicities of entangled organisms and environments in terms of the "touch of ecoconnectivity"; that is, the commingling of multiplicities "with a divergence of directions, with an indirection of consummation that is never One", but is a dynamic process of contingent entanglements and differentiations, *"eros* and *thanatos"*.[46] With tactful touch, integral sense stays in the middle, between sense and nonsense, direction and indirection, manifestations and essences, *eros* and *thanatos*, the tangible and the unattainable depths of the untouched. Becoming intermezzo, integral sense overcomes the false dichotomy between the sensible and the intelligible.

Efforts such as those of phenomenologists, feminists, and postmodern theorists support the emergence of a new sense of sense, an integral sense, for which the true world is right here in the middle of things. This new sense of the world challenges the inherited ideas, images, and stories that partition sense into fixed identities and dualistic schemas. This integral sense calls for participation in the generative processes whereby the multiplicities of sense are enacted, participation in the unfolding chaosmos. Such participation requires new ideas and images of the chaosmos and the place of humans therein. It requires new stories. For concepts to help us stay in the middle of things, stay tactfully in touch with the sense of the world, those concepts must transform the human imagination and facilitate the navigation of passages between stories.

"We are in between stories".[47] This sentence from Thomas Berry can be read in at least two ways. In one way, it means that the old narratives and images that oriented humans to the world no longer work, and that new narratives and images are required if humans are going to have a sustainable relationship with the Earth community. That seems to be the intended meaning of Berry's phrase. He thus goes on to say, "The old story, the account of how the world came to be and how we fit into it, is no longer effective".[48] There is another way to read Berry's phrase, a reading that complements the first way. In the first way, "in between" is a preposition, describing our place of transition from old to new stories. To read it differently, let "in between" be an adjective modifying "stories". We are in between stories. Humans not only have stories, we are stories—an unfolding material-semiotic process—and as stories, we stay in the middle, the in-between. In short, humans are liminal narratives, interstitial stories. Combining these two ways of reading the phrase, one gets the sense that the old narratives and images no longer work precisely because they suppress the in-between and prevent humans from becoming the liminal stories that we are. The old stories no longer work because they fail to stay in the middle, and instead they colonize the complex boundaries of material-semiotic processes with god tricks, judgements, and original identities.

Integral ecology calls for the development of stories that can help humans stay in the middle and dwell tactfully amid the dynamic multiplicities of sense. Staying in the middle, stories are not simply mythical as opposed to logical discourses. Rather, like the discourse on *chora* given in Plato's *Timaeus*, a story that stays in the middle is a strange, quirky, and hybrid discourse, a dreamy, wandering, wondering discourse that interrupts and cuts open dichotomies of myth/logic, sensible/intelligible, and belief/truth.[49] Furthermore, stories that stay in the middle cut open the human/nonhuman boundary, emerging from the sense of the world and not merely from the mind of a human author (*mens auctoris*). This resonates with Gregory Bateson's understanding of stories.

> Now I want to show you that whatever the word "story" means [. . .], thinking in terms of stories does not isolate human beings as something separate from the starfish and the sea anemones, the coconut palms and the primroses. Rather, if the world be connected, if I am at all fundamentally right in what I am saying, then thinking in terms of stories must be shared by all minds, whether ours or those of redwood forests and sea anemones [. . .], the evolutionary process through millions of generations whereby the sea anemone, like you and me, came to be—that process, too, must be of the stuff of stories.[50]

To conceive of stories as originating solely from humans is to colonize storytelling with a false dichotomy that separates the intelligible world of human language from the sensible and sensuous world. New concepts are needed to situate narrative imagination back into its place in the chaosmos.[51] Those concepts would support the development of new images and stories that orient humans towards a sustainable planetary civilization.

One such concept of imagination is proposed in the emancipatory political ecology that Michael Watts and Richard Peet call "liberation ecology". Watts and Peet recognize that human societies construct the ideas and images they use to understand the natural environment. However, this "social construction of nature" is not the whole story. It is situated in relation to a "natural construction of the social", such that social or psychological imagination is complemented with an "environmental imaginary" — "a way of imagining nature" that includes images of "those forms of social and individual practice which are ethically proper and morally right with regard to nature".[52] The environmental imaginary tends to be expressed in local forms of discourse that focus on the history of relations between a society and a specific natural environment. Through the notion of environmental imaginary, one experiences "nature, environment, and place as *sources* of thinking, reasoning, and imagining".[53] As the phrase *liberation ecology* indicates, there is an "emancipatory potential of the environmental imaginary", whereby the confluence of ecological engagements in "science, society, and environmental justice" brings together "natural as much as social agency" to resist unjust and unsustainable models of "development".[54] To map environmental imaginaries is to engage the co-constitutive relationality of imagination, which disturbs the partition of the sensible and thus empowers humans and nonhumans marginalized by development to become visible and audible, to make sense, to make a difference, which might look like a lot of nonsense.

For John Sallis, a turn towards environmental imaginaries or "elemental imagination" can be facilitated through deconstruction, for deconstruction accompanies a turn to the elemental, a turn that "would reinstall the human in wild nature and in its bearing on the earth and beneath the sky, returning human nature to nature".[55] With this elemental turn, deconstruction becomes ecological deconstruction, which David Wood describes as "econstruction — a living, developing, and materially informed deconstruction".[56] To facilitate the econstruction of imagination and the turn towards the elemental, new rigourous determinations of imagination are needed. As Sallis observes, this "makes phenomenology indispensable" to a deconstruction of imagination, because phenomenology provides rigourous determinations of things as they show themselves, thus holding in abeyance any preconceived notions, schemas, or determinations that efface what imagination shows.[57]

Phenomenology itself mutates as it is touched by the elemental force of imagination and the deconstruction of traditional philosophical categories. Such a mutation requires that phenomenology adhere more rigorously to the complexity and perplexity of what shows itself, and thus rather than confining phenomenology to appearances (i.e., phenomena), which are present to consciousness, phenomenology becomes open to that which exceeds the horizon of presence. This is not unlike what Gaston Bachelard calls "a phenomenology without phenomena".[58] In other words, phenomenology mutates into a "deconstructive phenomenology", which opens phenomenology and reactivates its sense of responsibility, exposed to the risks and pressures of the world.[59] This mutant phenomenology responds to the complexity, difference, absence, excess, and nonsense that are at work (but not simply present to consciousness) in the constitution of things as they show themselves.

Overflowing the limits of presence, images show themselves in an exorbitant sense of "showing" (from Latin, *monstrare*), which calls for phenomenology to become "monstrology".[60] Monstrology is open to what shows itself in its irreducible excess, anomaly, and paradox, which is to say, its "monstrosity" (from Latin, *monstrum*, "monster", "portentous sign"). Along similar lines as Haraway's sacramental consciousness (see "Opening" above), for which everything is like a monstrance—a ritual object for displaying the Flesh-Word of the Eucharistic host—monstrology does not reduce images to binary oppositions such as material/semiotic, subject/object, nature/culture, appearance/reality, matter/form, and sensible/intelligible. Undergoing a deconstructive mutation, phenomenology articulates imagination in terms of a monstrous force that impels things to show themselves, such that imagination is not exclusively human but is a generative force of sense. To impel things to show themselves, the force of imagination gathers together the multiplicities of sense, oscillating between the multivalent determinations of sense (e.g., subject/object, appearance/reality, matter/meaning). Following the concept of imagination given by the German idealist philosopher Johann Gottlieb Fichte, one can describe this gathering of sense as a "hovering" (*Schweben*) that wavers between the various determinations of sense while also wavering between these determinations and the radical indeterminacy and uncertainty of sense.[61] Imagination hovers in the middle, amidst the events of many senses of sense. Furthermore, imagination stays in the middle with the force of a beginning.

In gathering together the horizons in which things show themselves, imagination can be described as a beginning of things. Like a beginning, it is simultaneously originary and memorial: originary because imagination is a creative force that draws things into presence, and memorial because that which imagination creates does not emerge out of nothing but is drawn into presence and is thus already there virtually or implicitly before it is gathered into presence. Hovering between the determinations and indeterminacy of the originary/memorial, the semiotic/material, and the subjective/objective, the force of imagination draws things into the places where they show themselves: "imagination composes monstrosity".[62]

Imagination does not belong to humans or even to nonhuman subjects. Subjects belong to imagination. The force of imagination hovers amidst multiplicities and lets human and nonhuman things show themselves as vectors of the sense of the world. By disclosing the exorbitant sense of things as they show themselves, imagination can reinvent the human, such that the human is re-placed, placed back into nature, and nature likewise is re-placed, placed back into the complex boundaries of the chaosmos. In this sense, nature would be liberated from the overly ordered, harmonious, capitalized Nature that acts like an origin instead of a beginning. Faber describes such a chaosmic nature as "econature", which pertains to the wild becoming of all things in relations of mutual immanence, where "wildness" is not about "any identity of nature *or* culture" but is "in between", like *chora*, moving and shaking with the necessity of our constitutive contingency.[63] Wild econature is an elemental nature that encompasses and overflows the complex boundaries of things. It is what Sallis calls "a kind of hypernature within nature".[64] Restoring the sense of the world, elemental imagination reorients the human to its place, putting human nature back in the middle of the wild becoming of elemental nature.

RHIZOMES

Here in the middle of things, imagination opens onto a philosophy of nature or, more specifically, a philosophy of elemental nature. In this context, the term *elemental* does not refer to hydrogen, helium, carbon, or other elements on the period table. Elements are not building blocks that compose things. They are the beginnings from which all manifestations flow. As Sallis says, what is "required of philosophy at the limit is that it turn back to the elements as constituting the *from which*, not of composition, but of manifestation", thus recovering "an exorbitant sense of *element*", for which elements gather and express "the expanse of the self-showing of things themselves".[65] This reflects the sense of elements articulated in ancient Greek philosophy, not *stoicheia* ("components"), which is mentioned in the discussions of elements in Plato's dialogues, but *rhizomata* ("roots"). Along these lines, Sallis refers to the work of Empedocles, whose writings convey a sense of the four elements (fire, earth, air, and water) as "the roots that convey sustenance to all things, enabling natural things to grow, to come to light, to unfold into the open expanse bounded and configured by these very roots".[66]

Furthermore, the roots are divine, with Empedocles associating the four elements with Hera, Zeus, Nestis, and Aidoneus.[67] Empedocles did not only write about these divine roots, but also he engaged in transformative practises with them "to benefit humans and other creatures", including "shape-shifting" practises of becoming a bush, tree, or other natural beings, leading some scholars to suggest that Empedocles can be described as "a shaman or natural magician".[68]

A recovery of Empedocles's *rhizomata* has much to offer integral ecology. As David Macauley argues, Empedocles uses his concept of *rhizomata* to express a rudimentary theory of evolution, to convey a "deep sympathy with sentient organisms and nonhuman entities", to analyse the complex relationship between purity and pollution in nature, society, and human consciousness, and to affirm a commitment to take on the multiple perspectives of "naturalist, poet, religious prophet, philosopher" and "shaman-healer".[69] In this case, a philosophy for integral ecology could be described as "elemental philosophy", which does not stop at pre-Socratic concepts of elements but also includes the recovery of the elemental in twentieth-century philosophies (e.g., phenomenology, feminism, and poststructuralism).[70] To put it another way, a philosophy of integral ecology could be described as a philosophy of *rhizomata*, where *rhizomata* are not only elements in the Empedoclean sense but also rhizomes. In this sense, integral ecology has much to gain from the "reanimation of the notion of rhizomes in the post-structuralist work of Gilles Deleuze and Félix Guattari for new possible ways of thinking about the elements and our own environmental dilemmas".[71] The rhizomes of D&G are of central importance to the creation of concepts that open up to the middle of things. *Rhizome* is a term used in plant sciences (e.g., botany, dendrology, plant taxonomy). Also called rootstocks or creeping rootstocks, rhizomes are plant stems that grow horizontally and send out roots (below) and shoots (above) from their nodes. Examples include ginger, couch grass, bamboo, violets, and irises, and they are similar to tubers (e.g., potatoes) and bulbs (e.g., onions and garlic). The rhizome is the main stem of a plant, and it functions as an organ of vegetative reproduction, which is an asexual reproductive process whereby any piece cut off a rhizome can generate another plant. They often grow underground, but some grow above ground or on the surface (e.g., some irises and ferns).[72] In short, a plant with a rhizome has nodes generating knotty networks of horizontal and vertical growth, in which any part of the rhizome can become the source of a new plant.

D&G transform the rhizome into a philosophical concept, and it has become one of the most commonly referenced of the numerous concepts they developed together. They introduce the concept of the rhizome in the first chapter of *A Thousand Plateaus*, "Introduction: Rhizome". They extend the rhizome beyond one kind of plants to ask "whether plant life in its specificity is not entirely rhizomatic".[73] They extend the concept even beyond plant life, so that rhizomes refer to animals, burrows, and to any complex network of interconnections. Even a book "forms a rhizome with the world" (11).[74] Rhizomes take on "very diverse forms, from ramified surface extension in all directions to concretion into bulbs and tubers".[75] D&G enumerate six characteristics that define rhizomes. The first two are discussed together: "connection and heterogeneity", which indicate that "any point of a rhizome can be connected to anything other, and must be".[76] They describe these characteristics by critiquing the model of the tree—an arborescent structure, which serves as the basic model in many areas of study, including linguistics, where the tree is used for diagramming sentences. Sentence trees frame meaningful enunciations within the plotted points and fixed orders of noun and verb phrases. In contrast, a rhizome opens up semiotics beyond standard linguistics and thus connects heterogeneous species of meaning, including biological, political, artistic, perceptive, gestural, and others. A rhizomatic method analyses language by mapping its connections with varied and diverse dimensions and registers of meaning. The third characteristic is "multiplicity", which indicates that a rhizome is "a multiplicity of nerve fibers", indeed "multiplicities of multiplicities", like fractal puppet strings that are tied not to a puppet master but to other puppets.[77] Claims to unity, the One, totality, and more occupy transcendent or overcoding positions from which multiplicities are partitioned and divided into familiar dichotomies: subject/object, natural/spiritual, image/world. The overcoding partitions drawn by a transcendent One are "lines of segmentarity", and in contrast to those "oversignifying breaks", the fourth principle of the rhizome proposes another kind of break, "asignifying rupture", which occurs "whenever segementary lines explode into a line of flight".[78]

If the One overcodes the rhizome and turns it into segmented and stratified territories, lines of flight are decoding "lines of deterritorialization", which explode the overcoded rhizome, opening it up so that they might "start up again on one of its old lines, or on new lines", like an anthill rebuilding after being destroyed.[79] Every rhizome includes lines of segmentarity (territorialization) and lines of flight (deterritorialization). "These lines always tie back to one another. That is why one can never posit a dualism or dichotomy", such as the dualism for which lines of segmentarity are bad and deterritorialization is good; rather, it all depends on how the rhizome is being engaged: "Good and bad are only the products" of an ongoing selection process that "must be renewed".[80] This means that rhizomes are not necessarily opposed to stratifications that block connections. Rather, the connections of the rhizome can integrate closings, blockages, and impasses. It is important to "realize that even an impasse is good if it is part of the rhizome".[81] D&G *do not privilege destratification over stratification.* "Staying stratified—organized, signified, subjected—is not the worst that can happen; the worst that can happen is if you throw the strata into demented or suicidal collapse, which brings them back down on us heavier than ever".[82] The intertwining of territorialization and deterritorialization is exemplified in the coevolutionary relationship between pollinating insects and the plants they pollinate. D&G use the example of the orchid and the wasp.

> The orchid deterritorializes by forming an image, a tracing of a wasp; but the wasp reterritorializes on that image. The wasp is nevertheless deterritorialized, becoming a piece in the orchid's reproductive apparatus. But it reterritorializes the orchid by transporting its pollen. Wasp and orchid, as heterogeneous elements, form a rhizome.[83]

What takes place is symbiosis or *aparallel evolution*—"a becoming-wasp of the orchid and a becoming-orchid of the wasp".[84] To put it another way, wasp and orchid deconstruct one another to create a new complex entanglement, a rhizome in which each becomes with the other. The task of rhizomatic philosophy is not simply to deterritorialize, but to create rhizomes, following lines of flight so as to facilitate novel evolutionary connections: "Conjugate deterritorialized flows".[85] A rhizome does not rely on models to support the growth of rhizomes. A model (or framework or underlying generative structure) is like a tracing that reproduces or represents multiplicities with an overcoding system or underlying support structure. In contrast, the rhizome is "a *map and not a tracing*", which is the point of the fifth and sixth principles of the rhizome: "cartography and decalcomania".[86]

Cartography is a principle of map-making, and maps are distinguished from tracings insofar as maps are exploratory, "entirely oriented towards an experimentation in contact with the real". The map is about "performance, whereas the tracing always involves an alleged 'competence'" to mimic an original structure. The map is "part of the rhizome" — "open and connectable in all of its dimensions; it is detachable, reversible, susceptible to constant modification" and "always has multiple entryways".[87] The orchid and the wasp do not trace one another; they develop experimental maps whereby they enact transformative contact with one another. Again, as with lines of segmentarity, this does not mean that tracings (models, frameworks, etc.) are bad, but that tracings must be situated on the rhizome, like putting decals onto fabrics or pottery (i.e., decalcomania). If tracings are not rhizomatically situated, they enact god tricks, dominating multiplicities with an overcoding origin. "It is a question of method: *the tracing should always be put back on the map*". To follow the rhizome does not mean to abandon or destroy all tracings, trees, and lines of segmentarity, but to open novel modes of existence for those tracings, trees, and lines. "To be rhizomorphous is to produce stems and filaments that seem to be roots" or connect with roots, while putting those roots to "strange new uses".[88]

To summarize: "the rhizome connects any point to any other point", it integrates "very different regimes of signs" (language, politics, gestures, animals, sexuality, economics, arts, sciences, etc.), "and even nonsign states" (asignifying ruptures, nonsense); it is neither One nor multiple, but is a multiplicity composed of lines ("directions in motion"), including lines of territorialization and deterritorialization; and finally, it "pertains to a map" that has "multiple entryways and exists" and to "tracings that must be put on the map".[89] The rhizome brings into question relations to "all manner of 'becomings,'" opening relations up so that they stay in the middle of multiplicities instead of governing multiplicities with origins, judgements, or models that claim to be over and above multiplicities.[90]

The rhizome is of central importance for staying in the middle. "It has neither beginning nor end, but always a middle (*milieu*) from which it grows and which it overspills. . . . *It grows between*, among other things".[91] However, this does not mean that the rhizome is a hierarchical unity where the centre organizes or controls the periphery. Staying in the middle means staying between beginning and ending, and it also means staying between middles and margins. Staying in the middle is a way of becoming centred as well as eccentric. Amidst the world's multiplicities, the rhizome is paradoxically a middle without a determinate centre—"a centerless center".[92] In the middle, where there is no control centre, there is "an acentered multiplicity".[93] For D&G, "acentered systems" resist control centres without positing a dualism against centric or polycentric systems. Indeed, the rhizome is not reducible to any dualism. It opens up creative spaces of growth between the strata of all dualistic schemas and hierarchical trees: between beginning and ending, between central and peripheral, and even between dualism and nondualism. Not reducible to any dualism, the rhizome is not simply nondualistic either, for that would just amount to "a new or different dualism", a dualism between nondualism (rhizomatic) and dualism (arborescent).[94] Insofar as there is a dualism between rhizomes and trees, it is meant to challenge all dualistic models and bring theory and practise into contact with the multiplicities of the chaosmos. "We invoke one dualism only in order to challenge another. [. . .] in order to arrive at a process that challenges all models", or perhaps more appropriate, to arrive at a process that rearranges all models, as if dualisms and hierarchies are "the furniture we are forever rearranging".[95] The point is not to affirm nondualism over and above dualism but to stay in the middle of the ongoing rearranging process, following lines of flight as they open new modes of existence. In the middle of multiplicities, the arborescent and the rhizomatic fold into one another. "There are knots of arborescence in rhizomes and rhizomatic offshoots in roots".[96] The practise of rhizomatics is not *against* arborescent boundaries and stratified borderlines. Rather, it cuts through those borderlines to open new territories. The rhizome cuts open all boundaries, including the boundary between the bound and the unbound.[97]

If everything is situated in the rhizomatic multiplicities of the chaosmos, then rhizomatic approaches to philosophy prevent ontology from ever attaining an original foundation, they "overthrow ontology, do away with foundations", without, however, simply abandoning the metaphysical project of conceptualizing being (*ousia*) and beings (*onta*).[98] Indeed, Deleuze is not against the metaphysical task of theorizing the nature of being. He even describes himself as "a pure metaphysician".[99] Without a foundation, the *being* of foundational ontology is re-placed with *interbeing*, which is to say, it is placed back amidst multiplicities. Rhizomatic being is "always in the middle, between things, interbeing, *intermezzo*".[100] A world of interbeing is a chaosmos of what Higgins calls "interflowing multiplicities".[101] If interbeing is about interflowing multiplicities opening connections between boundaries, then the rhizomatic ontology of interbeing can be described as an ontology that adheres to "a logic of the AND" or, to put it more simply, "the rhizome is the conjunction, 'and . . . and . . . and . . . ' This conjunction carries enough force to shake and uproot the verb 'to be.'"[102]

> The whole of grammar, the whole of syllogism, is a way of maintaining the subordination of conjunctions to the verb to be, of making them gravitate around the verb to be. One must go further: one must make the encounter with relations penetrate and corrupt everything, undermine being, make it topple over. Substitute AND for IS. A *and* B. The And is not even a specific relation or conjunction, it is that which subtends all relations, the path of all relations, which makes relations shoot outside their terms and outside the set of their terms, and outside everything which could be determined as Being, One, or Whole. The AND as extra-being, inter-being.[103]

There is no start or finish to interbeing. As multiplicities proceed "from the middle, through the middle", they are "coming and going rather than starting or finishing".[104] Moreover, this coming and going is not a pure continuity, but is interrupted by lines of flight and asignifying ruptures. The rhizome is reducible to neither continuity nor discontinuity. It is a complex "and" that makes room for continuity (both/and) *and* discontinuity (either/or) while overflowing the limits of both.

By overthrowing foundational ontology and shifting towards interbeing, D&G create a concept that resonates with relational ontologies implicit in East-Asian religions, such as that articulated by the Vietnamese Zen Buddhist monk Thich Nhat Hanh, who uses the word *interbeing* to describe the interpenetration and interconnectedness of all things, which can be understood in terms of the Buddhist doctrine of "dependent co-arising" (Pali, *paticcasamuppada*; Sanskrit, *pratityasamutpada*).[105] Also translated as the "together-rising-up-of-things", this doctrine is generally viewed as supportive of ecological concerns and may even function as "a quintessential ecological virtue".[106] The contemporary Korean philosopher Hwa Yol Jung draws on Nhat Hanh's sense of interbeing along with other resources in East-Asian religions (Buddhism, Confucianism, and Daoism), phenomenology, postmodernism, and feminism to articulate a comparative philosophy that responds to contemporary ecological challenges through the development of a "relational ontology"; that is, a philosophy of interbeing, which is not only an ontology but also opens up a "new ethics" and "a new politics" of "ecopiety"—a conjunctive or *"inclusionist"* sense of reciprocity between human and Earth others.[107] Jung describes this philosophy with a term from D&G, *geophilosophy*: "Whenever and wherever there is Interbeing, there is also geophilosophy which is concerned with all matters of the earth in a single embrace". "Interbeing is the 'first law' of geophilosophy".[108] The connections between D&G's interbeing and East-Asian conceptions of interbeing are important for facilitating cross-cultural dialogue relevant to ecological issues. Although those connections are worth developing, which Jung's work shows, my concern here is not to elaborate on comparisons between D&G and East-Asian religions but to explicate D&G's philosophy of rhizomes—that is, geophilosophy.

For D&G, geophilosophy is a philosophy that is no longer dominated by subject and object, whether in opposition or with one term revolving around the other. Replacing subject-object schemas with open systems of multiplicities, D&G's geophilosophy integrates insights from the history of philosophy (including figures such as Spinoza, Marx, Nietzsche, and Bergson) and from complexity theory to map the creative and self-organizing processes at work in human, organic, and material systems.[109] Geophilosophy cultivates experimental contact with the real by staying in the middle, following lines of Earth and territory. Earth in this case is not "one element among others but rather brings together all the elements within a single embrace while using one or another of them to deterritorialize territory", which means that Earth is not itself a territory but is the opening of territories, carrying out "a movement of deterritorialization on the spot, by which it goes beyond any territory".[110] The aim of geophilosophy is to map lines of flight (Earth) and stratification (territory) so as to open new modes of existence for the Earth community, "*so as to summon forth a new earth, a new people*".[111] In this sense, the task of philosophical thinking is to experiment, and "experimentation is always that which is in the process of coming about—the new, remarkable, and interesting that replace the appearance of truth" with events.[112] Geophilosophy re-places philosophy, situating philosophy's apparent truths back into place, into a "milieu rather than an origin", into "a becoming instead of a history".[113] To create a geophilosophical concept is to create a becoming, which resists dominology by placing it in the open, in the middle of multiplicities. In other words, "becoming is the concept itself", which "has neither beginning nor end but only a milieu", a mid-place where "pure becomings, pure events" interrupt structures of domination.[114]

The movement of becoming is the movement of the middle. "The middle in not an average; it is fast motion, it is the absolute speed of movement. A becoming is always in the middle; one can only get it by the middle. A becoming is neither one nor two, nor the relation of the two; it is the in-between, the border or line of flight or descent running perpendicular to both".[115] The movement of becoming is the movement of transversality. Transversality transgresses and transforms the stratified lines of hierarchies to open possibilities for new alliances and connections. "Transversal communications between different lines scramble the genealogical trees", such that transversal becoming "sweeps one *and* the other away, a stream without beginning or end that undermines its banks and picks up speed in the middle".[116] Transversality scrambles the lines of the horizontal and the vertical in a way that opens those lines up to multiple movements of becoming, and not in a way that simply averages them out into a diagonal: "the transversal breaks free of the diagonal as a localizable connection between two points".[117] D&G's concept of transversality comes primarily through Guattari, whose work transforms Jean-Paul Sartre's concept of transversality. For Sartre, the boundary-crossing movement of transversality is centred on the intentionality of human consciousness. In contrast, Guattari emphasizes the role of transversality as a function of communicative praxis across multiple material and semiotic registers (i.e., the three ecologies of subjectivity, society, and environment), thus overcoming the human-centred and subject-centred transversality of Sartre's existentialist theory of consciousness.[118] Guattari's conception of transversality changed throughout his career, with various uses from his clinical work as a psychotherapist and his theoretical writings, and in his work with Deleuze, transversality becomes a *central* concept of rhizomatic philosophy.

Transversality is a concept for staying in the middle, amidst the complex boundaries of the world's interflowing multiplicities. Furthermore, as Leonardo Boff says (presumably influenced by Guattari), integral ecology calls for an understanding of transversality, which functions as a method for engaging the multidimensional and cross-disciplinary capacities of ecological knowledge.[119] Hwa Yol Jung makes a similar point in arguing that transversality opens up possibilities for a planetary approach to truth, wherein the centre of truth is not a unified control centre marginalizing different ways of knowing but is a centre that is everywhere, with its circumference nowhere.[120] Moreover, this entails that truth is not an elitist truth that coordinates professionals and experts from around the globe. If the centre of truth is everywhere, it is even in popular culture. Indeed, it is especially in popular culture, where multiplicities of styles, genres, and media circulate without being unified into any expert language. Accordingly, geophilosophy or rhizomatics can be engaged as an analysis of popular culture: "RHIZOMATICS = POP ANALYSIS".[121] What D&G call "pop" ("pop music, pop philosophy, pop writing") is an "escape for language, for music, for writing", an escape that makes use of the "polylingualism" of minorities and multiplicities to resist the "oppressive quality" of any regime of signs that wants to be "an official language" or "a master of the signifier".[122] Deleuze articulates a guiding principle of pop analysis when he describes a chaosmos in which "everything bathes in its difference".[123] Such philosophy enjoins us to plunge into multiplicity, to bathe in the multitude.[124]

A rhizomatic approach to integral ecology would not just integrate ecological research in the sciences and the humanities but would also develop experimental contact with the ecologies of social media, hip-hop music, sci-fi novels, hair salons, stand-up comedy, and other forms of expression that wander outside of the accepted boundaries of expert knowledge and high culture.[125] The point is not that pop methods have access to something that official discourses lack. The point is that, with pop methods, minorities and multitudes can shake things up and do things differently. Pop methods are thus of inestimable importance for efforts to nurture the diversity of planetary coexistence and abjure any system or language that would seek to control or efface that diversity. A geophilosophical approach to integral ecology would not see the wandering multiplicities of pop culture as erroneous, lost, or false, but as creative forces opening new modes of existence. Geophilosophy teaches us a lesson that is communicated in *The Lord of the Rings*, the popular trilogy of the English fantasy author J. R. R. Tolkien: *"Not all those who wander are lost"*.[126]

NOMADS

Geophilosophy is a philosophy of wandering, a philosophy of nomads, which D&G call "nomadology".[127] Like rhizomes, "nomads are there, on the land", anywhere a milieu opens up, growing wildly "in all directions", such that nomads can be described as "vectors of deterritorialization".[128] Just as rhizomatics overthrows foundational ontology with the relational connectivity of interbeing, nomadology escapes the bondage of foundational ontology (imperial essences) with politics of vagabondage (vague essences).[129] For D&G, "politics precedes being".[130] There is no articulation of being that is not already political. There is no being that is not already "traversed by lines, meridians, geodesics, tropics, and zones marching to different beats and differing in nature".[131] There is no individual or group that is not already negotiating its relations and navigating the conflicting demands of multiplicities. As a science, "nomad science" is rigourous without being exact (intelligible) or inexact (sensible). It stands in contrast to the control centre of any "State science" ("royal or imperial sciences") that would impose one way of knowing onto the multiplicities of knowledge.[132] In terms of politics, this suggests that nomadology resists hegemonic centrism and encourages social and political experiments to liberate events, keeping the flow between multiplicities open and free and subverting any forces that attempt to impose blocks or stratifications that inhibit their wandering.

Moreover, lest nomads be thought of exclusively as human nomads, it is important to mention that nomadology pertains to all beings, human and nonhuman. Nomadology maps the lines whereby every being opens out in complex connections with other events. D&G overthrow Leibniz's metaphysics of monads (i.e., beings as substantial units that are closed off from one another) and replaces it anagrammatically with a metaphysics of nomads. In place of a monadic distribution of events, there is a nomadic distribution of events, which are neither self-contained nor rigidly determined.[133] In place of a Leibnizian monadology, there is nomadology. The idea of a self-contained monad is abstracted from a vibratory event, a luminous wave that emerges from the creative forces of the chaosmos.[134] Every monad is a nomadic event, an open process wandering into relations with others. Whitehead makes a similar point about the process of "feeling" or "prehension" constitutive of monads. "Each monadic creature is a mode of the process of 'feeling' the world".[135] Prehending the world, all entities are open systems feeding into one another. Nomadic monads are thus mutually immanent. They have open windows, in contrast to Leibniz's monads, which are "windowless for each other" and only have windows that open in relation to God.[136] Feeling the world, nomads create novel relationships and new modes of existence by expressing their power to wander. For Whitehead, that "power of wandering" is evident in the capacities of animals and humans to adapt to the world, and to be sure, the power of wandering is dangerous, yet it is precisely such danger that makes it beneficial: "The very benefit of wandering is that it is dangerous and needs skill to avert evils".[137] Amidst the dangers of wandering, nomads become open to adaptations, adventures, and creative advances.

The affirmation of wandering in Whitehead and Deleuze indicates one of the convergences between the cosmologies expressed in process philosophy (Whitehead) and poststructuralism (Deleuze). As Keller observes, cosmological philosophies like those of Whitehead and Deleuze reject the concept of a world made up of self-identical substances closed off from one another, and they replace it with a concept of the chaosmos as a "a fluid nexus of mutually constitutive events"; that is, "an open universe of mutually constitutive relations".[138] Moreover, to say that the chaosmos is an open universe of mutually constitutive relations is not to say that there are no individual things. Nomads are thoroughly relational, but they are not reducible to relations. In other words, rhizomatics is not a relational reductionism that explains actual things (away) as if they are merely a sum of relations. "Every relation is external to its terms", such that every actual thing is not simply a sum of relations but is a singularity harbouring a virtual potency that cannot be fully defined or exhausted by any or all of its relations with other things, qualities, causes, and effects.[139] Every term is made up of relations, yet every relation or complex of relations is a term, an inexhaustible singularity. This position can be described as a pluralism and a realism, affirming a chaosmos teeming with real entities, which are entwined in mutually constitutive relations. This resonates with Whitehead's "ontological principle", according to which "actual entities are the only *reasons*; so that to search for a reason is to search for one or more actual entities".[140] Relations are not *merely* relations. They are actual entities, composing and being composed by relations that are themselves other actual entities, each of which wanders into and out of contact with the others. To forge relations with nomads is to forge relations that open upon real beings, singularities, which exhibit an alterity or rupture that cannot be fully manifested or appropriated. Relations to nomads are relations of alterity or interruption, what Derrida would call a "relation without relation", in which an encounter with any single other opens onto that which is wholly other: *tout autre est tout autre*, every other is wholly other, and the wholly other is every other.[141] Pure becoming is every single thing, and every single thing is pure becoming, an intact event, creative nonsense.

The relational cosmologies of Deleuze and Whitehead acknowledge that the chaosmos is not only a holistic network of relations but also that there are real things, nomadic others that can build and break relations. However, as Faber notes, pluralism is not the whole story, as "*both* philosophies arrive" at what D&G describe as "the magic formula we all seek—PLURALISM = MONISM".[142] If there is too much continuity between the becoming of an entity and other becomings, then pluralism gives way to a monism of becoming. If continuity is not continually tempered by pluralism, it becomes what Ian Bogost critiques as "firehose metaphysics"—the world as a continuous flow.[143] Deleuze and Whitehead are pluralists *and* monists. With their shared affirmation of the mutual immanence of all events, their pluralism is folded together with a monism: there are many events, and they are all within one another. As Faber notes, neither Deleuze nor Whitehead fully arrives at the equation of pluralism and monism. Although they both express ambivalent and subtle distinctions on this issue, Deleuze seems to be more of "the monist, always searching for a continuity of becoming", while Whitehead is more of "a pluralist".[144] "There is a becoming of continuity" for Whitehead, "but no continuity of becoming".[145]

Perhaps the question is whether we should even seek the magic formula equating monism and pluralism. Is it a way of staying in the middle of binary stratifications and opening up possibilities for new modes of existence, or is it a naïve attempt to have one's cake and eat it, too? For now, I want to stay in the middle of these questions, rather than attempting to give an answer or solution.[146] Even if the magical formula is doomed to fail, does that mean we should stop following it? If the formula fails and one falls into monism instead of pluralism, would one be less capable of accounting for the diversity and heterogeneity of beings? This is particularly problematic for integral ecology, which calls for attention to the diversity of ecological realities and the diversity of perspectives on the natural world.[147] Moreover, pluralism is by no means a guarantee that differences are truly being welcomed. It does not necessarily resist legitimating hierarchies, which partition and control the multiplicities of sense with claims to a unified origin or monolithic control centre. Affirming pluralism over monism could reify and totalize the multiple, installing plurality as a dominant origin, thereby reversing rather than subverting the system of domination. However dangerous and risky it is, D&G's magic formula might be more effective than pluralism alone for staying in the middle and replacing structures of domination with experimental contact that aims to liberate nomads and summon a new Earth and new people.

One could argue that D&G are trying to have their cake and eat it too with the magical equation of pluralism and monism and with their other rhizomatic concepts that stay in the middle. It might seem like they are trying to find an easy way out of hierarchies and dualisms. However, it is not easy, nor is it a way out of dualisms, since that would simply install another dualism anyway (the dualism-nondualism binary). It is more like a difficult engagement maintained through spiritual practise, as the phrase *magic formula* suggests. Staying in the middle, for practitioners of geophilosophy, means wandering amidst the multiplicities of the chaosmos while attending to processes of territorialization and deterritorialization with the aim of facilitating the liberation of beings. The rhizome does not "seek to do away with the strange, bumpy divisions between things".[148] For D&G, the rhizome is not a lukewarm average but is the transversal movement of nomadic becoming. Perhaps a better criticism of rhizomatics is not that it finds a lukewarm average between opposites, but that its experimentation with following lines of flight to create contact with the real is not average enough. More specifically, one could argue that rhizomatic experimentation is not sufficiently domestic or domesticated to support a vibrant planetary civilization. This problem is evident in D&G's first book, *Anti-Oedipus*, which takes destruction as its motto: "Destroy, destroy".[149] In 1980, almost a decade after *Anti-Oedipus* (originally published in 1972), D&G change to a more constructive tone in *A Thousand Plateaus*: "Creation! Creation"![150] Although D&G express numerous creative and affirmative concepts, they still have a wild side that impedes constructive efforts to find sustainable and just modes of mundane existence. Haraway notices this problem in her analysis of D&G's concept of "becoming-animal".[151]

Haraway appreciates that D&G's discussion of becoming-animal "works so hard to get beyond the Great Divide between humans and other critters to find the rich multiplicities" of the world. She appreciates D&G's critique of the Oedipal subject and patrilineal systems, for which the world is "a tree of filiations ruled by genealogy and identity".[152] She expresses a rhizomatic approach to building connections between the organic (lapdogs) and technological (laptops) when she says, "I seek my siblings in the nonarboreal, laterally communicative, fungal shapes of the queer kin group that finds lapdogs and laptops in the same commodious laps".[153] Although concepts of becoming-animal can be helpful for recognizing the complex boundaries between humans and other species, D&G fail to regard the boundary projects of mundane and domestic animal existence. They focus exclusively on one exceptional borderline, the boundary with the anomalous: "all that counts is the borderline—the anomalous".[154] Becoming-animal could be a concept for engaging respectfully in our multiplicities and attending to the complexities of interspecies relations, but for D&G, becoming-animal is a concept for forming an alliance with the anomalous, "the exceptional individual in the pack".[155] Haraway sees here a "scorn for all that is mundane and ordinary".[156] She goes on to say that D&G are expressing "a philosophy of the sublime, not the earthly".[157] Their distaste for normal, everyday, ordinary existence "feeds off a series of primary dichotomies figured by the opposition between the wild and the domestic", an opposition that Haraway notices in D&G's critique of Freud's famous analysis of a man who dreamt of wolves (called the "Wolf-Man" by Freud).[158]

D&G criticize Freud for reducing the wolves in the dream to a father figure instead of recognizing those wolves as a "call to become-wolf".[159] Yet in making an otherwise sound point, D&G take an extra step by opposing wolves (wild) to dogs (domestic), suggesting that Freud knew nothing of wolves or of becoming-animal and only knew of dogs: "The only thing Freud understood was what a dog is".[160] Perhaps this comment is just a joke at Freud's expense, but as Haraway observes, "the wolf/dog opposition is not funny".[161] Not only does that opposition subordinate the domestic and ordinary to the wild and exceptional, it also fails to recognize that "wolf-dog hybrids do exist rather widely".[162] Becoming humorous, a more effective response to Freud would trouble the boundaries of the wolf/dog opposition instead of simply reinforcing them. D&G make more disparaging comments about "family pets" in another context, unrelated to the discussion of Freud, and they even go so far as to say that *"anyone who likes cats or dogs is a fool"*: becoming-animal does not pertain to "the little cat or dog owned by an elderly woman who honors and cherishes it".[163] This is an unacceptably narrow conception of becoming-animal, one that fails to stay in the middle of the wild/domestic opposition, and thus also fails to practise rhizomatic philosophy. As Timothy Morton points out, referring to Haraway's critique of D&G, what is needed is an "ecological thought" that overcomes such narrow thinking, an ecological thought that eschews such a "masculine Nature" and welcomes interconnections with all beings. In other words, what is needed is a more welcoming concept of becoming-animal: "welcome grandmothers with dogs, and boo to philosophers who should know better who disparage grandmothers with dogs in favor of wolves".[164]

D&G facilitate growth in the middle of dualisms, even the dualism between duality and nonduality, yet the example of the wolf/dog opposition indicates that some of their expressions fail to stay in the middle and end up propagating hierarchies that facilitate subordination domination instead of tactful contact and liberation. Even the most nomadic nomads and the most twisted rhizomes may find themselves lodged in structures of domination, complicit in dualisms and hierarchies that overcode and control the interflowing multiplicities of the chaosmos. D&G's wolf/dog opposition does not negate the value of rhizomatics, geophilosophy, and nomadology. It is a teachable mistake, one that might serve as a reminder that rhizomatics calls for ongoing vigilance: open eyes, open minds, open hearts.

It is difficult to stay in the middle, even for D&G, but to do so can transform everything, opening up all of one's relationships. "It's not easy to see things in the middle, rather than looking down on them from above or up at them from below, or from left to right or right to left: try it, you'll see that everything changes".[165] From the middle, it is possible to transform hegemonic centrism and generate more liberated modes of existence for people and the entire Earth community.

OMNICENTRIC

Without a hegemonic control centre, the world is not simply awash in centreless chaos. Rhizomatic philosophy is acentred, but only in the sense that it resists claims to a single control centre, not in the sense that it negates centric and polycentric systems. To negate centric systems would turn acentred systems into an overcoding model dominating all modes of becoming. In the acentred systems of rhizomes, everything is a centreless centre, growing from the middle amidst multiplicities of multiplicities. To grow rhizomatic concepts is to "remake and unmake" them "from an always decentred centre".[166] That centre is everywhere. In other words, the rhizomatic sense of the world is multicentric or omnicentric. To elaborate on this omnicentrism, I introduce the rhizomatic concept of "quasi-objects", which Latour adapts from his teacher, Michel Serres. Following that, I discuss contributions to the concept of omnicentrism in the philosophies of Nicholas of Cusa (1401–1464) and Giordano Bruno (1548–1600) and adaptations of that concept in twentieth-century philosophy, theology, and science.

In an omnicentric universe, every single thing is a centre of the world. Nothing is merely on the margins of another being's horizons. Nothing is merely the passive recipient of another's actions. Every single thing is an actor, a dancer taking centre stage. As Nietzsche puts it, "all things themselves dance" in "the ring of existence", such that "the ball There rolls around every Here. The middle is everywhere".[167] Nietzsche's example of a ball is instructive. Consider a ballgame. The ball does not revolve around the players. The players revolve around the ball. Not merely a passive object receiving the players' actions, the ball also acts like a subject the players must follow. Serres gives an apt description of this example, showing that a ball is more than "an ordinary object":

> Ball isn't played alone. Those who do, those who hog the ball, are bad players and are soon excluded from the game. They are said to be selfish. The collective game doesn't need persons, people out for themselves. Let us consider the one who holds it. If he makes it move around him, he is awkward, a bad player. The ball isn't there for the body; the exact contrary is true: the body is the object of the ball; the subject moves around this sun. Skill with the ball is recognized in the player who follows the ball and serves it instead of making it follow him and using it. It is the subject of the body, subject of bodies, and like a subject of subjects. Playing is nothing else but making oneself the attribute of

the ball as a substance. The laws are written for it, defined relative to it, and we bend to these laws. Skill with the ball supposes a Ptolemaic revolution of which few theoreticians are capable, since they are accustomed to being subjects in a Copernican world where objects are slaves.[168]

The ball is a thing in the world, an object, but it is not an ordinary object, since it is an object with some agency, functioning as a subject altering the intentions of the players. In contrast to a Copernican world, in which the appearance of an object is shaped by human subjects (e.g., the sun seems to but does not actually rise), the soccer game shows a Ptolemaic world in which the object shapes human subjects and thereby reveals itself as another subject. Whereas Kant's Copernican revolution of consciousness disclosed a world in which things appear according to the laws of human rationality and processes of social construction, a ballgame discloses a world in which humans bend to the laws of things.

Neither object nor subject, the ball is what Serres calls a "quasi-object", which "is not an object, but it is one nevertheless, since it is not a subject, since it is in the world; it is also a quasi-subject, since it marks or designates a subject who, without it, would not be a subject".[169] Latour follows Serres in describing such an object-subject hybrid in terms of "quasi-objects", which slip through the cracks of the modern partition that opposes a natural world of objects to a social world of human subjects.[170] The quasi-object is not a social construct. It is a real thing in the world, yet it exhibits some agency or active participation in the world, so it is not simply natural if nature is understood in opposition to social or subjective agency. Along these lines, Latour calls quasi-objects "actors" or "actants".[171] Actors are not the "risk-free objects" of the modern partition, which have *"clear boundaries"* separating them from any perplexities or "unexpected consequences", relegated to "a *different* universe" of subjective, social, political, and all-too-human factors; rather, actors are *"risky attachments*, tangled objects", "tangled beings", which Latour follows D&G in describing as "rhizomes", which have "numerous connections, tentacles, and pseudopods that link them in many different ways" to other risky beings.[172]

For Latour, ecological crises are not crises of "matters of fact" in a nature separate from society. They are crises of "matters of concern", the proliferating rhizomes whose entanglements add more perplexing complexity to the world, with each tangled being occupying a centre of the world, calling for other actors to bend and conform to its uncertain actions and unexpected consequences.[173] To respond to ecological crises is to respond to rhizomatic centres of the world. Accordingly, an integral ecology that intends to address ecological crises as they intertwine consciousness, society, and the natural environment needs more than the anthropocentrism, biocentrism, and ecocentrism that have pervaded environmental philosophy since the 1970s. Integral ecology needs a concept of omnicentrism. Such a concept is formulated in the philosophies of Nicholas of Cusa and Giordano Bruno, both of whom conceptualized reality in terms of the "coincidence of opposites" (*coincidentia oppositorum*)—an influential concept repeated in many places, including Joyce's articulation of the chaosmos.[174] Consider, for example, the coincidence of centre and circumference.

For Cusa and Bruno, the universe is a sphere that has its "center everywhere" (*centrum ubique*) and its "circumference nowhere" (*circumferentia nullibi*).[175] As Cusa puts it, "The world machine will have, one might say, its centre everywhere and its circumference nowhere, for its circumference and centre is God, who is everywhere and nowhere".[176] Cusa finds this omnicentricity to be evident in the relativity of the sense of motion, according to which "every observer, whether on the earth, the sun, or another star" feels like "an immovable center of things" around which everything else moves.[177] This omnicentricity exceeds the limits of knowledge. Cusa mentions that, since God is infinite, God is incomprehensible, "above all affirmation and all negation" and "above all opposition".[178] If God's centre is everywhere, centred on everything and everyone, then knowing anything is ultimately a matter of knowing the incomprehensible infinite, which by definition cannot be done. To know anything amidst the whirling forces of an omnicentric universe, knowledge must open up to uncertainty, undecidability, and multiplicities of conjectures and opinions. Knowledge of an omnicentric universe must cultivate "learned ignorance" or "knowing ignorance" (*docta ignorantia*): "aided only by learned ignorance, you come to see that the world and its motion and shape cannot be grasped, for it will appear as a wheel in a wheel and a sphere in a sphere, nowhere having a center or a circumference".[179]

This is not a pantheism that simply equates God with all the things of the universe. It is a panentheism for which "God is in all things" and "all things are in God".[180] Cusa distinguishes God's infinity ("negatively infinite") from the universe, which is neither infinite (since it contains things that are not God) nor finite ("for nothing actually greater than it, in relation to which it would be limited, can be given") but is "privatively infinite", thus existing in "a contracted way": in short, the universe is "contracted infinity" — unbound (without circumference), yet not identical to the divine.[181] God is unfolded in the universe. Furthermore, "the universe is contractedly in all things", which implies that "every creature is, as it were, a finite infinity or a created god", and that all creatures are mutually immanent.[182] Every individual thing is a contraction of all the things composing the universe, "so that all things are in all things" — "a most wonderful connection".[183] The finite and the infinite are folded together, such that all things are enfolded in God, and God unfolds into all things.[184] The universe is an unbound process of divine folding, creating a complex (com-plex, "folding together") of contracted centres — finite infinities. Cusa's language of enfolding (*complicatio*) and unfolding (*explicatio*) is taken up by Bruno. Bruno elaborates on the folds of Cusa's omnicentrism while adding a twist, imploding the distinction between circumference and centre, such that "the universe is all centre and all circumference".[185] Just as much as everything is centre, each centre is itself an edge, on the verge of other centres. As Casey notes, Bruno's cosmology shows us that "we are always on the edge of things and of the world itself", which suggests that existing as a contracted centre does not entail unlimited freedom or access to any "beyond" or "outside", since the freedom of centres is "counter-poised with the inhibition of being hemmed in by a series of circumferences", something Bruno knew quite well as he was not only hemmed in by the Church but burned at the stake for his ideas.[186] Cusa's and Bruno's concepts of an omnicentric universe of folds have been further elaborated in philosophical, theological, and scientific developments of the twentieth century, many of which are folded into Keller's Deleuzian vision of "a trinity of folds": complicatio, explicatio, implicatio.[187]

Keller's trinity draws on Deleuze's trifold formula: "the trinity complication-explication-implication".[188] Deleuze follows the lineage of Cusa and Bruno to articulate his trinity of folds, which he also relates to Leibniz's theory of monads. Deleuze notes that the concept of monad originates in Neo-Platonic philosophy and is elaborated in Bruno's theory of *complicatio*, which itself derives from Cusa.[189] Cusa, Bruno, and Leibniz all attend to the reality of monads and, in different ways, they show how each monad folds together ("complicates") its unity as One and its series as Multiple; that is, "its envelopments and developments, its implications and explications".[190] For Deleuze's nomadic monads, what folds together the implications and explications is not God, but the chaotic opening of the chaosmos, and the enfolded oneness of all in all is not a simple identity but is differenciation—a relational process of constitutive difference.[191] "The trinity complication-explication-implication accounts for the totality of the system—in other words, the chaos which contains all, the divergent series which lead out and back in, and the differenciator which relates them one to another".[192] Things unfold themselves (the divergent series), and in the process of unfolding (the differenciator), they envelop and are enveloped by one another, prehending one another's prehensions in mutually immanent vibrations, and all of this unfolding and enveloping takes place "*in* this chaos which complicates everything".[193] This complex chaos resonates with the infinity of Cusa's *non aliud* ("not-other"), whose creative activity is, like Deleuze's differenciation, "a process of *infinite embodying* of difference", an activity in which God is what Faber calls "the event of theoplicity, of insistence on multiplicity".[194] A theoplicitous event, God is, in the *explicatio*, a "foldout God".[195]

This God-talk is not part of Deleuze's vocabulary. Although Deleuze's work is influenced deeply by esoteric spirituality, his philosophy is often quite hostile towards religion, specifically in light of religious appeals to a hegemonic transcendence, with God being the prime example.[196] However, not every religious expression appeals to transcendence, and not every appeal to transcendence imposes a logic of domination onto the world's multiplicities. As Keller shows, Deleuze's trinity is amenable to a theology of becoming, which is allied with ecological, feminist, process, and postcolonial theologies. She includes Deleuze's criticisms of transcendence while still affirming the terms and conditions of religion, specifically Christianity. Accordingly, she makes "a perversely theological use of this trinity", avoiding Deleuze's antireligious dogmatism while also displacing the homogenizing hegemony that marks Christianity.[197] Eschewing the anthropocentrism and androcentrism of the traditional trinity of God the Father, the Son, and the Holy Spirit, Keller's is not a trinity of "persons" but of "capacities", of *complicatio*, *explicatio*, and *implicatio*, which could be called "Infinity, Word and Spirit", or in more feminine terms, "the womb", "Sophia" (wisdom), and "Ruach" (spirit).[198] The first capacity—*complicatio*—is the "*capacity* of genesis", which is not to be identified with God but refers to "*the depth of God*"; that is, the generative chaos of the deep, Tehom, less of a Father than a "womb and place-holder of beginnings".[199] With the openness of beginnings, this first capacity is no transcendent origin, yet it is not simply opposed to transcendence either. For Keller, "the *complicatio* capacitates both the *implicatio* and the *explicatio*", which are respectively "the immanating and the transcending capacities" of the tehomic trinity.[200]

The second capacity—*explicatio*—can be called "the *difference of God*".[201] It has traditionally gone by names such as "Sophia, Elohim, Christ, Logos, *Verbum*".[202] The action of the verb transcends the deep, yet in its transcending movement of unfolding it does not commit any hegemonic separation that would partition and control the world. Rather, unfolding the differences implicit in the deep, it is a transcendence that "makes a difference", a transcendence that "moves *beyond—but always in relation to*—whatever already is". The third capacity—*implicatio*—names the mutual immanence that relates "the negativity of the infinite" (chaos) with "the positivity of its explications".[203] "So the third capacity thus signifies the relationality itself", and could thus be called "the *spirit of God*", the spirit vibrating over the face of the deep, intensifying differences by bringing explications into contact with their chaotic complication.[204] This complex sense of the world not only resonates with philosophical and theological tones. It also resonates with some of the revolutionary developments in sciences throughout the twentieth century. For instance, research in complexity theory uses the image of folding (*plicare*) to describe its object of study, com*plex* systems. Sean Kelly's proposal for a "complex holism" explicitly draws on Cusa and on new paradigms of thought emerging with twentieth-century scientific developments, including the "paradigm of complexity" expressed by Edgar Morin, who describes the universe as a unity and multiplicity of folds, "*unitas multiplex*".[205] Keller also draws out the scientific implications of these complex folds of thought. She mentions Whitehead's conception of mutual immanence, which engages quantum and relativity theories, and she mentions the concept of "the implicate order" developed by quantum physicist David Bohm.[206] She also remarks that the contracted infinity of Cusa's cosmos "may be read as anticipating the conundrums of cosmic immensity characteristic of contemporary astrophysics, with its speculations on the inflationary universe, the multiverse, the mind-busting quantities that constitute various relative infinities".[207] Indeed, it is from a contemporary cosmological context that I derive my use of the term *omnicentrism*, which comes from the cosmologist Brian Swimme.

According to Swimme, we inhabit "an omnicentric evolutionary universe, a developing reality which from the beginning is centred upon itself at each place of its existence. In this universe of ours to be in existence is to be at the cosmic centre of the complexifying whole".[208] Swimme derives his vision primarily from "two apparently mutually exclusive cosmological observations".[209] First, we can observe light from the big bang, which reaches us from billions of years and miles away, and second, the universe appears to be expanding, so that wherever one is appears to be a stable centre away from which everything else is moving.[210] The first observation implies that we are at the edge of the central origin of the universe. The second implies that we are at the centre of the universe. Together, this means that "the cosmos is centered on its own expansion".[211] The big bang is the centre of the universe, and so is Earth, Saturn, Jupiter, my sister, me, the Milky Way, a dog, a lamp, the Pinwheel Galaxy, a church, a mountain, a toaster, shoes, a potato, a national park, a cell phone, a city, a cigarette, and a compost heap. In short, *"The center of the cosmos is each event in the cosmos"*.[212] This cosmological observation compels humans to rethink their place in the world and their relationship to other beings. "A re-education of the mind is necessary to make sense of what we have discovered".[213] Such an omnicentric re-education could bring about a shared sense of "cosmic solidarity".[214] Along these lines, Barbara Holmes proposes that knowledge of the omnicentric universe could help foster needed change in systemic problems of marginalization and oppression, specifically in light of racial struggles and victimization. "Even the most malignant forces of domination cannot hold down a community that is cosmically on the move".[215] Forces of domination propagating ecological crises can be thwarted by the nomadic (non)sense of the organisms and environments they are destroying.

Perhaps a concept of the omnicentric chaosmos could facilitate integral approaches to environmental ethics that contact different centres on their own terms (whether material, living, or conscious) rather than focusing on human centres and marginalizing organisms and environments (anthropocentrism) or marginalizing humans and focusing on organisms (biocentrism) or environments (ecocentrism). With this ethical inflection, omnicentrism resonates with the approach to environmental ethics that Anthony Weston calls "multicentrism". Weston envisions *"diverse centers, shifting and overlapping but still each with its own irreducible and distinctive starting-point"*, each inhabiting "a world with separate though mutually implicated centers". [216] In this case, moral development is not about expanding from an anthropocentric to nonanthropocentric centre of value. It is about intensifying one's experience of the multiplicity of the world. Of course, in some sense, a multicentrism is not a centrism at all. There is no circumference to mark off the centre. Every centre is a centreless centre. As Weston puts it, the concept of multicentrism is "a kind of Trojan horse", offering "an alternative to the entire centric project as so far understood".[217] He goes on to suggest that, following Irene Klaver, becoming "*ex*-centric" might be a better possibility for environmental ethics.

Finding ourselves at and amidst multiple centres of the universe, we find our place in the chaosmos, our home, our *oikos*. Moreover, this is not a home that is isolated from strangers, neighbours, and others. Our home (*Heim*) is uncanny (*unheimlich*). It is a "strange situation".[218] In terms of Morton's ecological thought, our home is full of the "uncanniness of strange strangers".[219] The rhizomatic complexity of our home is eccentric, weird, wondrous, uncanny, astonishing, as it opens individual identities so that they might wander adventurously into other modes of existence.

> To enter the omnicentric unfolding universe is to taste the joy of radical relational mutuality. [. . .] Our astonishment at existence becomes indestructible, and we are home again in the cosmos as we reach the conviction that we could have been [and could become] an asteroid, or molten lava, or a man, or a woman, or taller or shorter, or angrier, or calmer, or more certain, or more hesitant, or more right or wrong.[220]

At home in the centre of the omnicentric chaosmos, the human being is not anthropocentric, but it is not simply nonanthropocentric either. Those choices presuppose a false dichotomy between a human centre and a nonhuman periphery. At home in a centre that is everywhere, amidst multiple folds of finite infinities, the human becomes a centreless centre, eccentric, anthropocosmic. "We are each the cosmic person, the Mahapurusha, the Great Person of Hindu India, expressed in the universe itself".[221]

ANTHROPOCOSMIC

In recent decades, it has become increasingly apparent that home cannot be taken for granted as a stable background upon which humans live their lives. Home is becoming increasingly unstable, uncertain, and uncanny, particularly in light of the proliferation of ecological crises threatening the future of life on Earth, crises composed of tangled objects like global climate change, a mass extinction event, freshwater scarcity, and pollution. If we humans are going to continue making ourselves at home on this planet, our sense of home must be revised. In short, ecological crises are compelling cultures to reevaluate and reconstruct their sense of home. A viable sense of home must be one that responds to the ecological challenges of our time out of joint.

A concept of home is central to ecology. Deriving from *oikos* and *logos*, ecology could be defined simply as "home-talk". For an ecological sense of home to become integral, it must account for the rhizomatic complexity of home. Although ecology is often associated with environmental sciences, the home of integral ecology cannot be articulated solely from scientific perspectives in ecology. To be sure, sciences are a necessary part of any effort to facilitate a more ecological sense of home, and sciences have already done much to raise awareness about the complex relationships and processes that make up our omnicentric chaosmos. However, even though sciences are necessary, they are not sufficient to imagine a sense of home that can provide humans with a rhizomatic sense of the world. In the middle of rhizomatic multiplicities, science (nature, fact, object) and society (culture, value, subject) are always already entangled in mutually constitutive contact. Accordingly, an integral ecological sense of home facilitates contact between the sciences and the humanities, which harbour philosophies, religions, literatures, and arts that can, together with science, nurture the efforts of humans to cultivate a planetary home in the omnicentric chaosmos.

Although scholars and researchers in the humanities have been developing ecological perspectives since the environmental movement of the 1960s, religious leaders and communities have been slower to reevaluate and reconstruct their perspectives to account for ecological issues. This has been noticed by Mary Evelyn Tucker, a founding figure in the interdisciplinary field of religion and ecology. "Religions have thus been late in coming to environmental discussions and they need to be in conversation with those individuals and groups who have been working on environmental issues for many decades".[222] Although religion is somewhat late to the scene, "there is growing evidence of the vitality of the emerging dialogue of religion and ecology" and of "grassroots environmental action inspired by religion".[223] Along these lines, I propose an integral ecological sense of home emerging in the field of religion and ecology. To do so, I briefly outline accounts of the anthropocentric attitudes towards home found throughout many religious traditions and the nonanthropocentric alternatives developed by scholars of environmental ethics. Showing the anthropocentric/nonanthropocentric opposition to be a false dichotomy, I draw on research in religious studies and phenomenology to introduce the "anthropocosmic" vision of religion and ecology, for which humans (*anthropoi*) and the world (*kosmos*) are intimately intertwined, such that they are not reducible to the mutually exclusive opposition implied in the dichotomy between anthropocentric and nonanthropocentric perspectives.

Traditionally, religious worldviews have tended to express anthropocentric attitudes, defining home primarily in terms of humans or human-divine relations and only engaging the natural world insofar as it is significant to humans or to human relations with the divine. Critiques of anthropocentric attitudes in religions became prevalent following Lynn White Jr.'s 1967 essay, "The Historical Roots of Our Ecologic Crisis", wherein White argues that technological and economic development are not the root causes of our ecological crisis.[224] Rather, such development is itself rooted in anthropocentric attitudes, which White finds at the foundations of the Western worldview, specifically in biblical religion. In a very anachronistic reading, projecting modern domination onto ancient agrarian people, White sees anthropocentrism exemplified in Genesis 1:28, where God tells humans to "subdue" and have "dominion" over creation, thus setting up a dualism between humans and nature that positions the human as superior and central while nature is inferior and marginalized. White's argument is to some extent an indictment of biblical religion in general, with Asian religions (specifically Buddhism) and indigenous traditions considered less anthropocentric and more harmonious with the natural world. White argues that, among biblical religions, Christianity is particularly flagrant in its anthropocentrism, with the exceptions of some Christians (specifically St. Francis of Assisi and Eastern Orthodox Christians) who recognize that creation is an equal partner and not an inferior object in relation to human participation in the divine. Many scholars of religious studies and of environmental ethics have disagreed with White, making important arguments that biblical religion is not as anthropocentric as White claims or that religious worldviews are not the only roots of the ecological crisis. In any case, many of those scholars still agree that anthropocentric attitudes are indeed a root of the ecological crisis and that, accordingly, a viable response to the ecological crisis should include a transition to a nonanthropocentric sense of the place of humans in the world.

The consensus among environmental philosophers has generally converged on the topic of critiquing anthropocentrism and embarking on "the project of constructing nonanthropocentric environmental ethics".[225]

Although White found anthropocentrism only in biblical religions, others have noticed that all religious traditions harbour tendencies to care for the natural world primarily in relation to what is important and valuable for humans. Warning against romanticizing and orientalist views, for which non-Western traditions are seen as more pure, innocent, and environmentally harmonious than Western traditions, many ecologically oriented scholars have pointed out that all traditions have been complicit in some environmentally destructive attitudes and behaviours throughout their history. There is no "ecological noble savage".[226] Even Buddhism (especially early Buddhism), a favored tradition among many environmental philosophers for its emphasis on the interdependent connectedness of all beings, includes a focus on one's personal quest for liberation and can thus be described as anthropocentric, or at least "weakly anthropocentric".[227] It has gradually become apparent among scholars of religious studies and of environmental ethics that all religious traditions include anthropocentric and nonanthropocentric tendencies, with the general consensus being that a turn towards the latter is the preferred direction for developing a viable approach to environmental ethics. However, there are considerable ethical limitations in the two main alternatives to anthropocentrism: biocentrism and ecocentrism.[228] Although they have brought much needed attention to the presence of values inherent in individual living organisms (biocentrism) and in whole ecosystems (ecocentrism), biocentrism and ecocentrism harbour tendencies to marginalize social issues like poverty, racism, sexism, education, and disenfranchisement. Whenever something is put at the centre of home (whether humans, organisms, or ecosystems), someone or something else is marginalized. A home that does injustice to its own people (a misanthropic home) is not a desirable replacement for a home that destroys its own environment.

This suggests that the problem with anthropocentrism is not *anthropos* but centrism, and not centrism in the sense of moderate or "third way" politics, but centrism in the sense of hegemonic centrism, where a central term subordinates a peripheral term. To facilitate the emergence of a vibrant Earth community marked by the mutual flourishing of humans and nonhumans, a sense of home is needed that does not set up a fundamental opposition for which *either* humanity *or* the natural world is the exclusive centre of ethical concern. Such a sense of home must overcome this either/or dichotomy and ground itself instead on the complex entanglement of *anthropos* in an omnicentric *kosmos*. Such a sense of home is anthropocosmic. Becoming anthropocosmic, the human self is no longer an isolated and independent being separate from the world (a separative self), but could be said to become an ecological self, as long as such a self is not conceived as existing in continuous unity with the cosmos (a soluble self) but in complex relationality (a connective self).[229] Along these lines, Val Plumwood criticizes notions of the ecological self that aim for a self/world "merger" (e.g., the eco-self of deep ecology), for that uncritically reverses the problem of the self/world "hyperseparation" and perpetuates a "false choice" between continuity and difference.[230] "The resolution of dualism", according to Plumwood, requires humans to recognize "a complex, interacting pattern of both continuity and difference".[231] Moreover, this pattern relates to the whole Earth community and not just to humans. Accordingly, to participate in this pattern is "to understand and affirm both otherness and our community in the earth".[232]

For the most part, the adjective *anthropocosmic* appears in the context of the study of religions, particularly following the work of the historian of religion Mircea Eliade (1907–1986), and also in phenomenological philosophy, specifically in the works of the twentieth-century French thinkers Gaston Bachelard, Gabriel Marcel, and Paul Ricoeur. To elaborate on the ways in which the field of religion and ecology is facilitating the emergence of an anthropocosmic sense of our planetary home, it is helpful to consider the meaning of the term in religious studies and phenomenology. In the context of religious studies, Eliade uses the terms *anthropocosmic* and *anthropocosmos* throughout many of his journal writings and published books, and he even expressed intentions to write a book called *Anthropocosmos*.[233] For Eliade, the symbolic transformation of humans in "magico-religious experience" allows humans to have what he calls "anthropocosmic experiences", wherein one becomes "a living cosmos open to all the other living cosmoses" that surround one's body.[234] In other words, magico-religious experiences manifest symbolic correspondences that break through the boundaries of human existence and open them up to intimate connections with the rest of the world. Anthropocosmic experiences support existential transformations that lead to a more encompassing and more meaningful sense of home, one that overcomes the alienation and one-dimensional superficiality that plagues the modern human condition. As Eliade says,

> Still with the aid of the history of religions, man might recover the symbolism of his body, which is an anthropocosmos. What the various techniques of the imagination, and especially poetic techniques, have realized in this direction is almost nothing beside what the history of religions might promise. [...] By regaining awareness of his own anthropocosmic symbolism—which is only one variety of the archaic symbolism—modern man will obtain a new existential dimension.[235]

Throughout his works, Eliade gives a variety of examples of anthropocosmic correspondences, including many symbols, myths, and rituals that open up porous boundaries between microcosms and macrocosms: texts that symbolize the intestines as a labyrinth, the eyes as sun and moon, or breathing as weaving; a yogic practitioner aligning spine, mountain, and axis mundi; an indigenous community symbolizing correspondences between a womb, tomb, house, village, and the cosmic womb of the Universal Mother; and numerous other homologies pervading the history of religions. In short, for Eliade, studying religions is not a matter of satisfying historical curiosity but of cultivating anthropocosmic experiences that enable humans to participate in the existential dimensions wherein a wholly other power (i.e., the sacred) intimately intertwines the multiple levels of the world, from the micro to the macro, the cultural to the natural, the human to the more than human.

To describe anthropocosmic experience and religious experience in general, Eliade draws on phenomenology, specifically the phenomenology of religion, with particular references to the Dutch phenomenologist and theologian Gerardus van der Leeuw and the depth psychologist Carl Jung, both of whom adopt Rudolf Otto's concept of the sacred as a wholly other power.[236] Accordingly, it is not surprising that, at the same time an anthropocosmic vision was being developed in religious studies, the term also came into use in phenomenological philosophy, specifically that of Gabriel Marcel, Paul Ricoeur, and Gaston Bachelard. Marcel speaks of "anthropocosmic relations" to describe the basic character of human existence as it is always already "in a situation"; that is, "oriented in a cosmological direction". Such relations are "established beyond the opposition of subject and object".[237] Furthermore, anthropocosmic relations are of ecological value. They are relations expressing the value of *oikos*—home, dwelling. Indeed, reflecting on Martin Heidegger's account of "dwelling", Marcel claims that "dwelling has anthropo-cosmic value", and the loss of this value is precisely what is currently making our world uninhabitable.[238] Whereas Marcel's sense of anthropocosmic relations echoes phenomenological concepts of being in a situation (such as Heidegger's concepts of "dwelling" and "being-in-the-world"), Paul Ricoeur brings those kinds of phenomenological insights together with Eliade's work to describe "sectors of anthropocosmic experience" that connect various forms of symbolism with the power of the sacred.[239] For Ricoeur, anthropocosmic experiences indicate that the sacred is not exclusively a matter of human-divine relations but is a matter of the cosmos, such that one "first reads the sacred *on* the world, *on* some elements or aspects of the world", *on* a "fragment of the cosmos" that gathers together the symbols of existence, symbols from poetry, dream, and religion.[240]

Marcel and Ricoeur contribute much towards a phenomenological understanding of a sense of home grounded in anthropocosmic relations, but it is in Gaston Bachelard's work that anthropocosmic images of home are most thoroughly developed, particularly in the "anthropo-cosmology" he develops in *The Poetics of Space*, in which he articulates a phenomenological account of the poetic imagination of inhabiting intimate spaces.[241] The house plays an important role in Bachelard's anthropocosmology. He considers it "a privileged entity for a phenomenological study of the intimate values of inside space".[242] The point is not to attend to the house as object, but to attend to "the house that has been experienced by a poet", and in doing so, "neglect nothing of the anthropo-cosmic tissue of a human life".[243] Poetic images disclose a house composed of anthropocosmic tissue intertwining humans with intimate spaces, from nests and shells to corners and drawers, extending to the immensity of the universe, which is experienced as an "inner immensity" or "intimate immensity".[244] Our anthropocosmic tissue is manifest in "anthropocosmic complexes"—ways of being that are even more fundamental than "parental complexes" in conditioning the ways that humans engage the world.[245] The "anthropocosmic ties" of those complexes become slack as one enters adulthood and starts learning to treat the world like an object.[246] Participation in imagination weaves together anthropocosmic ties and helps humans dwell amidst intimate immensities.

To put this in the terms of D&G, anthropocosmic ties are the rhizomatic lines that entangle and differentiate the human in relation to everything in the chaosmos. An anthropocosmic tie is "a

Universe fiber", and when a fiber opens (deterritorializes) its boundary, it can stretch and connect to the becomings of other nomads: "A fiber stretches from a human to an animal, from a human or an animal to molecules, from molecules to particles, and so on to the imperceptible. Every fiber is a Universe fiber".[247] "We become universes. Becoming animal, plant, molecular, becoming zero".[248] Moreover, this becoming-cosmic of the human happens through a process of contemplation (not unlike Cusa's contraction): "We become with the world, we become by contemplating it".[249] Bringing together D&G's contemplative nomads with the insights of Bachelard, Ricoeur, Marcel, and Eliade, one can discern a shared task of nomadologists, phenomenologists, and historians of religion: to renew a sense of poetic, oneiric, and sacred images so as to facilitate an existential transformation, a contemplation that weaves together the ties of anthropocosmic relations and thus brings humans and the world into profoundly intimate interrelationships. This is also the task of religion and ecology.

The anthropocosmic insights of Eliade and of the aforementioned French phenomenologists have been adapted by scholars in the field of religion and ecology, often in reference to the Confucian scholar Tu Weiming—one of the first scholars of religion and ecology to use the term *anthropocosmic*. Drawing on Eliade and Ricoeur, Tu discusses an "anthropocosmic" vision to describe the "ethicoreligious" implications of the Confucian worldview.[250] Tu brings attention to the Confucian understanding of a fundamental "unity of Heaven and humanity" (*tianrenheyi*), which is expressed in various Confucian texts, including the *Analects* and the *Doctrine of the Mean* (*Chung-yung*), and in various neo-Confucian writings, such as those of Chang Tsai (1020–1077) and Wang Yangming (1472–1529).[251] The anthropocosmic vision of Confucianism affirms a complex relationality uniting the human self with its community, the natural environment, and the cosmos as a whole. Furthermore, Tu highlights the ecological importance of this anthropocosmic vision, which he sees playing a significant role in the "ecological turn" currently taking place in contemporary Confucianism.[252] This ecological turn is happening in Chinese society in general, as indicated by the Chinese state using the idea of "ecological civilization" as a guiding model for development.[253]

Tu's work has been extended and applied in the study of other religious worldviews. For example, James Miller claims that another ancient Chinese religion, Daoism, also expresses an "anthropocosmic vision", which affirms "the mutual implication of human beings, their social systems, and their natural environment".[254] Humans and the cosmos are continuous with one another in the flow of the "Way" (*Dao*). This means that, for Daosim, a problem like global climate is also a problem for one's own local society and for one's own body. Extending Tu's work beyond Chinese religions, William Chittick address the Islamic philosophical tradition's accounts of the interconnectedness of the human world and the natural world.[255] Chittick also extends the anthropocosmic vision even further, claiming that his account of it presents "the Islamic version of a perspective that is normative for the human race".[256] This echoes the claims of Eliade and the phenomenologists, for whom anthropocosmic experience is articulated in terms of an existential dimension of fundamental importance for all humans. All human existence pulses with the imperative to become anthropocosmic, to learn to dwell, to come home to one's intimate interconnectedness with the omnicentric cosmos. This is the sense of home implicit in the anthropocosmic environmental ethics emerging in the field of religion and ecology.

Mary Evelyn Tucker, a founder of the Forum on Religion and Ecology at Yale, refers to Tu's use of the term *anthropocosmic* in her proposal for a movement towards anthropocosmic environmental ethics, which can facilitate the entrance of the world's religions into an ecological phase.[257] An anthropocosmic vision can assist religious responses to issues facing human society as well as issues facing "the larger macrocosm of the universe in which humans are a microcosm".[258] An anthropocosmic vision can assist the efforts of religious leaders and communities to help humans dwell, to help humans face the ecological and social challenges of our day by tightening the ties intimately intertwining the members of our species with one another, with the planet, and with the immensity of the cosmos. Tucker even uses Bachelard's phrase *intimate immensities* to describe an anthropocosmic response to the challenges of our current historical moment.[259] Religions and all humans are facing these challenges

> as we begin to take on our cosmological being, to dwell in intimate immensities. We are cracking open the shell of our anthropocentric selves and our particular religious traditions to move toward more expansive religious sensibilities that embrace both Earth and universe. New configurations of tradition and modernity will emerge, and with them will come retrieval of texts, reconstruction of theologies, renewal of symbols and rituals, and

re-evaluations of ethics, and, most importantly, a revivified sense of wonder and celebration.[260]

As the title of her book suggests, the anthropocosmic vision of religion and ecology is a vision of "worldly wonder", returning us once again to the beginning of philosophy—Socrates in silent wonder, receiving what opens from the interruptive discourse on *chora*.

Such wonder indicates that the anthropocosmic entanglement of humans with the world is not a simple homogeneity, but is abundantly other, strange, awesome, and mysterious, evoking a sense of the sacred; that is, a sense of a wholly other power that cracks open the boundaries habitually separating oneself from one's community, from other living beings, and from the universe. An anthropocosmic sense of human existence calls for the mutual flourishing of all beings in their uniqueness and difference, including human others and Earth others in a comprehensive sense of concern. Worldly wonder is becoming revivified as religious communities, poets, dreamers, philosophers, and others come to enter the ecological phase of their development and renew their engagement in the anthropocosmic ties of existence, the rhizomatic fibers that support the ongoing task of our species: to dwell, to inhabit the intimate spaces of our omnicentric chaosmos, to come home.

NOTES

1. *Hegemonic centrism* is a phrase Val Plumwood uses to refer to the logic whereby the terms of a relation are defined with a "primary-secondary pattern"—a primary centre set up in opposition to secondary "marginal Others"—where the marginalized Others are colonized and dominated by the centre (Plumwood, *Environmental Culture: The Ecological Crisis of Reason* [New York: Routledge, 2002], 101). Hegemonic centrism is another way of figuring the "logic of colonization" whereby one (primary) pole of a difference dominates the other (secondary) pole, as in dualisms of male/female, human/nature, white people/people of colour, self/other, reason/emotion, and civilized/primitive (Plumwood, *Feminism and the Mastery of Nature* [New York: Routledge, 1993], 43).
2. Luke Higgins, "Becoming through Multiplicity: Staying in the Middle of Whitehead's and Deleuze-Guattari's Philosophies of Life," in *Secrets of Becoming: Negotiating Whitehead, Deleuze, and Butler*, eds. Roland Faber and Andrea M. Stephenson (New York: Fordham University Press, 2011), 145.
3. Ibid., 154.
4. Roland Faber, "Becoming Intermezzo: Eco-Theopoetics after the Anthropic Principle," in *Theopoetic Folds: Philosophizing Multifariousness*, eds. Roland Faber and Jeremy Fackenthal (New York: Fordham University Press, 2013), 232.
5. Jean-Luc Nancy, "Interview: The Future of Philosophy," trans. Benjamin C. Hutchens, in *Jean-Luc Nancy and the Future of Philosophy*, by B. C. Hutchens

(Chesham: Acumen, 2005), 161. Nancy borrows the expression *crisis of sense* from Jan Patocka and Václav Havel (Nancy, *The Sense of the World*, trans. Jeffrey Librett [Minneapolis: University of Minnesota Press, 1997], 2).

6. Nancy, *The Sense of the World*, 8.

7. Ibid., 15.

8. "The partition of the sensible is the cutting-up of the world", a cutting-up that makes "a partition between what is visible and what is not, of what can be heard from the inaudible" (Rancière, "Ten Theses on Politics, trans. Davide Panagia, *Theory and Event* 5.3 [2001], http://muse.jhu.edu/journals/theory_and_event/toc/tae5.3.html). Rancière elaborates on the politics and aesthetics of this partition or "distribution" (*partage*) in *The Politics of Aesthetics: The Distribution of the Sensible*, trans. Gabriel Rockhill (New York: Continuum, 2004). The task of democracy is to reconfigure the sensible to represent the invisible and include the voice of the inaudible. While Rancière's focus is on the visibility and audibility of humans, Jane Bennett extends Rancière's democratic concerns to "a more (vital) materialist theory of democracy" that challenges the partition separating nonhuman others from humans (Bennett, *Vibrant Matter: A Political Ecology of Things* [Durham: Duke University Press, 2010], vii, 105–8). I address these questions of democracy in the following chapter, "Ending".

9. Murray Code, *Process, Reality , and the Power of Symbols: Thinking with A. N. Whitehead* (New York: Palgrave, 2007), 3. For Code, the "Grand Myth of Scientific Superrationality" is "imperialist" in Edward Said's sense of imperialism as "a political philosophy whose aim and purpose for being is territorial expansion and legitimation" (2). Said warns against considering "territory in too literal a way", for there are a variety of ways for "gaining and holding a domain", including operations for appropriating domains of land and people as well as domains of ideas, all "as a result of being able to treat reality appropriately" (Said, *The Question of Palestine* [New York: Vintage Books, 1992], 73).

10. Friedrich Nietzsche, *Twilight of the Idols*, trans. Richard Polt (Indianapolis: Hackett Publishing, 1997), 23–24.

11. Plato, *The Republic*, 2nd ed., trans. Allan Bloom (New York: Basic Books, 1991), 517c.

12. Nietzsche, *Twilight of the Idols*, 23.

13. According to Paul (Rom. 3:24), considerable effort is not enough to attain to the resurrection body; the grace of God "through the redemption that is in Christ Jesus" is also needed. Those that are initiated into Christ's reconciling redemption, through a rite such as baptism, "will certainly be united with him in a resurrection like his" (6:5). According to Joseph Tyson's account of early Christianity, although initiation into Christ does entail a new spiritual life for the believer, Paul "still regards the resurrection as future", such that the grace of God brings one into a life with Christ that will remain hidden until "Christ himself returns" (Tyson, *New Testament and Early Christianity* [New York: Mac-Millan, 1984], 334).

14. Nietzsche, *Twilight of the Idols*, 23.

15. Immanuel Kant, *Prolegomena to Any Future Metaphysics That Can Qualify as a Science*, trans. Paul Carus (Chicago: Open Court, 1997), 75.

16. Immanuel Kant, *Fundamental Principles of the Metaphysic of Morals*, trans. T. K. Abbott (Amherst: Prometheus Books, 1988), 11–12, 37–38.

17. Nietzsche, *Twilight of the Idols*, 23.

18. Ibid.

19. Nietzsche first used this phrase in *The Gay Science*, trans. Josefine Nauckhoff (New York: Cambridge University Press, 2001), 167, 181, 279; and it also

appears several times throughout *Thus Spoke Zarathustra: A Book for Everyone and No One*, trans. R. J. Hollingdale (New York: Penguin Books, 1969), 41, 114, 249.

20. Nietzsche, *Twilight of the Idols*, 24.

21. The loss of nature to forces of technoscientific modernization is the topic of many notable works of ecological thought. Two particularly influential accounts (first published in the 1980s) are those of the environmental activist Bill McKibben, for whom the challenges of climate change signal *The End of Nature*, and the ecofeminist theorist Carolyn Merchant, who describes how the rise of the modern worldview is characterized by *The Death of Nature*, which involves the domination of women, nonhuman species, and the material environment. These questions of endings are explored more in the "Ending" chapter. Bill McKibben, *The End of Nature* (New York: Random House, 2006); Carolyn Merchant, *The Death of Nature: Women, Ecology, and the Scientific Revolution* (San Francisco: HarperSanFrancisco, 1990).

22. Nietzsche, *The Will to Power*, trans. Walter Kaufmann and R. J. Hollingdale (New York: Vintage Books, 1968), 9.

23. Ibid., 14.

24. "Stay loyal to the earth. [. . .] May your bestowing love and your knowledge serve towards the meaning of the earth! Thus I beg and entreat you. [. . .] Lead, as I do, the flown-away virtue back to earth—yes, back to body and life: that it may give the earth its meaning, a human meaning"! (Nietzsche, *Thus Spoke Zarathustra*, 102). "To introduce a meaning [*Sinn*]—this task still remains to be done" (Nietzsche, *Will to Power*, 327).

25. Paul Ricoeur, *Husserl: An Analysis of His Phenomenology*, trans. E. G. Ballard and L. E. Embree (Evanston, IL: Northwestern University Press, 1967), 41.

26. Ibid., 89.

27. Maurice Merleau-Ponty, *Signs*, trans. Richard C. McCleary (Evanston: Northwestern University Press), 1964, 167; *The Visible and the Invisible*, trans. Alphonso Lingis (Evanston: Northwestern University Press, 1968), 250. For an overview of Merleau-Ponty's philosophy of sense, see Ted Toadvine, "Singing the World in a New Key: Merleau-Ponty and the Ontology of Sense," *Janus Head* 7.2 (2004): 273–83.

28. Luce Irigaray, *An Ethics of Sexual Difference*, trans. Carolyn Burke and Gillian C. Gill (London: Continuum, 2004), 127ff; Judith Butler, "Sexual Difference as a Question of Ethics: Alterities of the Flesh in Irigaray and Merleau-Ponty," in *Feminist Interpretations of Maurice Merleau-Ponty*, eds. Dorothea Olkowski and Gail Weiss (University Park: Pennsylvania State University Press, 2006); Elizabeth A. Grosz, *Volatile Bodies: Toward a Corporeal Feminism* (Bloomington: Indiana University Press, 1994), 11.

29. Leonard Lawlor, *Thinking through French Philosophy: The Being of the Question* (Bloomington: Indiana University Press, 2003), 142.

30. Deleuze, *The Logic of Sense*, trans. Constantin V. Boundas (New York: Columbia University Press, 1990), 141.

31. Ibid., 72.

32. Ibid., 71.

33. Ibid., vii.

34. Ibid., 123

35. Ibid., 136. Deleuze mentions Zen archery, drawing, gardening, flower arranging, tea ceremony, and fencing as examples of the event in "the Zen arts" (137).

36. Deleuze observes that "what is apprehended when we touch the surface of the object is perceived as residing in its innermost depth". Ibid., 274.

37. It is important to note that, although there are relays and resonances between Deleuze and Nancy, they have very different approaches to philosophy. The way Nancy puts it, he shares in Deleuze's "fold of thought", even suggesting that, currently, "one would not be thinking without taking something from this fold", which is not to say "that one must incline towards it, nor does it imply that there are not diverse ways of taking this fold, of folding it, unfolding and refolding it in turn" (Nancy, "The Deleuzian Fold of Thought," in *Deleuze: A Critical Reader*, ed. Paul Patton, 107–13 [Cambridge: Blackwell Publishers, 1996], 107). Nancy summarizes the difference between his and Deleuze's strains of thought in terms of their different concepts of sense. Deleuze articulates "sense as composition of a passage across a ground of chaos" (i.e., a chaosmic ground), and Nancy articulates "sense as the underlying tautology of what being there is" (112). Deleuze's sense is "a *becoming*, which moves in the middle of things", whereas Nancy's sense is a genesis moving "from an origin toward an end" (108). These two concepts of sense reflect different approaches to negativity. For Deleuze, "the negative has the simple plenitude of chaos", such that being does not harbour a lack but is a chaosmic process of folding and unfolding: "the fold is being itself" (112). In contrast, Nancy's negative is more Hegelian, as "it hollows out being's lack of itself". Deleuze and Nancy share an affirmation of "irreducible difference", "of distancing, or of spacing": for Deleuze, distancing is a "distribution" of events traversing the folds of the chaosmos, and for Nancy, distancing is a "dislocation" of being itself (113). Sharing in a fold of thought that affirms irreducible difference, Deleuze and Nancy share a "common opposition" to "everything which dissolves our freedom", a freedom that "shares itself through the fold and through the strange proximity of philosophical positions" (ibid.). Roland Faber notes a similar contrast between the conceptions of negativity in Deleuze, Whitehead, and Butler. Butler follows Hegel's dialectical negation while Deleuze and Whitehead are committed to a "*rejection of negation*" and an "affirmation of the 'Chaosmos,'" which is "the sheer affirmation of structures *harbored and nourished* in the 'Open' that is Relation in Chaos", where the heterogeneity of relation in chaos is not negativity but is the "the *mutual immanence* of *khora* and its harbored vibrating structures" (Faber, "Surrationality and Chaosmos: For a More Deleuzian Whitehead [with a Butlerian Intervention]," in *Secrets of Becoming: Negotiating Whitehead, Deleuze, and Butler*, eds. Roland Faber and Andrea M. Stephenson [New York: Fordham University Press, 2011], 169, 171–72). These different approaches to negativity correspond with different accounts of the chaos and openness of Plato's *chora*, which is figured either as a negative limit or as a field of mutually immanent forces (Faber, "Introduction: Negotiating Becoming," in *Secrets of Becoming: Negotiating Whitehead, Deleuze, and Butler*, eds. Roland Faber and Andrea M. Stephenson [New York: Fordham University Press, 2011], 30–36).

38. Nancy, *Sense of the World*, 63.

39. For a detailed account of Nancy's concept of touch and its relationship to related concepts throughout the history of philosophy, see Derrida, *On Touching—Jean-Luc Nancy*, trans. Christine Irizarry (Stanford: Stanford University Press, 2005). For Derrida, Nancy's philosophy of touch can be described as "post-deconstructive realism": postdeconstructive insofar as it attends to irreducible difference; realism insofar as it affirms a real world that exceeds what Derrida calls "humanualism", where reality is measured according to what is given to human consciousness or grasped by the human hand (46, 182). On the religious implications of touching for Derrida and Nancy, see the essays on "La/ Le Toucher (Touching Her/Him)", which is the concluding section of the anthol-

148   Chapter 3

ogy edited by Yvonne Sherwood and Kevin Hart, *Derrida and Religion: Other Testaments* (New York: Routledge, 2005).

40. Jean-Luc Nancy, *Noli Me Tangere: On the Raising of the Body*, trans. Sarah Clift, Pascale-Anne Brault, and Michael Naas (New York: Fordham University Press, 2008), 13–14.

41. Ibid., 48.

42. Ibid., 13.

43. Ibid., 37.

44. Ibid.

45. Rivera, *The Touch of Transcendence: A Postcolonial Theology of God* (Louisville, KY: Westminster John Knox Press, 2007), 5. Although Rivera draws on Nancy and Derrida, she refers her sense of touch not to them but to Irigaray's concept of *"touching upon"*, which is "a touching which respects the other", giving the other attentiveness and "a call to co-exist", never subjecting the other to "appropriation, capture, seduction—to me, toward me, in me—nor envelopment". Irigaray, *I Love to You: Sketch for a Possible Felicity in History*, trans. Alison Martin (New York: Routledge, 1996), 124–25.

46. Faber, "Becoming Intermezzo: Eco-Theopoetics after the Anthropic Principle," in *Theopoetic Folds: Philosophizing Multifariousness*, eds. Roland Faber and Jeremy Fackenthal (New York: Fordham University Press, 2013), 230.

47. Thomas Berry, *The Dream of the Earth* (San Francisco: Sierra Club Books, 1988), 123.

48. Ibid.

49. John Sallis, *Chorology: On Beginning in Plato's Timaeus* (Bloomington: Indiana University Press, 1999), 39, 118–20; Plato, *Timaeus*, trans. R. G. Bury (Cambridge: Harvard University Press, 2005), 26c–e, 52b.

50. Gregory Bateson, *Mind and Nature: A Necessary Unity* (New York: Dutton, 1979), 12.

51. On the ecological importance of embodied storytelling and the problematic separation of language from the sensuous world, see David Abram's popular work of ecophenomenology. Abram, *The Spell of the Sensuous: Perception and Language in a More-Than-Human World* (New York: Vintage Books, 1997).

52. Watts and Peet, "Towards a Theory of Liberation Ecology," in *Liberation Ecologies: Environment, Development, Social Movements*, eds. Richard Peet and Michael Watts (London: Routledge, 1996), 263. It should be noted that this essay by Watts and Peet appears only in the first edition of *Liberation Ecologies*.

53. Ibid.

54. Watts and Peet, "Liberating Political Ecology," in *Liberation Ecologies: Environment, Development, Social Movements*, 2nd ed., eds. Richard Peet and Michael Watts (London: Routledge, 2004), 15.

55. John Sallis, *Force of Imagination: The Sense of the Elemental* (Bloomington: Indiana University Press, 2000), 25, 172.

56. David Wood, "Specters of Derrida: On the Way to Econstruction," in *Ecospirit: Religions and Philosophies for the Earth*, eds. Laurel Kearns and Catherine Keller (New York: Fordham University Press, 2007), 286. Moreover, ecological deconstruction is not opposed to Derrida's sense of deconstruction but is actually implicit in Derrida's work, as Wood notices in Derrida's accounts of the alterity of animals, including an account of Derrida's own experience of "a face-to-face relation to his cat" (64). Timothy Morton's work also exemplifies ecological deconstruction. Promoting connections between ecology and deconstruction, Morton draws on Derrida to propose an ecology that is "without" the stable, self-identical, totalized background called "Nature" (Morton, *Ecology without Nature: Rethinking Environmental Aesthetics* [Cambridge: Harvard Uni-

versity Press, 2007], 6, 21, 48). Morton also adapts Derrida's conception of alterity to argue that ecology needs to recognize that beings are interconnected in a vast "mesh" and that those beings are uncanny, other, "the *strange stranger*" (Morton, *The Ecological Thought* [Cambridge: Harvard University Press, 2014], 40–41, 143n72). This ecological dimension of deconstruction shows that Derrida's work is not opposed to engagements with the real world or engagements with the natural sciences. This is further demonstrated in Michael Marder's account of Derrida as a postdeconstructive realist and in Vicki Kirby's use of deconstruction to conceptualize mathematics, biology, physics, and systems theories (Marder, *Event of the Thing: Derrida's Post-Deconstructive Realism* [Toronto: Toronto University Press, 2009]; Kirby, *Quantum Anthropologies: Life at Large* [Durham: Duke University Press, 2011]).

57. Sallis, *Force of Imagination*, 8. The word *phenomenology* is derived from the Greek words *phainomenon* and *logos*, with the former deriving from *phainesthai* ("to show itself"). Phenomenology is thus a discourse (*logos*) on that which shows itself. According to Heidegger's account of the etymological derivation of the word, phenomenology is a way of letting phenomena show themselves in their self-showing: *phenomenology* means "to let that which shows itself be seen from itself in the very way in which it shows itself from itself" (Heidegger, *Being and Time*, trans. John Macquarrie and Edward Robinson [New York: Harper & Row, 1962], 58).

58. Gaston Bachelard, *Poetics of Space*, trans. Maria Jolas (Boston: Beacon Press, 1994), 184.

59. The idea of "deconstructive phenomenology" comes from David Wood, *The Step Back: Ethics and Politics after Deconstruction* (Albany: SUNY Press, 2005), 131–37.

60. Sallis, *Force of Imagination*, 42.

61. According to Sallis, Fichte describes imagination as a "hovering" (*Schweben*), such that imagination "endeavors to unify what is not unifiable" by hovering "between determination and nondetermination". Sallis, *Force of Imagination*, 127. Imagination gathers together the monstrosity of sense by hovering between its various determinations and not resting with any one of them.

62. Ibid., 138–39.

63. Faber, "Becoming Intermezzo", 222, 228, 233.

64. Sallis, *Force of Imagination*, 158.

65. Ibid., 154–55.

66. Ibid., 153–54.

67. It is clear from Empedocles's writings that he uses these divine names to refer to the elements, yet there is no scholarly consensus on exactly which gods are correlated with which elements (Macauley, "The Flowering of Environmental Roots and the Four Elements in Presocratic Philosophy: From Empedocles to Deleuze and Guattari," *Worldviews* 9.3 [2005]: 284).

68. Ibid., 292.

69. Ibid., 282–83.

70. Such an ecologically engaged elemental philosophy is proposed in Macauley, *Elemental Philosophy: Earth, Air, Fire, and Water as Environmental Ideas* (Albany: SUNY Press, 2010).

71. Macauley, "Flowering of Environmental Roots", 282.

72. James D. Mauseth, *Botany: An Introduction to Plant Biology*, 4th ed. (Sudbury: Jones and Bartlett Publishers, 2009), 17, 88–118.

73. Deleuze and Guattari, *A Thousand Plateaus: Capitalism and Schizophrenia*, trans. Brian Massumi (Minneapolis: University of Minnesota Press, 1987), 6.

74. *A Thousand Plateaus* is itself a rhizome: "We are writing this book as a rhizome" (ibid., 22). A similar statement is made in D&G's work, *Kafka: Toward a Minor Literature*, trans. Dana Polan (Minneapolis: University of Minnesota Press, 1986): "This work is a rhizome" (3).
75. Deleuze and Guattari, *A Thousand Plateaus*, 7.
76. Ibid., 7.
77. Ibid., 35.
78. Ibid., 8–9. The "flight" of a line of flight translates the French "fuite", which has connotations of escaping, eluding, fleeing, flowing, disappearing, and leaking (xvi). Although the term does not imply the sense of flying expressed in the English word *flight*, it does not necessarily preclude a connotation with flying. Thus, D&G express a magical sense of flying when they discuss the decoding lines followed in the "dangerous exercise" called "thinking": "To think is always to follow the witch's flight" (Deleuze and Guattari, *What Is Philosophy?* trans. Hugh Tomlinson and Graham Burchell [New York: Columbia University Press, 1994], 41).
79. Deleuze and Guattari, *A Thousand Plateaus*, 9.
80. Ibid., 9–10.
81. Deleuze and Guattari, *Kafka*, 4.
82. Deleuze and Guattari, *A Thousand Plateaus*, 161.
83. Ibid., 10.
84. Ibid. This rhizomatic evolution also happens between the world and a book: "The book assures the deterritorialization of the world, but the world effects a reterritorialization of the book, which in turn deterritorializes itself in the world (if it is capable, if it can)" (ibid., 11).
85. Ibid., 11.
86. Ibid., 12.
87. Ibid., 12–13.
88. Ibid., 13, 15.
89. Ibid., 21.
90. Ibid.
91. Ibid., 19.
92. Higgins, "Becoming through Multiplicity", 145.
93. Deleuze and Guattari, *A Thousand Plateaus*, 17.
94. Ibid., 20.
95. Ibid., 21.
96. Ibid., 20. As an example of a rhizomatic offshoot of a tree, D&G mention the tree under which the Buddha attained enlightenment: "Buddha's tree itself becomes a rhizome" (ibid., 20).
97. In her proposal for adapting D&G's rhizome for conceptualizing complexity in natural systems, Beth Dempster suggests that the rhizome resonates with the relational and interactive "no-boundary-thinking" articulated by the Integral theorist Ken Wilber. Dempster, "Boundarylessness: Introducing a Systems Heuristic for Conceptualizing Complexity," in *Nature's Edge: Boundary Explorations in Ecological Theory and Practice*, eds. Charles S. Brown and Ted Toadvine (Albany: SUNY Press, 2007), 95–99, 105–8. For Wilber's account of boundaries and of the boundarylessness of ultimate reality, see Wilber, *No Boundary: Eastern and Western Approaches to Personal Growth* (Boston: Shambhala, 2001).
98. Deleuze and Guattari, *A Thousand Plateaus*, 25.
99. Deleuze, "Response to a Series of Questions," *Collapse* 3 (2007): 42. As a pure metaphysician, Deleuze mentions that he follows Bergson ("I am Bergsonian") in attempting to find the metaphysics for contemporary science, and he also says that the categories expressed in *A Thousand Plateaus* are not Kantian

but are proposed "in the style of Whitehead" (ibid., 41). To put it another way, Deleuze's metaphysics follows the lines of process philosophy.

100. Deleuze and Guattari, *A Thousand Plateaus*, 25.
101. Higgins, "Becoming through Multiplicity", 154.
102. Deleuze and Guattari, *A Thousand Plateaus*, 25.
103. Gilles Deleuze and Claire Parnet, *Dialogues*, 2nd ed., trans. Hugh Tomlinson and Barbara Habberjam (New York: Columbia University Press, 2002), 57.
104. Deleuze and Guattari, *A Thousand Plateaus*, 25.
105. Thich Nhat Hanh, *Interbeing: Fourteen Guidelines for Engaged Buddhism* (Berkeley, CA: Parallax Press, 1998), 27. *Interbeing* translates the Vietnamese *tiep hien*: *tiep* means "being in touch with" and "continuing." *Hien* means "realizing" and "making it here and now" (3). Moreover, interbeing is not merely an abstract principle, but is something that Nhat Hanh practises, as indicated by his work as a founder in the mid-1960s of a Buddhist order (the "Order of Interbeing") committed to the principle of interbeing (vii). It is important to note that the implications of dependent coarising for ecology and environmental ethics are contested, and that there is no consensus or single interpretation seen as authoritative (Pragati Sahni, *Environmental Ethics in Buddhism: A Virtues Approach* [New York: Routledge, 2008], 17–20).
106. Charles Taliaferro, "Vices and Virtues in Religious Environmental Ethics," in *Environmental Virtue Ethics*, eds. Ronald Sandler and Philip Cafaro (Lanham: Rowman & Littlefield, 2005), 166.
107. Hwa Yol Jung, *The Way of Ecopiety: Essays in Transversal Geophilosophy* (New York: Global Scholarly Publications, 2009), 14, 103.
108. Ibid., 19, 14.
109. Mark Bonta and John Protevi, *Deleuze and Geophilosophy: A Guide and Glossary* (Edinburgh: Edinburgh University Press, 2004), 3–5.
110. Deleuze and Guattari, *What Is Philosophy?*, 85.
111. Ibid., 99.
112. Ibid., 111.
113. Ibid., 96.
114. Ibid., 110.
115. Deleuze and Guattari, *A Thousand Plateaus*, 293. The "middle is by no means an average; on the contrary, it is where things pick up speed" (25).
116. Ibid., 11, 25.
117. Ibid., 297.
118. Calvin O. Schrag, *The Resources of Rationality: A Response to the Postmodern Challenge* (Bloomington: Indiana University Press, 1992), 152–53.
119. Leonardo Boff, *Cry of the Earth, Cry of the Poor*, trans. Phillip Berryman (Maryknoll: Orbis Books, 1997), 4; Mark Hathaway and Leonardo Boff, *The Tao of Liberation: Exploring the Ecology of Transformation* (Maryknoll: Orbis Books, 2009), 337. Boff's and Guattari's concepts of transversality are also discussed in the introduction to the present work.
120. Hwa Yol Jung, *Way of Ecopiety*, 10. Hwa Yol Jung here is adapting the formula of *omnicentrism* (i.e., "center is everywhere" and "circumference nowhere"), which is discussed in detail below in the section of the same name.
121. Deleuze and Guattari, *A Thousand Plateaus*, 24.
122. Deleuze and Guattari, *Kafka*, 26–27.
123. Deleuze, *Difference and Repetition*, trans. Paul Patton (New York: Columbia University Press, 1994), 243.
124. I am alluding here to Charles Baudelaire's prose-poem, "Crowds" ("*Les Foules*"), which begins with the following: "It is not given to every man to take a bath of multitude: to play upon crowds is an art" (Baudelaire, "Crowds", in

Baudelaire: His Prose and Poetry, ed. T. R. Smith [New York: Boni and Liveright, 1919], 46).

125. One example of an account of the ecological implications of pop culture comes from Noël Sturgeon, who focuses on images of nature in pop culture, particularly in light of the naturalization of social inequality, which can be seen in images that associate women with nature (e.g., "Mother Nature") or images that identify indigenous people with a more "natural" (and less civilized) way of life (Sturgeon, *Environmentalism in Popular Culture: Gender, Race, Sexuality, and the Politics of the Natural* [Tuscon: University of Arizona Press, 2009]).

126. J. R. R. Tolkien, *The Fellowship of the Ring* (London: Unwin Hyman, 1966), 182, 184, 260.

127. Deleuze and Guattari, *A Thousand Plateaus*, 25, 48.

128. Ibid., 382.

129. Nomadology articulates vague essences "in the etymological sense of 'vagabond': it is neither inexact like sensible things nor exact like ideal essences, but *an exact yet rigorous*" (ibid., 367). D&G's concept of nomadic essences draws on Husserl's discovery of "a region of *vague and material* essences (in other words, essences that are vagabond, an exact and yet rigorous)", which are "fuzzy aggregates" relating to a liminal process ("passage to the limit") irreducible to either term of the intelligible/sensible dualism (407). D&G take the terminology of "rigorous, anexact" from Michel Serres, *The Parasite*, trans. Lawrence R. Schehr (Minneapolis: University of Minnesota Press, 2007, 555).

130. Ibid., 203.

131. Ibid., 202.

132. Ibid., 367, 362–64.

133. Deleuze, *Logic of Sense*, 77, 102, 107, 113–14.

134. Deleuze, *The Fold: Leibniz and the Baroque*, trans. Tom Conley (Minneapolis: University of Minnesota Press, 1992), 78.

135. Alfred North Whitehead, *Process and Reality: An Essay in Cosmology*, corr. edition eds. David Ray Griffin and Donald W. Sherburne (New York: Free Press, 1978), 80. Whitehead says that he "adopted the term 'prehension,' to express the activity whereby an actual entity effects its own concretion" (52). Every prehension involves a prehending or feeling entity, a prehended datum, and the "subjective form" (the "how") whereby the entity prehends (23). Drawing on Whitehead, Deleuze describes an event as a "nexus of prehensions" and all prehension is "*already* the prehension of another prehension. [. . .] Prehension is naturally open, open onto the world, without having to pass through a window" (Deleuze, *Fold*, 78, 81).

136. Alfred North Whitehead, *Adventures of Ideas* (New York: Free Press, 1967), 133–34.

137. Alfred North Whitehead, *Science and the Modern World* (New York: Free Press, 1967), 207.

138. Catherine Keller, "Process and Chaosmos: The Whiteheadian Fold in the Discourse of Difference," in *Process and Difference: Between Cosmological and Poststructuralist Postmodernisms*, eds. Catherine Keller and Anne Daniell (Albany: SUNY Press, 2002), 56, 59–60.

139. Deleuze, *Empiricism and Subjectivity: An Essay on Hume's Theory of Human Nature*, trans. Constantin V. Boundas (New York: Columbia University Press, 1991), 99.

140. Whitehead, *Process and Reality*, 24.

141. Jacques Derrida, *The Gift of Death*, trans. David Wills (Chicago: University of Chicago Press, 1995), 78.

142. Roland Faber, "Surrationality and Chaosmos: For a More Deleuzian Whitehead (with a Butlerian Intervention)," in *Secrets of Becoming: Negotiating Whitehead, Deleuze, and Butler*, eds. Roland Faber and Andrea M. Stephenson (New York: Fordham University Press, 2011), 174; Deleuze and Guattari, *A Thousand Plateaus*, 20.

143. Ian Bogost, "Process vs. Procedure", paper presented at the Whitehead Research Project Conference, Claremont, California, December 2–4, 2010.

144. Faber, "Surrationality and Chaosmos", 177. Yet this formulation could be reversed, as Deleuze's relentless emphasis on multiplicity and difference favors pluralism in contrast to Whitehead's more monistic and monotheistic language of process, creativity, and God.

145. Whitehead, *Process and Reality*, 35.

146. Proponents of object-oriented ontology (OOO) attempt to give an answer to this question. They abandon the magic formula and side with pluralism of objects (not objects as opposed to subjects, but units or actors that entangle the subjective/interior and the objective/exterior). For instance, Levi Bryant's approach to OOO draws heavily from Deleuze, although he shifts away from what he considers Deleuze's schizophrenic ambivalence between monism and pluralism and moves towards an explicitly pluralist ontology, for which the virtual becoming of an object is not one preindividual continuum but is a dimension of the individual object (Bryant, *The Democracy of Objects* [Ann Arbor: Open Humanities Press, 2011], 94). Similarly, describing the metaphysics of actors articulated by Bruno Latour, Graham Harman claims that Latour is separated from Deleuze and Bergson insofar as the latter do not believe that "concrete actual entities are primary in the world", whereas Latour, OOO, and Whitehead ("surely Latour's closest philosophical ancestor") all posit a plurality of actual entities, such as is affirmed in Whitehead's ontological principle (Harman, *Prince of Networks: Bruno Latour and Metaphysics* [Melbourne, Australia: re.press, 2009], 101). Harman separates his own position from Whitehead and Latour in claiming that the latter identify entities with their accidents or relations and thereby fail to acknowledge a dimension of objects that withdraws from all relation (a relation without relation) (Harman, *Towards Speculative Realism: Essays and Lectures* [Winchester: Zero Books, 2010], 150). Faber has argued that Whitehead does acknowledge a dimension of actual entities in which all relations are sundered, the dimension of becoming (Roland Faber, "Touch: A Philosophic Meditation," paper presented at the Whitehead Research Project conference, Claremont, California, December 2–4, 2010). Harman's speculative realism of objects is in close contact with Whitehead's "provisional realism" or "organic realism". On provisional realism, see Whitehead, *Science and the Modern World*, 64, 68, 72, 91. On organic realism, see Whitehead, *Process and Reality*, 309.

147. The importance of pluralism for integral ecology and for Integral Theory in particular has been elaborated on by Sean Esbjörn-Hargens, who proposes "Integral Pluralism"—a pluralism of ways of being and knowing, thus including "epistemological, methodological, and ontological" pluralisms. In addressing climate change, this pluralist approach accounts for the many real objects or actors involved in climate change (e.g., carbon dioxide, methane, cars, glaciers, oceans, national economies, islands, politicians, environmental activists, fossil fuels, scientists, intergovernmental panels, free trade agreements, church groups, etc.), and it also accounts for the many ways that those actors interpret, translate, and enact one another from different perspectives (Esbjörn-Hargens, "An Ontology of Climate Change: Integral Pluralism and the Enactment of Multiple Objects", *Journal of Integral Theory and Practice* 5.1 [2010]: 146).

148. Morton, *Ecology without Nature*, 52. This is Timothy Morton's criticism of D&G's rhizome. Morton argues that concepts of the in-between are not beneficial to ecological thought insofar as they simply produce an ambience that fails to engage boundaries and differences. Morton is rightly suspicious of concepts that privilege nonhierarchical over hierarchical thinking and for any "wish to have it both ways", a wish that erases difference and risks "sheer nihilism" (54). However, as I show above, D&G's rhizome is much more complex than average or ambient concepts of the in-between. D&G's rhizome is mutually immanent with the arborescent, thus staying in the centreless centre of the dualism between dualistic oppositions and nondualistic betweens.

149. Deleuze and Guattari, *Anti-Oedipus: Capitalism and Schizophrenia*, trans. Robert Hurley, Mark Seem, and Helen R. Lane (Minneapolis: University of Minnesota Press, 1983), 311.

150. Deleuze and Guattari, *A Thousand Plateaus*, 338.

151. Haraway, *When Species Meet* (Minneapolis: University of Minnesota Press, 2008), 27–30. D&G discuss "becoming-animal" throughout *A Thousand Plateaus*, particularly in the tenth chapter, "1730: Becoming-Intense, Becoming-Animal, Becoming-Imperceptible . . ." (232–309).

152. Haraway, *When Species Meet*, 27–28.

153. Ibid., 10.

154. Deleuze and Guattari, *A Thousand Plateaus*, 245.

155. Ibid., 244.

156. Haraway, *When Species Meet*, 27.

157. Ibid., 28.

158. Ibid.

159. Deleuze and Guattari, *A Thousand Plateaus*, 28.

160. Ibid., 26.

161. Haraway, *When Species Meet*, 29.

162. Ibid., 36.

163. Deleuze and Guattari, *A Thousand Plateaus*, 240, 244.

164. Morton, *Ecological Thought*, 85–86.

165. Deleuze and Guattari, *A Thousand Plateaus*, 23.

166. Deleuze, *Difference and Repetition*, xxi. The decentred centre of rhizomatics is not unlike Morin's proposal for a "grand bricolage" that accounts for the complex intertwining of centrism, polycentrism, and acentrism, which also implies the intertwining of the correlative concepts of hierarchy, heterarchy, and anarchy. This aspect of Morin's thought is described by Kelly, "Participation, Complexity, and the Study of Religion," in *The Participatory Turn: Spirituality, Mysticism, Religious Studies*, eds. Jorge Ferrer and Jacob Sherman (Albany: SUNY Press, 2008), 126.

167. Nietzsche, *Thus Spoke Zarathustra*, 234.

168. Serres, *Parasite*, 225–6.

169. Ibid., 225.

170. Bruno Latour, *We Have Never Been Modern*, trans. Catherine Porter (Cambridge: Harvard University Press, 1993), 51.

171. Bruno Latour, *Politics of Nature: How to Bring the Sciences into Democracy*, trans. Catherine Porter (Cambridge: Harvard University Press, 2004), 237.

172. Ibid., 22–24.

173. Ibid.

174. Philip Kuberski, *Chaosmos: Literature, Science, and Theory* (Albany: SUNY Press, 1994), 76; Catherine Keller, *Face of the Deep: A Theology of Becoming* (New York: Routledge, 2003), 243.

175. This formula appeared as early as a twelfth-century pseudo-Hermetic book of anonymous philosophical contributions (*The Book of the XXIV Philosophers*), but Cusa and Bruno develop their concepts without any reference to this pseudo-Hermetic text. Edward S. Casey, *The Fate of Place: A Philosophical History* (Berkeley: University of California Press, 1997), 116–17. Germinal expressions of the omnicentric formula can surely be found earlier than the twelfth century, and the formula is also repeated in numerous modern philosophers, from Pascal to Nietzsche. However, my intention here is not to give a genealogy of omnicentric concepts but to map omnicentrism onto the philosophy of integral ecology.

176. Nicholas of Cusa, "On Learned Ignorance," in *Nicholas of Cusa: Selected Spiritual Writings*, trans. H. Lawrence Bond (New York: Paulist Press, 1997), 161.

177. Ibid.

178. Cusa, "On Learned Ignorance", 91–92.

179. Ibid., 160.

180. Ibid., 140.

181. Ibid., 130–31, 138.

182. Ibid., 134, 139.

183. Ibid., 141.

184. According to Cusa, insofar "as God is the enfolding" of things, "in God all things are God", and insofar "as God is the unfolding, God is in all things that which they are" (ibid., 137).

185. Giordano Bruno, *Cause, Principle and Unity: And Essays on Magic*, trans. Richard J. Blackwell and Robert de Lucca (New York: Cambridge University Press, 1998), 10. According to Bruno, "We may certainly affirm that the universe is entirely centre, or that the centre of the universe is everywhere, and the circumference nowhere insofar as it is different from the center; or else that the circumference is everywhere, but the centre is nowhere insofar as it differs from the circumference" (89).

186. Casey, *Fate of Place*, 123.

187. Keller, *Face of the Deep*, 231. Also see Keller, "Rumors of Transcendence: The Movement, State, and Sex of 'Beyond'", in *Transcendence and Beyond: A Postmodern Inquiry*, eds. John D. Caputo and Michael J. Scanlon (Bloomington: Indiana University Press, 2007), 143.

188. Deleuze, *Difference and Repetition*, 123.

189. Deleuze, *Fold*, 23f, 146n23.

190. Ibid., 23. "Explication-implication-complication form the triad of the fold, following the variations of the relation of the One-Multiple" (24).

191. Deleuze distinguishes between *différencier* and *différentier*, the latter of which is a mathematical term with no English equivalent. The terms are commonly rendered into English respectively as *differenciation* and *differentiation*. Differenciation is a process of the actualization of individual things, whereas differentiation refers to the virtual structure of such productive difference. "We call the determination of the virtual content of an Idea differentiation; we call the actualization of that virutality into species and distinguished parts differenciation. [. . .] Whereas differentiation determines the virtual content of the Idea as problem, differenciation expressed the actualization of this virtual and the constitution of solutions (by local integrations)" (Deleuze, *Difference and Repetition*, 207, 209).

192. Ibid., 123.

193. Ibid., 124.

194. Roland Faber, "Bodies of the Void: Polyphilia and Theoplicity," in *Apophatic Bodies: Negative Theology, Incarnation, and Relationality*, eds. Chris Boesel and Catherine Keller (New York: Fordham University Press, 2010), 202, 222.

195. Keller, *Cloud of the Impossible: Theological Entanglements*, forthcoming, 35.

196. For a collection of essays detailing, on the one hand, Deleuze's hostility to transcendent and judgemental tendencies in religion and, on the other hand, the points of convergence between Deleuze's thinking and pantheism, mysticism, scholastic theology, Buddhism, Neo-Platonism, and more, see Mary Bryden, *Deleuze and Religion* (New York: Routledge, 2001). On the esoteric spirituality and occult knowledge folded into Deleuze's thought, see the works of Christian Kerslake: *Deleuze and the Unconscious* (London: Continuum, 2007); *Immanence and the Vertigo of Philosophy: From Kant to Deleuze* (Edinburgh: Edinburgh University Press, 2009). Also see Joshua Ramey, The Hermetic Deleuze: Philosophy and Spiritual Ordeal (Durham, NC: Duke University Press, 2012). For reflections on the political and ethical implications of Deleuze's spirituality, see the special issue of the journal *SubStance* focusing on Deleuze's spiritual politics (Joshua Delpech-Ramey and Paul A. Harris, "Spiritual Politics after Deleuze: Introduction", *SubStance* 39.1 (2010): 3–7). On the relevance of Deleuze to liberation theology, see Kristien Justaert, *Theology after Deleuze* (New York: Continuum, 2012).

197. Keller, "Rumors of Transcendence", 143.

198. Ibid., 143, 145.

199. Keller, *Face of the Deep*, 231.

200. Keller, "Rumors of Transcendence", 144.

201. Keller, *Face of the Deep*, 231.

202. Keller, "Rumors of Transcendence", 144.

203. Ibid., 144–45.

204. Keller, *Face of the Deep*, 232.

205. Sean Kelly, *Coming Home: The Birth and Transformation of the Planetary Era* (Great Barrington: Lindisfarne Books, 2010), 133–36.

206. Keller, "Cloud of the Impossible", 40. Like Cusa's universe in which all things are in all things, Whitehead's "provisional realism" affirms a universe of mutual immanence in which "everything is everywhere at all times", such that nothing can be reduced to its "simple location" separate from other locations (Whitehead, *Science and the Modern World*, 91). Whitehead affirms mutual immanence on philosophical and scientific grounds. Thus, reflecting on the mutual immanence implied in Plato's concept of the receptacle (*hupodoche*, i.e., *chora*), Whitehead claims that twentieth-century physical sciences are closer to the concept of the receptacle than any science had been since Plato, particularly that Plato's concept supports a sense of the universe as an active process that generates a relationship of internal connectedness between all things, "but does not impose what that relationship shall be" (Whitehead, *Adventures of Ideas*, 150). Also drawing on twentieth-century physical sciences, David Bohm posits an "*implicate* order", in which "a *total order* is contained, in some *implicit* sense, in each region of space and time", and this total order is unfolded in the arrangements of objects and events in the "explicate order" (Bohm, *Wholeness and the Implicate Order* [Boston: ARK, 1983], 149f). The universe is a seamless fabric of flowing folds; that is, "Undivided Wholeness in Flowing Movement" (11). To emphasize that the movement of the universe is "unbroken and undivided", Bohm uses the term *holomovement* (151). Furthermore, this complex movement is infinite. According to Bohm, "The holomovement enfolds and unfolds in a multidimensional order, the dimensionality of which is effectively infinite" (189).

207. Keller, "Cloud of the Impossible", 39.
208. Brian Swimme, *The Hidden Heart of the Cosmos: Humanity and the New Story* (Maryknoll: Orbis Books, 1996), 85–86.
209. Kelly, *Coming Home*, 135.
210. The first phenomenon ("the light from the beginning of time") was discovered by Arno Penzias and Robert Wilson in the 1960s, and the second phenomenon (expansion) was discovered by Edwin Hubble in the 1920s (Swimme, *Hidden Heart of the Cosmos*, 63–64, 78, 83).
211. Ibid., 83.
212. Ibid., 112.
213. Ibid., 85.
214. Kelly, *Coming Home*, 135.
215. Barbara Ann Holmes, *Race and the Cosmos: An Invitation to View the World Differently* (Harrisburg: Trinity Press, 2002), 110.
216. Anthony Weston, *The Incompleat Eco-Philosopher: Essays from the Edges of Environmental Ethics* (Albany: SUNY Press, 2009), 89–90.
217. Ibid., 106.
218. Swimme, *Hidden Heart of the Cosmos*, 84.
219. Morton, *Ecological Thought*, 80.
220. Ibid., 111.
221. Thomas Berry, *The Great Work: Our Way into the Future* (New York: Bell Tower, 1999), 175.
222. Mary Evelyn Tucker, *Worldly Wonder: Religions Enter their Ecological Phase* (Chicago: Open Court Publishing, 2003), 20.
223. Ibid.
224. White, "Historical Roots of Our Ecologic Crisis", *Science* 155 (1967): 1203–7.
225. J. Baird Callicott and Michael P. Nelson, *American Indian Environmental Ethics: An Ojibwa Case Study* (Upper Saddle River: Prentice Hall, 2004), 4.
226. Douglas J. Buege, "Ecological Noble Savage Revisited", *Environmental Ethics* 18.1 (1996): 71–88.
227. Pragati Sahni, *Environmental Ethics in Buddhism: A Virtues Approach* (New York: Routledge, 2008), 88.
228. For an overview of anthropocentrism, biocentrism, and ecocentrism, see Christine E. Gudorf and James E. Huchingson, *Boundaries: A Casebook in Environmental Ethics*, 2nd ed. (Washington, DC: Georgetown University Press, 2010), 4–15.
229. I am drawing here from Keller, who integrates insights drawn on feminist theory, depth psychology, developmental psychology, process philosophy, and religious studies (1) to articulate the distinction between "separative" and "soluble" senses of self, which is the distinction that marks the dominant partition between male and female selves (and between reason/emotion, one/many, being/becoming, etc.), and (2) to complicate that distinction with a place between separative and soluble, the "connective self", which exists in complex relationship. Neither simply separate nor continuous with the world, the connective self is open to difference, multiplicity, and the rhythmic dance of polarities. Enjoining us to experiment with such a connective sense of self, Keller asks us to "imagine the radical choreography of all sentient beings. Perhaps we can at the same time begin to retrieve, in the name of connection, those freedoms and solitudes often held under the guardianship of separate selfhood. But then our subjectivity will never be the same" (Keller, *From a Broken Web: Separation, Sexism, and Self* [Boston: Beacon Press, 1986], 6).

230. Val Plumwood, *Feminism and the Mastery of Nature* (New York: Routledge, 1993), 179.
231. Ibid., 167.
232. Ibid., 137.
233. For a more comprehensive genealogy of the term, including citations to Eliade's many uses of the term in journals and books, see Sam Mickey, "Contributions to Anthropocosmic Environmental Ethics", *Worldviews: Environment, Culture, Religion* 11.2 (2007): 226–47.
234. Mircea Eliade, *Patterns in Comparative Religion*, trans. Rosemary Sheed (Cleveland: World Publishing, 1970), 455.
235. Eliade, *Images and Symbols: Studies in Religious Symbolism*, trans. Philip Mairet (Princeton, NJ: Princeton University Press, 1991), 36.
236. Ibid., 29. For an overview of van der Leeuw's phenomenology of religion and the concept of the sacred as "wholly other", see Sam Mickey, "On the Function of the Epoche in Phenomenological Interpretations of Religion", *PhaenEx: Journal of Existential and Phenomenological Theory and Culture* 3.1 (2008): 56–81.
237. Gabriel Marcel, "Phenomenological Notes about Being in a Situation", in *Creative Fidelity*, trans. Robert Rosthal (New York: Fordham University Press, 2002), 83.
238. Marcel, *Tragic Wisdom and Beyond*, trans. Stephen Jolin and Peter McCormick (Evanston: Northwestern University Press, 1973), 152. For more on the ecological implications of Heidegger's philosophy, see Bruce Foltz, *Inhabiting the Earth: Heidegger, Environmental Ethics, and the Metaphysics of Nature* (Amherst: Humanity Books, 1995).
239. Paul Ricoeur, *The Symbolism of Evil*, trans. Emerson Buchanan (New York: Harper & Row, 1967), 11–14.
240. Ibid., 10.
241. Bachelard, *Poetics of Space*, 47.
242. Ibid., 3.
243. Ibid., 22, 47.
244. Ibid., 183–85.
245. Bachelard, *The Poetics of Reverie: Childhood, Language, and the Cosmos*, trans. Daniel Russell (Boston: Beacon Press, 1971), 123.
246. Bachelard, *Poetics of Space*, 4.
247. Deleuze and Guattari, *A Thousand Plateaus*, 249.
248. Deleuze and Guattari, *What Is Philosophy?*, 169.
249. Ibid, 169. "Contraction is not an action but a pure passion, a contemplation that preserves the before in the after. [. . .] Contemplating is creating, the mystery of passive creation, sensation" (ibid., 212). Contemplation is not something that happens between humans and the world exclusively. It happens between all of the nomads traversing the folds of the chaosmos, "not only people and animals but plants, the earth, and rocks. [. . .] The plant contemplates by contracting the elements from which it originates—light, carbon, and the salts—and it fills itself with colors and odours that in each case qualify its variety, its composition: it is sensation in itself" (ibid.).
250. Weiming Tu, *Centrality and Commonality: An Essay on Chung-Yung* (Honolulu: University Press of Hawaii, 1976), 8; *Confucian Thought: Selfhood as Creative Transformation* (Albany: State University of New York Press, 1985), 64.
251. Tu, *Confucian Thought*, 10, 73–75, 137.
252. Weiming Tu, "The Ecological Turn in New Confucian Humanism: Implications for China and the World", *Daedalus* 130.4 (2001): 243–64.

253. For an overview of Chinese models of "ecological civilization", including the cooperative relationship that leaders and scholars in China are building with scholars of Whitehead and process thought, see Jay McDaniel, "Ecological Civilization", Jesus, Jazz, and Buddhism, http://www.jesusjazzbuddhism.org/ecological-civilization.html.

254. James Miller, "Envisioning the Daoist Body in the Cosmic Economy of Power", *Daedalus* 130.4 (2001): 279.

255. William Chittick, *The Heart of Islamic Philosophy: The Quest for Self-Knowledge in the Teachings of Afḍal al-dīn Kāshānī* (Oxford: Oxford University Press, 2001), 65–67, 316; "The Anthropocosmic Vision in Islamic Thought," in *God, Life and the Cosmos*, eds. Ted Peters, Muzaffar Iqbal, and Syed Nomanul Haq (Burlington: Ashgate, 2002).

256. Chittick, "Anthropocosmic Vision in Islamic Thought", 149.

257. Tucker, *Worldly Wonder*, 48.

258. Ibid., 49.

259. Ibid., 52, 98.

260. Ibid., 52.

FOUR
Ending

The Earth community is undergoing an ecological crisis. Trillions of beings face unprecedented risks and challenges. The material-semiotic multiplicities of the world are becoming threatened, endangered, extinct. This crisis is not only a crisis of natural environments but also a crisis of cultures and subjects. The crisis is transforming the very concepts with which humans live their lives and participate in the unfolding universe, including concepts that are themselves contributing factors in the ecological crisis. Morin aptly describes this aspect of the crisis in his observation that "it is obviously the whole structure of the system of thought that is finding itself thoroughly shaken and transformed. It is the whole of an enormous superstructure of ideas that is collapsing. This is what we must prepare for".[1] The challenge of a philosophy of integral ecology is to prepare—to empower responses to the ecological crisis by enacting creative and experimental encounters with concepts, engendering new concepts, and thereby opening up new possibilities for participating in planetary coexistence. It is the same challenge expressed by Tucker and Swimme in their call for a planetary civilization.

> The challenge now is to construct a responsive civilization that is truly planetary in its scope and sustainable in its functioning. [. . .] Beyond world wars and the cold war, there beckons the sense of a larger planetary whole—an emerging, multiform, planetary civilization. It is in participating in this transition mo-

ment that we will fulfill our role as humans on behalf of future generations.[2]

Some people might wonder whether this planetary response to the ecological crisis has started yet. Has this momentous transition to a new civilization already begun? Maybe, but even if that is the case, it nonetheless seems like the unsustainable civilization responsible for the ecological crisis has not finished ending. Indeed, some people wonder whether the ecological crisis has really started yet.

If the worst is still ahead, maybe we are only beginning to enter the crisis. Or are we already inside of it? Or is it already over and giving way to an emerging planetary civilization? The ecological thinker Timothy Morton notices that even asking such questions is indicative of how deeply immersed in this crisis we already are. There are still a lot of humans who think that they can attain some transcendent position to clearly determine to what extent we are in an ecological crisis. "The very worry about whether we are inside or outside becomes a symptom of how far *inside* we have gone—the inside/outside distinction has itself begun to be corroded".[3] The ecological crisis we are in is not an emergency happening out there to some singular thing called "Nature"—the background of human existence. There is no such "Nature".[4] We are inside the ecological crisis precisely insofar as we are forced to face the reality that there is no stable background clearly distinguished from a foreground. Upheavals traversing environments, cultures, and consciousness are forcing humans to face the perplexing complexity of foreground/background, inside/outside, and other dualisms (human/nature, science/society, organic/technological, facts/values, dualism/nondualism, etc.).

Deep inside our planetary ecological crisis, one hears apocalyptic tones from environmentalists. As Morton mentions, environmentalism "warns of, and wards off, the end of the world".[5] Again, the crisis is not so simple. Being inside the ecological crisis, the end of the world is not merely a future possibility or a present event. To be sure, it is both of those, and it is also more. It is something that has been happening, which is to say, "The end of the world has already happened. We sprayed the DDT. We exploded the nuclear bombs. We changed the climate. This is what it looks like after the end of the world. Today is not the end of history. We're living at the beginning of history".[6] As T. S. Eliot says, "to make an end is to make a beginning. / The end is where we start from".[7] The "end of the world" here does not just mean the end of the world as we humans know it. It does not refer only to the end of some species and ecosystems, the end of some cultures and languages, the end of the Cenozoic era. The scope of this end is infinite. To say that the end of the world has happened is to say that there is "no longer any sense of the world", as Nancy says, "no longer a *mundus*, a *cosmos*, a composed and complete order (from) within which one might find a place, a dwelling, and the elements of an orientation [. . .] no longer the "down here" of a world one could pass through toward a beyond or outside of this world".[8] We have lost the sense of the world ("beyond") along with the world of sense ("down here"). The modern era bore witness to the death of God and Nature. "*Along with the true world, we have also done away with the apparent*"![9]

We have lost the world, yet that loss is not over and done with. We are "after the End of the World", as Morton says.[10] However, what Morton does not say is that there is more than one way to be after something. After can be a matter of subsequence (e.g., tomorrow is after today), and it can also be a matter of seeking something or trailing along behind it (e.g., a predator is after prey). It is in that dual sense that we are after the past and after the future, a (non)sense moving in both directions at once. We are following the end of the world like tomorrow follows today and seeking it like predators follow prey, or perhaps more appropriately, like lovers follow their beloveds. It is tempting to put the end behind us and get it out of our future, but that would only amount to an inverse end, an end to all this talk of the end. No matter how much we want to, we cannot simply disavow the end of the world or relegate it to the past. Perhaps we will always be after the end of the world, and so we cannot just drop the end. In any case, there is nowhere to drop it off, no "away" to throw it. We're here in the middle of the world's ending, going after it. The end of the world is still unfolding into the meanings and matters of planetary existence: carbon dioxide emissions are increasing worldwide, evermore species and populations are going extinct, poverty and social unrest are spreading, cultural diversity is becoming homogenized, and freshwater is becoming increasingly scarce. The world ended, and we continue to live at its ending, inhabiting a world on edge.[11] Perhaps there is some good news at the end of the world: it compels humans to give up any pretension to dissociate from and control the rhizomatic boundaries of the chaosmos. Hopefully, this end opens new possibilities for humans to participate in the chaosmos in a way that affirms its whirling multiplicities instead of assimilating them into dualisms of truth/appearance, intelligible/sensible, spiritual/material, being/becoming.

The end of the world opens up new practises in which humans can participate in a world that does not have sense, but is sense. Accordingly, while we are mourning the loss of lives, livelihoods, ecosystems, cultures, and others, there is also room for gratitude, for the loss of the world opens possibilities for another world, a more democratic world not partitioned into the hierarchies that mark the logic of colonization. Consider Latour's political ecology, which celebrates the death of Nature (and of "God" and "man"). "Thank God, nature is going to die. Yes, the great Pan is dead. After the death of God and the death of man, nature, too, had to give up the ghost. It was time: we were about to be unable to engage in politics any more at all".[12] The reified totality of Nature short-circuits processes of experimentation and questioning. It oversimplifies the tangled rhizomes of ecology. What is needed now is for all humans not simply to gather together and say, "Let us protect nature"! but to stay amidst the perplexity of the experimental "situation of ignorance", saying, "No one knows what an environment can do".[13] This resonates with Deleuze, who follows Spinoza in calling out to us: "You do not know beforehand what good or bad you are capable of; you do not know beforehand what a body or a mind can do, in a given encounter, a given arrangement, a given combination".[14] In other words, "We do not even know what a body *can do* [. . .] what a body is capable of, what forces belong to it or what they are preparing for".[15] This situation of ignorance opens up new ways of engaging the body as a "relationship of forces", "a multiple phenomenon", and it thereby initiates "a new direction for the sciences and philosophy".[16]

The end of the world is the beginning of the democratic work of political ecology. The good news about the ecological crisis is precisely that it enables us to become ecological, affirming a complex relationality that displaces the logic of domination that pitted God against Nature, meaning against matter, transcendence against immanence. Displacing the logic of domination, humans are coming home to their place in the chaosmos. "Getting back into place", as Ed Casey says, is "the homecoming that matters most", and it "is an ongoing task that calls for continual journeying between and among places. [. . .] As travelers on such a voyage, we can resume the direction, and regain the depth, of our individual and collective life once again—and know it for the first time".[17] At the end of the world, we are beginning (again), getting (back) into the sense of the world. That sounds like good, if troubling, news. It is troubling to say that there is any good news in the suffering of real beings, especially when that suffering is undue or unjust. Indeed, there is something deeply troubling about all of this edgy "end of the world" talk. It resonates with violent tendencies of fanaticism, fundamentalism, terrorism, and militarism. More specifically, it resonates with the tones of apocalypse—the "disclosure" or "revelation" (*apokalupsis*) of the end of an unjust and destructive world and a hope for the arrival of a just world, a hope described in the book of Revelation as an expectation of the advent of "a new Heaven and a new Earth" where anyone who is thirsty can "come" and drink "the water of life" (Rev. 21:1–6, 22:17).

Although apocalypse might not seem like a crucial issue for integral ecology, there are actually many ways in which something like an apocalyptic tendency or predisposition becomes manifest in the responses people have to ecological problems. Consider a problem like the global crisis of freshwater scarcity.[18] There are many ways that people criticize the global injustices of water resource management while calling for the arrival of equitable and just water management. While some people call for privatization and free trade, others are criticizing privatization and promoting the democratization that represents water as a commons. Although these responses to global water issues do not necessarily seem apocalyptic, they do indeed harbour apocalyptic tendencies. They manifest what Keller refers to as an *"apocalypse script"*, *"apocalypse habit"* or, more generally, an *"apocalypse pattern"*.[19] These expressions are similar to Derrida's concept of an "apocalyptic *pli* [fold, envelope, letter, habit, message]"—a habit or script that brings forth apocalyptic tones, which convey an announcement or arrival of catastrophes that mark the end of the world, and like a double-edged sword, they also convey a desire for the vigilance of truth and light.[20]

We are all participants in the apocalyptic fold, some of us more wittingly than others. Apocalyptic tones resonate in any call for an end, for a new beginning, or for a decisive distinction separating the new from the old, the good from the evil, the innocent from the guilty. Even for those who are critical of the book of Revelation or critical of biblical religions or religion as such, becoming apocalyptic seems inescapable. For instance, consider the atheistic and secular aspirations of Marx, who nonetheless invoked an apocalyptic vision of a coming society that would attain "the consummated oneness in substance of man and nature—the true resurrection of nature—the naturalism of man and the humanism of nature both brought of fulfillment".[21] There is no escaping the apocalypse script. The desire to escape from apocalypse once and for all would itself be an apocalyptic desire: to end all apocalypses. Indeed, Derrida suggests that the apocalyptic *pli* might be the condition of all discourse and all experience, as every word and action addresses some other (person, thing, event), engaging the other, which, by its very otherness, remains to come.[22] Every word and every action harbours the apocalyptic call. Come! This is not unlike T. S. Eliot saying that every poem is an epitaph and every action is "a step to the block, to the fire, down the sea's throat / Or to an illegible stone: and that is where we start".[23]

In some instances, as in contemporary religious fundamentalisms, people are explicit about their tendencies to perform the script of apocalypse. In other cases, as with global economic development or scientific and technological progress, these habits are often at work implicitly or unknowingly as functions of our *"apocalyptic unconscious"*.[24] The apocalypse pattern often becomes manifest with extraordinary violence, domination, and destruction, which are supposed to usher in the arrival of a rejuvenated and just world. However, there are some examples in which apocalyptic habits promote love, justice, and partnership, while countering or minimizing the catastrophic destruction that typically characterizes the performance of the apocalypse script. For instance, the book of Revelation contains descriptions of events that devastate and ultimately annihilate the Earth, making way for the arrival of a new Earth (Rev. 8, 16, 21:1), but for the twelfth-century Christian visionary Hildegard of Bingen, the cataclysmic destruction that precedes the rejuvenation of the world is less of an annihilation and more of a constructive destruction—an apocalypse that "will be brought forth with gentle words" on the last day, when God will "wash the four elements clean".[25] To resist and overcome those aspects of the apocalypse habit that currently threaten the continuation of life on Earth, we must not escape apocalypse but repeat the apocalypse pattern with a difference, perform a more tactful script, one that resonates with an integral apocalyptic tone that calls for the emergence of a vibrant planetary civilization, which nurtures viable and mutually enhancing relations between the multifarious inhabitants and habitats of the planet. To repeat the apocalypse pattern with a difference, it is important to understand how the apocalypse habit has been performed throughout history and how those performances are being reiterated in contemporary global society. Accounting for these folds of apocalypse supports the development of a concept of the planetarity that characterizes the emerging planetary civilization, a concept that resonates with concepts of love and of the ongoing work and play of cosmopolitan democracy.

APOCALYPSE

Disclosure, revelation, uncovering, unveiling: these are all translations of the Greek word *apokalupsis*. Apocalypse can involve a catastrophic vision of the end of time or the end of the world, but more specifically, apocalypse is a matter of an unveiling or revelation, often a revelation of the sovereignty of God. The pattern of this revelation can be defined in terms of a morality that pits good and light against evil and darkness in a battle of cosmic proportions, where one identifies oneself with the good, which is oppressed and victimized by the diabolical forces of the enemy. Keller describes the apocalypse pattern in terms of an "either/or morality" that supports expectations of a catastrophe or cataclysm in which, with the aid of God or some transcendent force, good must achieve victory over evil and "live forever after in a fundamentally new world", even at the expense of the complete destruction of the current world.[26] With the continuous deferral of the final triumph of good over evil, the apocalypse script is performed with a sense of time that tends to be oriented towards the future or towards some sort of millennial expectation. With regards to apocalyptic senses of place, it is especially relevant to the present investigation to note that the apocalypse pattern has a planetary and cosmic scale, as it involves expectations of the destruction of the world and the creation of a new world. Although the global scale of the apocalypse script is evident in premodern apocalyptic texts, of which the book of Revelation is paradigmatic, performances of the apocalypse script have had increasingly global effects within the last five hundred years as processes of globalization (e.g., colonization, industrialization, and "free market" capitalism) have disseminated the values of Christianity and biblical religion throughout the entire planet. Before I discuss this globalization of the apocalypse pattern, I investigate some of the different ways this pattern has become manifest throughout its history.

Historically, the apocalypse pattern emerged from a more general eschatology pattern, which is concerned with "edges", *eskhata*— the ends of things, end times, the end of the world. Paul Hanson provides an account of how the religious perspective of apocalyptic eschatology emerged out of developments in Jewish prophetic eschatology.[27] Prophetic and apocalyptic perspectives are not mutually exclusive but are more like two poles on a continuum of eschatology. Prophetic eschatology is characterized by its visionary critique of injustice and its call for a future renewal of justice in the world. Apocalyptic eschatology also calls for justice and criticizes injustice, but it differs from prophetic eschatological perspectives in its view of the historical conditions of injustice. For prophetic eschatology, it is possible to translate the call for justice into the terms of the historical and political reality that appears unjust. For apocalyptic eschatology, which developed in the postexilic conditions of the fifth century BCE, the historical and political conditions of reality appear so inhospitable to justice that the call for justice can no longer be translated into the terms of the unjust reality. In short, for apocalyptic eschatology, the call for justice demands a final destruction of the present world. However, this is not the whole story. The apocalypse pattern evident in the developments of Jewish prophetic eschatology can lead one to turn back to inquire about early beginnings. Indeed, germinal expressions of the apocalypse pattern appear prior to prophetic eschatology. For instance, in the seventh century BCE, the moral and cosmological dualism of the apocalypse pattern is expressed by Zoroaster and his followers, for whom the history of the world is understood according to the relation between the god of goodness and light (Ahura Mazda) and the god of evil and darkness (Angra Mainyu), who battle with one another throughout a series of four trimillennial periods, culminating in the final triumph of good over evil and the regeneration of the world.[28]

The apocalyptic habit is also prefigured in the sense of place expressed by many premodern and indigenous peoples. As Keller notes, expressions of apocalyptic expectations can be found in varying degrees among peoples who are dissociated or detached from a sense of place in the cosmos, including peoples in urban environments, where alienation from nature and place is common, and nonurban peoples for whom practises of horticulture, agriculture, or nomadic pastoralism are accompanied by some sense of detachment from the environment or a sense of guilt about controlling and manipulating the environment with these practises.[29] Unlike peoples who live according to simple hunter-gatherer practises, which are relatively harmonious with natural cycles, peoples living amidst agricultural or industrial societies have a more intense and complicated impact on the environment and thus often have a deeper sense of disconnection from the world, a disconnection that is expressed through apocalyptic expectations of a new, just world to come. These apocalyptic expectations are particularly pronounced in Christian eschatology. It is within Christianity that apocalyptic writings came to be explicitly understood as such, particularly insofar as Christianity explicitly introduced a text as an *apokalupsis*: the book of Revelation in the New Testament.[30] There are innumerable interpretations and adaptations of this text, with its elaborate visions of the triumphant return of Jesus in the final battle between good and evil, and its account of the catastrophic violence, destruction, and omnicide that precede this final triumph. This text has fueled the apocalyptic habits of many famous figures throughout the history of the West, including Christopher Columbus, Isaac Newton, Joseph Priestly, Joseph Fourier, Robert Owen, William Butler Yeats, Ronald Reagan, and George W. Bush, to name but a few.[31]

The scenes described by John of Patmos in the book of Revelation are definitive expressions of the apocalypse script, particularly insofar as they disclose a strict dichotomy between good and evil and an expectation that good must ultimately triumph over the diabolical forces of evil. Evil is represented in Revelation by the imperial forces of Rome, alluded to with the misogynistic image of "the great whore" of Babylon (Rev. 17–18). Furthermore, this disclosure of an either/or morality is envisioned on a planetary scale, with earthquakes, plagues, storms of hail and fire, and other tribulations afflicting everyone and everything, including people—even those who hide—as well as mountains and islands that lose their place, waters that turn bitter or become blood, and a heaven and an Earth that are destroyed and then replaced with a new heaven and Earth (Rev. 6:12; 8; 16; 21:1). The planetary scale of these events has led many scholars to reflect on the relationship between the book of Revelation and current issues involving the global ecological crisis.[32] Different interpretations of the apocalypse script reflect different interpretations of the role of human beings in responding to problems that threaten the future of the planet, which is to say, problems that threaten the future of human individuals and communities as they are embedded in ecosystems and intertwined with the Earth as a whole. The apocalyptic implications of the global water crisis thus correspond with different interpretations of the apocalypse script. The differences between the various performances of the apocalypse script that have taken place throughout the last five hundred years of globalization can be understood in terms of some salient differences between the interpretation of apocalypse articulated by St. Augustine (354–430) and that articulated by the Italian Cistercian monk, Joachim of Fiore (1135–1202).

Augustine's interpretation of Revelation rejects any literalized reading of this text. In his *City of God*, Augustine makes a clear distinction between the city of human beings and the city of God, such that the arrival of the city of God will never literally take place in the historical reality of the city of humans. As Eugen Weber notes, Augustine's allegorical reading of Revelation held that "millenarian perfection could only be attained in another life".[33] Cataclysms and catastrophes occur regularly all over the world, but these are not to be interpreted as literal signs of the arrival of the city of God. Augustine argues that Revelation has not only been misunderstood but "has even been turned into ridiculous fables" by millenarian materialists who imagine that "those who have risen again" will indulge in "the most unrestrained material feasts".[34] According to Augustine, one need not hope for justice or salvation within the historical and earthly city of humans. Rather, the Christian faith looks ahead to what is "promised as eternal in the future, making use of earthly and temporal things like a pilgrim in a foreign land".[35] This does not mean that Augustine was entirely opposed to the possibility of any sort of immanent eschatology. In some sense, the heavenly city already arrived on Earth with the arrival of Jesus and the foundation of his church. Although the heavenly city is not yet manifest and will not arrive until the end of the earthly and temporal city of humans, this "not yet" is present "already" within the church. In 431, the Council of Ephesus adopted Augustine's position, thus making it the official position of the church: there is no collective salvation in history, and insofar as there is any earthly salvation, it is already present in the church.[36] With this gesture, the apocalypse pattern came to be interpreted in terms that emphasized not revolutionary justice but nontemporal salvation, which is represented on Earth not in an anti-imperial community but in a Christian church that, since Constantine, was allied with imperial Rome.

It is paradoxical that the anti-imperial text written by John of Patmos should be canonical within a very proimperial church. Moreover, this paradox has not gone unnoticed. Beginning at least as early as the fourteenth century, many people declared that the pope himself is the diabolic figure of the Antichrist envisioned in John's apocalyptic text. This is tantamount to associating the Messiah with the great whore of Babylon. Furthermore, such associations were not uncommon. In seventeenth-century England, it was the norm to consider the pope to be the Antichrist.[37] However, this paradoxical imperial apocalypse, which became the dominant interpretation of the history of the world, was not the only interpretation. For instance, Keller argues that the vision of apocalypse articulated by Joachim of Fiore is a presentation of an "anti-Augustinian alternative", or maybe more accurately, a counter-Augustinian alternative for the interpretation of history.[38] As Sean Kelly notes, Joachim appears to be the first person to explicitly articulate the structure of history in terms of the Christian Trinity.[39] For Joachim, salvation can occur within history, as history moves towards a "third age" by progressing from the age of the Father, to the age of the Son, and finally, to the age of the Spirit. Through elaborate speculations, Joachim correlates these three ages with the seven seals of Revelation.[40] Joachim describes the historical progression of these three ages in various ways, including the following three-fold patterns: from slavery and servitude to liberty, from fear and faith to love, from old men and young men to children, and from slaves and sons to a community of friends.[41] Patriarchal and imperial images of slavery, servitude, masculinity, and fear are thus overcome in the age of the Spirit, which is characterized by liberty, friendship, and love. In the age of the Spirit, homogenizing hegemonies give way to something different, becoming other.[42]

This apocalyptic hope for a liberated and loving community to occur within history is radically different from the proimperial interpretation of apocalypse adopted by the church from Augustine, and although it was not adopted as the official interpretation of the church, the Joachite vision has influenced many apocalyptic expectations, including those of Dante Alighieri, Saint Francis of Assisi, and the Comte de Saint-Simon.[43] Nietzsche's Zarathustra can be heard echoing the Trinitarian progression: "Once spirit was God, then it became man, and now it is even becoming mob".[44] The Joachite third age is also invoked by Deleuze, who describes *Difference and Repetition* as "an apocalyptic book (the third time in the series of times)".[45] Deleuze's apocalyptic book affirms the profound difference and complexity of the chaosmos so as "to overcome the alternatives temporal/non-temporal, historical/eternal and particular/universal", such that the third time is "more profound than time and eternity" and is more like what Nietzsche calls "the untimely".[46] Untimely philosophy involves "acting counter to our time and thereby acting on our time and, let us hope, for the benefit of a time to come".[47] The tension between the imperial (Augustinian) and counterimperial (Joachite) folds of apocalypse is evident in the performances of the apocalypse script that have taken place throughout the last five centuries of globalization, which have been sites of global imperialism as well as places of hope and love. Such places can support efforts to counter the apocalypses of our time for the benefit of becoming other, the benefit of a time to come—"the people to come and the new earth".[48]

FROM GLOBE TO PLANET

Around five hundred years ago, Christopher Columbus embarked on a series of voyages that facilitated the emergence of globalized performances of the apocalypse script. Columbus was influenced by Joachite interpretations of a coming third age, but he was less interested in the Joachite vision of an egalitarian age of the Spirit than he was in a more imperial vision that involved the colonization of the world, the commodification of resources, and the exploitation and violent oppression of women and indigenous peoples.[49] In short, a concern for conquest and the acquisition of gold preoccupied Columbus far more than did any concern for liberty, love, or friendship, although this is not to say that his missionary and messianic drive was completely devoid of authentic religious expression. This is indicative of what the economist David Korten calls the "golden rule" of Empire: "He who has the gold rules".[50] Columbus's voyages of "discovery"—another translation of *apokalupsis*—have provided a foundation for a subsequent epoch of global imperialism characterized by faith in progress and the unending conquest of paradise.

In the contemporary global situation, the processes of colonization and commodification that characterize the imperial apocalypse of Columbus have mutated, expanding their reach throughout the planet, such that colonial domination has become postcolonial and neocolonial, and commodification is now a matter of global capitalism. Furthermore, the conquest of paradise has expanded its imperial reach throughout the planet with the help of the progressive rationality of modern science and technology. This is not to say that the apocalyptic implications of colonization, global capitalism, and modern technoscience take place consciously or explicitly. Rather, the apocalyptic implications of these global processes often remain unconscious, as do the apocalyptic implications of movements that resist the hegemony of the global Empire. Furthermore, sometimes cryptoapocalyptic habits even take on explicitly antiapocalyptic tones, calling (cryptoapocalyptically) for truth and light while trying (antiapocalyptically) to eliminate any trace of an apocalyptic tone.

Before elaborating on the apocalyptic habits of the current global Empire and of movements resisting its global hegemony, it is important first to clarify what it means to refer to the current global "Empire". In defining imperial tendencies in general, Korten notes that the rule of Empire assumes the necessity of a coercively imposed social order and emphasizes "the human capacity for hatred, exclusion, competition, domination, and violence in the pursuit of domination".[51] Furthermore, the specific character of Empire today is different from the imperialism of nation-states. "Empire", which is the "new form of global sovereignty" according to the Deleuzian political philosophers Michael Hardt and Antonio Negri, is different from earlier forms of imperialism because it rules not by concentrating on a nation-state or some such "territorial center of power" that could be marked off with fixed borders, but by functioning as "a *decentered* and *deterritorializing* apparatus of rule that progressively incorporates the entire global realm within its open, expanding frontiers".[52]

Empire transgresses boundaries and limits as it incorporates the world into an interdependent network held together through militarism and economic globalization. In terms of Peter Sloterdijk's philosophical theory of globalization, empire can be described as "a planetary palace of consumption", an immense "hothouse that has drawn inwards everything that was once on the outside".[53] Empire expresses power as climate control in the planetary hothouse. To live in Empire is to live in an atmosphere of domination. Empire dominates "the entirety of social relations" while also extending "throughout the depths of the consciousness and bodies of the population".[54] Supplementing Hardt and Negri's definition of Empire, Keller adds further that Empire is not only deterritorializing, for it also expresses power through rigid borders and territorial limits, particularly through the imperial power of the United States.[55] This became particularly evident after the initial publication of *Empire* in the year 2000. Subsequent to the events of September 11, 2001, a new manifestation of Empire has emerged with an expansionist United States that is "aggressively *nationalistic* and boundary-fixated" in many of its policies, while still supporting military and economic projects that transgress modern interpretations of boundaries, laws, and borders.[56] Although Keller made that point during the administration of U.S. president George W. Bush, it is still true as I write today, during the last years of Barack Obama's administration.

The importance of boundaries for Empire is evident in postcolonial theory, which attempts to examine the use of boundaries and binaries with which colonizers have dominated subaltern peoples throughout the globe. Through the efforts of people like Columbus, modern colonialism has often identified itself with the apocalyptic light that needs to conquer the darkness and evil in the world. This is particularly evident in the Christian missionary efforts that have accompanied colonization. For example, consider the missionary activity of nineteenth-century German pietists among the Ewe-speaking people in Ghana. Rather than doubting or denying the efficacy or reality of the religious worldview of these people, the missionaries interpreted them as manifestations of the evil and diabolical darkness that must be converted to the truth and light of Christianity.[57] This apocalypse script of conversion is performed with a more secular tone in the rhetoric that describes colonized or postcolonial peoples as uncivilized others of the developing world (the Third or Fourth World), who need to be lifted up into civilization through industrialization and free market capitalism.

Like Columbus, proponents of global capitalism identify with principles of goodness and liberation as they impose on the world the values of commodification and free trade. Korten notes that faith in a global free market capitalist economy is particularly characteristic of the conservative political movement that emerged in the latter half of the twentieth century as "the New Right".[58] As a transnational movement of global exchange, acts of privatization and market deregulation by the New Right are decentred and deterritorializing processes of Empire; but in many places—the United States in particular—privatization and market regulation are also territorializing processes insofar as they attempt to secure the global hegemony of a Pax Americana—an American "peace" akin to the imposed "peace" of the Pax Romana, grounded in the hegemonic domination of an expansionist nation-state.[59] Moreover, the domination is not just a domination of humans. Global capitalism is a driving force of the ecological crisis, as its unregulated extraction and consumption of resources involves little or no concern for the profound ecological devastation that accompanies these processes.[60]

The apocalyptic pattern manifest in global capitalism is particularly evident in Francis Fukuyama's well-known neoconservative declaration that history (in a somewhat Hegelian sense of a dialectical development) has come to its end through the success of liberal democracy throughout the world in the late 1980s (especially November 9, 1989), and that "good news has come" as the economic principles of the "free market" have spread throughout the globe.[61] Fukuyama thus announces the final triumph of goodness and liberation, despite the vast number of people who have been economically disenfranchised by the capitalist deregulation of markets, and despite the collateral damage that economic development has inflicted upon the planet's ecosystems. Furthermore, Fukuyama discusses how modern technoscience "guides us to the gates of the Promised Land of liberal democracy", particularly insofar as the technological advances facilitated by the development of modern science make possible, for those who have access to them, "military advantages" and "the limitless accumulation of wealth". However, technoscience "does not deliver us to the Promised Land itself", for that can only be accomplished through economic production.[62]

As with resistance to the colonizing forces of Empire, movements to resist the capitalistic and technoscientific processes of Empire run the risk of reinforcing Empire by invoking the same apocalyptic either/or morality they are trying to resist. Rather than taking an antiapocalyptic tone, it is possible to develop a tone that Keller describes as "counter-apocalyptic", which subverts the apocalyptic script of Empire not with an antiapocalyptic script, but by consciously mimicking and overwriting the script it is subverting.[63] In short, a counterapocalyptic tone would ironically mimic and mock Empire, repeating it with a difference and not opposing it. In other words, rather than opposing the global hegemony of capitalism and technoscience, a counterapocalyptic perspective works "to tease the either/or logic of apocalypse towards a more sustainable wisdom".[64] The counterapocalypse is similar to what Derrida calls "the apocalypse *without* apocalypse", which has no eschatology except for "Come" (*Viens*)—a tone that calls for the arrival of an underivable event, the arrival of a truth that is irreducible to the dichotomies of good/evil and true/false that qualify any particular apocalypse.[65] Such a counter-apocalypse is suggested in Gayatri Chakravorty Spivak's deconstructive call for planetarity: "Today it is planetarity that we are called to imagine".[66] "Planet-thought" mimics globalization, but rather than simply supporting the globalization of capitalist commodification and technoscientific objectification, it transgresses and overwrites their global hegemony by embracing the entire range of human relations with the planet, from "aboriginal animism" to "postrational science".[67]

Spivak's deconstructive postcolonial theory works towards, on one hand, analyzing the processes whereby the entire world has been subjected to the imperial dominance of colonial power and, on the other hand, considering possibilities for subverting or countering the power of Empire.[68] Postcolonial theory often fails to counter Empire because it tends to reduce the decentred and deterritorializing power relations of global Empire to the centralized rule of imperial nations, and it tends to recapitulate the same rigid binaries and either/or morality that it seeks to subvert. To subvert the apocalypse script of Empire, postcolonial theory must account for the global scale of Empire, in its territorializing and deterritorializing aspects; and furthermore, postcolonial strategies of subversion must not be simply anti-imperial or antiapocalyptic, for such strategies would only recapitulate the either/or logic of imperial apocalypse instead of disclosing the deconstruction of that logic. As Keller rightly observes, Spivak is an example of a postcolonial thinker who adeptly articulates subversive strategies that account for the global scale of Empire while avoiding any simple either/or axioms.[69] Spivak's concept of planetarity is one such subversive strategy.

Spivak calls for those academic disciplines that cross boundaries (e.g., Comparative Literature, Area Studies) to think of themselves as "planetary" instead of thinking of themselves as "continental, global, or worldly".[70] The globe is not a space that can be inhabited. "The globe is on our computers. No one lives there".[71] The globe is the uninhabitable "gridwork of electronic capital", such that processes of globalization enact "the imposition of the same system of exchange everywhere": to live in Empire is to be colonized by "rationalized global financialization".[72] What can be done? Are passive acceptance and futile resistance the only options, or is there some other way of responding to global imperialism? Along these lines, Spivak imagines the planet. Different from (yet not opposed to) the globe, the planet is other than any mere object or calculable entity. The planet is "in the species of alterity, belonging to another system; and yet we inhabit it, on loan".[73] Other, uncanny, and different, the planet is "underived" and irreducible to any given category. Rather than simply negating or opposing the globally interconnected network Empire, Spivak proposes "the planet to overwrite the globe", which requires a "planet-talk"—a discourse of planetarity that "can work in the interest of this globalization" by engaging its decentred grids and its shifting boundaries and can also work in the interest of overcoming this global hegemony, writing over it with an "inexhaustible taxonomy" of names for the planet and for the intact alterity of its "undivided 'natural' space".[74] Planetarity is *not opposed* to the financialized globe but is much more complex. It is folded together with globalization. In other words, planetarity is complicit in the global imposition of economic exchange.[75] This means that planetarity does not necessarily entail opposition to the things normally associated with globalization, such as corporations and the privatization of natural resources.[76] Likewise, planetarity does not necessarily entail opposition to the kinds of knowledge associated with globalization, which privilege generalizations and abstract categories over particularity and concrete contexts.[77]

Spivak's sense of planetarity encourages people to imagine themselves as "planetary subjects rather than global agents, planetary creatures rather than global entities".[78] Such planetary subjects subvert the interconnectedness of global Empire not by opposing globalization, but by overwriting it with the names of another order, with the taxonomy of planetary interconnectedness. For Spivak, this planetary interconnectedness is a matter of learning to engage nature with multiple ways of knowing, from "aboriginal animism" to "postrational science".[79] This also includes theology, particularly liberation theology, as it is the approach to theology most explicitly oriented towards planetary issues of ecological justice. Furthermore, Spivak suggests that whatever planetary thinking can learn from the wisdom of animism, theology, sciences, and hybrids like "animist liberation theologies", the work of planetary transformation must be supplemented by love.[80]

PLANETARY LOVE

Describing how scholars and activists need to learn from liberation theology and from the indigenous wisdom of the "original practical ecological philosophies of the world", Spivak mentions that such "learning can only be attempted through the supplementation of collective effort by love".[81] For Spivak, the invocation of love for the sake of ecological justice is part of an effort to use the mobilizing discourse of justice not only for the uplift of the poor, the oppressed, and the Fourth World, but also for all planetary subjects. What, then, does Spivak name with the word *love*? "What deserves the name love is an effort—over which one has no control yet at which one must not strain": neither controlling nor straining, love is "slow, attentive on both sides".[82] Love patiently attends to both sides, whatever these sides might be: self and other, male and female, ecology and economy, planet and globe, science and politics, animist and theologian.

As Keller points out, Spivak is in some ways not attentive enough to both sides of this "new liberation-animist eco-hybrid", for Spivak considers Christian theology to be too complicit in religious appeals to an individualist and transcendent reality to help bring about ecological justice.[83] To an extent, Spivak's critique is valid, since Christian ideas of love are implicated in the history of colonialism, sexism, the overexploitation of the natural environment, and other forms of domination. Love is put to use by the logic of colonization, as in Platonic philosophy, which assimilates love into a dualistic hierarchy where rational love of the Idea is promoted at the expense of supposedly lower kinds of love, which are seen as inferior precisely insofar as they are material, animal, sensual, reproductive, and so on.[84] The task for philosophers and theologians is to recover a sense of love that runs counter to the logic of colonization, a planetary love that would stay in the middle and resist any logic of colonization. Such a love is invoked by Irene Klaver, who describes love as "a boundary project, an edge effect, a transition zone" that "takes the other seriously" and is therefore "a most powerful engine for transition or transformation".[85] Without love, differences are effaced in favor of sameness, and the creative becomings of transition and transformation are assimilated into a homogenizing hegemony. Love requires ongoing openness to difference and alterity. In this sense, "Love is a never-ending practice, an ongoing invitation to change, to adjust to the other. [. . .] To love is to find the transitions in boundaries".[86] Love finds naturalcultural transitions between significant others, including humans and nonhumans. Following a line from William Carlos Williams, Klaver considers the place of love at the boundary of a rose. "It is at the edge of the petal that love awaits".[87] Furthermore, love can be found in all kinds of boundaries, "not only of the charismatic rose but also of the greening of the grass. To love is to find the special in the everyday. Look: It is at the edge of the grass that love awaits".[88]

The love of the everyday finds and creates transitions between boundaries, resisting any imperial love that dominates from on high. This is the sense of love Plumwood calls for by quoting the French philosopher Simone Weil: "Let us love the land of Here Below: it is real—it offers resistance to love".[89] Morin also considers the possibility of recovering a more earthly and mortal love. "Could we not, as it were, thaw the huge amount of love petrified in religions and abstractions and devote it to the mortal, no longer to the immortal"?[90] Keller shows how expressions of Spivak's "love-supplement" can be sustained by a theology that promotes planetary love and resists Empire, more specifically, a "constructive theology of becoming", which accounts for the flows of immanence, alterity, multiplicity, impossibility, and difference in the relations between humans, the sacred, and planetary subjects.[91] Becoming more attentive to both sides of the animist-liberation hybrid, Keller engages Spivak's planetarity in terms of a "theopolitics of planetary love", which affirms planetarity in a theological context that counters the imperial tendencies of globalization by supporting a complex relational love—an *"ecology of love"*.[92] In other words, efforts to open globalization into planetarity need to be supplemented by efforts of love, and such efforts are folded into a rhizomatic complexity that is ecological ("planetary ecology") as well as spiritual (*"planetary spirituality"*).[93] Ecospiritual love is a constructive and transformative force, not merely a feeling or passion. Thus, Spivak says that love is "mindchanging on both sides", facilitating responsibility for an ethical singularity that cannot be appropriated or ascertained.[94] Love capacitates responses to the singularity of planetary subjects, and it does so with intimate contact rather than resorting to coercion, imposition, or crisis. The collective efforts of ecological justice movements are working "to change laws, relations of production, systems of education, and health care", but these efforts cannot achieve anything unless they are supplemented by love; that is, supplemented by "mind-changing one-on-one responsible contact".[95] Love is tactful contact, one-on-one, transforming both sides. Love approaches responsible contact with the ethical singularity of planetary others "when responses flow from both sides".[96] The one-on-one contact requires the lover and beloved to let one another be other, neither romanticizing the other as unconditionally admirable nor infantilizing the other as needy or as "better off" because of one's love.

Of course, introducing the word *love* may sound overly sentimental or simply frivolous in the context of ecological justice movements negotiating the boundaries of global capitalism. This is addressed by Hardt and Negri in their call for the people—more specifically, the "multitude" (i.e., people as a multiplicity)—to counter the global Empire: "People today seem unable to understand love as a political concept, but a concept of love is just what we need to grasp the constituent power of the multitude".[97] Hardt and Negri propose a "material and political sense of love", claiming "that love serves as the basis for our political projects in common and the construction of a new society. Without this love, we are nothing".[98] The forces of the multitude can work against the global Empire insofar as "being-against" Empire is a "being-for"; that is, "a resistance that becomes love and community".[99] In this sense, love is a creative force that opens up a shared world, just as D&G's wasp and orchid create a mutually transformative milieu through their love.[100] "Every act of love is an ontological event in that it marks a rupture with existing being and creates new being [. . .] it produces the common".[101] Moreover, the common is not just the human commonwealth. It is "an ecology of the common—an ecology focused equally on nature and society, on humans and the nonhuman world in a dynamic of interdependence, care, and mutual transformation".[102] Love is the transformative force by which the multitude can subvert Empire and recuperate the common.

The political sense of love vibrating in the work of Spivak, Keller, Hardt, and Negri converges in some ways with Morin's account of the history of modernization as "an evolution toward a planetary consciousness", an evolution of "the Planetary Era".[103] The awareness that humans are intertwined with the one another and with the Earth began emerging in the last five centuries through processes of imperialism, colonization, militarism, and economic globalization. These processes of modernization have been sites for the emergence of global social and ecological crises, but they have also been sites for the emergence of what Morin calls "planetary solidarity", according to which globalization becomes contextualized within the horizon of the planet.[104] Such solidarity is uncertain and finite, touching on the anxiety at the core of human existence. "Love is the antidote, the counterthrust" that empowers humans to cultivate planetary solidarity in the face of anxiety, ignorance, and uncertainty.[105] Cultivating such planetary love is not easy. Indeed, the "planetary union" that Morin invokes is a "possible impossible"—a planetary utopia, an impossible realism, which accounts for probabilities and improbabilities while it *"grounds itself in the uncertainty of the real"*.[106] This is similar to Spivak's affirmation of the "(im)possibility" of a planetary intuition.[107] The cultivation of love and planetary consciousness is a matter of engaging the uncertainty and alterity that characterize the complex unity of humanity and the planet. The planet "is mysterious and discontinuous—an experience of the impossible"; "I cannot offer a formulaic access to planetarity. No one can".[108] Spivak's "prayer for planetarity" is thus a prayer for the possibility of the impossible.[109] Along these lines, a viable political theology of planetary love must include what Keller calls a "theopolitics of uncertainty", which, like the *"knowing ignorance"* (*docta ignorantia*) of Nicholas of Cusa, considers uncertainty, chaos, turbulence, and "not-knowing" to be fundamental to the folds of our complex relations with the planet.[110] As Morin says, the "human fellowship" that constitutes our awareness of participating in "the complex web of the Planetary Era" does not presuppose any mastery or control over nature or over ourselves; on the contrary, this fellowship is based on a realization that "we are lost"—a realization that humans are nomads, "gypsies of the cosmos, vagabonds of the unknown adventure".[111]

Referring to the impossibility of a planetary civilization is not meant to be disempowering, as if to suggest that it cannot happen. It is meant to convey the arrival of a sustainable planetary civilization that would transform the very partition between the possible and impossible, re-placing the grid of globalization. Eschewing the arborescent hierarchies of the logic of domination, a planetary civilization is rhizomatic, taking place in the chaosmos.[112] Accordingly, it is found precisely insofar as we realize we are lost. It is possible precisely insofar as it is open to nomadic events, which wander outside of any determinable coordinates of the possible. In other words, a planetary civilization functions precisely insofar as it is open to the chaos of dysfunction.[113] "Another world is possible" insofar as its otherness shocks and transforms our sense of the limits of possibility.[114] To say that planetarity is impossible is to say that a planetary future is not possible as an orderly programme that needs to be applied but is only possible as a coming event that shocks our systems, opening our concepts and practises so that people and Earth become other, become different. This resonates with Luce Irigaray's statement: "I am, therefore, a political militant of the impossible. [. . .] I want what is yet to be as the only possibility of a future".[115]

To open up to the uncertain elements of the real, Morin's (im)possible planetary realism engages in "complex thinking", which "endeavors to connect that which was separate while preserving distinctiveness and differences".[116] Complex thinking is an "ecologized thinking", which conceives of the world's circuitous and recursive relations of interactions and retroactions, while also considering the "hologrammatic character" of these relations, according to which the whole (e.g., the planet) and the parts (e.g., humans) are internally interconnected, each being implicated within the constitution of the other. Furthermore, the complex thinking of planetary realism resonates with a counterapocalyptic tone, as

Morin announces a "gospel of doom" that overwrites the apocalypses of other-worldly salvation (e.g., the Roman church, contemporary religious fundamentalisms) as well as this-worldly salvation (e.g., Marxism, free market capitalism) with "an earthly religion of the third type"—a planetary religion that holds people together in the doom of their terrestrial finitude.[117] This is a religion for which salvation—if there is salvation—lies in the efforts of "consciousness, love, and fellowship", particularly insofar as these efforts do not mean "to escape doom", but "to dodge the worst, to find out what is best".[118] The Joachite "third age" resonates in Morin's religion of the "third type"—a religion that seeks to awaken love and fellowship within history. This resonates with the call for planetary love by Spivak and Keller. From these perspectives, the apocalyptic habit of Empire is to be overcome not through opposition or antiapocalyptic tones, but through a counterapocalyptic call for the creative contact of love, which overwrites Empire by embracing all human beings and bringing them into an (im)possible and complex interconnectedness with each other and with the planet.

Planetary love supports the efforts of integral ecology to engage ecological realities in all of their discontinuity, impossibility, and mystery. An organism, a river, a species, or a climate is a rhizomatic reality and not merely an object of commodification or technoscientific control, yet rather than merely opposing the objectifying, reductive, and simplifying habits of Empire, planetary love complexifies and overwrites them with the inexhaustible taxonomy of planetary subjects. Those planetary subjects count. The great work of our time is to count and be counted on by all planetary subjects, thus carrying out a transition whereby humans can cease being a destructive force on the planet and can "become integral with the larger Earth Community".[119] The counterapocalyptic tones of planetary love thus call for "a cosmopolitan democracy"—a relational solidarity that, not unlike Morin's "planetary solidarity", is supported by the "planetary web of interdependent diversity".[120] Such democratic solidarity expresses the conviviality and mutuality that empower ongoing negotiations between friends and enemies who are seeking to live together in interdependence.[121] Although this cosmopolitan democracy is still to come, the "good news" is that "the signs of it are planetary".[122] Planetary practises that reflect this democracy are occurring throughout the planet, slowly overwriting the Empire of the globe with a complex relationality—"a cosmically democratized ideal of co-creativity". The rhizomatics of such co-creativity involve a "spiritual pluralism" that "respects the particular ecologies of every species as the context for any body's agency; it deterritorializes and reterritorializes socio-religious contexts in the interest of a counter-apocalypse that is at the same time a counter-globalization".[123]

Counterapocalyptic and counterglobal, one could say that planetary love is a globalization "from below", standing in contrast to imperial globalization "from above". Arjun Appadurai calls such globalization from below "grassroots globalization".[124] At the edge of the grass, planetary love perhaps awaits. However, it is important to distinguish between grasses without rhizomes (e.g., shorthair reedgrass, *Calamagrostis breweri*) and rhizomatic grasses (e.g., couch grass, *Cynodon dactylon*). The grass of globalization from below puts too much emphasis on roots. A knottier image of a grass rhizome provides a better guide than grassroots, so that planetarity becomes a milieu of transversal movements cutting across the opposition between globalization from above and from below. Like a rhizome, planetary love "*grows between*, among other things" and proceeds "from the middle, through the middle".[125] In the process, practises of planetary love—"just love"—are "rediscovering the *cosmos* of cosmopolitanism".[126]

COSMOPOLITICS

It is no longer possible (if it ever was) to account for the world in terms of dualisms that neatly categorize things into oppositions: local and global; natural and technological; individual and collective; masculine and feminine; self and other. In our contemporary global civilization, these categories do not function well. They overflow and rupture as uncertainty, alterity, and complexity pervade their boundaries. Accordingly, it is impossible to give any clear distinctions or exact counts that would identify all of the actors on the world's stage. This dysfunction and impossibility provocatively enjoin humans to think and act differently, becoming different, becoming other, becoming planetary. Staying in the middle of this dysfunction and impossibility, a new sense of the world opens up, one in which the meanings and matters of human and nonhuman beings are thoroughly intertwined in an omnicentric and chaotic cosmos. Staying in the middle, humans are entangled amidst rhizomatic multiplicities of material forces, living organisms, technologies, signs, media, institutions, and cultures, all shaping and being shaped by one another.

Instead of affirming this rhizomatic chaosmos, there are interminable debates predicated on a false dichotomy that divides the world neatly into a realm of human politics (society, culture, subjectivity, values) and a realm of the nonhuman cosmos (matter, nature, objectivity, facts). However, if the rhizomatic boundaries of the chaosmos are taken into account, then it appears that *polis* and *kosmos* are not opposed, but are intimately intertwined in networks of mutually constitutive relations. Facing the implosion of the *kosmos/polis* distinction in a world on edge, how can humans work together to build a just and sustainable planetary civilization? If the world is pervaded by mutually constitutive relations between the values and constructions normally labeled as "politics", on the one hand, and facts normally labeled as "cosmos", on the other, then such a global society will have to be built with attention to the unstable, ambiguous, and dynamic boundaries of those relations. We need something better than a two-level approach that separates the realm of politics from the factual realm of the cosmos. We need a model of world building that affirms a complex and uncertain relationality between humans and nonhumans. We need a cosmopolitan democracy that takes seriously all the entangled human and nonhuman others in the universe, "the democracy of creation" (Keller), "a democracy of fellow creatures" (Whitehead), "a democracy extended to things themselves" (Latour).[127] In other words, we need what the French philosopher Isabelle Stengers calls *cosmopolitics*—an inventive "ecology of practices" that displaces cosmos/politics dualisms and aims to compose a common world by attending to the complex and uncertain boundaries of different and diverging modes of existence.

To engage in cosmopolitics is to cultivate a knowledge that affirms ambiguous boundaries instead of hastily excluding any boundary projects that appear strange or assimilating them into dichotomous hierarchies. In Stengers's terms, to participate in cosmopolitics is to cultivate pharmacological knowledge, where the word *pharmacological* alludes to the ambiguous way the ancient Greek word *pharmakon* means "poison" and "remedy". The cultivation of pharmacological knowledge supports cosmopolitical engagements, which open possibilities for the coming of another world, a just and sustainable planetary civilization. Before saying more about pharmacological knowledge, it is important to distinguish Stengers's concept of cosmopolitics from other uses of the term. The word *cosmopolitics* has roots in the Cynic and Stoic philosophies of ancient Greece. Diogenes Laertius reports that the Cynic philosopher Diogenes of Sinope, having been asked "where he came from", responded, "I am a citizen of the world (*kosmopolitês*)".[128] Subsequently, developing cosmopolitics into a concept, Stoic philosophers defined identity in terms of concentric circles that would include personal and national levels of identity within an encompassing circle of cosmic rationality (*logos*) embracing all humans. The Stoics used the concept of cosmopolitics "to express an affiliation to no city in particular but to humanity in general".[129] That concept is taken up and elaborated in a modern context by Kant in his proposal for a *jus cosmopoliticum*—a cosmopolitical law that promotes "perpetual peace" between all humans through a universal hospitality.[130]

Stengers develops her concept of cosmopolitics explicitly "in contrast to Kant".[131] In that sense, she is similar to Levinas and Derrida, both of whom propose a revision of Kant's cosmopolitics of hospitality, such that it is not based on a universal law (which assimilates the otherness and differences of people into a horizon of meaning) but on responsible encounters with others (encounters that honor the otherness and particular differences that exceed any horizon of meaning). Whereas Kantian cosmopolitics assimilates differences into the perpetually peaceful horizon of a universal moral law, the Levinasian and Derridean versions call for a peace and justice grounded in a welcoming of difference.[132] However, although Levinas and Derrida overcome the homogenizing tendency of a universal law that secures a final peace, they are often (but not always) talking about hospitality to human others, thus falling into the same old dualism that makes politics a matter of humanity and assigns nonhumans into a separate realm of nature.[133] Stengers develops a concept of cosmopolitics that also welcomes differences and, more than Levinas and Derrida, she articulates this concept in a way that puts the cosmos back in cosmopolitics, thus welcoming human as well as nonhuman others in their unpredictable entanglement. As Latour notes, cosmopolitics "acquired a deeper meaning through its use by Isabelle Stengers to mean the new politics that is no longer framed inside the modernist settlement of nature and society".[134]

For Stengers, a cosmopolitical engagement takes place amidst multiplicities of different, diverse, divergent networks of humans and nonhumans, such that "the cosmos refers to the unknown constituted by these multiple divergent worlds, and to the articulations of which they could eventually be capable, as opposed to the temptation of a peace intended to be final".[135] The cosmos is not a determinate unity, nor is it simply given. It is an unknown common world in the process of constitution amidst multiplicities capable of various articulations. As Donna Haraway points out, the cosmopolitical unknown resonates with the figure of the idiot, which is embraced by Deleuze and Guattari:

> the one who knew how to slow things down, to stop the rush to consensus or to a new dogmatism or to denunciation, in order to open up the chance of a common world. Stengers insists we cannot denounce the world in the name of an ideal world. Idiots know that. For Stengers, the cosmos is the possible unknown constructed by multiple, diverse entities. Full of the promise of articulations that diverse beings might eventually make, the cosmos is the opposite of a place of transcendent peace.[136]

Furthermore, Stengers's cosmopolitical proposal joins "feminist communitarian anarchism" and Whitehead's speculative philosophy in affirming a commitment to responsible decisions, which "must take place somehow in the presence of those who will bear their consequences. [. . .] To get "in the presence of" demands work, speculative invention, and ontological risks. No one knows how to do that in advance of coming together in composition".[137]

Cosmopolitics is the task of attending to the cosmopolitical unknown, the task of "learning to play with strangers", which entails remaining open and questioning amidst the divergent multiplicities of the world: "Cosmopolitical questions arise when people respond to seriously different, felt and known, finite truths and must cohabit well without a final peace".[138] There is no final answer to the ongoing decisions of cohabitation with strangers, and there is no position that is innocent or separate from complicity in those decisions. "Forbidding both the dream (and nightmare) of a final solution and also the fantasy of transparent and innocent communication, cosmopolitics is a practice for going on, for remaining exposed to consequences, for entangling materially with as many of the messy players as possible".[139]

The messy players of cosmopolitics are human and nonhuman actors, such that agency is not restricted to an exclusively human realm. Cosmopolitics involves practises for going on and entangling with "heterogeneous actors", practises of "ontological choreography".[140] The dance of these actors is full of action and passion, and learning to dance together means "sharing suffering", sharing in the troubling decisions of the "worlding game on earth", "articulating bodies to some bodies and not others, nourishing some worlds and not others, and bearing the mortal consequences".[141] Insofar as actors are strangers or others, there are always multiple asymmetries complicating the boundary negotiations of cosmopolitics, following along lines such as species, gender, sex, geography, nationality, race, class, ethnicity, age, and ability. Cosmopolitical questions are matters "of learning to be 'polite' in responsible relation to always asymmetrical living and dying, and nurturing and killing".[142]

"The challenge of the cosmopolitical unknown", for Stengers, calls for us to remain open, "reinventing questions wherever we have been converted to believing the power of answers".[143] This does not mean questioning beliefs in favor of facts, but of questioning the very definitions of beliefs, facts, and the boundaries between them. Thus, Latour, who is deeply influenced by Stengers, notes that cosmopolitics involves putting away the hammer of the iconoclast (or critical theorist) and honoring multiple ontologies. Indeed, "setting aside the iconoclast's hammer allows us to see that we have always been involved in *cosmopolitics*":

> It is only through an extraordinary shrinking of the meaning of politics that it has been restricted to the values, interests, opinions, and social forces of isolated, naked humans. The great advantage of letting facts merge back into their disheveled networks and controversies, and of letting beliefs regain their ontological weight, is that politics then becomes what is has always been, anthropologically speaking: the management, diplomacy, combination, and negotiation of human and nonhuman agencies.[144]

For Latour, the challenge of the cosmopolitical unknown is the challenge of composing the "collective" — "that which *collects us all* in the cosmopolitics envisaged by Isabelle Stengers":

> If nonhumans are to be assembled into a collective, it will be the *same* collective, and within the *same* institutions, as the humans whose fate the sciences have brought nonhumans to share. Instead of this bipolar power source — nature and society — we will have only one, clearly identifiable source of politics for humans and nonhumans alike, and one clearly identifiable source for new entities socialized into the collective.[145]

In this context, the "role of the intellectual" is "to *protect the diversity* of ontological status against the threat of its transformation into facts and fetishes, beliefs and things".[146]

The ontological diversity of the world is not divisible into facts and fetishes. It is made up of rhizomatic actors or *factishes*. "Thus another political model is offered, [. . .] one that entertains as many practical ontologies as there are factishes".[147] This means engaging ontological diversity in all of its human and nonhuman expressions, not lumping nonhumans together into a totalized Nature opposed to Society. Cosmopolitics follows actors in their specificity and heterogeneity, not following Nature and Society but following frogs, forests, cities, corporations, slogans, concepts, black holes, mushrooms, waterways, governments, rainstorms, wildfires, planets, hydroelectric dams, seeds, cars, laptops, lapdogs, and innumerable others. Even God(s) are considered in the cosmopolitical collective, as long as the considered deity is conceived neither as a social construct nor as a given fact separate from processes of construction, but as a "factish god", which is real *and* constructed in networks of human and nonhuman actors.[148] Invoking Heraclitus, Latour affirms that even in our supposedly disenchanted global technoculture, "Here too the gods are present" (*Einai gar kai entautha theous*).[149]

Whether a deity, animal, plant, a stone, or a computer, a factish is not reducible to fact/belief dichotomies or, for that matter, to anything whatsoever. Its heterogeneity is irreducible. No actor is reducible to anything else, although actors can translate and connect with one another in heterogeneous assemblages. Actors are neither reducible nor simply irreducible.[150] They are heterogeneous participants in the composition of the collective. The ontological heterogeneity of the collective resonates with Jane Bennett's proposal for a democracy of human and nonhuman agencies. "Theories of democracy that assume a world of active subjects and passive objects begin to appear as thin descriptions at a time when the interactions between human, viral, animal, and technological bodies are becoming more and more intense".[151] If humans and nonhumans are all actors enmeshed in rhizomatic assemblages, "then it seems that the appropriate unit of analysis for democratic theory is neither the individual human nor an exclusively human collective but the (ontologically heterogeneous) 'public' coalescing around a problem".[152] How, then, can we nurture the emergence of such a public?

The ongoing democratic work of composing such a public requires the cultivation of ways of knowing that are sensitive to complexity and difference, sensitive to the ontological choreography of significant others. Knowledge that protects ontological diversity is knowledge that is open to the uncertain and complex boundaries of heterogeneous actors: nomads, companion species, human-nonhuman assemblages, factishes, actors, things, and others. Instead of foreclosing the composition of the collective with a bipolar constitution that opposes *kosmos* (facts and things) to *polis* (beliefs and fetishes), such knowledge is pharmacological, affirming the pervasive ambiguities of boundaries. By cultivating pharmacological knowledge, the cosmopolitical intellectual facilitates the composition of the collective, protecting the practical ontologies, the ontological choreography of heterogeneous actors.

Stengers defines the *pharmakon* as

> a drug that may act as a poison or a remedy. [. . .] The lack of a stable and well determined attribute is the problem posed by any *pharmakon*, by any drug whose effect can mutate into its opposite, depending on the dose, the circumstances, or the context, any drug whose action provides no guarantee, defines no fixed point of reference that would allow us to recognize and understand its effects with some assurance.[153]

Although the word is Greek, the *pharmakon* is not unique to Western society but is part of every society. "Every human culture recognizes the intrinsic instability of certain roles, certain practices, certain drugs". What is unique in the Western context is "the intolerance of our tradition in the face of this type of ambiguity, the anxiety it arouses. We require a fixed point, a foundation, a guarantee. We require a stable distinction between the beneficial medicament and the harmful drug, between rational pedagogy and suggestive influence, between reason and opinion".[154]

Having unassured effects with no fixed point of reference, the *pharmakon* is comparable to the "historical sophists" — "the philosopher's other" who "bartered the truth" through reliance upon "changing and malleable" opinion.[155] The exclusion of the sophists from philosophy is an example of the intolerance that our tradition has for the *pharmakon*. The exclusion of the *pharmakon* also takes place in numerous modern practises ("scientific, medical, political, technological, psychoanalytic, pedagogical") that were introduced as "disqualifying their other — charlatan, populist, ideologue, astrologer, magician, hypnotist, charismatic teacher".[156] Stengers mentions that, in some sense, "the *pharmakon* refuses to be excluded"; the instability of the subject-object distinction haunts practises that purport to be objective yet fail to escape from "subjective persuasion". The "factishes" of scientific practises "have a very pharmacological instability". In this sense, the *pharmakon* can never be excluded. It persists as "a symptom in the heart of whatever tries to distinguish itself from it". However, Stengers's point is not simply to define the *pharmakon* as an instability that cannot be completely excluded, but also to recognize that such a definition runs the risk of separating "us" (we who understand the dynamics of the *pharmakon*) from traditional misunderstandings of the *pharmakon*, such that our definition of the *pharmakon* is precisely "our definition", constructed through practises "that have disqualified and, therefore, transformed, if not destroyed, the traditional ways in which this instability we associate with the *pharmakon* was managed".[157] In other words, even when we define the *pharmakon* as a recalcitrant instability that cannot be excluded from knowledge, that definition still works within one "form of 'truth telling' without bringing into existence other ways of telling. And this 'truth telling' locks us into a setting whose only horizon is what *we* call *pharmakon*".[158]

Instead of simply showing how modern or Western practises exclude the *pharmakon* or how the *pharmakon* refuses such exclusion, Stengers proposes that our knowledge of pharmacological instability should help us learn to play with strangers and bring into existence other ways of telling, other practises, other ways of managing the *pharmakon*. Our knowledge of pharmacological instability should make us capable of the composition of a cosmopolitical collective (what Latour calls a "'cult' of factishes"), which celebrates "the event that brings a new being or a new method or measurement into existence".[159] This is a problem of becoming ecological, as it requires an engagement with the dynamic relations whereby new beings and practises emerge. It requires deciding how, how much, and in what cases to intervene in ecological situations, which entails knowing that "not all 'ecological' situations are equal".[160] Some of the shoots and roots of the rhizome are more important to cultivate than others, and some are more important to cut away. Cosmopolitics does not celebrate equally every event. It accounts for events ecologically, studying the ways each event is situated in different relations and processes, studying "multiplicities, disparate causalities, and unintentional creations of meaning". Moreover, "the ecological perspective", especially insofar as humans are involved, "communicates directly with the question" of "pharmacological instability".[161] Whereas human societies can sometimes justify their practises while "forgetting the price paid for their choices", the ecological perspective generates pharmacological knowledge of the instability of human-nonhuman relations. Ecology generates "a memory of the unintentional processes" connecting heterogeneous assemblages of humans and nonhumans, which is also a memory "of the ravages caused by our simplistic industrial, and even 'scientific,' strategies (the 'DDT strategy')": "this memory is now part of the present. In that sense, we can say that our present is cultivating the growth of "pharmacological knowledge", a science of processes where good intentions risk turning into disasters".[162] In terms of that knowledge, "no action has an identity independent of the whole that stabilizes it", but can cause that whole to become other, "to change its meaning".[163]

Cultivating pharmacological knowledge faces the "challenge of the cosmopolitical unknown", which is to say, "the challenge of 'thinking with' unknowns", thinking with ambiguities, exclusions, instabilities, and unintentional processes.[164] Putting the cosmos back into cosmopolitics means opening up politics to the rhizomatic complexity of coexistence. The cosmos of cosmopolitics is different than a universal law and different than a universe objectified by sciences. It is different than anything known. It is "the unknown affecting our questions that our political tradition is at significant risk of disqualifying":

> It creates the question of possible nonhierarchical modes of coexistence among the ensemble of inventions of nonequivalence, among the diverging values and obligations through which the entangled existences that compose it are affirmed. Thus, it integrates, problematically, the question of an ecology of practices that would bring together our cities, where politics was invented, and those other places where the question of closure and transmission has invented other solutions for itself. Cosmopolitics is emphatically not "beyond politics", it designates our access to a question that politics cannot appropriate.[165]

Cosmopolitics is an ongoing question. It is the problem of becoming open to others, playing with strangers, integrating multiplicities of ecologies. It is "the mode in which the problematic copresence of practices may be actualized: the experience, always in the present, of the one into whom the other's dreams, hopes, and fears pass".[166]

For Stengers, "the cosmopolitical question" is "directed at the modern tradition" and "its fear of the pharmakon", and thus calls for a pharmacological approach to knowledge, which would aim to "sustain the obligation to resist the code words" that impose themselves on the ecology of practises, the obligation to resist anything that short-circuits the democratic composition of the collective.[167] The failure to develop pharmacological knowledge hinders the creative potentials of planetary existence. It arrests the inventive and uncertain boundary projects of cosmopolitics by imposing onto divergent worlds the boundary projects of one particular representation of the world. This is what is happening with the "infernal alternatives" imposed by the "capitalist sorcery" of militarized neoliberal models of globalization.[168]

To cultivate pharmacological knowledge is to resist such global imposition and nurture a more just and sustainable world by attending to uncertain boundaries and unintentional processes whereby heterogeneous actors cohabit and entangle with one another, creating and being created by one another in the movements of ontological choreography. To cultivate pharmacological knowledge is to practise experimental contact with unstable wanderings and unpredictable becomings in joyous celebration of the risky invention of new events, new ways of getting on together in the cosmopolitical composition of another world—a peaceful, just, and sustainable planetary civilization. Drawing on the work of the neopagan witch Starhawk, Stengers suggests that such a joyous celebration of risky invention is a practise of witchcraft, a sorcery that empowers humans to stay in the middle, in alliance with multiplicities, thus countering the sorcery of Empire, which captures planetary subjects in the infernal logic of domination.[169] D&G might agree: "that is our way, fellow sorcerers. [. . .] That is how we sorcerers operate", by cultivating a "symbiosis of or passage between heterogeneities", living "at the edge" and "at the borderline" so that they can "haunt the fringes" between worlds, mapping lines of flight to make rhizomes, to create new modes of existence: "So experiment".[170] "To think is always to follow the witch's flight".[171]

Following witches, *pharmaka*, rhizomes, nomads, and undecidably numerous others in an omnicentric chaosmos, a philosophy of integral ecology supports the emergence of a planetary civilization by facilitating the practise of a craft—creating concepts *"so as to summon forth a new earth, a new people"*.[172] With its craft, philosophy is opening new possibilities for existing together in a world on edge. In the middle of multiplicities at the end of the world, a new beginning is coming. Imagine. Decide. Become different, become other, with love.

NOTES

1. Edgar Morin, *On Complexity*, trans. Robin Postel (Cresskill: Hampton Press, 2008, 35). The collapsing superstructure of ideas is a collapse of the hegemonic homogeneity of Western civilization, including Western philosophy and the imperialism whereby Western philosophy infected the whole planet, for

better and for worse. Foucault makes this point. "The crisis of Western thought is identical to the end of imperialism. [. . .] it is the end of the era of Western philosophy. Thus, if philosophy of the future exists, it must be born outside of Europe or equally born in consequence of meetings and impacts between Europe and non-Europe". Michel Foucault, *Religion and Culture*, trans. Richard Townsend (New York: Routledge, 1999), 110–14.

2. Mary Evelyn Tucker and Brian Swimme, "The Evolutionary Context of an Emerging Planetary Civilization", *Kosmos: An Integral Approach to Global Awakening* 5.1 (2005), http://www.kosmosjournal.org/article/the-evolutionary-context-of-an-emerging-planetary-civilization/.

3. Morton, *Ecology without Nature: Rethinking Environmental Aesthetics* (Cambridge: Harvard University Press, 2007), 27. To articulate the complexity of inside/outside and foreground/background boundaries, Morton engages Derrida's writings on margins, with specific attention to his concept of the "re-mark", which indicates that boundaries are demarcated through an undecidable and recursive process of differentiation according to which nothing is ever simply inside or simply outside (or both inside and outside, or neither inside nor outside) (40, 48). On the re-mark, see Jacques Derrida, *Dissemination*, trans. Barbara Johnson (Chicago: University of Chicago Press, 1981), 54, 104, 205, 208, 222, 253.

4. Morton is among many other theorists who are proposing an "ecology without nature" or a postnatural ecology. Slavoj Žižek is one of them. "Indeed, what we need is an ecology without nature: the ultimate obstacle to protecting nature is the very notion of nature we rely on" (Žižek, *In Defense of Lost Causes* [New York: Verso, 2008], 445). Similarly, Jozef Keulartz draws on the works of Latour and Haraway to call for "a 'post-naturalist' turn in environmental philosophy" (Keulartz, *Struggle for Nature: A Critique of Radical Ecology*, trans. Rob Kuitenbrouwer [New York: Routledge, 1998], 2). Sean Esbjörn-Hargens and Michael E. Zimmerman claim that "Integral Ecology is a post-natural approach: nature is not simply given, independent of our observation, nor are we the sole generators of nature" (Esbjörn-Hargens and Zimmerman, *Integral Ecology: Uniting Multiple Perspectives on the Natural World* [Boston: Integral Books, 2009], 276). In other words, "We live in a time in human history when nature and culture are so intermixed that we cannot rightly speak of the natural world without implicating ourselves in it. [. . .] we champion a post-naturalism in which nature is intertwined with culture, culture is shot through with nature" (272). This postnaturalism is related to the emphasis on "denaturalization" in much postmodern theory and cultural studies for decades. Although there are benefits to conceiving of ecology without or after nature, it has its limits. Along those lines, Judith Butler calls for recognition of "the limits of denaturalization as a critical strategy" in gender discourses. Butler indicates how denaturalization is not inherently emancipatory. It can subvert norms but can also support oppressive hegemonies (Judith Butler, *Bodies That Matter: On the Discursive Limits of "Sex"* [New York: Routledge, 1993], 93). Applying this insight to ecological concerns, Catherine Keller and Laurel Kearns note that, although denaturalization "is no more driven by antienvironmentalism than by environmentalism", it can have the effect of a "condescending boredom with the nonhuman materialities in which the human materializes" (Keller and Kearns, "Introduction: Grounding Theory—Earth in Religion and Philosophy", in *Ecospirit: Religions and Philosophies for the Earth*, eds. Laurel Kearns and Catherine Keller [Fordham, NY: Fordham University Press, 2007], 8).

5. Morton, *Ecological Thought* (Cambridge: Harvard University Press, 2010), 98.

6. Ibid.

7. Eliot, "Little Gidding", line 215, in *Four Quartets* (Orlando: Harcourt, 1971), 58.

8. Jean-Luc Nancy, *The Sense of the World*, trans. Jeffrey Librett (Minneapolis: University of Minnesota Press, 1997), 4.

9. Friedrich Nietzsche, *Twilight of the Idols*, trans. Richard Polt (Indianapolis: Hackett Publishing, 1997), 24.

10. Timothy Morton, *Hyperobjects : Philosophy and Ecology after the End of the World* (Minneapolis: University of Minnesota Press, 2013), 3.

11. The role of edges in the human inhabitation of the world is explored by many environmental philosophers. For a variety of approaches to engaging ecological edges, see Charles Brown and Ted Toadvine, *Nature's Edge: Boundary Explorations in Ecological Theory and Practice* (Albany: SUNY Press, 2007). For a specific example, consider Ed Casey, who accounts for ways in which humans, by attending to the edges of the world, ethically inhabit their environments. For Casey, ethical responsibility towards the environment is a matter of perceiving the surfaces of landscapes (more generally, placescapes) in a way that attends to their alterity. Casey thereby extends to nonhumans the ethics of responsibility proposed by Emmanuel Levinas, who focused on the alterity of the human face. Every sur*face* can harbour a *face* in its occluding edges (Casey, "Taking a Glance at the Environment: Preliminary Thoughts on a Promising Topic", in *Eco-Phenomenology: Back to the Earth Itself*, eds. Charles S. Brown and Ted Toadvine [Albany: SUNY Press, 2003]). For Levinas's account of an ethical metaphysics of the face, see Levinas, *Totality and Infinity: An Essay on Exteriority*, trans. Alphonso Lingis (Dordrecht: Kluwer Academic Publishers, 1991). Extending Levinas's phenomenology to the environment, Casey adopts J. J. Gibson's ecological psychology and develops concepts of the perception of the "layout" of "surfaces" and their "occluding edges" (Gibson, *The Ecological Approach to Visual Perception* [Boston: Houghton Mifflin, 1979], 307–8). For more on the implications of edges for environmental philosophy, see the writings of Irene Klaver, who emphasizes the roles of paradox and mutually constitutive relationality in boundary projects (Klaver, "Boundaries on the Edge", in *Nature's Edge: Boundary Explorations in Ecological Theory and Practice*, eds. Charles S. Brown and Ted Toadvine [Albany: SUNY Press, 2007]).

12. Latour, *Politics of Nature: How to Bring the Sciences into Democracy*, trans. Catherine Porter (Cambridge: Harvard University Press, 2004), 25–26.

13. Ibid., 80.

14. Deleuze, *Spinoza: Practical Philosophy*, trans. Robert Hurley (San Francisco: City Lights Books, 1988), 125. According to Spinoza, "No one has yet determined what the Body can do" (Benedict de Spinoza, *Ethics*, in *Collected Works of Spinoza, Vol. 1*, 2nd printing with corrections, ed. and trans. Edwin Curley [Princeton: Princeton University Press, 1988], IIIP2S).

15. Deleuze, *Nietzsche and Philosophy*, trans. Hugh Tomlinson (New York: Columbia University Press, 2006), 39.

16. Ibid., 40, 39.

17. Casey, *Getting Back into Place: Toward a Renewed Understanding of the Place-World* (Bloomington: Indiana University Press, 1993), 314.

18. Water is becoming increasingly scarce around the world: lakes are shrinking and disappearing, aquifers are being overpumped, and rivers are failing to reach the sea. Lester Brown, founder and president of the Earth Policy Institute, describes the current planetary situation as a "global water deficit" (Lester Brown, *Plan B 2.0: Rescuing a Planet under Stress and a Civilization in Trouble* [New York: Norton, 2006], 42). Furthermore, the deficit is growing. This vast water scarcity is of recent historical origin, due in large part to the increased demands

for water from a growing population of humans, the increased amounts of water pollution that accompany processes of urbanization and industrialization, and the unpredictable effects of global climate change on precipitation and other aspects of the hydrological cycle (United Nations World Water Assessment Program, *Water: A Shared Responsibility* (New York: UNESCO and Berghahn Books, 2007), 120–31). The crisis also involves the inequitable distribution of water due to the oversimplified definition of water as a commodity, such as the definition expressed at the March 2000 World Water Forum in The Hague, where water was defined explicitly as a commodity by representatives of governments that have "helped pave the way for private corporations to sell water, for profit, to the thirsty citizens of the world" (Maude Barlow and Tony Clarke, *Blue Gold: The Fight to Stop the Corporate Theft of the World's Water* [New York: New Press, 2002], xiii). According to Laura Donaldson, the unsustainable and ecologically destructive effects of water privatization amount to killing water—"aquacide" (Donaldson, "Covenanting Nature: Aquacide and the Transformation of Knowledge", *Ecotheology* 8.1 (2003): 100–18). The objectification of water as a commodity has been accompanied by an objectification of water by technoscientific developments that aim to increase the certainty with which people gain access to and accumulate water. Along with advances in privatization and commodification, the use of technological advances in methods of water capture, storage, and distribution to secure certain access to water has often led to problems that increase the uncertainty of access to water and, in some cases, has led to devastating effects for the civilization employing these technological means. For instance, techniques of desalinization increase access to water in a way that is more ecologically viable than damming and irrigation, but the costs of desalinization preclude most of the planet's population from making use of any water made available through this process (Bruce Simmons, Robert Woog, and Vladimir Dimitrov, "Living on the Edge: A Complexity-Informed Exploration of the Human–Water Relationship". *World Futures* 63.3 [2007]: 280). The objectification of water ignores the complexity and uncertainty constitutive of the individual, social, and environmental systems involved in relations between humans and the hydrologic cycle.

19. Keller, *Apocalypse Now and Then: A Feminist Guide to the End of the World* (Boston: Beacon Press, 1996), 4, 11.

20. Derrida, "On a Newly Arisen Apocalyptic Tone in Philosophy", trans. John Leavy Jr., in *Raising the Tone of Philosophy: Late Essays by Immanuel Kant, Transformative Critique by Jacques Derrida*, ed. Peter Fenves (Baltimore: Johns Hopkins University Press, 1993), 157.

21. Karl Marx, *Economic and Philosophic Manuscripts of 1844*, trans. Martin Milligan (Amherst: Prometheus Books, 1988), 104. As Derrida says, Marx is among those who "formed the canon of the modern apocalypse", which involves the announcements of many ends ("end of History, end of Man, end of Philosophy"), which were heralded in the writings of Hegel, Marx, Nietzsche, Heidegger, and Kojève (Derrida, *Specters of Marx: The State of the Debt, the Work of Mourning, and the New International*, trans. Peggy Kamuf [New York: Routledge, 1994], 15).

22. Derrida asks, "Wouldn't the apocalyptic be a transcendental condition of all discourse, of all experience even, of every mark or every trace"? (Derrida, "On a Newly Arisen Apocalyptic Tone", 156).

23. Eliot, "Little Gidding", line 218, 58.

24. Keller, *God and Power: Counter-Apocalyptic Journeys* (Minneapolis: Augsburg Fortress, 2005), viii.

25. Keller, *Apocalypse Now and Then*, 115–16.

26. Ibid., 11.

27. Paul Hanson, *The Dawn of the Apocalyptic: The Historical and Sociological Roots of Jewish Apocalyptic Eschatology*, rev. ed. (Philadelphia: Fortress Press, 1979), 11.

28. Eugen Weber, *Apocalypses: Prophesies, Cults, and Millennial Beliefs through the Ages* (Cambridge: Harvard University Press, 1999), 39.

29. Keller, *Apocalypse Now and Then*, 148–50.

30. John J. Collins, *The Apocalyptic Imagination: An Introduction to Jewish Apocalyptic Literature*, 2nd ed. (Grand Rapids: Eerdmans Publishing, 1998), 3.

31. Most of these figures are discussed in Weber, *Apocalypses*. For a discussion of Bush's apocalyptic habit, see Keller, *God and Power*, 18–27.

32. Keller, *Apocalypse Now and Then*; Richard Woods, "The Seven Bowls of Wrath: An Ecological Parable", *Ecotheology* 5.7 (1999): 8–21; Paul Halpern, *Countdown to Apocalypse: A Scientific Exploration of the End of the World* (New York: Basic Books, 2001); David J. Hawkin, "The Critique of Ideology in the Book of Revelation and Its Implications for Ecology", *Ecotheology* 8.2 (2003): x.

33. Weber, *Apocalypses*, 45.

34. Augustine, *City of God*, trans. Henry Bettenson (London: Penguin Books, 2003), 2.20.17.

35. Ibid., 2.19.17.

36. Weber, *Apocalypses*, 34, 46.

37. Ibid., 57, 64–66, 77.

38. Keller, *Apocalypse Now and Then*, 27.

39. Sean Kelly, *Coming Home: The Birth and Transformation of the Planetary Era* (Great Barrington: Lindisfarne Books, 2010), 46.

40. Keller, *Apocalypse Now and Then*, 106. Multiplying correlations, one might wonder whether the third age might be correlated to the third thing of Plato's *chora*.

41. Ibid., 107.

42. "We shall not be what we have been, but we shall begin to be other". Joachim von Fiore, Psalterium Decem Cordarum Abbatis Joachim (Frankfurt: Minerva, 1965), 260, column a, quoted in Frank Edward Manuel, *Shapes of Philosophical History* (Stanford, CA: Stanford University Press, 1965), 40.

43. Weber, *Apocalypses*, 52–54.

44. Nietzsche, *Thus Spoke Zarathustra: A Book for Everyone and No One*, trans. R. J. Hollingdale (New York: Penguin Books, 1969), 67.

45. Deleuze, *Difference and Repetition*, trans. Paul Patton (New York: Columbia University Press, 1994), xxi.

46. Ibid.

47. Nietzsche, *Untimely Meditations*, trans. R. J. Hollingdale (New York: Cambridge University Press, 1997), 60.

48. Deleuze and Guattari, *What Is Philosophy?*, trans. Hugh Tomlinson and Graham Burchell (New York: Columbia University Press, 1994), 109.

49. Keller, *Apocalypse Now and Then*, 152–62.

50. David Korten, *The Great Turning: From Empire to Earth Community* (Bloomfield: Kumarian Press and Berrett-Koehler, 2006), 35.

51. Ibid., 33.

52. Hardt and Negri, *Empire* (Cambridge: Harvard University Press, 2001), xii.

53. Sloterdijk, *In the World Interior of Capital: For a Philosophical Theory of Globalization*, trans. Weiland Hoban (Malden: Polity Press, 2013), 12.

54. Hardt and Negri, *Empire*, 24.

55. Keller, *God and Power*, 118–21.

56. Ibid., 120.
57. Birgit Meyer, "Christianity and the Ewe Nation: German Pietist Missionaries, Ewe Converts and the Politics of Culture", *Journal of Religion in Africa* 32.2 (2002): 167–99.
58. Korten, *Great Turning*, 219, 225.
59. Ibid., 231.
60. To give examples of contemporary critics of capitalism's ecologically destructive tendencies, I would refer to three figures: (1) the libertarian socialist and founder of social ecology, Murray Bookchin, who criticizes capitalism for harming society and nature through the exploitation, overconsumption, and inequitable distribution of resources; (2) the environmental lawyer and co-founder of the Natural Resources Defense Council, James Gustave ("Gus") Speth, who calls for nonsocialist alternatives to capitalism while criticizing the harmful effects of capitalism on consciousness, society, and the natural environment; and (3) the philosopher and cultural critic, Slavoj Žižek, whose critique of today's capitalism, which he calls biocapitalism, suggests that the ecological problems on the horizon are so risky and threatening to the human species that these problems preclude trust in the mechanisms of the market. For an overview of Bookchin's thought, see Andrew Light, *Social Ecology after Bookchin* (New York: Guilford Press, 1998). Regarding Speth's proposal for a nonsocialist system beyond today's capitalism, see Speth, *Bridge at the Edge of the World: Capitalism, the Environment, and Crossing from Crisis to Sustainability* (New Haven: Yale University Press, 2008). On Žižek's critique of biocapitalism and his claim the ecological crisis undermines the rationality of market solution, see Žižek, *In Defense of Lost Causes* (New York: Verso, 2008), 357, 421. For Žižek's account of the apocalyptic dimensions of global capitalism, of which the ecological crisis is one of the "four riders of the apocalypse" along with biogenetic technology, increases in social inequities and rifts, and "imbalances within the system itself" (e.g., struggles over intellectual property and resources), see Žižek, *Living in the End Times* (London: Verso, 2011), x.
61. Francis Fukuyama, *The End of History and the Last Man* (New York: Avon Books, 1992), xi–xiii.
62. Ibid., xiv–xv.
63. Keller, *God and Power*, 62–63, 87–88; Keller, *Apocalypse Now and Then*, passim.
64. Keller, *Apocalypse Now and Then*, 309.
65. Derrida, "On a Newly Arisen Apocalyptic Tone", 167.
66. Gayatri Chakravorty Spivak, *Death of a Discipline* (New York: Columbia University Press, 2003), 81.
67. Ibid., 73.
68. Keller, *God and Power*, 121–26.
69. Ibid., 126–31.
70. Spivak, *Death of a Discipline*, 72.
71. Ibid. Of course, the globe did not begin with the invention of the computer. Spivak notes that globalization has "a long history" that can be traced to "ancient world systems" (73). A consideration of this long history is a crucial part of the task of rethinking globalization, but particularly important for this discussion are the current flows of economic globalization, which are "relatively autonomous" insofar as they rely on computer technologies and information systems that were not present in those ancient world systems. The current form of the globe is "the computerized globe".
72. Ibid., 72, 38.

73. In a different vein, Eugene Thacker also emphasizes the alterity of the planet, thereby distinguishing *Planet* from the subjective *World* ("world-for-us") and the objective *Earth* ("world-in-itself"). Thacker, *In the Dust of This Planet*, Vol. 1 of *Horror of Philosophy* (Alresford: Zero Books, 2011), 6. "The Planet (the world-without-us) is, in the words of darkness mysticism, the 'dark intelligible abyss' that is paradoxically manifest as the World and the Earth" (8). Conceiving of the Planet is a way of conceiving of a world that is becoming "increasingly unthinkable"; that is, "a world of planetary disasters, emerging pandemics, tectonic shifts, strange weather, oil-drenched seascapes, and the furtive, always-looming threat of extinction" (1). Furthermore, conceiving of the planet is a matter of "horror", not simply as a genre of literature or as an emotion but as a philosophical practise (or a "negative philosophy" or "non-philosophy" at the edge of philosophy). "Horror is about the paradoxical thought of the unthinkable" (9). Along with fiction like that of the horror writer H. P. Lovecraft, Thacker engages demonology, occultism, and esotericism to think of the unthinkable. He invokes "a kind of mysticism that can only be expressed in the dust of this planet" (159).

74. Spivak, *Death of a Discipline*, 71–74.

75. Drawing on the etymology of the word *complicity* (related to *complexity*), Spivak suggests that to be in a "complicitous" relationship is to be "folded together" (Spivak, *A Critique of Postcolonial Reason: Toward a History of the Vanishing Present* [Cambridge: Harvard University Press, 1999], 361).

76. Consider the conflicts of management around the Edwards Aquifer—an underground body of freshwater that provides water to south-central Texas, including San Antonio (Irene Klaver and John Donahue, "Whose Water Is It Anyway? Boundary Negotiations on the Edwards Aquifer in Texas", in *Globalization, Water, and Health: Resource Management in Times of Scarcity*, eds. Linda Whiteford and Scott Whiteford [Santa Fe: School of American Research Press, 2005], 108). Although the aridity of much of the south-central Texas climate has forced people to adapt to their embeddedness within the uncertain complexities of the hydrological cycle, the city of San Antonio avoids dealing with the complexity of water management in a semiarid climate by relying on the rechargeable aquifer beneath the city for 99 percent of its municipal supply. Currently, the Edwards Aquifer is something like a "battleground" where multiple and varied interests converge, including geographical and hydrological interests, social and political concerns, corporate and industrial demands for water, and federal and local environmental organizations (113). In other words, the Edwards Aquifer is a "boundary object"—a vehicle of translation that constitutes a "meeting ground" for ongoing negotiations and makes possible "coherence across social worlds" (110, 114).

To facilitate translations and negotiations of the boundaries of the Edwards Aquifer, Klaver and Donahue propose a concept of public property, which would itself function as a vehicle of translation that would make it possible for interested parties to arrive together at the meeting ground of the aquifer. Water has been conceived of as a commons in premodern societies and as a commodity in Empire, but perhaps the emergence of a counterapocalyptic "third age" characterized by planetarity calls for a conception of water that moves from commons and commodity into a "third space". Although Klaver and Donahue do not make any explicitly apocalyptic or eschatological references, they do invoke a "third space": "Water as public property could be seen as a 'third space'" or a "middle path" that occurs with the intersection of the space of a commons and that of private property (116, 124). The concept of public property works towards "a broad partnership" of all the interests intersecting in the aquifer, thus embracing corporations and opening them up to the complexity of their planetary context, specifically through a model of "integrative management" that coordinates heterogeneous interests to arrive at "cooperative decisions" by engaging in negotiations that account for the entangled relations between humans, societies, natural systems, and their respective health issues (108–9, 117, 124).

77. This strategic deployment of generalizations is related to Spivak's concept of "strategic essentialism". She describes "a *strategic* use of positivist essentialism" that she claims is at work in the scholarly efforts of Subaltern Studies (Spivak, *In Other Worlds: Essays in Cultural Politics* [New York: Routledge, 1988], 205). Long-term efforts for addressing ecological issues must take the risk of deploying essentialist determinations found in names like "Earth community", "nature", "animal", "human", and so on. The task of "strategic essentialism" is to make these strategies critically self-conscious so that they do not fall into oppressive tendencies whereby essentialisms efface difference and alterity. "The strategic use of an essence as a mobilizing slogan or masterword like *woman* or *worker* or the name of the nation is, ideally, self-conscious for all mobilized. This is the impossible risk of a lasting strategy. Can there be such a thing?" Spivak, *Outside in the Teaching Machine* (New York: Routledge, 1993), 3.

78. Spivak, *Death of a Discipline*, 72.
79. Ibid., 73.
80. Spivak, *Critique of Postcolonial Reason*, 382.
81. Ibid., 383.
82. Ibid.
83. Keller, *God and Power*, 131.
84. Val Plumwood, *Feminism and the Mastery of Nature* (New York: Routledge, 1993), 81.
85. Klaver, "Boundaries on the Edge", 129.
86. Ibid.
87. William Carlos Williams, "The Rose (The Rose Is Obsolete)", in *1909–1939, Vol. 1 of The Collected Poems of William Carlos Williams*, eds. A. Walton and Christopher MacGowan (New York: New Directions, 1986), 195.
88. Klaver, "Boundaries on the Edge", 129.
89. Plumwood, *Feminism and the Mastery of Nature*, 81.
90. Edgar Morin, *Homeland Earth: A Manifesto for the New Millennium*, trans. Sean M. Kelly and Roger LaPointe (Cresskill: Hampton Press, 1999), 136.
91. Keller, *God and Power*, 131, 150–51. Although Spivak is continually critical of theological traditions, she is also deepening her engagement with theologians, particularly on the topic of planetary love. This is particularly evident in the anthology of essays that grew out of the seventh Transdisciplinary Theological Colloquium at Drew University in New Jersey, which included Spivak and Keller among the participants (Stephen Moore and Mayra Rivera, *Planetary Loves: Spivak, Postcoloniality, and Theology* (New York: Fordham University Press, 2011).
92. Keller, *God and Power*, 116–17. For more on the concept of an "ecology of love", which suggests a relational conversion of divine and cosmic creative processes, see Roland Faber, *God as Poet of the World: Exploring Process Theologies*, trans. Douglas W. Scott (Louisville, KY: Westminster John Knox Press, 2008), 152–57. In their "common creative process, God and world as so interwoven that they continually are one in the other and yet simultaneously exceed or pass beyond each other" (165). Although the ecology of love has roots in Whitehead, it is "a concept rarely discussed in process theology" (152).
93. Keller, *God and Power*, 130–32.

94. Spivak, *Critique of Postcolonial Reason*, 383.
95. Ibid.
96. Ibid., 384.
97. Michael Hardt and Antonio Negri, *Multitude: War and Democracy in the Age of Empire* (New York: Penguin, 2004), 351.
98. Ibid., 351–52.
99. Hardt and Negri, *Empire*, 361.
100. D&G enjoin us to become nomads and follow rhizomes so that our "loves will be like the wasp and orchid" (Deleuze and Guattari, *A Thousand Plateaus*, 25). Furthermore, Deleuze's experiments with love as a rhizomatic coupling of multiplicities is not unlike the experience of the impossibility of love expressed by Derrida. For both of them, love forges relations not through identification or parallelism with the other but through mutual differentiation. For more on the concepts of love at work in Deleuze's and Derrida's writings, see John Protevi, "Love", in *Between Deleuze and Derrida*, eds. Paul Patton and John Protevi (London: Continuum Press, 2003). Along similar lines as D&G, Charles Darwin expresses a coevoutionary sense of love, according to which humans and all social animals are not only guided by instinct but are also "impelled by mutual love and sympathy" (Darwin, *The Descent of Man, and Selection in Relation to Sex* [New York: Penguin Group, 2004], 133).
101. Hardt and Negri, *Commonwealth* (Cambridge: Harvard University Press, 2009), 181.
102. Ibid., 171.
103. Morin, *Homeland Earth*, 6, 24. Morin's view of the evolution of the planetary era is analogous to the account of the emerging planetary civilization given by Tucker and Swimme, who recognize that humans are "being called to the next stage of evolutionary history" as we participate "in a transition from an era dominated by competing nation states to one that is birthing a sustainable planetary civilization" (Tucker and Swimme, "Evolutionary Context of an Emerging Planetary Civilization").
104. Ibid., 106, 116, 130.
105. Ibid., 135.
106. Morin, *Homeland Earth*, 106–8.
107. Spivak, *Death of a Discipline*, 72.
108. Ibid., 102, 78.
109. Ibid., 114. To figure the (im)possibility of planetary collectivities, Spivak refers to Derrida (specifically *The Politics of Friendship*, trans. George Collins [New York: Verso, 20]), who often engages in prayers for the impossible (Spivak, *Death of a Discipline*, 27–32). Derrida opens *The Politics of Friendship* by repeating the impossible question, "How many of us are there?" (1–2). How can we count the collective? Who counts and who is counted? How much? These questions open onto the underived alterity of every other, such that "every other is altogether other" (*tout autre est tout autre*) (22). There are always more others to come, and every other harbours more otherness to come. Inevitably, something or someone gets left out of the count, excluded, homogenized, or subordinated. If counting the collective were not impossible, it would be, as Derrida says, "a poor possible"—calculated and assimilated into some grid, programme, or formula (29). It is as impossible to decide upon the collective as it is to decide whom one loves: "What knowledge could ever measure up to the injunction to choose between those whom one loves, whom one must love, whom one can love"? (22). Spivak follows Derrida in claiming that the impossible figure of planetarity is only possible if it is "opened up with the question 'How many are we'?" (Spivak, *Death of a Discipline*, 102).

110. Keller, *God and Power*, 148–51.
111. Morin, *Homeland Earth*, 144–46.
112. Not incidentally, a critique of imperialism and an affirmation of an emerging planetary culture are persistent themes of Joyce's *Finnegans Wake*, where he coined the term *chaosmos*. On those themes, see Philip Kuberski, *Chaosmos: Literature, Science, and Theory* (Albany: SUNY Press, 1994), 55, 58, 141.
113. Such an affirmation of the creative force of impossibility and dysfunction is a shared commitment of Deleuze and Whitehead (Faber, "'O Bitches of Impossibility!'—Programmatic Dysfunction in the Chaosmos of Deleuze and Whitehead", in Deleuze, Whitehead, Bergson: Rhizomatic Connections , ed. Keith Robinson [New York: Palgrave Macmillan, 2009]). Morin also affirms the function of dysfunction. "*Complexity emerges, therefore, at the heart of Oneness simultaneously as relativity, relationality, diversity, alterity, duplicity, ambiguity, uncertainty, antagonism, and in the union of these notions which are each in reference to the others complementary, concurrent, and antagonistic.* [. . .] There is no organization without anti-organization. There is no functioning without dysfunction". Morin, *Method: Towards a Study of Humankind. Vol. 1 of The Nature of Nature*, trans. J. L. Roland Bélanger (New York: Peter Lang, 1992), 146.
114. "Another world is possible" is the slogan of the World Social Forum, an annual meeting (first held in Brazil in 2011) of people and organizations committed to resisting imperialism and neoliberalism and to building another world, a more peaceful, just, and sustainable world. To put it in Deleuzian terms, this slogan expresses a cry for the event. In this tone, Stengers and Philippe Pignarre say together that "another world is possible" is "a cry" and not merely "a thesis or a program, whose value would be judged by its plausibility. [. . .] We say that this cry is the name of an event, and that the force of this event is the manner in which it makes this question exist for those who respond to it: how is one to inherit, to prolong, to become the child of the event"? Pignarre and Stengers, *Capitalist Sorcery: Breaking the Spell* (New York: Palgrave Macmillan, 2011), 4.
According to Deleuze, the cry "All is event!" has resounded three times in the history of philosophy, in the ancient world it was the Stoics, in the modern world Leibniz, and most recently in the constructive postmodernism of Whitehead. Deleuze, "Cours Vincennes", para. 7, Les Cours de Gilles Deleuze, April 29, 1980, http://www.webdeleuze.com/php/texte.php?cle=55&groupe=Leibniz&langue=2. For more on Deleuze's "cry for the event", see Faber, "Introduction", 12.
115. Irigaray, *I Love to You: Sketch for a Possible Felicity in History*, trans. Alison Martin (New York: Routledge, 1996), 10. Furthermore, Irigaray's sense of the future also resonates with the apocalyptic tone of the Joachite third age. Gesturing towards a theology of becoming, Irigaray invokes an age of the couple to follow the ages of the Father and the Son. "The third era of the West might, at last, be the era of the *couple*: of the spirit and the bride? [. . .] The spirit and the bride invite beyond genealogical destiny to the era of the wedding and the festival of the world. To the time of a theology of the breath in its horizontal and vertical becoming, with no murders". Irigaray, *An Ethics of Sexual Difference*, trans. Carolyn Burke and Gillian C. Gill (London: Continuum, 2004), 148–49.
116. Morin, *Homeland Earth*, 114.
117. Ibid., 130, 141.
118. Ibid., 142.
119. Thomas Berry, *The Great Work: Our Way into the Future* (New York: Bell Tower, 1999), 48.
120. Keller, *God and Power*, 110; Morin, *Homeland Earth*, 106.

121. Keller, *Apocalypse Now and Then*, 218–22.
122. Keller, *God and Power*, 110.
123. Ibid., 51–52.
124. Appadurai, "Grassroots Globalization and the Research Imagination", *Public Culture* 12.1 (2009): 1–19.
125. Deleuze and Guattari, *A Thousand Plateaus*, 19, 25.
126. Keller, *God and Power*, 52. The term *just love* has a few different meanings, connoting a justice shaped by mercy and compassion, a love that is all you need, and a love that requires justice. "Not only does this term suggest a justice tempered by mercy and warmed by compassion, but while 'all you need is love,' as the Beatles crooned, it is also true that love without justice is not love but abuse" (164).
127. Keller, *God and Power*, 135; Whitehead, *Process and Reality: An Essay in Cosmology*, corr. ed. eds. David Ray Griffin and Donald W. Sherburne (New York: Free Press, 1978, 50); Latour, *We Have Never Been Modern*, trans. Catherine Porter (Cambridge: Harvard University Press, 1993), 142.
128. Diogenes Laertius, *Lives of Eminent Philosophers. Vol. 2*, trans. R. D. Hicks (Cambridge: Harvard University Press, 1970), 6.63.
129. Latour, *Pandora's Hope: Essays on the Reality of Science Studies* (Cambridge: Harvard University Press, 1999), 305.
130. Kant there claimed that the expansion of hospitality with regard to "use of the right to the earth's surface which belongs to the human race in common" would "finally bring the human race ever closer to a cosmopolitan constitution" (Kant, "Toward Perpetual Peace", in *Practical Philosophy: Cambridge Edition of the Works of Immanuel Kant*, trans. M. J. Gregor [Cambridge: Cambridge University Press, 1999], 329 [8:358]).
131. Stengers, *Cosmopolitics I*, trans. Robert Bononno (Minneapolis: University of Minnesota Press, 2010), 79.
132. Aiming to overcome "the objectivism of war" and "the totality it reveals", Levinas proposes a peaceful subjectivity that breaks through totalizations with the otherness of infinity, and he defines that "subjectivity as welcoming the Other, as hospitality" (Levinas, *Totality and Infinity*, 25, 27). While Levinas focuses primarily on the ethics of hospitality, Derrida elaborates on the connections between this sense of hospitality and politics, proposing a cosmopolitanism of welcoming the profound otherness of every other. On Derrida's proposal for a "concept of hospitality" that facilitates a "new ethic" and "new cosmo*politics*", see Derrida, *On Cosmopolitanism and Forgiveness*, trans. Mark Dooley and Michael Hughes (New York: Routledge, 2001), 5.
133. Although Levinas and Derrida both discuss human others primarily, there are many places in Derrida's writings where he articulates the ethically compelling otherness of nonhumans, particularly nonhuman animals, including much discussion of his cat. On the ecological implications of Derrida's philosophy, see David Wood, "Specters of Derrida: On the Way to Econstruction", in *Ecospirit: Religions and Philosophies for the Earth*, eds. Laurel Kearns and Catherine Keller (New York: Fordham University Press, 2007), and "Thinking with Cats", in *Animal Philosophy: Essential Readings in Continental Philosophy*, eds. Matthew Calarco and Peter Atterton (London: Continuum, 2004).
134. Latour, *Pandora's Hope*, 305.
135. Stengers, "The Cosmopolitical Proposal", in *Making Things Public: Atmospheres of Democracy*, eds. Bruno Latour and Peter Weibel (Cambridge: MIT Press, 2005), 995.
136. Donna Haraway, *When Species Meet* (Minneapolis: University of Minnesota Press, 2008), 83. For D&G's articulation of the "conceptual persona" of the

idiot, which resonates with Dostoevsky, Augustine, Cusa, and others, see Deleuze and Guattari, *What Is Philosophy?*, 61–63.
137. Haraway, *When Species Meet*, 83.
138. Ibid., 243, 299.
139. Ibid., 106.
140. Ibid., 65, 256. Haraway adapts the phrase *ontological choreography* from Charis Thompson, *Making Parents: The Ontological Choreography of Reproductive Technologies* (Cambridge: MIT Press, 2005).
141. Haraway, *When Species Meet*, 19, 88.
142. Ibid., 42.
143. Stengers, *Cosmopolitics I*, 83.
144. Latour, *Pandora's Hope*, 290. Latour's indebtedness to Stengers is indicated in his *Politics of Nature*, which is dedicated to Stengers (and to Vinciane Despret and David Western), "three true practitioners of cosmopolitics" (v). Latour says that his writing on his project of political ecology "shamelessly looted Stengers' *Cosmopolitics*" (viii).
145. Latour, *Pandora's Hope*, 297.
146. Ibid., 290–91. This effort to protect ontological diversity is the focus of Latour's latest work, *An Inquiry into Modes of Existence*, which is a collaborative and multimedia affirmation of ontological pluralism. As Latour puts it, "We may benefit from an ontological pluralism that will allow us to populate the cosmos in a somewhat richer way, and thus allow us to begin to compare worlds, to weigh them, on a more equitable basis" (Latour, *An Inquiry into Modes of Existence: An Anthropology of the Moderns*, trans. Catherine Porter [Cambridge: Harvard University Press, 2013], 21).
147. Latour, *Pandora's Hope*, 290.
148. For Latour's concept of factish gods, see Latour, *On the Modern Cult of the Factish Gods*, trans. Catherine Porter and Heather MacLean (Durham: Duke University Press, 2010). "The words 'fetish' and 'fact' have the same ambiguous etymology", deriving from Latin *facere* ("to make", "to do"), which simultaneously connotes an external or objective reality (fact) and the subjective process or making or believing in reality (fetish) (21). "Joining the two etymological sources, we shall use the label *factish* for the robust certainty that allows practice to pass into action without the practitioner ever believing in the difference between construction and reality, immanence and transcendence" (22).
149. Latour, *We Have Never Been Modern*, 65. Latour is criticizing Heidegger's contempt for modernity, which has supposedly forgotten about Being.

> And yet—"here too the gods are present": in a hydroelectric plant on the banks of the Rhine, in subatomic particles, in Adidas shoes as well as in the old wooden clogs hollowed out by hand, in agribusiness as well as in timeworn landscapes, in shopkeepers' calculations as well as in Hölderlin's heartrending verse. [. . .] Has someone, however, actually forgotten about Being? Yes: anyone who really thinks that Being has really been forgotten. (66)

Latour's theology is thus an actor-oriented theology or "object-oriented theology" (Adam Miller, *Speculative Grace : Bruno Latour and Object-Oriented Theology* [New York: Fordham University Press, 2013]). It resonates with Nicholas of Cusa's claim that "every creature is, as it were, a finite infinity or a created god" (Nicholas of Cusa, "On Learned Ignorance", in *Nicholas of Cusa: Selected Spiritual Writings*, trans. H. Lawrence Bond [New York: Paulist Press, 1997], 134). In the chaosmos, every actor is a created god, and God is an actor, a rhizomatic event. Thus, in Whitehead's chaosmos, God is not the origin of the creative process of becoming. "God is its primordial, non-temporal, accident" (Whitehead, *Process and Reality*, 7). This nontemporal event is "at once a creature of creativity and a condition for creativity. It shares this double character with all creatures" (31). What sets God apart from other actors is that God is the nontemporal limit of becoming. "God is *the limit* of the Event of Becoming, the *impossible* Event [. . .] the *infinite process of intensification itself*" (Faber, "Introduction: Negotiating Becoming", 47). God is "the *limit* of the *most intense dis/harmony of the Chaosmos*" (49). In Deleuzian terms, this impossible Event is the pure event, pure becoming, the non-sensical limit of sense, which Deleuze sometimes refers to as the "Body without Organs" (abbreviated as BwO) (46). Deleuze's BwO and Whitehead's God name the same activity, "the apophatic bodying of multiplicity", which resonates with "the pair of *complication/explication*" in Nicholas of Cusa's unfolding God (Faber, "Bodies of the Void: Polyphilia and Theoplicity", in *Apophatic Bodies: Negative Theology, Incarnation, and Relationality*, eds. Chris Boesel and Catherine Keller [New York: Fordham University Press, 2010], 222). The BwO-God connection is discussed in Faber, "'O Bitches of Impossibility!'" On the BwO, see Deleuze and Guattari, *Thousand Plateaus*, 149–66.

150. This is related to a fundamental principle of Latour's philosophy of actors, which is expressed in *Irreductions* (which is published in English as part of *The Pasteurization of France*, trans. Alan Sheridan and John Law [Cambridge: Harvard University Press, 1988]): "Nothing is, by itself either reducible or irreducible to anything else" (158). For an overview of this principle and of *Irreductions*, see Graham Harman, *Prince of Networks: Bruno Latour and Metaphysics* (Melbourne, Australia: re.press), 2009, 11–32.

151. Jane Bennett, *Vibrant Matter: A Political Ecology of Things* (Durham: Duke University Press, 2010), 108. Bennett is attempting to shift away from anthropocentric theories of democracy towards "a more (vital) materialist theory of democracy" (106). Bennett's materialism does not posit a world devoid of vitality or meaning but "a knotted world of vibrant matter", in which all beings are actors or agents in interconnected assemblages (13). "The political project" of Bennett's work is "to encourage more intelligent and sustainable engagements with vibrant matter and lively things" (viii).

152. Ibid., 108.

153. Stengers, *Cosmopolitics I*, 29. Stengers acknowledges Derrida's "magisterial text" in which he examines the functions of the *pharmakon* in Plato (specifically in Plato's *Phaedrus*), although she does "not necessarily accept the point of view proposed, where the multiplicity of *pharmaka* is subtly channeled toward the overarching question of writing" (264–5). On Derrida's reading of the *pharmakon*, see "Plato's Pharmacy", in Derrida, *Dissemination*, 61. It is worth noting that Derrida does not only associate *pharmaka* with human artifacts but also with nonhuman matters. For instance, Derrida associates the liquidity of water with the *pharmakon*. "In liquid, opposites are more easily mixed. Liquid is the element of the *pharmakon*. And water, pure liquidity, is most easily and dangerously penetrated then corrupted by the *pharmakon*, with which it mixes and immediately unites" (152). The connection between water and the *pharmakon* is at work in Plato's *Phaedrus*, wherein Socrates and Phaedrus speak to one another along the river Ilissus while making various references to the *pharmakon* (229c, 230d, 268c, 274e), including mention of Oreithyia, who was blown into the abyss while playing along the river with Pharmacea (229a–d).

154. Stengers, *Cosmopolitics I*, 29.
155. Ibid., 28.
156. Ibid., 30.

157. Ibid., 31.
158. Ibid., 30.
159. Ibid., 32.
160. Ibid.
161. Ibid., 34, 36.
162. Ibid., 35.
163. Ibid.
164. Ibid., 83, 72.
165. Stengers, *Cosmopolitics II*, trans. Robert Bononno (Minneapolis: University of Minnesota Press, 2011), 356.
166. Ibid., 372.
167. Stengers, *Cosmopolitics I*, 80.
168. According to Pignarre and Stengers, capitalist sorcery operates with techniques of capture that impose "infernal alternatives" onto planetary subjects, propagating a "set of situations that seem to leave no other choice than resignation or a slightly hollow sounding denunciation", passive acceptance or futile resistance (Pignarre and Stengers, *Capitalist Sorcery*, 24). Such capture is called magic or sorcery insofar as it is a mysterious process of transformation that exceeds market or scientific rationality. On the concept of "magical capture", see Deleuze and Guattari, *A Thousand Plateaus*, 460. On Stengers's transformation of D&G's concept into her concept of "reciprocal capture", see Stengers, *Cosmopolitics I*, 35–37.
169. Stengers says that "joy is an event" that relates to "the sorceresses' Goddess who, they say, is everywhere that joy, invention, and connection are. When new possibilities of thinking and acting appear, it is an ontological, or cosmological, event that we must learn to celebrate, even if it's precarious, precisely because it's precarious" (Stengers, "History through the Middle: Between Macro and Mesopolitics; Interview with Isabelle Stengers, 25 November 2008", *Inflexions: A Journal for Research Creation* 3 (2009): 1–15, http://www.senselab.ca/inflexions/volume_3/node_i3/stengers_en_inflexions_vol03.html#1, 10). An integral ecology must take seriously the practises of neopaganism, magic, and sorcery. "Don't say witches are regressive, seeking to reanimate a spirituality condemned by history. I think that their practices make them capable of connecting with what is unique in our epoch, including the threat of new types of powers for which we lack a concept and have never experienced" (11). The relevance of Starhawk's craft for countering the capture apparatus of capitalism is explored in more detail in Stengers, "Experimenting with Refrains: Subjectivity and the Challenge of Escaping Modern Dualism", *Subjectivity* 22 (2008): 38–59. Also see Pignarre and Stengers, *Capitalist Sorcery*, 34–41.
170. Deleuze and Guattari, *A Thousand Plateaus*, 241, 246, 250–51.
171. Deleuze and Guattari, *What Is Philosophy?*, 41.
172. Ibid., 99.

FIVE
Conclusion

Integral ecology engages ecological realities in their rhizomatic complexity, crossing boundaries between disciplines and, more than that, opening those boundaries up to new events, new modes of planetary coexistence. It counters the dominant partitions of time ("temporal/nontemporal, historical/eternal, and particular/universal"), and it opens them up to a new time, a "third time", what Deleuze, following Nietzsche, calls "the untimely".[1] Practicing the craft of integral ecology means "acting counter to our time and thereby acting on our time and, let us hope, for the benefit of a time to come".[2] Untimely practises are nevertheless quite timely. They are called for now more than ever, now, in our disjointed time of so much domination, injustice, despair, and extinction. Guattari calls for such practises in his ecological vision. "Ecological praxes strive to scout out" possibilities for liberation, seeking "something that runs counter to the 'normal' order of things, a counter-repetition" or "creative repetition" that opens a rhizomatic "rupture" in the boundaries of the current system and thus "invokes other intensities to form new existential configurations".[3] Through its beginning, middle, and ending, this book aligns the emerging field of integral ecology with philosophical concepts like those expressed by Deleuze, Guattari, and others who are variously affiliated with them (e.g., Whitehead, Derrida, Keller, Stengers), concepts that resonate with the transversal movement of counterrepetition, aiming to open possibilities for the new Earth and new people composing a planetary civilization.

The conclusion to an academic book or essay often includes a summary, which repeats the concepts and connections laid out in the rest of the book. This conclusion, too, repeats. More specifically, this conclusion attempts a creative repetition; that is, a repetition with a difference. One difference is the introduction of D&G's concept of the refrain, which is related to Deleuze's concept of repetition. Following that difference, there are others: compost, the SF mode, and the verge. Each of those concepts is not introduced in the previous chapters, yet each resonates with the other concepts proposed throughout this work. Like rhizomes, imagination, nomadology, decision, chaosmos, planetary love, and so on, those concepts create modes of existence that stay in the middle of the world's multiplicities, affirming the irreducible complexity of their boundaries and resisting any logic of domination that would partition multiplicities into dualistic hierarchies that legitimate oppression and violence against human and Earth others.

As stated in the "Beginning" chapter of the present work, beginning is a boundary project: edgy, liminal. It never happens out of nothing. It does not emerge from a self-identical subject or object. It takes place amidst the entangled boundaries of the chaosmos. Beginning is always beginning again, taking place in the open, emerging out of the profound complexities of pure difference—the "chaos which complicates everything".[4] In short, every beginning is a repetition of difference. Harboured in difference itself is the "power of beginning and beginning again"; accordingly, it could be said that "the true philosophical beginning, Difference, is in-itself already Repetition".[5] The beginning is already a repetition. To begin is to repeat. As Deleuze notes, this is related to "the idea of philosophy as a Circle", which rediscovers at the end what was already present in the beginning; however, "this circle is truly not tortuous enough".[6] Insofar as it repeats *difference*, repetition never returns to the *same* as what was already there, but opens out into the new. Repetition is difference itself in the complex process of making a difference, the transformative activity of unfolding and enfolding new events. Deleuze's concept of *pure difference* thus coalesces with his concept of *complex repetition*. Furthermore, these concepts are not just concepts of beginning. They are concepts of ending, making Deleuze's *Difference and Repetition* "an apocalyptic book", which works to counter the dominant dualisms given in this present era (e.g., particular/universal, sensible/intelligible, copy/model) and thereby invoke new modes of existence that stay in the open, in the middle of multiplicities.[7] The beginning, middle, and ending of all things pulses with complex repetition and pure difference.

Repeating differences, differentiating repetitions, everything in the chaosmos vibrates with the song of complex repetition and pure difference. "A single voice raises the clamour of being. [. . .] A single and same voice for the whole thousand-voiced multiple, a single and same Ocean for all the drops, a single clamour of Being for all beings".[8] That oceanic voice resonates in *The Universe Story* of Swimme and Berry: "There is eventually only one story, the story of the universe. Every form of being is integral with this comprehensive story. Nothing is itself without everything else".[9] Along these lines, Nicholas of Cusa remarks that "all things are in all things", Whitehead speculates that "everything is everywhere at all times", and Deleuze claims that "Being is the unique event in which all events communicate with one another", "the void of all events in one", "the nonsense of all senses in one", "a single voice for every hum of voices and every drop of water in the sea".[10] All things and their milieus are folded together in the mutually transformative becomings of a single song (uni-verse). "Climate, wind, season, hour are not of another nature than the things, animals, or people that populate them, follow them, sleep and awaken within them".[11] There is a single great song for every little ditty vibrating in the chaosmos. This is the beginning and ending of the chaosmos and everything in it. "Everything begins with refrains. [. . .] and everything comes to an end at infinity in the great Refrain". A single great Refrain raises the clamor of all refrains. D&G describe the great Refrain as a cosmic song, "the song of the universe", which also resonates as "a powerful song of the earth—the deterritorialized".[12]

REFRAIN

In music, a refrain is a repeating line, such as the chorus of a song. Consider the well-known refrains of songs by the Beatles. "All you need is love". "Let it be". Deriving from the Latin *refringere* ("to repeat"), the English word *refrain* translates D&G's French *ritournelle*, which is also translated into English with the Italian word *ritornello* ("little return")—a term used in Baroque music to denote a recurring line or theme.[13] D&G transform the musical meaning of refrains into a philosophical concept of complex repetition and difference. Like the rhizome, the differential process of the refrain can be described as an interactive movement between territorialization and deterritorialization. These movements are evident in the three main components of every refrain: territorializing, territorialized, and deterritorializing.

First, the territorializing component "jumps from chaos to the beginnings of order in chaos and is in danger of breaking apart at any moment", as when a terrified child lost in the dark sings, opening up a "center in the heart of chaos".[14] Territorializing components sketch out and maintain a centre amidst chaos, mapping a territory, drawing "a circle around that uncertain and fragile center".[15] Second, the space sketched out by the first components is organized and stratified by territorialized components. If the first components help make a home, the second components organize the home, stabilize its boundaries (e.g., put up a fence, trim hedges, tend the lawn), and support efforts to do things in the home. Now at home, the "child hums to summon the strength for the schoolwork she has to hand in".[16] Third, the refrain deterritorializes the circle organized by the first two components, thus opening up to new possibilities to let someone or something in or out. Deterritorialization does not mean reopening onto the chaos that was previously encircled and organized. It does not regress, but opens out "in order to join with the forces of the future, cosmic forces. One launches forth, hazards an improvisation [. . .] to join with the World, or meld with it". For example, the child doing schoolwork starts singing in a band, such that her individual territory becomes different and converts into a new thing: a band. The child matures and starts dating, and her "territorial assemblage" opens again to a new assemblage, "the courtship assemblage".[17] In conveying the coevolutionary inventiveness of refrains, the example of courtly love touches on another inventive refrain: planetary love. Imagine the imperial global assemblage opening onto a cosmic force, transforming into a cosmopolitical assemblage that cultivates loving contact between planetary creatures. Along those lines, imagine humans worldwide opening onto cosmic forces, transforming into anthropocosmic assemblages. As citizens (*polites*), as humans (*anthropoi*), this is our task: becoming cosmic.

When deterritorialization becomes absolute, it opens onto the infinity of the great Refrain. "At infinity, these refrains must rejoin the songs of the Molecules, [. . .] becoming cosmic", becoming "an immense deterritorialized refrain".[18] Our cosmopolitical and anthropocosmic tasks are not oriented towards building systems or models (*nor towards opposing* such buildings), but to forging alliances with the forces of our chaotic and omnicentric cosmos.[19]

Moreover, becoming cosmic happens somewhere.[20] It is not a final end to Earth or people, nor is it a retreat to an origin. Beginning and beginning again, becoming cosmic happens in the middle of multiplicities of humans and nonhumans. It takes place. The great Refrain becomes contracted in the little refrains of particular territories, such that every refrain folds together rhythm (repetition) and chaos (pure difference), enacting different assemblages, different modes of the great Refrain of "rhythm-chaos or the chaosmos".[21]

It is by opening up to the infinity of the great Refrain that territories emerge, develop, and are restored.[22] Participating in the powerful songs of Earth, the Molecules, the Cosmos, and other places of the great Refrain, we can participate in the restoration of the territories of our planetary home. The vibrations of D&G's refrains can be heard in Rachel Carson. "There is something infinitely healing in the repeated refrains of nature—the assurance that dawn comes after night, and spring after the winter".[23] There are many ways to open up territories to restorative potentials and new connections. Sciences, arts, governments, businesses, and religions all have ways of composing a world in which all planetary creatures contact the generative and restorative processes of the chaosmos. In this work, I have focused on the contributions of philosophy for efforts to compose such a world, philosophy for a planetary civilization.

By opening up the refrains of philosophical concepts that are marked by the dualistic logic of domination (e.g., natural/cultural, sensible/intelligible, and the either/or morality of apocalypse), those refrains can be restored or recuperated. For example, the refrains of sense can be recuperated from their confines in the sensible/intelligible binary. A counterapocalypse can be restored, an apocalypse without a violent either/or morality. Becoming restored, those concepts become restorative, capable of resisting domination and facilitating encounters with the infinitely healing power of refrains. In this sense, philosophy for a planetary civilization is about experimenting with *healing refrains*, which has a double meaning, a double movement: (1) by bringing healing to philosophical refrains, (2) our refrains can become infinitely healing.[24] By healing our concepts of boundaries (beginnings, middles, endings), we can participate in a creative repetition of concepts and thereby open up new possibilities for integral ecology to map the rhizomatic lines of planetary actors and facilitate the composition of peaceful, just, and sustainable modes of planetary coexistence, "*to summon forth a new earth, a new people*".[25] It is by participating in the counterrepetition of refrains that humans can respond creatively to the challenges of the ecological crisis, nurturing "the creation of a future new earth".[26]

By repeating the refrains of our time in a creative way, in a way that brings them into the open, into contact with the generative matrix of the chaosmos, it becomes possible to transform those refrains so that they resist the global hegemony of domination and imperial judgement and nurture a time to come, a time of a vibrant planetary civilization. It becomes possible to creatively transform our participation in the song of the planet and the song of the chaosmos, or in Berry's terms, our "participation in the dream of the Earth" and "the *story* of the universe".[27] Such participation empowers us to perform the great work of our time, "to carry out the transition from a period of human devastation of the Earth to a period when humans would be present to the planet in a mutually beneficial manner".[28]

COMPOST

The great work of our time is to become untimely, to enact counter-repetitions, creative refrains, which make way for a new sense of the world and a new sense of the place of humans therein. Such refrains would make way for practises that "reinvent the human *at the species level*".[29] In other words, they would make way for recycling the human, composting all of the boundary projects of our species history. This way of imagining composting is expressed in Keller's account of working and playing with a compost heap in El Salvador in an "international, multiracial group of Drew University theological students with *indigenous* peasants" working with Marta Benevides, a *feminist* activist organizing the project and "working to reclaim a bit of *land* and thereby to teach an *ecological* praxis" for the sake of independence from neocolonial structures.[30] The joyous "dance of the compost heap" involves the ontological choreography of actors entangled in so many relations, so many differences: sexual, ecological, socioeconomic, racial, international, political, religious. By giving our boundary projects over to the compost heap, we "recycle our history and our common ground", such that their boundaries come undone, and in that undoing, they become places of new beginnings, open to the emergence and development of new humus, new humans, new relations, new actors.[31] Moreover, not everything gets recycled. Some things are too toxic, too imperial, too dangerous to risk including in the process. Who is included?

There is no final answer or certainty. There is only the ongoing decisions of cosmopolitics, the ongoing effort of accounting for multiplicities of actors and creating a collective together. There is only the ongoing work and play of composting.

"The compost heap", according to Keller, "offers a metaphoric answer to our situation" amidst the destruction of our disjointed time:

> We cannot escape from our own world. But we need not. We need rather to take account of where we are, who we are, who we are with, and what we are for and thus proceed with our own recycling of ourselves and our cultures. One does not then hope for purification, for any unambiguous alternative space, either within our lives our within which we may live.[32]

Recycling ourselves, reinventing the human, who are we? What is becoming of humans as we participate in the process of becoming different, becoming planetary? If humanity is *com-post*, then it could be said that the human is now *with post*. Are humans becoming posthuman? Already in an era of postcolonialism and postmodernism, an era of posthumanism is also on its way. Humanism is giving way to posthumanism. Posthumanism composts the sovereign individual subject that defines the humanism of secular modernity as well as religious humanisms, where the exceptional power of humans is granted by an omnipotent God or some such origin or original order. In other words, the deconstruction of humanism, according to Faber, takes place in proximity to "the composting of the 'dead body of God'".[33] Recycling humanism means that all humanisms must be re-situated, re-placed, which entails troubling the boundaries of humans and nonhumans as well as the boundaries stratifying sacred and secular modes of existence. In the sacred-secular compost, posthumanism could be described more specifically as *postsecular posthumanism*—a phrase indicating that, amidst the vibrating refrains of the omnicentric chaosmos, the boundaries between human/nonhuman and sacred/secular are unpredictable, complex, and open-ended.

Posthumanism is what comes after humanism, particularly as humanism is defined in "Western" philosophy, from the classical humanism of ancient Greece through Renaissance humanism and modern humanism. Posthumanism comes after the humanism of Socrates in Plato's *Phaedrus*, where he says that trees and country places have nothing to teach him, only people in the city do.[34] It comes after Kant, who says that only humans are ends in themselves and that animals only deserve respect indirectly, as disrespecting them might lead one to disrespect humans.[35] It comes after existentialists for whom the human is the lonely arbiter of meaning in the world. In each of these humanisms, the human species has a central or exceptional status in opposition to the rest of the cosmos, whether as the primary focus of intellectual and moral concern, the pinnacle of creation, or the only and lonely source of meaning in the world.

Humanism is complicit in human exceptionalism, which could be described variously as speciesism, species narcissism, anthropocentrism, human chauvinism, and a human superiority complex. It presupposes a fundamental divide separating humans from other organisms, culture from nature, meaning from matter, word from flesh, politics from cosmos. Noticing that humanism cannot account for the complex relations connecting humans with technologies, environments, and other species, posthumanists seek something different. In some cases, posthumanists are "transhumanists", aiming to transform the human species through technological enhancements that can increase human capacities and transcend limitations like ageing and sickness. However, the sense of posthumanism I'm discussing is not predicated on desires to improve the human condition through technology, but is predicated upon critiques of human exceptionalism that have been developed in recent decades of critical theory, feminist theory, science and technology studies, religion and ecology, animal studies, "New Paradigm" thought, and environmental ethics.[36] Posthumanism integrates those critiques in efforts to re-place the human of anthropocentrism, which is to say, place the human back into its complex context—an entanglement of cultural, technological, semiotic, ecological, and evolutionary becomings.

Posthumanists challenge dualisms that oppose the human to the rest of the cosmos (e.g., animal/human, nature/culture, material/semiotic, *kosmos/polis*, body/mind, organic/technological). The human of posthumanism is constituted by its contact with the unruly edges of multiplicities of humans and nonhumans. Mapping such "unruly edges", the anthropologist Anna Tsing makes the following declaration: "Human nature is an interspecies relationship".[37] "In truth", as D&G put it, "there are only inhumanities, humans are made exclusively of inhumanities, but very different ones, of very different natures and speeds".[38] This entails that humanity is not the sole or primary centre of value (i.e., nonhumans are centres, too), and human centres are themselves constituted by relations to nonhuman actors and material forces. Consider Bachelard, who recognizes that "the world gravitates about a *value*" and that the centre of gravity is everywhere, not just in humans and not just in animals or organisms, but in everything, even a lamp: "The evening lamp on the family table is also the center of a world".[39] With posthumanism, research in the humanities becomes posthumanities, such that scholarly investigations into human cultures, meanings, and symbols account for the ways in which human phenomena are intimately intertwined with heterogeneous nonhuman actors. Drawing on Deleuze and Darwin, Elizabeth Grosz calls for such an approach to the humanities. "A new humanities becomes possible once the human is placed in its properly inhuman context", and these new humanities are connected to "the open varieties of life" (including human life) and "generate critical ecologies" that map human-nonhuman assemblages.[40]

Haraway's work is particularly relevant for recycling the human at the *species* level, as that book explicates the rambunctious category of companion species. That category figures the "naturalcultural contact zones" ("material-semiotic nodes or knots") whereby species become intimately entangled with one another in mutually constitutive relationships.[41] Species do not preexist the ontological choreography of their relational becoming. For a human, this means that "I am who I become with companion species", with "significant others" who call for respectful responses, with dance partners in the choreography of "species", which includes the dance between species as kinds and species as specifics as well as the dance between natural and cultural "species": "Not much is excluded from the needed play" of companion species, "not technologies, commerce, organisms, landscapes, peoples, practices".[42] That multidimensional and coevolutionary sense of the human species seems to be what posthumanism is all about. Recycling the human at the species level, the human becomes posthuman—a multispecies companion. To some extent, this "post" is not new. Throughout the entire development of the species, humans have always already been entwined in material-semiotic knots with other species. Humans have domesticated other species and have been domesticated by other species. My sensing, feeling, thinking, and speaking all express an implosion of the human and nonhuman. Just as Latour argues that "we have never been modern" insofar as moderns never really separated nature from society, Haraway says that "we have never been human and so are not caught in the cyclopean trap of mind and matter, action and passion, actor and instrument. Because we have never been the philosopher's human, we are bodies in braided, ontic, and antic relatings".[43] Moreover, this complex interspecies dance is not only figured in the category of companion species. It is also figured in many other concepts explicated in the present work: rhizomes, planetarity, and cosmopolitics. Furthermore, those concepts are all in contact with theological and religious concepts: love, witchcraft, panentheism, counterapocalypse. This does not mean that posthumanism is religious or committed to belief in anything sacred. Yet posthumanism is not quite secular either.

Posthumanism is postsecular. Just like posthumanism involves the implosion and transformation of the dualisms separating the human from the cosmos, the terms *postsecularism* and *postsecular* describe "a deconstruction or breakdown of any strict opposition between the religious and the secular".[44] It involves a deconstruction of the boundaries between spiritual and material as well as the boundaries separating religion from the public sphere in modernity. If we have never been modern and never been human, postsecularism joins in the conversation to say that we have never been disenchanted and never been secular.[45] Sacred and secular are not mutually exclusive opposites but are woven into one another. This recognition has become increasingly widespread throughout the twentieth century as religion has returned to the public sphere (e.g., the Israel-Palestine conflict, the Iranian revolution in 1979, the emergence of the religious right in the United States, the spread of fundamentalisms worldwide).[46]

The response of postsecularism to the implosion of the sacred-secular dualism is described by John Caputo (drawing on Derrida) as "religion without religion".[47] Postsecularism is *without religion* insofar as it joins the efforts of secularization to facilitate a democratic world free from the hegemony of any religion. Postsecularism nurtures *religion* without religion insofar as it uncovers the religious powers woven into secular politics and technoscience and facilitates participation in the mystery, wonder, and enchantment characteristic of the sacred. This religion without religion is evident in Derrida's call for an "apocalypse *without* apocalypse".[48] Committed to a justice to come, Derrida participates in the apocalyptic structure of the "to come" while holding in abeyance all commitments to particular apocalypses and apocalyptic traditions, which often harbour judgemental and violent tendencies. In short, postsecularists engage the sacred-secular networks of our global civilization to open possibilities for a more just or democratic world. This resonates with the sacramental consciousness of Haraway's Catholicism without

Catholicism (see "Opening" above), affirming the intertwining of the sacred and the mundane while also criticizing the god tricks performed in the sacred-secular web of the globalized world.[49]

I want to propose an analogy to summarize postsecular posthumanism. In Derrida's autobiographical *Circumfession*, he expresses his religion without religion by drawing on Augustine's *Confessions*, replacing the prefix *con-* with *circum-* so as to indicate a cut (circumcision) that marks multiple differences, including his religious difference from secularism, his Jewish difference from Augustine's Christianity, his atheist difference from Judaism (Jewish without Judaism). A related transformation of Augustine is put into play with Haraway. Instead of changing the prefix of *Confessions*, let us imagine that she changes the root, so that it is no longer "with fess" (*con-fess*; fessing up) but is with mess, with bread, *cum panis*. Augustine's "confessions" undergoes a rhizomatic multispecies transmutation, becoming St. Donna's "companions". Like Augustine, Haraway expresses her sense of self and of the sacred, but unlike Augustine, she does not confess to the wholly Other God of transcendental monotheism. She companions with the significant otherness of messmates.

This postsecular posthumanist transformation of Augustine is evident in the first of the two guiding questions in *When Species Meet*, "Whom and what do I touch when I touch my dog"?[50] This resonates with the question from Augustine's *Confessions*, "What, therefore, do I love when I love my God"?[51] There are significant differences between these questions. Haraway replaces Augustine's "God" with "dog", an anagrammatical shift indicating that "posthumanities" is "another word for 'after monotheism'".[52] Yet this is not a simply secular "after". Haraway affirms the religious tone of this anagram as it is expressed in the common bumper-sticker slogan, "Dog is my co-pilot".[53] Along with the dog-God reversal, she also switches love to touch, such that Augustine's transcendent and Neo-Platonic love is brought down to Earth, into the naturalcultural contact zones of touch, thus engendering a more worldly, tender, and tactful love. "To be in love means to be worldly".[54] Haraway declares that "love prepared me for meeting my companion species, who are my maker".[55] Loving messmates means practicing the cosmopolitics of planetary love, where "cosmopolitics is a practice for going on, for remaining exposed to consequences, for entangling materially with as many of the messy players as possible".[56]

Concepts like companion species express the convergence of postsecularism and posthumanism by facilitating respectful engagements in interspecies worlding, engagements that attend to the perplexing complexity of the material-semiotic entanglements of heterogeneous actors. However, to some extent, these "postal" discourses might prevent the very engagements that they aim to facilitate. After all, going postal is hardly a good thing. An idiom in American English, "going postal" means becoming uncontrollably angry and violent, particularly in the workplace. The phrase emerged in light of multiple incidents in the 1980s and 1990s in which U.S. Postal Service employees suffering from work-related rage committed acts of mass murder at their workplace, shooting and killing other workers and public citizens. People enraged by a system acting out violently against that system: isn't this what happens in the scolding critique generated by the "post" talk of recent decades, with the numerous and varied calls for something postmodern, postcolonial, postmetaphysical, postsecular, postdisciplinary, and posthuman?

Haraway, Derrida, D&G, and many of the other philosophers engaged in the present work are complicit in these postal discourses. However, in many ways their works contrast sharply with postal discourses. For instance, many postsecular and posthumanist discourses use tools of critical theory to rage against the system (i.e., the hegemonic Man and his modern structures of domination), such that one sees total domination covering the planet, with no place of escape. Too much critique and one goes postal, reacting against the system instead of responding constructively to the play of heterogeneous actors. For D&G, there are always more places to move than we realize. Every refrain can crack open to the virtual powers of the great Refrain and create new events. "The most closed system still has a thread that rises toward the virtual, and down which the spider descends".[57] Structures of domination cannot totally close off the play, chaos, and openness of becoming.

Rhizomes, nomads, companion species, and cosmopolitics keep boundary projects open-ended and in play. In contrast, postsecular posthumanism closes up shop and gives us a definitive answer about the direction we are and/or should be headed: after humanism, after the human, towards new and improved hybrids. To the point, Haraway says, "I never wanted to be posthuman, or posthumanist, any more than I wanted to be postfeminist".[58] Haraway's aim is trying to rethink the becoming with of species, "not getting beyond one troubled category for a worse one even more likely to go postal".[59] Haraway's position here is exemplary for any philosophy of integral ecology. It is in tension *and* alliance with "post" efforts to overcome the dualisms propagated by humanism and secularism.[60] In other words, the world of companion species is, as she puts it, a world "inoculated against post-humanism but rich in compost, inoculated against human exceptionalism but rich in humus, ripe for multispecies storytelling".[61] By facilitating counterrepetitions of traditional philosophical refrains, the philosophy of integral ecology is recycling the human species, building alliances *with postal* discourses (*com-post*) while simultaneously resisting the reactionary criticism and violence of going postal.

THE SF MODE

Rich in com-post, the philosophy of integral ecology has a sense of the "post" that does not go postal. The postal system is no longer about going postal in the postmodern, postcolonial, postsecular, posthumanist. Rather, the postal system becomes the ontological choreography of giving and receiving patterns, messages, packages. The postal system becomes what the science fiction author Ursula Le Guin calls a "carrier bag" approach to fiction, which sees technoscience as a "cultural carrier bag rather than weapons of domination", thus cultivating a "strange realism" that experiments speculatively with whatever is going on, opening up to the possibilities coming from the entangled temporalities of our world, "this womb of things to be and tomb of things that were".[62] In contrast to the quite plausible story told by postsecular posthumanism, the carrier bag is more strange and experimental in its worlding practises. Plausible stories are too closed and are not strange or farfetched enough to open up cosmopolitical possibilities for composing the new Earth and people of a planetary civilization. With the carrier bag, the postal system is not about going postal. It transforms into another mode, the SF mode. SF means sci-fi or science fiction, and it means so much more. It is a mode and not just a literary genre.[63] It is a way of worlding that takes on many meanings, such that "SF" functions as a backronym, standing for open-ended configurations of words, from "science fiction" to "so far".

Haraway described the SF mode in her acceptance of the Pilgrim Award from the Science Fiction Research Association in 2011.

> Again and again, SF has given me the ideas, the stories, and the shapes with which I think ideas, shapes, and stories in feminist theory and science studies. [. . .] SF is that potent material-semiotic sign for the riches of speculative fabulation, speculative femi-

nism, science fiction, speculative fiction, science fact, science fantasy—and, I suggest, string figures. In looping threads and relays of patterning, this SF practice is a model for worlding. Therefore, SF must also mean "so far", opening up what is yet-to-come in protean entangled times' pasts, presents, and futures.[64]

Enacting "a game of cat's cradle or string figures", the SF mode is a game of

> giving and receiving patterns, dropping threads and so mostly failing but sometimes finding something that works, something consequential and maybe even beautiful, that wasn't there before, of relaying connections that matter [. . .] to craft conditions for flourishing in the Earth community.[65]

I would add a couple of extra explications. First, the SF mode is a San Francisco mode, where San Francisco (the area in which I presently live and work) is a place full of string figures, including relays between practises of global technoculture and countercultural practises resisting that dominant culture. Second, the "s" in SF is undecidably sacred and/or secular, such that the SF mode participates in the wondrous mystery and significant otherness of the sacred while staying situated in mundane relationships and eschewing god tricks.

If our stories are not undergoing the relays and counterrepetitions of the SF mode, then even concepts of complexity, hybridity, cosmopolitics, and chaosmos end up impeding respectful engagements with significant others. Critiques of god tricks become god tricks themselves, the nonoppositional rhizome and planet become *opposed* to the root and the globe, and the beginnings, middles, and endings of stories are used for dominating and destroying instead of imagining the sense of the world. The SF mode is crucial to the philosophy of integral ecology. To get a better sense of what this mode involves, consider two concepts: "farfetching" and "talking backward". These terms come from Le Guin and are transformed in Sha LaBare's work articulating the SF mode and its relevance for developing a viable ecological ethics that overcomes the limitations of human exceptionalism.[66]

The SF mode uses certain effects (fx) as a way of opening up to other ways of thinking and becoming with others. Far more than putting *post-* prefixes on troubling terms, SF fx involve new words and new languages that evoke alien worlds. With these fx, the SF mode puts into play a generative nonsense that cuts through common sense and opens its horizon. In this respect, a vital part of the

SF mode is talking backwards and having your head on backwards, which are images Le Guin uses in *Always Coming Home*.[67] In Le Guin's usage, talking backwards can be summarized as the wrong-headedness of anthropocentrism. However, even the most anthropocentric terms can be reterritorialized for nonanthropocentric uses. The differences between right-headedness and wrong-headedness are unpredictable and complex. Noticing this, LeBare decides to make "a virtue of necessity by transforming talking backwards from a judgment of wrong-headedness into an sf fx vital to the evocation of new and alien worlds".[68] In LeBare's counterrepetition of Le Guin's refrain, talking backwards itself becomes a concept of counterrepetition. It is a way of contacting others (alien worlds) by creating new codes and meanings out of codes and meanings that are complicit in the current world order.

By talking backwards and connecting with nonhuman others, one cannot abide human exceptionalism, yet one is not simply against human exceptionalism. Rather, one opens up to alternate boundary projects, alternative worldings, while acknowledging complicity in human exceptionalism. In the SF mode, the question is not whether you are guilty of human exceptionalism. It is not about an either/or judgement determining innocence or guilt. The SF mode opens questions about what relays you and your companions are giving and receiving, what rhizomatic connections you are breaking or forging, and how much you are responding to the heterogeneity of actors. Acknowledging complicity, talking backwards is a practise of remembrance for the ongoing significance of past others and histories. Talking backwards is a way of tracking our becomings. Following those tracks is not unlike following the Dreaming tracks discussed by the anthropologist Deborah Bird Rose, who explores the profound ethical implications of living during the current mass extinction event, which humans are causing. Rose opens questions about the human species by crossing boundaries between sciences and humanities while looking backwards to the knowledges of Aboriginal people in Australia and to the first contact of their multispecies kin groups during an ancestral time of Dreaming, the tracks of which traverse the land: "The desert is crisscrossed with Dreaming tracks".[69] The Aboriginal people follow those tracks by singing the refrains of territories, refrains known as "songlines"—lines of the song of the earth, which "bring a body to earth and the land to the body, enabling one to touch the very core of the other, singing the story of a past while bringing about a new future, a new marking of the earth, a new inscription of bodies and territories".[70]

Turning our heads backwards to follow Dreaming tracks with Aboriginal refrains, we can also turn back to follow tracks by experimenting with the refrains of neopaganism, as in Stengers's experiments with "a refrain crafted by the contemporary neo-pagan witch Starhawk, a refrain that challenges us to connect with the burning times, when witches were burnt in Europe".[71] "The smoke of the burned witches still hangs in our nostrils".[72] Witchcraft is not a belief to be accepted or debunked. It is an Earth-based spiritual practise of real existing human beings who were systematically excluded and exterminated throughout centuries of modern history. The point of Starhawk's refrain is not to convert anyone into believing in magic but to empower a practise, a craft that effectively transforms our relationships, composting our histories and our common ground and opening new possibilities for building another world. This backwards-talking refrain does not yield a scolding postal discourse that tells moderns how guilty they are. It is a challenge to stay in touch and track our becomings, our naturalcultural contact zones, cultivating loving planetary practises amidst the risky and complex encounters of cosmopolitics.

Talking backwards to open up to the heterogeneous actors of cosmopolitical encounters, the SF mode is farfetched. Indeed, "farfetching" is an integral component of SF practises of worlding. Another term from Le Guin, *farfetching* is a practise of a "rather high-flown speculation" that produces "an intuitive perception of a moral entirety", which tends to become expressed in metaphors (not rational symbols).[73] In LaBare's *Farfetchings*, he claims that such intuitive perceptions are needed for humans (or "?humans") "to not only survive but thrive on this planet. With our powers having so far outgrown our ethics, ?humans now have the opportunity to pay close attention to our" ecological coexistence—our "togetherness in the great, omniversal collective that is our home".[74] The *speculation* involved in such moral or ethical intuitions recalls the "s" of the SF mode: speculative fiction, speculative fabulation, speculative feminism. Along these lines, the SF mode renews the task of speculative thought after centuries of post-Kantian prohibitions against metaphysics.

The present work might best be described as an experiment with speculative feminism, experimenting with the refrains of theorists such as Haraway, Stengers, Grosz, and Keller, each of whom engages with speculative philosophy (with attention to Whitehead and/or Deleuze) to create concepts that address the contemporary challenges of resisting the dualisms of the logic of domination and bringing together heterogeneous human and nonhuman actors into a cosmopolitical collective. In particular, Keller's speculative feminist theology of becoming, which sustains a political theology of planetary love and cosmopolitan democracy, resonates throughout every chapter of this book, in the explication of concepts that complexify the boundaries of beginnings, middles, and endings. Experimenting with the refrains of speculative feminism empowers humans to creatively engage with the complexity and significant otherness of actors, species, and nomads, wandering together through the cosmopolitical unknown in the planetary era.

Deep inside the ecological crisis, in our time out of joint, there is no assurance that we have reached or will reach the "after" or "end" of the dominant divides that oppose humanity to animality, sacred to mundane, masculine to feminine, identity to difference, culture to nature, semioticity to materiality, cosmos to chaos. By talking backwards with the refrains of farfetching experiments, the speculative philosophy of integral ecology becomes rich in regenerative compost, reinventing the human while resisting the postsecular posthumanist temptation to go postal. The philosophy of integral ecology creates concepts for staying in the open, staying in the middle of multiplicities and calling for another world to come. Open, tactful, and loving, it is a world of intact planetary subjects, an integral Earth community. In short, the philosophy of integral ecology is philosophy for a planetary civilization. To repeat: we are creating concepts to empower participation in the speculative operations of cosmopolitics, tracking the perplexing complexity and complicity of our entangled becomings and, let us hope, forging the becomings of a flourishing Earth community, with love.

ON THE VERGE

After the end of the world, we inhabit a world on edge, yet nonetheless, we are always coming home.[75] We are learning that we do not know who "we" are, and that is precisely who we are: knowing ignorance. "How many of us are there"?[76] Who counts? We try to say "we" for as many beings as we can, and more, compelled by the alluring possibility of counting their effulgent diversity, letting all actors count. *"Let us say we for all being, that is, for every being, for all beings one by one, each time in the singular of their essential plural"*.[77]

Inclusions and exclusions are inevitable, as are ambiguities and uncertainties. The process of making decisions is ongoing. The cosmopolitical unknown is still to come, always in the making, in the process of composition.

In the middle of an unprecedented ecological crisis affecting the natural environment, society, and consciousness, we are beginning and beginning again, on edge. According to Gus Speth, an environmental lawyer, advocate, and cofounder of the Natural Resources Defense Council, there is hope for our world on edge, but there is no time to waste. "Yes, we can save what is left. Yes, we can repair and make amends. We can reclaim nature and restore ourselves. There is a bridge at the edge of the world. But for many challenges, like the threat of climate change, there is not much time".[78] Humans are at a fork on our evolutionary path as we proceed "hollowing out nature, ourselves, and our society", and either path we traverse leads to "the end of the world as we have known it": one path continues with business as usual, which is heading us "toward a ruined planet" and "into the abyss", while the other path "leads to a bridge across the abyss".[79] What carries us across the bridge? For Speth, "We are carried forward by hope, a radical hope, that a better world is possible and that we can build it".[80] Let us hope that humans are making changes in their lives and deciding to transition from crisis to sustainability, from globe to planetarity, from isolated monads to mutually constitutive nomads, from anthropocentric to anthropocosmic and omnicentric. "It is again time to give the world a sense of hope".[81]

In the present work, I explicate a variety of philosophical concepts in an effort to contribute to the renewal of hope for another world and contribute to the transition from the edge of the world to a vibrant planetary civilization. The concepts introduced in this work are very different from one another, yet the contrasts produced by their juxtaposition convey a shared sense of direction: affirming the irreducible complexity of boundaries and eschewing any dualistic hierarchies or hegemonic homogeneities that propagate domination. That is what those concepts are "of" or "on". They can thus be said to be concepts on boundaries, on edge, or on the verge. Accordingly, a philosophy of integral ecology that supports a transition to a sustainable planetary civilization is a philosophy on the verge of a planetary civilization.[82] To be on the verge of a planetary civilization is to encounter the complex boundaries of coexistence in our planetary era. Furthermore, being on the verge of something can also mean that something is almost happening or close to happening: on the verge of tears, on the verge of revolution, on the verge of insanity. A philosophy of integral ecology is almost happening, and a planetary civilization is on its way. In that sense, humans are on the verge of the great work of our time. "We are here to become integral with the larger Earth Community".[83] To become integral with the Earth community requires humans to become different, reinventing and recycling themselves so as to re-place themselves, placing themselves into their complex entanglement with one another and with all planetary creatures. In other words, the task of becoming integral calls for humans to stop thinking and acting as if they are the exclusive centre of value in the universe and start coming home to the omnicentric chaosmos. It calls for humans to get back into their rhizomatic milieus, their middles; that is to say, get back on the verge, on the boundaries, edges, and limits whereby beings wander with and through one another in mutually transformative contact.

The two senses of being *on the verge* converge. A planetary civilization (together with accompanying philosophical refrains) is *almost happening*, on the verge of transforming humans and the Earth community, and its emergence requires a creative encounter with the complexity *of boundaries*. It is on the verge that the current work is situated, with hope for another world to come, hope for the composition of the cosmopolitical unknown. Furthermore, writing on the verge, I am writing, as Deleuze says, "at the frontiers of our knowledge, at the border which separates our knowledge from our ignorance and transforms the one into the other".[84]

Writing philosophy on the verge is a craft, a practise of cultivating pharmacological knowledge, which opens new possibilities by attending to the unpredictable and ambiguous boundaries of events. It is a practise of knowing ignorance (*docta ignorantia*), cultivating and learning a profound unknowing that empowers learning and knowledge. Staying on the verge, at the limits of knowledge, is a practise of ethics, but not an ethics of calculations or rules. It is like a "negative capability" that does not prescribe or proscribe an action but opens us up to the significant otherness of every other, the alterity of every planetary creature.[85] It is a practise of wonder, becoming astonished by the very existence of things. This is analogous to the sense of ethics expressed by Wittgenstein, who recognized that humans have "the impulse to run up against the limits of language", as in the example of "the *astonishment* that anything exists. [. . .] Kierkegaard, too, saw that there is this running up against something, and he referred to it in a fairly similar way (as running up against paradox). This running up against the limits of language is *ethics*.[86]

To stay on the verge is to follow the rhizome, the interconnected milieu of the in-between, the middle. The rhizome is never simply given. In subterranean processes of becoming, it has to be found, composed, and created. It is difficult to stay on the verge. For Aristotle, staying on the verge is precisely what makes ethics difficult. The verge is the virtuous mean between the vices of excess and deficiency. It is that towards which virtuous action aims, and it is "easy to miss the target and difficult to hit it".[87] Like all practises of staying in the middle, the creative task of philosophy is not easy, which might help to explain why philosophical writing can be so difficult to read or understand, including many of the writings referred to in the present work. Deleuze, Guattari, Derrida, Whitehead, and Stengers are far from easy to read, but not through some deficiency on their part. They are difficult because they stay in the middle, on the verge, attending to the thresholds from which philosophy opens out. Along these lines, I follow David Wood in aiming "to vindicate a certain species of *difficulty* in philosophy", a restless difficulty that comes from the complexities engaged by philosophy and from the critical dimension of philosophy, whereby philosophy perennially exceeds itself and turns back on itself.[88] The restless difficulty is a necessary part of philosophy. It emerges at the limit marking the edges of whatever conception of philosophy is dominant at a given time. Although it "*may* disturb the theatre of their performance", the task of mapping the difficult limits of philosophy is done with the "hope that it will increase the demand for seats".[89]

The point of difficult styles, in other words, is not to make philosophy hard but to initiate more people into the ongoing work of creating concepts to summon a new Earth and new people. The "*difficult* styles" of philosophy can thus be seen as "setting up *initiatory thresholds* to prevent any understanding below a certain level of active recognition and participation".[90] Difficult styles are trickster styles. Like the coyote figures of Native American traditions, these styles make and break boundaries to facilitate encounters with the troubling ambiguities, paradoxes, and disturbances that make up the world.[91] The general outline of this book expresses a trickster style, as chapters on beginning, middle, and ending deploy numerous concepts for which the boundaries of beginning, middle, and ending become intertwined in rhizomatic knots.

At its best, philosophy keeps us in the middle, always engaging thresholds, breaking and building boundaries, folding, unfolding, enfolding, refolding, beginning, and beginning again. Philosophy attends to boundaries between concepts as well as many other boundaries, including boundaries between beings, between philosophy and multiple disciplines of research and inquiry, between historical changes and epochs, between concepts and language, between concepts and experience (including "limit-experiences" where we run up against the limits of thought and language, opening the horizons of our organized territories).[92] It also attends to the boundaries between boundaries and boundarylessness, limited and unlimited, infinite and finite. The aim of the present work resonates with Wood's *Philosophy at the Limit*:

> Philosophy is an everlasting fire, sometimes damped down by setting itself limits, then flaring into new life as it consumes them. Every field of inquiry is limited, but philosophy has an essential relation to the question of limits, to its own limits. [. . .] The book is devoted to the results of confronting some of these limits. Perhaps "negotiating" would be better than "confronting". For one of the central issues is whether overcoming such limits is not itself an illusion, a burden — a limitation.[93]

The difficult style of facilitating encounters with the complexity of limits requires "the transformation of philosophical style into a performance".[94] For a philosophy of integral ecology, the question is this: How do you perform an act of staying in the middle, dwelling amidst multiplicities in an omnicentric chaosmos? This performance of liminality resonates with the concept of ritual and theatrical performance articulated by the anthropologist Victor Turner, for whom all performance is a liminal experience — an experience of transformative transitions and threshold-crossings, an experience that makes possible the creation of new structures and modes of coexistence. To some extent, all experience involves performances of liminality, as people are continually crossing borders of different social structures while playing various roles in the drama of social existence.[95] "Liminality implies that the high could not be high unless the low existed, and he who is high must experience what it is like to be low".[96]

Turner derives his concept of the liminality of performance from the anthropologist Arnold van Gennep's concept of *rites de passage* ("rites of passage"), which are initiatory rites that involve three phases: (1) preliminal (separation); (2) liminal (transition); and (3) postliminal (incorporation).[97] Also drawing on this conception of ritual, the mythologist Joseph Campbell describes the pattern of liminal experience as the *monomyth*, a term coined by Joyce in *Finnegans Wake*.[98] For Campbell, the monomyth is the pattern of *separation-initiation-return*, which pervades the world's mythologies, such as myths of figures like Prometheus, Odysseus, Moses, Jesus, and the Buddha, all of whom have to leave their places of origin (separation) to seek sacred or divine knowledge (initiation) that can be brought back for the benefit of humanity (return).[99] The monomyth is the great Refrain pulsing in the beginning, middle, and ending of all things in the chaosmos.[100] Sean Kelly shows how the liminal pattern expressed in the monomyth can be discerned in the transition from premodern (religious) and modern (secular) civilization to the emerging planetary civilization.[101]

As a performance, the philosophy of integral ecology is an attempt to raise the clamor of the chaosmos, creatively repeating the refrain of liminality with the aim of opening up possibilities for more actors to participate in the composition of a planetary civilization. Such philosophy is not just theory, but theory that takes place, becoming theatrical.[102] It could be described in terms of participatory theatre, which undoes the usual partition between performers and audience members, so that all are active participants in the performance. However, many forms of participatory theatre only include human performers and audience members as participants. The philosophy of integral ecology is more anthropocosmic than that, thus resembling the theatrical performance process developed by Nicolás Núñez, who articulates "schemes of participatory theatre which are based on the idea of anthropocosmic theatre", schemes that "give back to our organism its capacity to be the echo box of the cosmos".[103] As an anthropocosmic performance, the philosophy of integral ecology becomes "a way of 'opening up' the stage" so as to let each participant become an actor that can sustain its action "without being forced, manipulated or exploited in the service of the show".[104] The show is the cosmopolitical process of composing a planetary civilization. It is the "performance commons" that humans share with other organisms and environments.[105]

At its best, a philosophy of integral ecology is a performance of anthropocosmic theatre. It is philosophy taking place in the performance commons. To put it another way, the performative dimension of philosophy is not only a matter of using trickster humour and difficult styles to facilitate participation in the complexity of boundaries. It is also a matter of going into the field. Consider the following comment of the environmental philosopher Robert Frodeman:

> In addition to the scholar's study, philosophy also makes its home in the field. [...] wandering trails that lead into the heart of our wilderness—both natural and cultural. The terrains covered are quite varied and involve the cultivation of the eye or hand or limb in concert with a tool or proscenium or landscape. Examples of such terrains include the violin, cabinetry-making, and surgery; field biology, athletics, and dance; and teaching, writing, and research.[106]

In the field, philosophy is a craft. Not primarily discursive or linguistic, it is a craft of creating concepts for facilitating participation in new events, new becomings, new modes of planetary coexistence. For D&G, the field on which philosophy creates concepts is a field or plane of mutually immanent events in the chaosmos, and it can "be explored only by legwork".[107] The craft of philosophy involves mapping the rhizomatic lines of the field to invoke new possibilities for people and Earth. The craft requires "groping experimentation", going out into the prephilosophical plane of immanence and returning with something different, returning with possibilities for becoming other.[108] To think philosophically is to practise an experimental craft of "becoming something else" (e.g., "an animal, a molecule, a particle").[109]

Practises of groping experimentation are not necessarily met with public approval. They do not always fit within respectable academic standards or the limits of reason. "These measures belong to the order of dreams, of pathological processes, esoteric experiences, drunkenness, and excess. We head for the horizon, on the plane of immanence, and we return with bloodshot eyes, yet they are the eyes of the mind. [...] To think is always to follow the witch's flight".[110] Mapping the rhizomatic lines of the plane of immanence, philosophers become other, nomadic, wandering outside the coordinates of reason and public approval, going out of their way to create concepts. Philosophers even go out of their minds to create concepts, disorganizing consciousness so as to open its doors to what Leibniz calls "minute perceptions" (*petites perceptions*), which disclose multiplicities of differences swarming beneath the surface of conscious perception.[111] Such is the difficult and risky work of creating consciousness-raising concepts.

In the present work, I attempt to stay on the verge, in the field, undertaking the task of participating in the creation of concepts of integral ecology, which is to say, concepts that facilitate engagements with ecological realities by mapping complex boundaries entangling multiplicities of environments, societies, and subjectivities. The process of creating concepts of integral ecology "calls for a future form, for a new earth and people that do not yet exist".[112] Although some of my conceptual explications are new to integral ecology, the field of integral ecology has been developing for decades, with important contributions from liberation theology (Boff), complex thought (Morin), Integral theory (Esbjörn-Hargens and Zimmerman), and the new cosmology (Berry and Swimme), which themselves draw in various degrees on many of the philosophical sources I explore in this volume (e.g., speculative philosophy, postmodernism, feminist theory). Although it already contains robust rhizomatic offshoots, integral ecology is still relatively unknown. Many ecological theories and practises have yet to open up to the vast scope and transdisciplinary orientation of its rhizomatic knots. It is still to come, on the verge.[113] It is my hope that the concepts introduced in the present work contribute to its coming and, in doing so, contribute to the arrival of a planetary civilization. Imagine: a homecoming for humans and for the entire Earth community. Homecoming does not mean attaining a final peace or ultimate conclusion. It is much more restless, difficult, and tricky than that. Our journey home is thoroughly uncanny. It is an ongoing adventure of cultivating and composting complex connections with planetary others in all of their strangeness. We are arriving at the ongoing cosmopolitical work of composing a planetary *oikos* together, in the open. Beginning and beginning again, we are always coming home.

NOTES

1. Gilles Deleuze, *Difference and Repetition*, trans. Paul Patton (New York: Columbia University Press, 1994), xxi.
2. Friedrich Nietzsche, *Untimely Meditations*, trans. R. J. Hollingdale (New York: Cambridge University Press, 1997), 60.
3. Félix Guattari, *The Three Ecologies*, trans. Ian Pindar and Paul Sutton (London: Ahtlone Press, 2000), 45. For Aldo Leopold, working against the normal order of things is a matter of ecological practise and also of hobbies and even nonhuman evolutionary processes. For Leopold, any "good hobby" is "a rebellion" or "revolt against the commonplace"; "nonconformity is the highest evo-

lutionary attainment of social animals" (Leopold, *Round River: From the Journals of Aldo Leopold* [New York: Oxford University Press, 1993], 8).

4. Deleuze, *Difference and Repetition*, 124.
5. Ibid., 136, 129.
6. Ibid., 129
7. Ibid., xx–xxi.
8. Ibid., 35, 304. Since the phrase *clamor of being* is the title of Alain Badiou's book on Deleuze, it is important to distinguish what is being said here from Badiou's reading. Badiou reads Deleuze as a monist. "Deleuze's fundamental problem is most certainly not to liberate the multiple but to submit thinking to a renewed concept of the One" (Badiou, *Deleuze: The Clamor of Being*, trans. Louise Burchill [Minneapolis: University of Minnesota Press, 2000], 10). However, as I discuss in the section on "Nomads", Deleuze harbours pluralist *and* monist tendencies, ultimately affirming "the magic formula we all seek—PLURALISM = MONISM" (Deleuze and Guattari, *A Thousand Plateaus: Capitalism and Schizophrenia*, trans. Brian Massumi [Minneapolis: University of Minnesota Press, 1987], 20). Although Deleuze can be viewed as more monist than pluralist, his work does engage the political project of liberating multiplicities. For a reading that defends Deleuze against Badiou's claims that Deleuze is a politically irrelevant monist, see Clayton Crockett, *Deleuze Beyond Badiou: Ontology, Multiplicity, and Event* (New York: Columbia University Press, 2013). With his emphasis on multiplicity, Deleuze can be allied with Whitehead's more pluralistic realism of actual entities or with Keller's proposal for "a pluralism not of many separate ones but of plurisingularities, of interdependent individuations, constantly coming, flowing, *through* one another" (Catherine Keller, *Face of the Deep: A Theology of Becoming* [New York: Routledge, 2003], 179). Keller's pluralism resonates with Nancy's claim that "the singular-plural constitutes the essence of Being", such that Being is defined as "singularly plural and plurally singular" (Jean-Luc Nancy, *Being Singular Plural*, trans. Robert D. Richardson and Anne E. O'Byrne [Stanford: Stanford University Press, 2000], 28f).
9. Brian Swimme and Thomas Berry, *The Universe Story: From the Primordial Flaring Forth to the Ecozoic Era—A Celebration of the Unfolding of the Cosmos* (San Francisco: HarperCollins, 1992), 268.
10. Nicholas of Cusa, "On Learned Ignorance", in *Nicholas of Cusa: Selected Spiritual Writings*, trans. H. Lawrence Bond (New York: Paulist Press, 1997), 141; Alfred North Whitehead, *Science and the Modern World* (New York: Free Press, 1967), 91; Deleuze, *The Logic of Sense*, trans. Constantin V. Boundas (New York: Columbia University Press, 1990), 180.
11. Deleuze and Guattari, *A Thousand Plateaus*, 263.
12. Deleuze and Guattari, *What Is Philosophy?* trans. Hugh Tomlinson and Graham Burchell (New York: Columbia University Press, 1994), 189, 191.
13. Guattari, *The Three Ecologies*, 45.
14. Deleuze and Guattari, *A Thousand Plateaus*, 311.
15. Ibid. Although the previous example focused on a human refrain, D&G deploy the concept of refrain in relationship to the becoming of all organisms and organized entities, human and nonhuman. They devote particular attention to birds, and not just the songs of birds, but also other expressive functions, like those of the brown stagemaker, which turns leaves upside down every morning so that the "paler underside" of the leaves "stands out against the dirt: inversion produces a matter of expression" (315).
16. Ibid., 311.
17. Ibid., 324.
18. Ibid., 327.

19. "Produce a deterritorialized refrain, [. . .] release it in the Cosmos—that is more important than building a new system. Opening the assemblage onto a cosmic force" (ibid., 350).

20. "Absolute deterritorialization does not take place without reterritorialization" (Deleuze and Guattari, *What Is Philosophy?*, 101).

21. Deleuze and Guattari, *A Thousand Plateaus*, 313.

22. "Movements of deterritorialization are inseparable from territories that open onto an elsewhere; and the process of reterritorialization is inseparable from the earth [the deterritorialized], which restores territories" (Deleuze and Guattari, *What Is Philosophy?* 85–86).

23. Rachel Carson, *The Sense of Wonder* (New York: Harper & Row, 1965), 88–89.

24. The double meaning of healing refrains echoes the double meaning of James Hillman's *Healing Fiction*, in which he argues that the human psyche needs fictions to heal its wounds and that, in order to produce such healing fictions, we must heal our relationship to fiction and cease equating fictions and lies (Hillman, *Healing Fiction* [Woodstock: Spring Publications, 1983]).

25. Deleuze and Guattari, *What Is Philosophy?*, 99. "The creation of concepts in itself calls for a future form, for a new earth and people that do not yet exist" (108).

26. Ibid., 88.

27. Thomas Berry, *The Great Work: Our Way into the Future* (New York: Bell Tower, 1999), 163, 165.

28. Ibid., 3.

29. Ibid., 160.

30. Catherine Keller, "Composting Our Connections", in *The Greening of Faith: God, the Environment, and the Good Life*, eds. John E. Carroll, Paul Brockelman, and Mary Westfall (Hanover: University Press of New England, 1997), 165.

31. Ibid., 165–66.

32. Ibid., 167.

33. Roland Faber, "Becoming Intermezzo: Eco-Theopoetics after the Anthropic Principle", in *Theopoetic Folds: Philosophizing Multifariousness*, eds. Roland Faber and Jeremy Fackenthal (New York: Fordham University Press, 2013), 220.

34. Plato, *Phaedrus*, trans. Albert A. Anderson (Millis: Agora Publications, 2002), 30d.

35. For Kant, "We have duties toward the animals because thus we cultivate the corresponding duties toward human beings. [. . .] animals must be regarded as man's instruments. [. . .] Our duties towards animals, then, are indirect duties toward mankind", and likewise, "duties toward inanimate objects" are "indirectly duties towards mankind" (Immanuel Kant, *Lectures on Ethics*, trans. Louis Infield [Indianapolis: Hackett Publishing, 1963], 240–41).

36. For an overview of posthumanism, see Cary Wolfe, *What Is Posthumanism?* (Minneapolis: University of Minnesota Press, 2010). I follow Wolfe's claim that "posthumanism is the *opposite* of transhumanism" insofar as the latter intensifies human exceptionalism while the former "opposes the fantasies of disembodiment and autonomy, inherited from humanism itself" (xv).

37. Tsing, "Unruly Edges: Mushrooms as Companion Species", para. 9, http://tsingmushrooms.blogspot.com.

38. Deleuze and Guattari, *A Thousand Plateaus*, 190.

39. Gaston Bachelard, *The Poetics of Space*, trans. Maria Jolas (Boston: Beacon Press, 1994), 171.

40. Grosz, *Becoming Undone*: Darwinian Reflections on Life, Politics, and Art (Durham, NC: Duke University Press, 2011), 21. This new humanities is explored in a book series of the University of Minnesota Press, "Posthumanities", the main editor of which is Cary Wolfe, who himself has a book in that series, *What Is Posthumanism?* (Minneapolis: University of Minnesota Press, 2010). I have referred to other books in that series in earlier chapters of the present work, including Stengers's two-volume *Cosmopolitics* (*Cosmopolitics I*, trans. Robert Bononno [Minneapolis: University of Minnesota Press, 2010] and *Cosmopolitics II*, trans. Robert Bononno [Minneapolis: University of Minnesota Press, 2011]), Michel Serres's *The Parasite* (trans. Lawrence R. Schehr [Minneapolis: University of Minnesota Press, 2007]), and Donna Haraway's *When Species Meet* (Minneapolis: University of Minnesota Press, 2008).

41. Haraway, *When Species Meet*, 7.

42. Ibid., 15, 19.

43. Ibid., 165.

44. Crockett, *Radical Political Theology: Religion and Politics after Liberalism* (New York: Columbia University Press, 2011), 160.

45. How could we be capable of disenchanting the world, when every day our laboratories and our factories populate the world with hundreds of hybrids stranger than those of the day before? Is Boyle's air pump any less strange than the Arapesh spirit houses"? (Bruno Latour, *We Have Never Been Modern*, trans. Catherine Porter [Cambridge: Harvard University Press, 1993], 115). Echoing Heraclitus, Latour argues that our global technoculture is not disenchanted. "Here too the gods are present" (*Einai gar kai entautha theous*) (65).

46. On the return of religion to the public sphere, see the essays collected in the anthology edited by Eduardo Mendieta and Jonathan Vanantwerpen, *The Power of Religion in the Public Sphere* (New York: Columbia University Press, 2011).

47. Caputo, *On Religion* (New York: Routledge, 2001), 2.

48. Derrida, "On a Newly Arisen Apocalyptic Tone in Philosophy", trans. John Leavy Jr., in *Raising the Tone of Philosophy: Late Essays by Immanuel Kant, Transformative Critique by Jacques Derrida*, ed. Peter Fenves (Baltimore: Johns Hopkins University Press, 1993), 167.

49. Ibid., 2.

50. Haraway, *When Species Meet*, 3. Moreover, Haraway does not mention Augustine at all in *When Species Meet*, and she might not have intentionally or consciously phrased that question in response to Augustine.

51. Augustine, *The Confessions of Saint Augustine*, trans. John K. Ryan (New York: Doubleday, 1960), X.7.

52. Ibid., 245.

53. Ibid., 12.

54. Ibid., 97.

55. Ibid., 4.

56. Ibid., 106.

57. Deleuze and Guattari, *What Is Philosophy?*, 122.

58. Haraway, *When Species Meet*, 17.

59. Ibid.

60. Haraway says this in an interview: "Companion species is my effort to be in alliance and in tension with posthumanist projects". Nicholas Gane and Donna Haraway, "When We Have Never Been Human, What Is to Be Done?" *Theory, Culture and Society* 23.7–8 (2006): 135–58, 140.

61. Donna Haraway, "SF: Science Fiction, Speculative Fabulation, String Figures, So Far", Pilgrim Award acceptance talk presented at the Science Fiction Research Association (SFRA) Conference, Lublin, Poland, July 7, 2011, 10.

62. Le Guin, "The Carrier Bag Theory of Fiction", in *Dancing at the Edge of the World: Thoughts on Words, Women, Places* (New York: Grove Press, 1989), 170.

63. Sha LaBare, "Chronicling Martians", in *Visions of Mars: Essays on the Red Planet in Fiction and Science*, eds. Howard V. Hendrix, George Slusser, and Eric S. Rabkin (Jefferson: McFarland, 2011), 158–59.

64. Haraway, "SF: Science Fiction", 5, 12.

65. Ibid., 13.

66. LaBare, *Farfetchings: On and in the SF Mode*, PhD dissertation, University of California, Santa Cruz, 2011. Haraway references LaBare, saying that he taught her "to pay attention to the sf tones of 'species'" (Haraway, *When Species Meet*, 310).

67. Le Guin, *Always Coming Home* (Berkeley: University of California Press, 2001), passim.

68. LaBare, *Farfetchings*, 55.

69. Deborah Bird Rose, *Wild Dog Dreaming: Love and Extinction* (Charlottesville: University of Virginia Press, 2011), 13, 18.

70. Elizabeth A. Grosz, *Chaos, Territory, Art: Deleuze and the Framing of the Earth* (New York: Columbia University Press, 2008), 49–50. For more on the songlines of Aboriginal peoples, see Bruce Chatwin, *The Songlines* (New York: Viking Press, 1987).

71. Isabelle Stengers, "Experimenting with Refrains: Subjectivity and the Challenge of Escaping Modern Dualism", *Subjectivity* 22 (2008): 40.

72. Starhawk, *Dreaming the Dark: Magic, Sex, and Politics* (Boston: Beacon Press, 1982), 219.

73. Le Guin, *The Left Hand of Darkness* (New York: Ace Books, 1969), 147.

74. LaBare, *Farfetchings*, 1.

75. The phrase *always coming home* is a three-ring circus of an allusion. It alludes to a book by the SF author Ursula K. Le Guin (*Always Coming Home*), in which she attempts to transform the boundaries of binaries and overcome the oppressive structures that have been perpetuated insofar as "the principle mode of our thinking is binary" (500). This phrase also alludes to an oft-quoted saying from Novalis: "Where are we going? Always home" (*Wo gehn wir denn hin? Immer nach Hause*) (Novalis, *Heinrich von Ofterdingen*, 3rd ed. [Munich: Beck, 1987], 267). The phrase also resonates with Sean Kelly's *Coming Home* (the Novalis quotation functions as one of the epigraphs), which inspires my own call for a creative transformation of the planetary era. Kelly, *Coming Home: The Birth and Transformation of the Planetary Era* (Great Barrington: Lindisfarne Books, 2010).

76. Derrida, *Politics of Friendship*, trans. George Collins (New York: Verso, 2001).

77. Nancy, *Being Singular Plural*, 3.

78. James Gustave Speth, *The Bridge at the Edge of the World: Capitalism, the Environment, and Crossing from Crisis to Sustainability* (New Haven: Yale University Press, 2008), 13.

79. Ibid., 237.

80. Ibid.

81. Ibid., 232.

82. This resonates with the philosophy that John Sallis articulates on the verge, where the verge is the generative matrix that opens possibilities for new modes of existence. "All determination in and through which something is brought about that is entirely unprecedented takes place on the verge" (Sallis,

The Verge of Philosophy [Chicago: University of Chicago Press, 2008], 3). Moreover, a verge is not just a static boundary but harbours dynamic and perhaps even revolutionary tendencies, as indicated by its derivation from the Latin verb *vergere* ("to turn, tend towards"), which comes from the Proto-Indo-European root *werg-* ("to turn, bend") (Calvert Watkins, ed., *The American Heritage Dictionary of Indo-European Roots*, rev. 2nd ed. [Boston: Houghton Mifflin, 2000], 99).

83. Berry, *The Great Work*, 48. Berry makes many other references to an integral Earth community (xi, 4, 64, 80, 98, 138, 147, 162, 193ff).

84. Deleuze, *Difference and Repetition*, xxi.

85. David Wood takes the term *negative capability* from the English Romantic poet John Keats to describe a postdeconstructive approach to ethics and politics. "Negative capability here means letting go of the seemingly attractive idea of reaching an end, never having to struggle again. Negative capability is both a conceptual and an existential achievement—the recognition of ongoing contingent engaged temporality as the plane on which we all must make our fragile sense" (Wood, *The Step Back: Ethics and Politics after Deconstruction* [Albany: SUNY Press, 2005], 7). Keats offers the following definition of "Negative Capability": it is "when a man is capable of being in uncertainties, mysteries, doubts, without any irritable reaching after fact and reason" (Keats, *The Love Poems of John Keats: In Praise of Beauty*, ed. David Stanford Burr [New York: St. Martin's Press, 1990], xi).

86. Ludwig Wittgenstein, *Wittgenstein and the Vienna Circle: Conversations Recorded by Friedrich Waismann*, ed. B. F. McGuinness, trans. J. Schulte (Oxford: Blackwell, 1979), 68. Wittgenstein makes a similar remark elsewhere. In his "Lecture on Ethics", he says the following: "Astonishment at the fact of the world. Every attempt to express it leads to nonsense", and yet humans are inclined to express it anyway and thus "run against the limits of language. This running against them signalizes ethics" (ibid., 93).

87. Aristotle, *Nicomachean Ethics*, trans. Joe Sachs (Newburyport: Focus Publishing, 2002), 1106b31.

88. David Wood, *Philosophy at the Limit* (London: Unwin Hyman, 1990), 153.

89. Ibid.

90. Ibid., 96–97.

91. Haraway describes her engagement with trickster figures of coyotes, which are part of the same litter as other figures populating her works (e.g., companion species, cyborgs, OncoMouse, primates). "The coyote is about the world as a place that is active in terms that are not particularly under human control, but it is not about the human on the one side and the natural on the other. [...] The coyote disturbs the nature/culture ontologies" (Haraway, "Interview with Donna Haraway", in *Chasing Technoscience: Matrix for Materiality*, eds. Don Ihde and Evan Selinger [Bloomington: Indiana University Press, 2003], 53).

92. Limit-experience is a common theme in Heidegger, Derrida, Levinas, Nancy, and other twentieth-century philosophers. Wood describes it as

> a negative (or liminal, or aporetic) experience, an experience of interruption, or (as Wittgenstein called it) a coming-up against limits. Heidegger, for example, had described *Angst* as the experience of the "slipping-away of the world as a whole": It is an experience that can only happen to a being constitutively bound up in a world. And if such an interruption does not in a flash light up everything it puts in question, it does open up a path of reflection, one aimed at interpreting such an experience. (Wood, "Topologies of Transcendence", in

Transcendence and Beyond: A Postmodern Inquiry, eds. John D. Caputo and Michael J. Scanlon [Bloomington: Indiana University Press, 2007], 183)

93. Wood, *Philosophy at the Limit*, xiii, xv.
94. Ibid., 142.
95. Victor Turner, *From Ritual to Theatre: The Human Seriousness of Play* (New York: PAJ Publications, 1982), 46.
96. Victor Turner, *The Ritual Process: Structure and Anti-Structure* (Chicago: Aldine Publishing, 1969), 97.
97. van Gennep, *The Rites of Passage*, trans. M. B. Vizedom and G. L. Caffee (Chicago: University of Chicago Press, 1960), 11, 21.
98. "And then and too the trivials! And their bivouac! And his monomyth! Ah ho! Say no more about it! I'm sorry! I saw. I'm sorry! I'm sorry to say I saw"! (Joyce, *Finnegans Wake*, [New York: Penguin Books, 1982], 581).
99. Joseph Campbell, *Hero with a Thousand Faces*, 2nd ed. (Princeton: Princeton University Press, 1973), 10–34. Furthermore, these heroic journeys often take on a patriarchal tone, as is particularly evident in Homer's *Odyssey* (19:136–37), wherein the hero Odysseus goes on his journey and Penelope stays at home in Ithaca weaving and unweaving the web of her wiles as she is pursued by various suitors. Thus Penelope says, "I waste away at the inward heart, longing for Odysseus. These men try to hasten the marriage. I weave my own wiles". *The Odyssey of Homer*, trans. Richmond Lattimore (New York: Harper Perennial, 1999).
100. Turner does not use the term *chaosmos*, but he does describe how conventional structures are constituted through "anti-structure" (Turner, *The Ritual Process*, 94–97). See also Turner, *From Ritual to Theatre*, 24–28.
101. Kelly discerns the liminal pattern in the transitions between those eras and also within those eras. Kelly is thus describing "a fractal repetition" of the monomythic shape, which means that "there exists a 'self-similarity' between the properties of the overall or larger-scale shape and the parts or regions of which this shape is constituted", like the fractal repetition in "the edge of a coastline as seen from space as compared to a much smaller part of the same edge viewed from closer up" (Kelly, *Coming Home*, 45).
102. Theory (*theoria*) derives from Greek words for viewing (*thea*) and seeing (*oros*). A theatrical theory conveys a viewing that takes place, a *theatron* (the suffix *-tron* connotes "place") (*Oxford English Dictionary*).
103. Núñez, *Anthropocosmic Theatre: Rite in the Dynamics of Theatre*, trans. R. J. Fitzsimons (Amsterdam: Routledge Harwood, 1996), xvii–xviii.
104. Ibid., 97–98.
105. The "performance commons" is a concept developed in the "performance ecology" (or "theatre ecology") of Baz Kershaw, who argues that humans in contemporary technoculture need to transform their relationship to performance, learning to share in participatory performance and thus overcoming the "performance addiction" that treats environmental and social crises like spectacles to be observed by alienated human spectators (Kershaw, *Theatre Ecology: Environments and Performance Events* [New York: Cambridge University Press, 2007], 14).
106. Frodeman, "Philosophy in the Field", in *Rethinking Nature: Essays in Environmental Philosophy*, eds. Bruce Foltz and Robert Frodeman (Bloomington: Indiana University Press, 2004), 149.
107. Deleuze and Guattari, *A Thousand Plateaus*, 371.
108. Deleuze and Guattari, *What Is Philosophy?*, 41.

109. Ibid., 42.
110. Ibid., 41.
111. In a seminar on Leibniz, Deleuze describes minute perceptions. They can be encountered in "an unconscious lived experience", which occurs "under certain conditions of disorganization in my consciousness", such that

> minute perceptions force open the door of my consciousness [. . .] when my consciousness is disorganized. At that moment, a flow of minute unconscious perceptions invades me. It's not that these minute perceptions stop being unconscious, but it's me who ceases being conscious. [. . .] I do not represent them, I do not perceive them, but they are there, they swarm in these cases. (Deleuze, "Cours Vincennes—St. Denis: 1 Évènement, Whitehead", Les Cours de Gilles Deleuze, October 3, 1987, para. 37, http://www.webdeleuze.com/php/texte.php?cle=140&groupe=Leibniz&langue=1)

According to Ed Casey, "petite perception" is "always already at work" in ethical relations with the heterogeneity and alterity of human and nonhuman others (Casey, "Taking a Glance at the Environment: Preliminary Thoughts on a Promising Topic", in *Eco-Phenomenology: Back to the Earth Itself*, eds. Charles S. Brown and Ted Toadvine [Albany: SUNY Press, 2003], 190).

112. Deleuze and Guattari, *What Is Philosophy?*, 108.

113. The coming paradigm of integral ecology can be understood as a rupture in the current paradigm, articulating new horizons for ecological research. It can also be understood as a gradual evolution that refines and intensifies integrative impulses already at work in other ecological approaches. Integrative impulses can be found in germinal forms since the beginnings of ecology with Haeckel, whose sense of ecology is political and theological, not just biological. These two ways of viewing the development of integral ecology (paradigm shift and gradual evolution) apply to other developments in ecology as well. For a collection of essays by ecologists and philosophers exploring mixtures of paradigm shifts and gradual evolutions throughout the history of ecology, see Kim Cuddington and Beatrix Beisner, eds. *Ecological Paradigms Lost: Routes of Theory Change* (Burlington: Elsevier, Academic Press, 2005).

References

Abram, David. *The Spell of the Sensuous: Perception and Language in a More-Than-Human World*. New York: Vintage Books, 1997.

Adorno, Theodor. *Negative Dialectics*. Translated by E. B. Ashton. New York: Seabury Press, 1973.

Agamben, Giorgio. *The Open: Man and Animal*. Translated by Kevin Attell. Stanford, CA: Stanford University Press, 2004.

Appadurai, Arjun. "Grassroots Globalization and the Research Imagination". *Public Culture* 12.1 (2009): 1–19.

Aristophanes. *Clouds*. Translated by Jeffrey Henderson. Cambridge: Harvard University Press, 1998.

Aristotle. *Nicomachean Ethics*. Translated by Joe Sachs. Newburyport: Focus Publishing, 2002.

———. *Physics: Books I–IV*. Translated by P. H. Wicksteed and F. M. Cornford. Cambridge: Harvard University Press, 1957.

Augustine. *City of God*. Translated by Henry Bettenson. London: Penguin Books, 2003.

———. *The Confessions of Saint Augustine*. Translated by John K. Ryan. New York: Doubleday, 1960.

Bachelard, Gaston. *The Poetics of Reverie: Childhood, Language, and the Cosmos*. Translated by Daniel Russell. Boston: Beacon Press, 1971.

———. *The Poetics of Space*. Translated by Maria Jolas. Boston: Beacon Press, 1994.

Badiou, Alain. *Deleuze: The Clamor of Being*. Translated by Louise Burchill. Minneapolis: University of Minnesota Press, 2000.

Barad, Karen. *Meeting the Universe Halfway: Quantum Physics and the Entanglement of Matter and Meaning*. Durham: Duke University Press, 2007.

Baring, Anne, and Jules Cashford. *The Myth of the Goddess: Evolution of an Image*. London: Penguin Books, 1993.

Barlow, Maude, and Tony Clarke. *Blue Gold: The Fight to Stop the Corporate Theft of the World's Water*. New York: New Press, 2002.

Bateson, Gregory. *Mind and Nature: A Necessary Unity*. New York: Dutton, 1979.

Baudelaire, Charles. *Baudelaire: His Prose and Poetry*. Edited by T. R. Smith. New York: Boni and Liveright, 1919.

Bauman, Whitney. *Theology, Creation, and Environmental Ethics: From Creatio Ex Nihilo to Terra Nullius*. New York: Routledge, 2009.

Bauman, Whitney, Richard Bohannon, and Kevin O'Brien. "Ecology: What Is It, Who Gets to Decide, and Why Does It Matter"? In *Grounding Religion: A Field Guide to the Study of Religion and Ecology*, edited by Whitney Bauman, Richard Bohannon, and Kevin O'Brien, 49–63. New York: Routledge, 2011.

Beckett, Samuel. *Watt*. New York: Grove Press, 2009.

Bekoff, Marc. *Minding Animals: Awareness, Emotions, and Heart*. New York: Oxford University Press, 2002.

Bélanger, J. L. Roland. "Chaosmos: Edgar Morin's Basic Analogue for Viewing Life". *French Cultural Studies* 8.24 (1997): 375–86.
Bennett, Jane. *Vibrant Matter: A Political Ecology of Things*. Durham: Duke University Press, 2010.
Berry, Thomas. *The Christian Future and the Fate of Earth*. Maryknoll: Orbis Books, 2009.
———. *The Dream of the Earth*. San Francisco: Sierra Club Books, 1988.
———. *The Great Work: Our Way into the Future*. New York: Bell Tower, 1999.
Boff, Leonardo. *Cry of the Earth, Cry of the Poor*. Translated by Phillip Berryman. Maryknoll: Orbis Books, 1997.
———. "Ecology". LeonardBoff.com, accessed December 10, 2013. http://leonardoboff.com/site-eng/lboff.htm.
Boff, Leonardo, and Virgilio Elizondo. "Ecology and Poverty: Cry of the Earth, Cry of the Poor". *Concilium: International Journal of Theology* 5 (1995): ix–xii.
Bogost, Ian. "Process vs. Procedure". Paper presented at the Whitehead Research Project Conference, Claremont, California, December 2–4, 2010.
Bohm, David. *Wholeness and the Implicate Order*. Boston: ARK, 1983.
Bonta, Mark, and John Protevi. *Deleuze and Geophilosophy: A Guide and Glossary*. Edinburgh: Edinburgh University Press, 2004.
Bottomore, Tom, ed. *A Dictionary of Marxist Thought*. 2nd ed. Malden: Blackwell, 1991.
Brereton, Pat. *Hollywood Utopia: Ecology in Contemporary American Cinema*. Portland: Intellect Books, 2005.
Brown, Charles S., and Ted Toadvine, eds. *Nature's Edge: Boundary Explorations in Ecological Theory and Practice*. Albany: SUNY Press, 2007.
Brown, Lester. *Plan B 2.0: Rescuing a Planet under Stress and a Civilization in Trouble*. New York: Norton, 2006.
Bruno, Giordano. *Cause, Principle and Unity: And Essays on Magic*. Translated by Richard J. Blackwell and Robert de Lucca. New York: Cambridge University Press, 1998.
Bryant, Levi. *The Democracy of Objects*. Ann Arbor: Open Humanities Press, 2011.
Bryant, Levi, Nick Srnicek, and Graham Harman, eds. *The Speculative Turn: Continental Materialism and Realism*. Melbourne: re.press, 2011.
Bryden, Mary, ed. *Deleuze and Religion*. New York: Routledge, 2001.
Buchanan, Ian, and Claire Colebrook, eds. *Deleuze and Feminist Theory*. Edinburgh: Edinburgh University Press, 2000.
Buege, Douglas J. "The Ecological Noble Savage Revisited". *Environmental Ethics* 18.1 (1996): 71–88.
Butler, Judith. *Bodies That Matter: On the Discursive Limits of "Sex"*. New York: Routledge, 1993.
———. "Sexual Difference as a Question of Ethics: Alterities of the Flesh in Irigaray and Merleau-Ponty". In *Feminist Interpretations of Maurice Merleau-Ponty*, edited by Dorothea Olkowski and Gail Weiss, 107–25. University Park: Pennsylvania State University Press, 2006.
Butler, Katy. "Winning Words: George Lakoff Says Environmentalists Need to Watch Their Language". *Sierra* 89.4 (2004): 54.
Calarco, Matthew. *Zoographies: The Question of the Animal from Heidegger to Derrida*. New York: Columbia University Press, 2008.
Callicott, J. Baird, and Michael P. Nelson. *American Indian Environmental Ethics: An Ojibwa Case Study*. Upper Saddle River: Prentice Hall, 2004.
Campbell, Joseph. *The Hero with a Thousand Faces*. 2nd ed. Princeton: Princeton University Press, 1973.

Caputo, John D. *The Insistence of God: A Theology of Perhaps*. Bloomington: Indiana University Press, 2013.
———. *More Radical Hermeneutics: On Not Knowing Who We Are*. Bloomington: Indiana University Press, 2000.
———. *On Religion*. New York: Routledge, 2001.
———. *The Weakness of God: A Theology of the Event*. Bloomington: Indiana University Press, 2006.
Carson, Rachel. *The Edge of the Sea*. New York: Houghton Mifflin, 1998.
———. *The Sea Around Us*. New York: Oxford University Press, 2003.
———. *The Sense of Wonder*. New York: Harper & Row, 1965.
———. *Silent Spring*. Boston: Mariner Books, 1962, 2002.
Casey, Edward S. *The Fate of Place: A Philosophical History*. Berkeley: University of California Press, 1997.
———. *Getting Back into Place: Toward a Renewed Understanding of the Place-World*. Bloomington: Indiana University Press, 1993.
———. "Taking a Glance at the Environment: Preliminary Thoughts on a Promising Topic". In *Eco-Phenomenology: Back to the Earth Itself*, edited by Charles S. Brown and Ted Toadvine, 187–210. Albany: SUNY Press, 2003.
Chatwin, Bruce. *The Songlines*. New York: Viking Press, 1987.
Chisholm, Dianne, ed. "Deleuze and Guattari's Ecophilosophy". *Rhizomes* 15 (2007). Retrieved from http://www.rhizomes.net/issue15/index.html.
Chittick, William. "The Anthropocosmic Vision in Islamic Thought". In *God, Life and the Cosmos*, edited by Ted Peters, Muzaffar Iqbal, and Syed Nomanul Haq, 125–49. Burlington: Ashgate, 2002.
———. *The Heart of Islamic Philosophy: The Quest for Self-Knowledge in the Teachings of Afḍal al-dīn Kāshānī*. Oxford: Oxford University Press, 2001.
Code, Murray. *Process, Reality, and the Power of Symbols: Thinking with A. N. Whitehead*. New York: Palgrave, 2007.
Collins, John J. *The Apocalyptic Imagination: An Introduction to Jewish Apocalyptic Literature*. 2nd ed. Grand Rapids: Eerdmans Publishing, 1998.
Combs, Allan. *The Radiance of Being: Understanding the Grand Integral Vision; Living the Integral Life*. 2nd ed. St. Paul: Paragon House, 2002.
Critchley, Simon. *Infinitely Demanding: Ethics of Commitment, Politics of Resistance*. London: Verso, 2007.
Crockett, Clayton. *Deleuze Beyond Badiou: Ontology, Multiplicity, and Event*. New York: Columbia University Press, 2013.
———. *Radical Political Theology: Religion and Politics after Liberalism*. New York: Columbia University Press, 2011.
Crockett, Clayton, and Jeffrey Robbins. *Religion, Politics, and the Earth: The New Materialism*. New York: Palgrave Macmillan, 2012.
Cubitt, Sean. *EcoMedia*. New York: Rodopi, 2005.
Cuddington, Kim, and Beatrix Beisner, eds. *Ecological Paradigms Lost: Routes of Theory Change*. Burlington: Elsevier, Academic Press, 2005.
Cullinan, Cormac. *Wild Law: A Manifesto for Earth Justice*. Devon: Green Books, 2011.
Darwin, Charles. *The Descent of Man, and Selection in Relation to Sex*. New York: Penguin Group, 2004.
Deleuze, Gilles. "Cours Vincennes". *Les Cours de Gilles Deleuze*, April 29, 1980. http://www.webdeleuze.com/php/texte.php?cle=55&groupe=Leibniz&langue=2.
———. "Cours Vincennes—St. Denis: 1 Évènement, Whitehead". *Les Cours de Gilles Deleuze*, October 3, 1987. http://www.webdeleuze.com/php/texte.php?cle=140&groupe=Leibniz&langue=1.

———. *Desert Islands and Other Texts 1953–1974*. Translated by Michael Taormina. Los Angeles: Semiotext(e), 2004.

———. *Difference and Repetition*. Translated by Paul Patton. New York: Columbia University Press, 1994.

———. *Empiricism and Subjectivity: An Essay on Hume's Theory of Human Nature*. Translated by Constantin V. Boundas. New York: Columbia University Press, 1991.

———. *Essays Critical and Clinical*. Translated by Daniel W. Smith and Michael A. Greco. London: Verso, 1998.

———. *The Fold: Leibniz and the Baroque*. Translated by Tom Conley. Minneapolis: University of Minnesota Press, 1992.

———. *The Logic of Sense*. Translated by Constantin V. Boundas. New York: Columbia University Press, 1990.

———. *Negotiations, 1972–1990*. Translated by Martin Joughin. New York: Columbia University Press, 1995.

———. *Nietzsche and Philosophy*. Translated by Hugh Tomlinson. New York: Columbia University Press, 2006.

———. "Response to a Series of Questions". *Collapse* 3 (2007): 39–43.

———. *Spinoza: Practical Philosophy*. Translated by Robert Hurley. San Francisco: City Lights Books, 1988.

———. *Two Regimes of Madness: Texts and Interviews 1975–1995*. Translated by Ames Hodges and Michael Taormina. New York: Semiotext(e), 2007.

Deleuze, Gilles, and Félix Guattari. *Anti-Oedipus: Capitalism and Schizophrenia*. Translated by Robert Hurley, Mark Seem, and Helen R. Lane. Minneapolis: University of Minnesota Press, 1983.

———. *Kafka: Toward a Minor Literature*. Translated by Dana Polan. Minneapolis: University of Minnesota Press, 1986.

———. *A Thousand Plateaus: Capitalism and Schizophrenia*. Translated by Brian Massumi. Minneapolis: University of Minnesota Press, 1987.

———. *What Is Philosophy?* Translated by Hugh Tomlinson and Graham Burchell. New York: Columbia University Press, 1994.

Deleuze, Gilles, and Claire Parnet. *Dialogues*. 2nd ed. Translated by Hugh Tomlinson and Barbara Habberjam. New York: Columbia University Press, 2002.

Delpech-Ramey, Joshua, and Paul A. Harris. "Spiritual Politics after Deleuze: Introduction". *SubStance* 39.1 (2010): 3–7.

Demen, Vitaly. "Is It Possible to Rethink Possible"? *EMG Strategy Consulting*, April 2010. Retrieved from http://www.eamesmgmt.com/Is_it_possible_to_Rethink_Possible.shtml.

Dempster, Beth. "Boundarylessness: Introducing a Systems Heuristic for Conceptualizing Complexity". In *Nature's Edge: Boundary Explorations in Ecological Theory and Practice*, edited by Charles S. Brown and Ted Toadvine, 93–110. Albany: SUNY Press, 2007.

Derrida, Jacques. *Acts of Religion*. Edited by Gil Anidjar. New York: Routledge, 2002.

———. *The Animal That Therefore I Am*. Edited by Marie-Louise Mallet, translated by David Wills. New York: Fordham University Press, 2008.

———. *Circumfession: Fifty-Nine Periods and Periphrases*. In *Jacques Derrida*, Geoffrey Bennington and Jacques Derrida, 3–315. Chicago: University of Chicago Press, 1993.

———. *Deconstruction in a Nutshell: A Conversation with Jacques Derrida*. Edited by John D. Caputo. New York: Fordham University Press, 1997.

———. *Demeure: Fiction and Testimony*. Translated by Elizabeth Rottenberg. Stanford: Stanford University Press, 2000.

——. *Dissemination*. Translated by Barbara Johnson. Chicago: University of Chicago Press, 1981.
——. *The Gift of Death*. Translated by David Wills. Chicago: University of Chicago Press, 1995.
——. *Monolingualism of the Other: Or, the Prosthesis of Origin*. Translated by Patrick Mensah. Stanford: Stanford University Press, 1998.
——. *Of Grammatology*. Translated by Gayatri Chakravorty Spivak. Baltimore: Johns Hopkins University Press, 1976.
——. "On a Newly Arisen Apocalyptic Tone in Philosophy". Translated by John Leavy, Jr. In *Raising the Tone of Philosophy: Late Essays by Immanuel Kant, Transformative Critique by Jacques Derrida*, edited by Peter Fenves, 117–71. Baltimore: Johns Hopkins University Press, 1993.
——. *On Cosmopolitanism and Forgiveness*. Translated by Mark Dooley and Michael Hughes. New York: Routledge, 2001.
——. *On the Name*. Edited by Thomas Dutoit. Stanford: Stanford University Press, 1995.
——. *On Touching—Jean-Luc Nancy*. Translated by Christine Irizarry. Stanford: Stanford University Press, 2005.
——. *The Politics of Friendship*. Translated by George Collins. New York: Verso, 2005.
——. "Psyche: Inventions of the Other". Translated by Catherine Porter and Phillip Lewis. In *Reading De Man Reading*, edited by Lindsay Waters and Wlad Godzich, 25–65. Minneapolis: University of Minnesota Press, 1989.
——. *Specters of Marx: The State of the Debt, the Work of Mourning, and the New International*. Translated by Peggy Kamuf. New York: Routledge, 1994.
Descartes, René. *Discourse on the Method*. Translated by George Heffernan. Notre Dame: Notre Dame Press, 1994.
Diogenes Laertius. *Lives of Eminent Philosophers*. Vol. 2. Translated by R. D. Hicks. Cambridge: Harvard University Press, 1970.
Donaldson, Laura. "Covenanting Nature: Aquacide and the Transformation of Knowledge". *Ecotheology* 8.1 (2003): 100–18.
Earth Charter Associates. "The Earth Charter Initiative". Accessed July 18, 2013. http://www.earthcharterinaction.org/content/.
——. "Read the Charter". Accessed July 18, 2013. http://www.earthcharterinaction.org/content/pages/Read-the-Charter.html.
Eaton, Heather, ed. *The Intellectual Journey of Thomas Berry: Imagining the Earth Community*. Lanham: Lexington Books, 2014.
Edwards, Bill, and Jan P. van Eijk. "The Two Coyotes: A Humorous Lillooet Story". In *Salish Myths and Legends: One People's Stories*, edited by M. Terry Thompson and Steven M. Egesdal, 305–6. Lincoln: University of Nebraska Press, 2008.
Eliade, Mircea. *Images and Symbols: Studies in Religious Symbolism*. Translated by Philip Mairet. Princeton, NJ: Princeton University Press, 1991.
——. *Patterns in Comparative Religion*. Translated by Rosemary Sheed. Cleveland: World Publishing, 1970.
Eliot, T. S. "Little Gidding". In *Four Quartets*, 49–63. Orlando: Harcourt, 1971.
Esbjörn-Hargens, Sean. "Ecological Interiority: Thomas Berry's Integral Ecology Legacy". In *Thomas Berry, Dreamer of the Earth: The Spiritual Ecology of the Father of Environmentalism*, edited by Ervin Laszlo and Allan Combs, 92–104. Rochester: Inner Traditions, 2011.
——. "An Ontology of Climate Change: Integral Pluralism and the Enactment of Multiple Objects". *Journal of Integral Theory and Practice* 5.1 (2010): 143–74.

Esbjörn-Hargens, Sean, and Michael E. Zimmerman. *Integral Ecology: Uniting Multiple Perspectives on the Natural World*. Boston: Integral Books, 2009.
Evanoff, Richard. *Bioregionalism and Global Ethics: A Transactional Approach to Achieving Ecological Sustainability, Social Justice, and Human Well-Being*. New York: Routledge, 2011.
Evernden, Neil. *The Natural Alien: Humankind and the Environment*. Toronto: University of Toronto Press, 1985.
Faber, Roland. "Becoming Intermezzo: Eco-Theopoetics after the Anthropic Principle". In *Theopoetic Folds: Philosophizing Multifariousness*, edited by Roland Faber and Jeremy Fackenthal, 212–35. New York: Fordham University Press, 2013.
———. "Bodies of the Void: Polyphilia and Theoplicity". In *Apophatic Bodies: Negative Theology, Incarnation, and Relationality*, edited by Chris Boesel and Catherine Keller, 200–23. New York: Fordham University Press, 2010.
———. *God as Poet of the World: Exploring Process Theologies*. Translated by Douglas W. Scott. Louisville, KY: Westminster John Knox Press, 2008.
———. "Introduction: Negotiating Becoming". In *Secrets of Becoming: Negotiating Whitehead, Deleuze, and Butler*, edited by Roland Faber and Andrea M. Stephenson, 1–49. New York: Fordham University Press, 2011.
———. "'O Bitches of Impossibility!'—Programmatic Dysfunction in the Chaosmos of Deleuze and Whitehead". In *Deleuze, Whitehead, Bergson: Rhizomatic Connections*, edited by Keith Robinson, 200–19. New York: Palgrave Macmillan, 2009.
———. "Surrationality and Chaosmos: For a More Deleuzian Whitehead (with a Butlerian Intervention)". In *Secrets of Becoming: Negotiating Whitehead, Deleuze, and Butler*, edited by Roland Faber and Andrea M. Stephenson, 157–77. New York: Fordham University Press, 2011.
———. "Touch: A Philosophic Meditation". Paper presented at the Whitehead Research Project conference, Claremont, California, December 2–4, 2010.
Faber, Roland, and Andrea M. Stephenson, eds. *Secrets of Becoming: Negotiating Whitehead, Deleuze, and Butler*. New York: Fordham University Press, 2011.
Fisher, Andy. *Radical Ecopsychology: Psychology in the Service of Life*. Albany: SUNY Press, 2002.
Foltz, Bruce. *Inhabiting the Earth: Heidegger, Environmental Ethics, and the Metaphysics of Nature*. Amherst: Humanity Books, 1995.
Foucault, Michel. *Religion and Culture*. Translated by Richard Townsend. New York: Routledge, 1999.
Freydberg, Bernard. *Philosophy and Comedy: Aristophanes, Logos, and Eros*. Bloomington: Indiana University Press, 2008.
Frodeman, Robert. "Philosophy in the Field". In *Rethinking Nature: Essays in Environmental Philosophy*, edited by Bruce Foltz and Robert Frodeman, 149–64. Bloomington: Indiana University Press, 2004.
Fukuyama, Francis. *The End of History and the Last Man*. New York: Avon Books, 1992.
Gane, Nicholas, and Donna Haraway. "When We Have Never Been Human, What Is to Be Done"? *Theory, Culture and Society* 23.7–8 (2006): 135–58.
Gibson, James J. *The Ecological Approach to Visual Perception*. Boston: Houghton Mifflin, 1979.
Girardot, Norman J. *Myth and Meaning in Early Taoism*. Berkeley: University of California Press, 1983.
Gleick, James. *Chaos: Making a New Science*. Rev. ed. New York: Penguin Books, 2011.

Grau, Marion. *Of Divine Economy: Refinancing Redemption.* New York: T&T Clark, 2004.
Grim, John, and Mary Evelyn Tucker. *Ecology and Religion.* Washington, DC: Island Press, 2014.
Grosz, Elizabeth A. *Becoming Undone: Darwinian Reflections on Life, Politics, and Art.* Durham, NC: Duke University Press, 2011.
———. *Chaos, Territory, Art: Deleuze and the Framing of the Earth.* New York: Columbia University Press, 2008.
———. *Volatile Bodies: Toward a Corporeal Feminism.* Bloomington: Indiana University Press, 1994.
Guattari, Félix. *Chaosmosis: An Ethico-Aesthetic Paradigm.* Translated by Paul Bains and Julian Pefanis. Bloomington: Indiana University Press, 1995.
———. *Molecular Revolution: Psychiatry and Politics.* Translated by Rosemary Sheed. New York: Penguin Books, 1984.
———. *The Three Ecologies.* Translated by Ian Pindar and Paul Sutton. London: Ahtlone Press, 2000.
Gudorf, Christine E., and James E. Huchingson. *Boundaries: A Casebook in Environmental Ethics.* 2nd ed. Washington, DC: Georgetown University Press, 2010.
Haeckel, Ernst. *Monism as Connecting Religion and Science: The Confession of Faith of a Man of Science.* Translated by J. Gilchrist. London: Adam and Charles Black, 1895.
Halpern, Paul. *Countdown to Apocalypse: A Scientific Exploration of the End of the World.* New York: Basic Books, 2001.
Hanson, Paul. *The Dawn of the Apocalyptic: The Historical and Sociological Roots of Jewish Apocalyptic Eschatology.* Rev. ed. Philadelphia: Fortress Press, 1979.
Haraway, Donna J. "Birth of the Kennel: A Lecture by Donna Haraway". *The European Graduate School*, August 2000. Retrieved from http://www.egs.edu/faculty/haraway/haraway-birth-of-the-kennel-2000.html.
———. "How Like a Leaf: An Interview with Thyrza Nichols Goodeve". New York: Routledge, 2000.
———. "Interview with Donna Haraway". In *Chasing Technoscience: Matrix for Materiality*, edited by Don Ihde and Evan Selinger, 47–57. Bloomington: Indiana University Press, 2003.
———. *Modest_Witness@Second_Millennium.FemaleMan©_Meets_OncoMouse*^{TM}. New York: Routledge, 1997.
———. "SF: Science Fiction, Speculative Fabulation, String Figures, So Far". Pilgrim Award acceptance talk presented at the Science Fiction Research Association (SFRA) Conference, Lublin, Poland, July 7, 2011.
———. "Situated Knowledges: The Science Question in Feminism and the Privilege of Partial Perspective". In *Simians, Cyborgs, and Women: The Reinvention of Nature*, 183–201. New York: Routledge, 1991.
———. "'There Are Always More Things Going on Than You Thought!' Methodologies as Thinking Technologies: Interview with Donna Haraway". In *Bits of Life: Feminism at the Intersections of Media, Bioscience, and Technology*, edited by Anneke Smelik and Nina Lykke, 32–41. Seattle: University of Washington Press, 2008.
———. *When Species Meet.* Minneapolis: University of Minnesota Press, 2008.
Hardt, Michael, and Antonio Negri. *Commonwealth.* Cambridge: Harvard University Press, 2009.
———. *Empire.* Cambridge: Harvard University Press, 2001.
———. *Multitude: War and Democracy in the Age of Empire.* New York: Penguin, 2004.

Harman, Graham. *Guerrilla Metaphysics: Phenomenology and the Carpentry of Things*. Chicago: Open Court, 2005.

———. *Prince of Networks: Bruno Latour and Metaphysics*. Melbourne, Australia: re.press, 2009.

———. *Towards Speculative Realism: Essays and Lectures*. Winchester: Zero Books, 2010.

Hart, John. "Catholicism". In *The Oxford Handbook of Religion and Ecology*, edited by Roger Gottlieb, 65–91. New York: Oxford University Press, 2006.

Hathaway, Mark, and Leonardo Boff. *The Tao of Liberation: Exploring the Ecology of Transformation*. Maryknoll: Orbis Books, 2009.

Hawkin, David J. "The Critique of Ideology in the Book of Revelation and Its Implications for Ecology". *Ecotheology* 8.2 (2003): 161–72.

Haxton, Brooks. *Fragments: The Collected Wisdom of Heraclitus*. New York: Viking Press, 2001.

Hegel, G. W. F. *Phenomenology of Spirit*. Translated by A. V. Miller. Oxford: Oxford University Press, 1977.

Heidegger, Martin. *Being and Time*. Translated by John Macquarrie and Edward Robinson. New York: Harper & Row, 1962.

———. "Building Dwelling Thinking". In *Poetry, Language, Thought*, translated by Albert Hofstadter, 145–61. New York: Harper & Row, 1971.

———. "The Origin of the Work of Art". In *Off the Beaten Track*, translated by Julian Young and Kenneth Haynes, 1–56. Cambridge: Cambridge University Press, 2002.

Herzogenrath, Bernd, ed. *Deleuze/Guattari & Ecology*. London: Palgrave Macmillan, 2009.

———. *An [Un]Likely Alliance: Thinking Environment[s] with Deleuze/Guattari*. Newcastle upon Tyne: Cambridge Scholars, 2008.

Hickory, Shagbark. "Everyday Environmental Ethics as Comedy and Story: A Collage". *Ethics and the Environment* 8.2 (2003): 80–105.

Hickory, Shagbark, Peter Koci, Violet Wood, and Sorrel Oxalis. "Further Thoughts on Everyday Environmental Ethics as Comedy and Story: A Conversation with Shagbark Hickory". *Canadian Journal of Environmental Education* 9.1 (2004): 82–91.

Higgins, Luke. "Becoming through Multiplicity: Staying in the Middle of Whitehead's and Deleuze-Guattari's Philosophies of Life". In *Secrets of Becoming: Negotiating Whitehead, Deleuze, and Butler*, edited by Roland Faber and Andrea M. Stephenson, 142–54. New York: Fordham University Press, 2011.

———. "Toward a Deleuze-Guattarian Micropneumatology of Spirit-Dust". In *Ecospirit: Religions and Philosophies for the Earth*, edited by Laurel Kearns and Catherine Keller, 252–63. New York: Fordham University Press, 2007.

Hillman, James. *Healing Fiction*. Woodstock: Spring Publications, 1983.

Holmes, Barbara Ann. *Race and the Cosmos: An Invitation to View the World Differently*. Harrisburg: Trinity Press, 2002.

Homer. *The Odyssey of Homer*. Translated by Richmond Lattimore. New York: Harper Perennial, 1999.

Ingram, David. *Green Screen: Environmentalism and Hollywood Cinema*. Exeter: University of Exeter Press, 2004.

Irigaray, Luce. *An Ethics of Sexual Difference*. Translated by Carolyn Burke and Gillian C. Gill. London: Continuum, 2004.

———. *I Love to You: Sketch for a Possible Felicity in History*. Translated by Alison Martin. New York: Routledge, 1996.

———. *The Speculum of the Other Woman*. Translated by Gillian C. Gill. Ithaca, NY: Cornell University Press, 1985.

Joachim von Fiore. *Psalterium Decem Cordarum Abbatis Joachim*. Frankfurt: Minerva, 1965.
Joyce, James. *Finnegans Wake*. New York: Penguin Books, 1982.
Jung, Hwa Yol. *The Way of Ecopiety: Essays in Transversal Geophilosophy*. New York: Global Scholarly Publications, 2009.
Justaert, Kristien. *Theology after Deleuze*. New York: Continuum, 2012.
Kahn, Charles H. *The Art and Thought of Heraclitus: An Edition of the Fragments with Translation and Commentary*. Cambridge: Cambridge University Press, 1979.
Kant, Immanuel. *Critique of Pure Reason*. Translated by Paul Guyer and Allen Wood. Cambridge: Cambridge University Press, 1998.
———. *Fundamental Principles of the Metaphysic of Morals*. Translated by T. K. Abbott. Amherst: Prometheus Books, 1988.
———. *Lectures on Ethics*. Translated by Louis Infield. Indianapolis: Hackett Publishing, 1963.
———. *Prolegomena to Any Future Metaphysics That Can Qualify as a Science*. Translated by Paul Carus. Chicago: Open Court, 1997.
———. "Toward Perpetual Peace". In *Practical Philosophy: Cambridge Edition of the Works of Immanuel Kant*, translated by M. J. Gregor, 311–52. Cambridge: Cambridge University Press, 1999.
Keats, John. *The Love Poems of John Keats: In Praise of Beauty*. Edited by David Stanford Burr. New York: St. Martin's Press, 1990.
Keller, Catherine. *Apocalypse Now and Then: A Feminist Guide to the End of the World*. Boston: Beacon Press, 1996.
———. "The Cloud of the Impossible: Embodiment and Apophasis". In *Apophatic Bodies: Negative Theology, Incarnation, and Relationality*, edited by Chris Boesel and Catherine Keller, 25–44. New York: Fordham University Press, 2010.
———. *Cloud of the Impossible: Theological Entanglements*. Forthcoming.
———. "Composting our Connections". In *The Greening of Faith: God, the Environment, and the Good Life*, edited by John E. Carroll, Paul Brockelman, and Mary Westfall, 165–73. Hanover: University Press of New England, 1997.
———. *Face of the Deep: A Theology of Becoming*. New York: Routledge, 2003.
———. *From a Broken Web: Separation, Sexism, and Self*. Boston: Beacon Press, 1986.
———. *God and Power: Counter-Apocalyptic Journeys*. Minneapolis: Augsburg Fortress, 2005.
———. "Process and Chaosmos: The Whiteheadian Fold in the Discourse of Difference". In *Process and Difference: Between Cosmological and Poststructuralist Postmodernisms*, edited by Catherine Keller and Anne Daniell, 55–72. Albany: SUNY Press, 2002.
———. "Rumors of Transcendence: The Movement, State, and Sex of 'Beyond'". In *Transcendence and Beyond: A Postmodern Inquiry*, edited by John D. Caputo and Michael J. Scanlon, 129–50. Bloomington: Indiana University Press, 2007.
———. "Talking Dirty: Ground Is Not Foundation". In *Ecospirit: Religions and Philosophies for the Earth*, edited by Laurel Kearns and Catherine Keller, 63–76. New York: Fordham University Press, 2007.
Keller, Catherine, and Anne Daniell, eds. *Process and Difference: Between Cosmological and Poststructuralist Postmodernisms*. Albany: SUNY Press, 2002.
Keller, Catherine, and Laurel Kearns. "Introduction: Grounding Theory—Earth in Religion and Philosophy". In *Ecospirit: Religions and Philosophies for the Earth*, edited by Laurel Kearns and Catherine Keller, 1–17. Fordham, NY: Fordham University Press, 2007.

Keller, Catherine, and Laurel C. Schneider. "Introduction". In *Polydoxy: Theology of Multiplicity and Relation*, edited by Catherine Keller and Laurel C. Schneider, 1–15. New York: Routledge, 2011.

Kelly, Sean. *Coming Home: The Birth and Transformation of the Planetary Era*. Great Barrington: Lindisfarne Books, 2010.

———. "Participation, Complexity, and the Study of Religion". In *The Participatory Turn: Spirituality, Mysticism, Religious Studies*, edited by Jorge Ferrer and Jacob Sherman, 113–34. Albany: SUNY Press, 2008.

Kershaw, Baz. *Theatre Ecology: Environments and Performance Events*. New York: Cambridge University Press, 2007.

Kerslake, Christian. *Deleuze and the Unconscious*. London: Continuum, 2007.

———. *Immanence and the Vertigo of Philosophy: From Kant to Deleuze*. Edinburgh: Edinburgh University Press, 2009.

Keulartz, Jozef. *The Struggle for Nature: A Critique of Radical Ecology*. Translated by Rob Kuitenbrouwer. New York: Routledge, 1998.

Kirby, Vicki. *Quantum Anthropologies: Life at Large*. Durham: Duke University Press, 2011.

Klaver, Irene. "Boundaries on the Edge". In *Nature's Edge: Boundary Explorations in Ecological Theory and Practice*, edited by Charles S. Brown and Ted Toadvine, 113–31. Albany: SUNY Press, 2007.

———. "The Implicit Practice of Environmental Philosophy". In *Environmental Philosophy and Environmental Activism*, edited by Don Marietta Jr. and Lester Embree, 67–78. Lanham: Rowman & Littlefield, 1995.

Klaver, Irene, and John Donahue. "Whose Water Is It Anyway? Boundary Negotiations on the Edwards Aquifer in Texas". In *Globalization, Water, and Health: Resource Management in Times of Scarcity*, edited by Linda Whiteford and Scott Whiteford, 107–26. Santa Fe: School of American Research Press, 2005.

Korten, David. *The Great Turning: From Empire to Earth Community*. Bloomfield: Kumarian Press and Berrett-Koehler, 2006.

Krupat, Arnold. "Native American Trickster Tales". In *Comedy: A Geographic and Historical Guide*, Vol. 2, edited by Maurice Charney, 447–61. Westport: Greenwood Publishing Group, 2005.

Kuberski, Philip. *Chaosmos: Literature, Science, and Theory*. Albany: SUNY Press, 1994.

LaBare, Sha. "Chronicling Martians". In *Visions of Mars: Essays on the Red Planet in Fiction and Science*, edited by Howard V. Hendrix, George Slusser, and Eric S. Rabkin, 152–61. Jefferson: McFarland, 2011.

———. *Farfetchings: On and in the SF Mode*. PhD dissertation, University of California, Santa Cruz, 2011.

Latour, Bruno. *An Inquiry into Modes of Existence: An Anthropology of the Moderns*. Translated by Catherine Porter. Cambridge: Harvard University Press, 2013.

———. "Interview with Bruno Latour". In *Chasing Technoscience: Matrix for Materiality*, edited by Don Ihde and Evan Selinger, 15–26. Bloomington: Indiana University Press, 2003.

———. *On the Modern Cult of the Factish Gods*. Translated by Catherine Porter and Heather MacLean. Durham: Duke University Press, 2010.

———. *Pandora's Hope: Essays on the Reality of Science Studies*. Cambridge: Harvard University Press, 1999.

———. *The Pasteurization of France*. Translated by Alan Sheridan and John Law. Cambridge: Harvard University Press, 1988.

———. *Politics of Nature: How to Bring the Sciences into Democracy*. Translated by Catherine Porter. Cambridge: Harvard University Press, 2004.

———. "The Promises of Constructivism". In *Chasing Technoscience: Matrix for Materiality*, edited by Don Ihde and Evan Selinger, 27–46. Bloomington: Indiana University Press, 2003.

———. *We Have Never Been Modern*. Translated by Catherine Porter. Cambridge: Harvard University Press, 1993.

Lawlor, Leonard. *Thinking through French Philosophy: The Being of the Question*. Bloomington: Indiana University Press, 2003.

Le Guin, Ursula K. *Always Coming Home*. Berkeley: University of California Press, 2001.

———. "The Carrier Bag Theory of Fiction". In *Dancing at the Edge of the World: Thoughts on Words, Women, Places*, 165–70. New York: Grove Press, 1989.

———. *The Left Hand of Darkness*. New York: Ace Books, 1969.

Leopold, Aldo. *Round River: From the Journals of Aldo Leopold*. New York: Oxford University Press, 1993.

———. *A Sand County Almanac and Sketches Here and There*. London: Oxford University Press, 1968.

Levinas, Emmanuel. *Totality and Infinity: An Essay on Exteriority*. Translated by Alphonso Lingis. Dordrecht: Kluwer Academic Publishers, 1991.

Light, Andrew, ed. *Social Ecology after Bookchin*. New York: Guilford Press, 1998.

Llewelyn, John. *Margins of Religion: Between Kierkegaard and Derrida*. Bloomington: Indiana University Press, 2009.

Lyotard, Jean-François. *The Postmodern Condition: A Report on Knowledge*. Translated by Geoff Bennington and Brian Massumi. Minneapolis: University of Minnesota Press, 1984.

Macauley, David. *Elemental Philosophy: Earth, Air, Fire, and Water as Environmental Ideas*. Albany: SUNY Press, 2010.

———. "The Flowering of Environmental Roots and the Four Elements in Presocratic Philosophy: From Empedocles to Deleuze and Guattari". *Worldviews* 9.3 (2005): 281–314.

Manuel, Frank Edward. *Shapes of Philosophical History*. Stanford, CA: Stanford University Press, 1965.

Marcel, Gabriel. "Phenomenological Notes about Being in a Situation". In *Creative Fidelity*, translated by Robert Rosthal, 82–103. New York: Fordham University Press, 2002.

———. *Tragic Wisdom and Beyond*. Translated by Stephen Jolin and Peter McCormick. Evanston: Northwestern University Press, 1973.

Marder, Michael. *The Event of the Thing: Derrida's Post-Deconstructive Realism*. Toronto: Toronto University Press, 2009.

Marx, Karl. *Economic and Philosophic Manuscripts of 1844*. Translated by Martin Milligan. Amherst: Prometheus Books, 1988.

Mauseth, James D. *Botany: An Introduction to Plant Biology*. 4th ed. Sudbury: Jones and Bartlett Publishers, 2009.

McDaniel, Jay. "Ecological Civilization". *Jesus, Jazz, and Buddhism*. Accessed April 11, 2013. http://www.jesusjazzbuddhism.org/ecological-civilization.html.

McKibben, Bill. *The End of Nature*. New York: Random House, 2006.

McKirahan, Richard D. *Philosophy before Socrates: An Introduction with Texts and Commentary*. Indianapolis: Hackett Publishing, 1994.

Meeker, Joseph. *The Comedy of Survival: Literary Ecology and a Play Ethic*. 3rd ed. Tuscon: University of Arizona Press, 1997.

Meillassoux, Quentin. *After Finitude: An Essay on the Necessity of Contingency*. Translated by Ray Brassier. New York: Continuum, 2008.

Mendieta, Eduardo, and Jonathan Vanantwerpen, eds. *The Power of Religion in the Public Sphere*. New York: Columbia University Press, 2011.
Merchant, Carolyn. *American Environmental History: An Introduction*. New York: Cambridge University Press, 2007.
———. *The Death of Nature: Women, Ecology, and the Scientific Revolution*. San Francisco: HarperSanFrancisco, 1990.
Merleau-Ponty, Maurice. *Signs*. Translated by Richard C. McCleary. Evanston: Northwestern University Press, 1964.
———. *The Visible and the Invisible*. Translated by Alphonso Lingis. Evanston: Northwestern University Press, 1968.
Meyer, Birgit. "Christianity and the Ewe Nation: German Pietist Missionaries, Ewe Converts and the Politics of Culture". *Journal of Religion in Africa* 32.2 (2002): 167–99.
Mickey, Sam. "Contributions to Anthropocosmic Environmental Ethics". *Worldviews: Environment, Culture, Religion* 11.2 (2007): 226–47.
———. "Cosmological Postmodernism in Whitehead, Deleuze, and Derrida". *Process Studies* 37.2 (2008): 24–44.
———. "On the Function of the Epoche in Phenomenological Interpretations of Religion". *PhaenEx: Journal of Existential and Phenomenological Theory and Culture* 3.1 (2008): 56–81.
Mickey, Sam, Adam Robbert, and Sean Kelly, eds. *Integral Ecologies: Nature, Culture, and Knowledge in the Planetary Era*. Forthcoming.
Millennium Ecosystem Assessment (MEA). *Ecosystems and Human Well-Being: Synthesis*. Washington, DC: Island Press, 2005.
Miller, Adam. *Speculative Grace: Bruno Latour and Object-Oriented Theology*. New York: Fordham University Press, 2013.
Miller, James. "Envisioning the Daoist Body in the Cosmic Economy of Power". *Daedalus* 130.4 (2001): 265–82.
Miller, Paul D. (DJ Spooky That Subliminal Kid). *Rhythm Science*. Cambridge: MIT Press, 2004.
Mooney, Tim. "Derrida and Whitehead". In *God, Literature, and Process Thought*, edited by Darren J. Middleton, 29–46. Aldershot: Ashgate, 2002.
Moore, Hilary B. *Marine Ecology*. New York: Wiley, 1958.
Moore, Stephen D., and Mayra Rivera, eds. *Planetary Loves: Spivak, Postcoloniality, and Theology*. New York: Fordham University Press, 2011.
Morin, Edgar. *Homeland Earth: A Manifesto for the New Millennium*. Translated by Sean M. Kelly and Roger LaPointe. Cresskill: Hampton Press, 1999.
———. *Method: Towards a Study of Humankind*. Vol. 1 of *The Nature of Nature*. Translated by J. L. Roland Bélanger. New York: Peter Lang, 1992.
———. *On Complexity*. Translated by Robin Postel. Cresskill: Hampton Press, 2008.
Morton, Timothy. *The Ecological Thought*. Cambridge: Harvard University Press, 2010.
———. *Ecology without Nature: Rethinking Environmental Aesthetics*. Cambridge: Harvard University Press, 2007.
———. *Hyperobjects: Philosophy and Ecology after the End of the World*. Minneapolis: University of Minnesota Press, 2013.
Murray, Robin L., and Joseph K. Heumann. *Ecology and Popular Film: Cinema on the Edge*. Albany: SUNY Press, 2009.
Nancy, Jean-Luc. *Being Singular Plural*. Translated by Robert D. Richardson and Anne E. O'Byrne. Stanford: Stanford University Press, 2000.
———. "The Deleuzian Fold of Thought". In *Deleuze: A Critical Reader*, edited by Paul Patton, 107–13. Cambridge: Blackwell Publishers, 1996.

―――. *The Inoperative Community*. Translated by Peter Connor, Lisa Garbus, Michael Holland, and Simona Sawhney. Minneapolis: University of Minnesota Press, 1991.

―――. "Interview: The Future of Philosophy". Translated by Benjamin C. Hutchens. In *Jean-Luc Nancy and the Future of Philosophy*, by B. C. Hutchens, 161–66. Chesham: Acumen, 2005.

―――. *Noli Me Tangere: On the Raising of the Body*. Translated by Sarah Clift, Pascale-Anne Brault, and Michael Naas. New York: Fordham University Press, 2008.

―――. *The Sense of the World*. Translated by Jeffrey Librett. Minneapolis: University of Minnesota Press, 1997.

Nhat Hanh, Thich. *Interbeing: Fourteen Guidelines for Engaged Buddhism*. Berkeley, CA: Parallax Press, 1998.

Nicholas of Cusa. "On Learned Ignorance". In *Nicholas of Cusa: Selected Spiritual Writings*, translated by H. Lawrence Bond, 85–206. New York: Paulist Press, 1997.

Nietzsche, Friedrich. *Beyond Good and Evil*. Translated by Walter Kaufmann. New York: Vintage Books, 1966.

―――. *The Gay Science*. Translated by Josefine Nauckhoff. New York: Cambridge University Press, 2001.

―――. *Selected Letters of Friedrich Nietzsche*. Edited and Translated by Christopher Middleton. Indianapolis: Hackett Publishing, 1996.

―――. *Thus Spoke Zarathustra: A Book for Everyone and No One*. Translated by R. J. Hollingdale. New York: Penguin Books, 1969.

―――. *Twilight of the Idols*. Translated by Richard Polt. Indianapolis: Hackett Publishing, 1997.

―――. *Untimely Meditations*. Translated by R. J. Hollingdale. New York: Cambridge University Press, 1997.

―――. *The Will to Power*. Translated by Walter Kaufmann and R. J. Hollingdale. New York: Vintage Books, 1968.

Nigianni, Chrysanthi, and Merl Storr, eds. *Deleuze and Queer Theory*. Edinburgh: Edinburgh University Press, 2009.

Novalis. *Heinrich von Ofterdingen*. 3rd ed. Munich: Beck, 1987.

Núñez, Nicolás. *Anthropocosmic Theatre: Rite in the Dynamics of Theatre*. Translated by R. J. Fitzsimons. Amsterdam: Routledge Harwood, 1996.

Olkowski, Dorothea. *Gilles Deleuze and the Ruin of Representation*. Berkeley: University of California Press, 1999.

Oxford English Dictionary Online. Accessed December 18, 2013. http://www.oed.com/.

Patton, Paul, and John Protevi. "Introduction". In *Between Deleuze and Derrida*, edited by Paul Patton and John Protevi, 1–14. London: Continuum Press, 2003.

Pignarre, Philippe, and Isabelle Stengers. *Capitalist Sorcery: Breaking the Spell*. New York: Palgrave Macmillan, 2011.

Plato. *Epistles*. Translated by R. G. Bury. Cambridge: Harvard University Press, 2005.

―――. *Phaedrus*. Translated by Albert A. Anderson. Millis: Agora Publications, 2009.

―――. *The Republic*. Translated by Allan Bloom. 2nd ed. New York: Basic Books, 1991.

―――. *Theaetetus*. Translated by Seth Benardete. Chicago: University of Chicago Press, 1986.

———. *Timaeus*. Translated by R. G. Bury. Cambridge: Harvard University Press, 2005.
Plumwood, Val. *Environmental Culture: The Ecological Crisis of Reason*. New York: Routledge, 2002.
———. *Feminism and the Mastery of Nature*. New York: Routledge, 1993.
Prigogine, Ilya, and Isabelle Stengers. *Order Out of Chaos: Man's New Dialogue with Nature*. New York: Bantam Books, 1984.
Protevi, John. "Love". In *Between Deleuze and Derrida*, edited by Paul Patton and John Protevi, 183–94. London: Continuum Press, 2003.
Ramey, Joshua. *The Hermetic Deleuze: Philosophy and Spiritual Ordeal*. Durham, NC: Duke University Press, 2012.
Rancière, Jacques. *The Politics of Aesthetics: The Distribution of the Sensible*. Translated by Gabriel Rockhill. New York: Continuum, 2004.
———. "Ten Theses on Politics". Translated by Davide Panagia. *Theory and Event* 5.3 (2001). http://muse.jhu.edu/journals/theory_and_event/toc/tae5.3.html.
Rees, Martin. *Our Cosmic Habitat*. Princeton: Princeton University Press, 2001.
Ricoeur, Paul. *Husserl: An Analysis of His Phenomenology*. Translated by E. G. Ballard and L. E. Embree. Evanston, IL: Northwestern University Press, 1967.
———. *The Symbolism of Evil*. Translated by Emerson Buchanan. New York: Harper & Row, 1967.
Rivera, Mayra. *The Touch of Transcendence: A Postcolonial Theology of God*. Louisville, KY: Westminster John Knox Press, 2007.
Rolston, Holmes, III. *A New Environmental Ethics: The Next Millennium for Life on Earth*. New York: Routledge, 2012.
Rose, Deborah Bird. *Wild Dog Dreaming: Love and Extinction*. Charlottesville: University of Virginia Press, 2011.
Rubenstein, Mary-Jane. *Strange Wonder: The Closure of Metaphysics and the Opening of Awe*. New York: Columbia University Press, 2008.
———. *Worlds without End: The Many Lives of the Multiverse*. New York: Columbia University Press, 2014.
Sahni, Pragati. *Environmental Ethics in Buddhism: A Virtues Approach*. New York: Routledge, 2008.
Said, Edward W. *Beginnings: Intention and Method*. New York: Columbia University Press, 1985.
———. *The Question of Palestine*. New York: Vintage Books, 1992.
Sallis, John. *Chorology: On Beginning in Plato's* Timaeus. Bloomington: Indiana University Press, 1999.
———. *Force of Imagination: The Sense of the Elemental*. Bloomington: Indiana University Press, 2000.
———. *Platonic Legacies*. Albany: SUNY Press, 2004.
———. *The Verge of Philosophy*. Chicago: University of Chicago Press, 2008.
Schrag, Calvin O. *The Resources of Rationality: A Response to the Postmodern Challenge*. Bloomington: Indiana University Press, 1992.
Serres, Michel. *The Parasite*. Translated by Lawrence R. Schehr. Minneapolis: University of Minnesota Press, 2007.
Shakespeare, William. *Hamlet*. Edited by Ann Thompson and Neil Taylor. London: Thomson Learning, 2006.
Sherwood, Yvonne, and Kevin Hart, eds. *Derrida and Religion: Other Testaments*. New York: Routledge, 2005.
Simmons, Bruce, Robert Woog, and Vladamir Dimitrov. "Living on the Edge: A Complexity-Informed Exploration of the Human–Water Relationship". *World Futures* 63.3 (2007): 275–85.

Sloterdijk, Peter. *In the World Interior of Capital: For a Philosophical Theory of Globalization*. Translated by Weiland Hoban. Malden: Polity Press, 2013.

Smith, Anthony Paul. *A Non-Philosophical Theory of Nature: Ecologies of Thought*. New York: Palgrave Macmillan, 2013.

———. "Believing in This World for the Making of Gods: Ecology of the Virtual and the Actual". *SubStance* 39.1 (2010): 103–14.

Smith, Daniel W. "Deleuze, Kant, and the Theory of Immanent Ideas". In *Deleuze and Philosophy*, edited by Constantin V. Boundas, 43–61. Edinburgh, UK: Edinburgh University Press, 2006.

Smith, Mick. *Against Ecological Sovereignty: Ethics, Biopolitics, and Saving the Natural World*. Minneapolis: University of Minnesota Press, 2011.

Snyder, Gary. *The Practice of the Wild: Essays*. Washington, DC: Shoemaker & Hoard, 1990.

Speth, James Gustave. *The Bridge at the Edge of the World: Capitalism, the Environment, and Crossing from Crisis to Sustainability*. New Haven: Yale University Press, 2008.

Spinoza, Benedict de. *Ethics*. In *Collected Works of Spinoza, Vol. 1*, 2nd printing with corrections. Edited and translated by Edwin Curley. Princeton: Princeton University Press, 1988.

Spivak, Gayatri Chakravorty. *A Critique of Postcolonial Reason: Toward a History of the Vanishing Present*. Cambridge: Harvard University Press, 1999.

———. *Death of a Discipline*. New York: Columbia University Press, 2003.

———. *In Other Worlds: Essays in Cultural Politics*. New York: Routledge, 1988.

———. *Outside in the Teaching Machine*. New York: Routledge, 1993.

Starhawk. *Dreaming the Dark: Magic, Sex, and Politics*. Boston: Beacon Press, 1982.

Stark-Merklein, Brigitte. "Rap Star Jay-Z's Video Diary to Spotlight Water Crisis in Angola and Worldwide". *UNICEF*, October 11, 2006.http://www.unicef.org/wash/angola_36135.html.

Stengers, Isabelle. "The Cosmopolitical Proposal". In *Making Things Public: Atmospheres of Democracy*, edited by Bruno Latour and Peter Weibel, 994–1003. Cambridge: MIT Press, 2005.

———. *Cosmopolitics I*. Translated by Robert Bononno. Minneapolis: University of Minnesota Press, 2010.

———. *Cosmopolitics II*. Translated by Robert Bononno. Minneapolis: University of Minnesota Press, 2011.

———. "Experimenting with Refrains: Subjectivity and the Challenge of Escaping Modern Dualism". *Subjectivity* 22 (2008): 38–59.

———. "Gilles Deleuze's Last Message". Accessed July 3, 2011. http://www.recalcitrance.com/deleuzelast.htm.

———. "History through the Middle: Between Macro and Mesopolitics; Interview with Isabelle Stengers, 25 November 2008". *Inflexions: A Journal for Research Creation* 3 (2009): 1–15. Accessed November 9, 2011, http://www.senselab.ca/inflexions/volume_3/node_i3/stengers_en_inflexions_vol03.html -1.

———. "Thinking with Deleuze and Whitehead: A Double Test". In *Deleuze, Whitehead, Bergson: Rhizomatic Connections*, edited by Keith Robinson, 28–44. New York: Palgrave Macmillan, 2009.

———. *Thinking with Whitehead: A Free and Wild Creation of Concepts*. Translated by Michael Chase. Cambridge: Harvard University Press, 2011.

Sturgeon, Noël. *Environmentalism in Popular Culture: Gender, Race, Sexuality, and the Politics of the Natural*. Tuscon: University of Arizona Press, 2009.

Swimme, Brian. *The Hidden Heart of the Cosmos: Humanity and the New Story*. Maryknoll: Orbis Books, 1996.

Swimme, Brian, and Thomas Berry. *The Universe Story: From the Primordial Flaring Forth to the Ecozoic Era—A Celebration of the Unfolding of the Cosmos*. San Francisco: HarperCollins, 1992.

Taliaferro, Charles. "Vices and Virtues in Religious Environmental Ethics". In *Environmental Virtue Ethics*, edited by Ronald Sandler and Philip Cafaro, 159–72. Lanham: Rowman & Littlefield, 2005.

Tamsin, Lorraine. *Irigaray and Deleuze: Experiments in Visceral Philosophy*. Ithaca: Cornell University Press, 1999.

Taylor, Mark C. *After God*. Chicago: University of Chicago Press, 2007.

Thacker, Eugene. *In the Dust of This Planet*. Vol. 1 of *Horror of Philosophy*. Alresford: Zero Books, 2011.

Thompson, Charis. *Making Parents: The Ontological Choreography of Reproductive Technologies*. Cambridge: MIT Press, 2005.

Toadvine, Ted. "Singing the World in a New Key: Merleau-Ponty and the Ontology of Sense". *Janus Head* 7.2 (2004): 273–83.

Tolkien, J. R. R. *The Fellowship of the Ring*. London: Unwin Hyman, 1966.

Tsing, Anna. "Unruly Edges: Mushrooms as Companion Species". Accessed March 20, 2013. http://tsingmushrooms.blogspot.com.

Tu, Weiming. *Centrality and Commonality: An Essay on Chung-Yung*. Honolulu: University Press of Hawaii, 1976.

———. *Confucian Thought: Selfhood as Creative Transformation*. Albany: State University of New York Press, 1985.

———. "The Ecological Turn in New Confucian Humanism: Implications for China and the World". *Daedalus* 130.4 (2001): 243–64.

Tucker, Mary Evelyn. *Worldly Wonder: Religions Enter Their Ecological Phase*. Chicago: Open Court Publishing, 2003.

Tucker, Mary Evelyn, and Brian Swimme. "The Evolutionary Context of an Emerging Planetary Civilization". *Kosmos: An Integral Approach to Global Awakening* 5.1 (2005). http://www.kosmosjournal.org/article/the-evolutionary-context-of-an-emerging-planetary-civilization/.

Turner, Victor. *From Ritual to Theatre: The Human Seriousness of Play*. New York: PAJ Publications, 1982.

———. *The Ritual Process: Structure and Anti-Structure*. Chicago: Aldine Publishing, 1969.

Tyson, Joseph B. *The New Testament and Early Christianity*. New York: MacMillan, 1984.

United Nations Environment Programme. *Global Environmental Outlook (GEO-4): Environment for Development*. Valletta, Malta: Progress Press, 2007.

United Nations World Water Assessment Program. *Water: A Shared Responsibility*. New York: UNESCO and Berghahn Books, 2007.

van Gennep, Arnold. *The Rites of Passage*. Translated by M. B. Vizedom and G. L. Caffee. Chicago: University of Chicago Press, 1960.

Vico, Giambattista. *New Science: Principles of the New Science Concerning the Common Nature of Nations*. Translated by David Marsh. London: Penguin Books, 2000.

Vitousek, P. M., H. A. Mooney, J. Lubchenco, and J. M. Melillo. "Human Domination of Earth's Ecosystems". *Science* 277 (1997): 494–99.

Walljasper, Jay. "Winona LaDuke: Voice of Native Cultures". In *Visionaries: The 20th Century's 100 Most Important Inspirational Leaders*, edited by Satish Kumar and Freddie Whitefield, 156–57. White River Junction, VT: Chelsea Green Publishing, 2007.

Warren, Karen. *Ecofeminist Philosophy: A Western Perspective on What It Is and Why It Matters*. Lanham, MD: Rowman & Littlefield, 2000.

Watkins, Calvert, ed. *The American Heritage Dictionary of Indo-European Roots*. Rev. 2nd ed. Boston: Houghton Mifflin, 2000.
Watts, Michael, and Richard Peet. "Liberating Political Ecology". In *Liberation Ecologies: Environment, Development, Social Movements*, 2nd ed., edited by Richard Peet and Michael Watts, 3–43. London: Routledge, 2004.
———. "Towards a Theory of Liberation Ecology". In *Liberation Ecologies: Environment, Development, Social Movements*, edited by Richard Peet and Michael Watts, 260–69. London: Routledge, 1996.
Weber, Eugen. *Apocalypses: Prophesies, Cults, and Millennial Beliefs through the Ages*. Cambridge: Harvard University Press, 1999.
Weizman, Eyal. "Walking through Walls: Soldiers as Architects in the Israeli-Palestine Conflict". *Radical Philosophy* 136 (2006): 8–22.
Weston, Anthony. *The Incompleat Eco-Philosopher: Essays from the Edges of Environmental Ethics*. Albany: SUNY Press, 2009.
White, Lynn, Jr. "The Historical Roots of our Ecologic Crisis". *Science* 155 (1967): 1203–7.
Whitehead, Alfred North. *Adventures of Ideas*. New York: Free Press, 1967.
———. *Dialogues of Alfred North Whitehead*. Boston: David R. Godine, 2001.
———. *Modes of Thought*. New York: Free Press, 1968.
———. *Process and Reality: An Essay in Cosmology*. Corr. ed. edited by David Ray Griffin and Donald W. Sherburne. New York: Free Press, 1978.
———. *Science and the Modern World*. New York: Free Press, 1967.
Whiteside, Kerry H. *Divided Natures: French Contributions to Political Ecology*. Cambridge: MIT Press.
Whitman, Walt. *Leaves of Grass*. New York: Oxford University Press, 2005.
Wilber, Ken. *No Boundary: Eastern and Western Approaches to Personal Growth*. Boston: Shambhala, 2001.
———. *Sex, Ecology, Spirituality: The Spirit of Evolution*. 2nd rev. ed. Boston: Shambhala Publications, 2000.
———. *The Spectrum of Consciousness*. Wheaton: Quest Books, 1977.
———. *A Theory of Everything: An Integral Vision for Business, Politics, Science, and Spirituality*. Boston: Shambhala Publications, 2000.
Williams, William Carlos. "The Rose (The Rose is Obsolete)". In *1909–1939*, Vol. 1 of *The Collected Poems of William Carlos Williams*, edited by A. Walton and Christopher MacGowan, 195. New York: New Directions, 1986.
Wimberley, Edward T. *Nested Ecology: The Place of Humans in the Ecological Hierarchy*. Baltimore: Johns Hopkins University Press, 2009.
Wittgenstein, Ludwig. *Wittgenstein and the Vienna Circle: Conversations Recorded by Friedrich Waismann*. Edited by B. F. McGuinness. Translated by J. Schulte. Oxford: Blackwell, 1979.
Wolfe, Cary. *What Is Posthumanism?* Minneapolis: University of Minnesota Press, 2010.
Wood, David. *Philosophy at the Limit*. London: Unwin Hyman, 1990.
———. "Specters of Derrida: On the Way to Econstruction". In *Ecospirit: Religions and Philosophies for the Earth*, edited by Laurel Kearns and Catherine Keller, 264–87. New York: Fordham University Press, 2007.
———. *The Step Back: Ethics and Politics after Deconstruction*. Albany: SUNY Press, 2005.
———. "Thinking with Cats". In *Animal Philosophy: Essential Readings in Continental Philosophy*, edited by Matthew Calarco and Peter Atterton, 129–44. London: Continuum, 2004.

———. "Topologies of Transcendence". In *Transcendence and Beyond: A Postmodern Inquiry*, edited by John D. Caputo and Michael J. Scanlon, 169–87. Bloomington: Indiana University Press, 2007.

Woods, Richard. "The Seven Bowls of Wrath: An Ecological Parable". *Ecotheology* 5.7 (1999): 8–21.

Worster, Donald. *Nature's Economy: A History of Ecological Ideas*. 2nd ed. New York: Cambridge University Press, 1994.

Žižek, Slavoj. *In Defense of Lost Causes*. New York: Verso, 2008.

———. *Living in the End Times*. London: Verso, 2011.

———. "Occupy First. Demands Come Later". *The Guardian*, October 26, 2011. http://www.theguardian.com/commentisfree/2011/oct/26/occupy-protesters-bill-clinton.

———. *Tarrying with the Negative: Kant, Hegel, and the Critique of Ideology*. Durham: Duke University Press, 1993.

Index

Aboriginal, 175, 177, 221–222
actors, 31, 33, 128–129, 186, 203n149, 228
Adorno, Theodor, 25
alterity, 61, 124, 176, 178–180, 194n11. *See also* otherness; wholly other
animism, 175, 177–178
Anthropocene, 71. *See also* planetary era
anthropocentric, 3, 88n14, 130, 134–138, 214, 221
anthropocosmic, 135, 137, 139–144, 228
atheism, 54, 165, 217
St. Augustine, 170, 217
Australia, 52, 221

Bachelard, Gaston, 111, 141, 143, 215
Berry, Thomas, 17–19, 21, 57, 71, 108, 209, 212
Big Bang, 45, 134
Boff, Leonardo, 19–22, 28, 121
boundaries, 8, 24–28, 46–48, 117, 121, 178, 224–227
Bruno, Giordano, 128, 130–131
Buddhism, 119, 138, 156n196; Zen, 107, 118

capitalism, 14, 172, 174–175, 192
Carson, Rachel, 64, 66, 211
centre, 117, 121, 128–131, 134–135, 215
centrism, 51, 102, 122, 127, 138
chaos, 63, 80–83, 132–133, 181
chiasm, 56, 81, 85

Christianity, 41n92, 107, 132, 137, 169, 174, 217; Catholic, 21, 54
climate change, 146n21, 153n147, 194n18. *See also* global warming
clouds, 26, 60, 66
community, 15, 22, 74, 86, 134, 142, 144; Earth, 58, 71, 120, 139, 225; integral, 17–19, 223, 235n83; loving, 171, 180; new, 46, 68
companion species, 49, 53, 215–219
complexity, 20, 38n38, 82, 133, 194n18, 198n75, 201n113
concepts, 2–3, 28, 32, 120, 161, 211, 227; the creation of, 1, 4–8, 29, 31, 229–230
Confucian, 119, 142
cosmogenesis, 18, 20–21, 23, 75
cosmology, 17, 21, 57, 76, 86, 123–124, 134
crisis, 5, 95n121, 102, 137, 161–162, 164, 224
Cusa, Nicholas of, 128, 130–133, 135, 181, 203n149, 209

Dao, 84, 143
Daoism, 85, 119, 142. *See also* Dao
deconstruction, 2–3, 7, 65, 110, 216
Deleuze, Gilles, 1, 25, 59, 79, 85, 118, 124, 208
democracy, 21, 145n8, 165, 175, 182, 184, 188, 216
Derrida, Jacques, 1, 7, 61–63, 148n56, 175, 216–217
deterritorialization, 115–117, 119, 122, 173, 176, 210
disciplinary, 1, 13, 22, 84, 121; postdisciplinary, 84, 218;

transdisciplinary, 36n9, 84–85, 230
diversity, 4, 71, 121, 125, 182, 187–188
dog, 49, 65, 126–127, 217
domesticated, 125, 215
domination, 50, 69–70, 82, 134, 172–173, 218–219; logic of, 51–52, 65, 103, 164, 192, 208
dream, 77, 126, 141, 186, 212, 221, 229
dualism, 51, 62, 117, 125, 127, 168, 216

The Earth Charter, 20–21, 34
ecofeminism, 27, 51, 146n21
ecological civilization, 142
ecological noble savage, 64, 138
ecology, 7, 10–16, 30, 63, 102, 136, 179–180; environmental, social, and mental, 14, 20, 22; deep, 16, 20, 139; integral, 14, 16–24, 49, 79, 84, 113, 130, 207; political, 110, 164; religion and, 9, 21, 136, 142–144
element, 76, 95n129, 110–113, 119, 166
Empedocles, 69, 113
empire. *See* imperialism
ethics, 15, 26, 40n81, 119, 134–135, 143, 225
event, 32, 59, 86, 96n142, 106–107, 120, 122–124, 190, 201n114
extinction, 71, 198n73, 221

Faber, Roland, 86–87, 102, 108, 112, 124, 132, 213
fact, 32–33, 44n126, 74, 129, 184, 187–188
fiction, 2, 198n73, 219–220, 222
feminist, 41n92, 49, 65, 78, 105, 186, 212–223. *See also* ecofeminism
fold, 9, 65, 72, 131–133, 147n37, 165, 198n75

genetic, 53, 57–58, 71, 197n60
globalization, 49, 167, 172–177, 183
global warming, 72
God, 50–54, 62, 76, 83, 104, 130–133, 188, 217
Grosz, Elizabeth, 49, 65, 70, 215
Guattari, Félix, 1, 3, 13–15, 22, 78, 120–121, 207

Haraway, Donna, 27, 48–49, 52–55, 126–127, 215, 217, 219
Harman, Graham, 2, 43n125, 153n146
Heraclitus, 46, 49–50, 69, 188
Heidegger, Martin, 46, 48, 140–141, 149n57, 235n92
hermeneutics, 74, 76, 84, 97n165
Hindu, 135
history, 43n122, 53, 74, 82, 120, 162, 170–171, 174
home, 1, 7, 135–136, 140–141, 210, 223, 230
hospitality, 7, 185
human exceptionalism, 3, 5, 214, 219–221. *See also* anthropocentric
humanities, 12–13, 33, 136, 215, 217

imagination, 30, 90n54, 109–112, 140–141
immanence, 86, 97n157, 108, 124, 133, 229
imperialism, 103, 122, 169–176, 192n1
impossible, 180–181
indigenous, 17, 26–27, 137, 168, 172, 177, 212. *See also* ecological noble savage
interbeing, 102, 118–119, 122
Islam, 143

Joachim of Fiore, 170–171
joy, 28, 69, 135, 192, 212
Joyce, James, 81–82, 85, 201n112, 228
judgement, 59–61, 109, 117, 212, 221

Index

justice, 9, 20–21, 39n68, 62, 93n106, 110, 168; ecological, 38n47, 177–179

Kant, Immanuel, 34, 56, 59, 65, 104, 129, 185, 213
Keller, Catherine, 36n9, 50–51, 83–84, 131–133, 157n229, 212, 223
Kierkegaard, 56, 61, 225
Klaver, Irene, 46, 48, 50, 135, 178, 198n76
knowledge, 5, 11, 25, 53, 61–62, 130; ecological, 22, 121; pharmacological, 184, 188–192, 221, 225

Latour, Bruno, 31–33, 129, 153n146, 187–188, 215
Leibniz, Gottfried Wilhelm, 122–123, 131, 201n114, 229
Le Guin, Ursula, 219–222
Leopold, Aldo, 67–68, 230n3
Levinas, Emmanuel, 91n76, 105, 185, 194n11
liberation, 21–22, 28, 69, 87, 110, 138, 177–179
liminality, 46, 109, 227–228
lines of flight, 115, 117–119, 125, 192
logos, 74–75, 133, 136, 149n57, 185
love, 14, 69, 107–108, 171, 177–183, 210, 217

Marcel, Gabriel, 139–141
magic, 113, 124–125, 139, 150n78, 189, 205n168–205n169, 222
messianic, 53, 92n83, 170, 172
monism, 76, 124–125, 231n8
Morin, Edgar, 38n38, 82, 133, 154n166, 161, 178, 180–182
Morton, Timothy, 127, 135, 148n56, 162–163
multitude, 121, 179–180
myth, 51–52, 73–75, 85, 228. *See also* story; narrative

Nancy, Jean-Luc, 95n133, 102, 107, 163, 231n8
narrative, 55, 90n54, 108–109. *See also* story; myth
nature, 45, 59, 104, 110, 127, 129, 162–164; and culture, 3, 47, 214. *See also* ecology; element; wild
Nietzsche, Friedrich, 28–29, 82, 103–105, 171, 207
nonsense, 106–108, 111, 116, 124, 209, 220, 235n86

object, 2, 18, 33, 111, 128–129, 153n146, 203n149. *See also* actors
omnicentrism, 128, 130–134, 151n120
Ontology, 85, 97n157, 118–119, 122, 153n146
opposites, 47, 54, 59, 125, 130, 204n153
origin, 17, 27, 50–53, 56, 65, 75–76, 106, 112
otherness, 61, 106–107, 185, 202n132, 217

panentheism, 130, 216
performance, 116, 166, 226–228
pharmakon, 184, 189–190
phenomenology, 44n126, 105–106, 110–111, 139–141, 194n11
philosophy, 1–10, 49, 59–60, 75, 105, 112, 171, 208; constructive, 32–33, 125, 201n114; critical, 34, 187, 214, 218, 226; ecological, 1, 13, 34; geo-, 3, 119–122, 125, 127; process, 123, 150n99, 157n229; speculative, 29–34, 153n146, 186, 222–223
place, 67, 72–79, 110, 112, 120, 164; apocalyptic sense of, 167–169
planetary era, 180–181, 223–224, 234n75
Plato, 5–6, 73–79, 86, 103, 204n153, 213
play, 7, 24–29, 128, 186, 212, 227

Index

Plumwood, Val, 51, 139, 144n1, 178
pluralism, 47, 76, 123–125, 182, 203n146, 231n8
politics, 14, 47, 77–78, 103, 119, 122, 164; cosmo-, 42n112, 183–191, 217; theo-, 179, 181
postcolonial, 41n92, 50, 108, 172, 174, 176, 213
posthuman, 33, 213–218
postmodern, 90n54, 106, 193n4, 201n114, 213, 218, 230
postsecular, 54, 213, 216–219, 223
prehension, 86, 123, 132
privatization, 165, 174
prophet, 113, 168

Rancière, Jacques, 103
relations, 10, 51, 62, 86, 118, 123–124
religion, 40n81, 51, 107, 118, 137, 139, 182, 216; biblical, 61, 83, 137, 167; Chinese, 84, 142; history of, 139–140. *See also* Buddhism; Christianity; Confucian; Daoism; Hindu; indigenous; spirituality
Ricoeur, Paul, 105, 141–142
roots, 113–114, 116–117, 183

sacramental, 54, 111, 216
sacred, 51–54, 81, 216
science, 2, 11–13, 86, 122, 136, 175, 219
secret, 60, 62, 98n178
sense, 93n89, 102–103, 105–108, 112, 163, 211
singularity, 15, 61–62, 64, 106, 179
Sloterdijk, Peter, 173
solidarity, 134, 180, 182
spirit, 132–133, 171
spirituality, 11, 22, 132, 179, 205n169
Snyder, Gary, 63, 78
Spivak, Gayatri Chakravorty, 175–180

Stengers, Isabelle, 7, 29–32, 184–187, 190–192
Stoic, 184
story, 9–10, 27, 108–110, 209, 219. *See also* narrative
subjectivity, 14, 18–20, 23, 61, 105
Swimme, Brian, 18, 57, 71, 133, 161, 200n103, 209

tact, 18–19, 107–109, 127, 166, 179
Tehom, 83–84, 132
territory, 105, 210. *See also* deterritorialization
theatre, 226–228
theology, 21–22, 50, 84, 96n142, 132, 177–179, 203n149, 223
touch, 17–19, 107–108, 217
transcendence, 52, 97n157, 101, 108, 132–133, 164
transversality, 22, 120–121
trickster, 26–28, 48, 226, 235n91
trinity, 131–132, 171

uncertainty, 8, 27, 29, 58, 111, 130, 180, 201n113, 235n85

wandering, 75–78, 85, 106, 121, 122–125
war, 46, 60, 68–70, 161, 202n132
water, 12, 67, 83, 165, 169, 198n76, 204n153
Whitehead, Alfred North, 30, 33, 43n115, 45, 55, 86–87, 123–124
wholly other, 62, 124, 140
Wilber, Ken, 22–23, 150n97
wild, 7, 32, 71, 110, 112, 126, 229
Wisdom, 17, 132, 175, 177
witchcraft, 192, 222, 229
wonder, 26, 75, 78, 131, 144, 225
Wood, David, 110, 149n59, 226–227, 235n85

Žižek, Slavoj, 48, 68, 193n4, 197n60